THE WATERLOO ARCHIVE

THE WATERLOO ARCHIVE

Previously unpublished or rare journals and letters
regarding the Waterloo campaign and
the subsequent occupation of France

Volume IV
British Sources

Edited by Gareth Glover

**Foreword by Joanna Hill,
a direct descendant of Sir Rowland Hill**

FRONTLINE
BOOKS

The Waterloo Archive: Volume IV

This edition published in 2012 by Frontline Books,
an imprint of
Pen & Sword Books Limited, 47 Church Street,
Barnsley, S. Yorkshire, S70 2AS
www.frontline-books.com
email info@frontline-books.com

© Gareth Glover, 2012
Foreword © Joanna Hill, 2012

ISBN: 978-1-84832-655-2

For more information on our books, please visit
www.frontline-books.com, email info@frontline-books.com
or write to us at the above address.

Typeset by Palindrome in Stempel Garamond 10½/12 pt

Printed by CPI Group (UK) Ltd, Croydon, CR0 4YY

CONTENTS

List of Illustrations   vii
Foreword by Joanna Hill   ix
Acknowledgements   xi
Introduction   xiii

The Staff of the Army   1
The Cavalry   32
  1st Brigade of Major General Lord Edward Somerset 32
  1st Life Guards   32
  2nd Life Guards   34
  1st or King's Dragoon Guards   49
  2nd Brigade of Major General Sir William Ponsonby 51
  1st or Royal Dragoons   53
  2nd (Royal North British) Dragoons, Scots Greys   55
  4th Brigade of Major General Sir John Vandeleur   57
  12th Light Dragoons   57
  6th Brigade of Major General Sir Hussey Vivian   61
  18th Hussars   67
  7th Brigade of Colonel Sir Frederick Arenschildt 96
  13th Light Dragoons   96
The Artillery   121
  The Staff   121
  Foot Artillery   128
  Major Lloyd's Battery, Royal Artillery   128
The Infantry   131
  First Division of Major General George Cooke   131
  1st Brigade of Major General Peregrine Maitland   131
  2nd Battalion 1st Foot Guards   133
  3rd Battalion 1st Foot Guards   141
  2nd Brigade of Major General Sir John Byng   143
  2nd Battalion Coldstream Guards   145

Third Division of Lieutenant General Baron Alten 150
5th Brigade of Major General Sir Colin Halkett 150
2nd Battalion 33rd Foot 150
2nd Battalion 69th Foot 151
Fourth Division of Lieutenant General Sir Charles Colville 175
4th Brigade of Colonel Mitchell 175
1st Battalion 23rd Foot 175
Fifth Division of Lieutenant General Sir Thomas Picton 194
8th Brigade of Major General Sir James Kempt 194
1st Battalion 95th Foot 197
Reserve Forces 224
54th Foot 224
The Support Services 228
Royal Staff Corps 228
Medical Services 230
Not at Waterloo 241
Armed Forces 241
Civilians 250

Bibliography 255
Index of Correspondents 257
Index of Officers and Places 259

ILLUSTRATIONS

William Mudford wrote an early history of Waterloo in 1817 and published a number of superb plates of the battlefield by James Rouse. This volume is extremely rare and expensive (upwards of £1,500) and I must thank Mick Crumplin for providing copies of all the plates, five of which, plates 1–5, are published in this volume.

Colour Plates

Plate 1   Entrance to the Forest of Soignes

Plate 2   The interior of the chapel at Waterloo

Plate 3   The wood at Hougoumont

Plate 4   The ruins of Château Hougoumont

Plate 5   The ruins of the village of Ligny

Plate 6   Private Thomas Playford and a drawing of a Life Guard

Plate 7   Drawings of Private Wanstell and Samuel Pritchard

Plate 8   Napoleon on board HMS *Bellerophon*

FOREWORD

The Duke of Wellington pointed out in his Foreword to the first volume of Gareth Glover's impressive 'Waterloo Archive' series that we are fast approaching the bicentenary of the great battle. After two hundred years, you might have thought that general reader interest would have begun to wane a little; not so! In 2011 alone at least a dozen new titles were published. I do not know how many accounts of Waterloo will be appearing before 18 June 2015, but the genuinely exciting thing about this period of history is that there is such a wealth of material that still lies hidden, waiting to be unearthed, in dusty archives, private houses and even uncatalogued in various libraries. Of course, there is a great deal that is now in the public domain in county record offices, although even this is sometimes difficult to find as it may be bundled with other material of the period, in the National Archives, the British Library and the National Library of Scotland among others.

Today, one of the most interesting sources of new material, as Gareth has proved once more, are the letters written home by enlisted men. These are relatively rare, when compared to those written by their officers, partly because the majority of such men could not read or write. However, there was among them, fortunately, a number who had taken the king's shilling, and who had received some education; their opinions of the battles, of their officers, the food, the ghastly injuries, the enemy and their fellow soldiers are fascinating. The most vivid are, of course, those written immediately following the action, before the writer's pride and imagination had added facts and aggrandised his own role in events; after all, the Prince Regent himself became convinced that he had won the great battle at Waterloo virtually single-handed! Gareth Glover, in this fourth volume of the Waterloo Archive, has once again managed to search out an interesting selection of previously unpublished letters. These letters were, principally, written to family members back in Britain, as events unfolded in the Netherlands and, subsequent to the battle itself, in and around Paris. The personal details of everyday campaigning, some fairly trivial in themselves, when added to graphic accounts of the 'blood and guts' of warfare in 1815, bring both the men and the entire Waterloo Campaign very vividly to life.

Gareth Glover opens his fourth volume with an introduction which, among other events, refers to (later Sir) Digby Mackworth's account of 18 June and the events surrounding it. This was written as night fell on an exhausted, battered Allied army. Mackworth, as far as it is possible to tell two hundred years later, wrote his description of the battle in a hut he shared with nine others, including his general, Rowland Hill. There seems no reason to suppose that he fabricated any part of what he wrote but, of course, in his description of the battle itself, it was his own view of events, those that he had seen for himself as a member of the 2nd Corps, which he recorded. The 2nd Corps was commanded by Lieutenant General Lord Hill to whom, Mackworth was an ADC. Mackworth's description of events in and around Brussels both before and after 18 June add richly to accounts already in the public domain.

Lord Hill has received little notice for the part that he played in the events of the great day; Mackworth and Orlando Bridgeman, another of Hill's ADCs and the general's fellow Salopian, have gone some way to redress this oversight. Hill was a very modest man, popular and beloved of the private soldiers thanks to the care and compassion that he demonstrated towards them. It is obvious that Bridgeman and Mackworth both felt great affection and admiration for 'their' general.

Joanna Hill

ACKNOWLEDGEMENTS

As with the previous volumes of this series, a large number of people, particularly in the various archives of this country, deserve special thanks for helping me unearth such valuable material, providing copies for me to work on at my leisure and eventually kindly granting me permission to publish. Each particular memoir or series of letters indicates its source and particular reference; but a few people have been exceptionally gracious of their time and support. Those who deserve special mention are Iain Brown of the National Library of Scotland, which holds a number of gems; Dr Alistair Massie of the National Army Museum; Brian Owen of the Royal Welch Fusiliers Museum; Eunice Shanahan and Andrew Prince, both of Australia, for permission to use material in their possession and Alan Lagden, who has provided material from his own collection. I must also thank the *Journal of The Society for Army Historical Research* (JSAHR) and the Wellcome Trust for allowing me to utilise their material.

But what heartens me more than anything else is the incredible support of fellow enthusiasts and I must particularly mention Mick Crumplin for his medical expertise, Ron McGuigan for his encyclopaedic knowledge of service records and seemingly endless ability to discover references for anything, always answering even the most obscure questions I challenge him with; and Pedro Ramiro whose language skills are tested frequently. Such tireless devotion to the general drive to improve our understanding of Napoleonic history never fails to amaze me and reaffirms my faith in a community that to outsiders can sometimes appear at war with itself and full of cranks. As usual I must thank Philip Haythornthwaite for checking my text and suggesting numerous corrections/improvements from his encyclopaedic knowledge.

I must also thank my wife, Mary, who never ceases to encourage and support me in all I do and my two now adult children, Sarah and Michael, who inspire me to strive to introduce a new generation to this fascinating subject.

Gareth Glover

INTRODUCTION

I have explained in previous volumes that a great deal has been written on the subject of the Battle of Waterloo and the campaign that surrounds it and that there is even a smattering of works that deal with the subsequent three-year occupation of France by the Allied powers. However, during my studies of this fascinating campaign, I have become painfully aware that much modern material has become a stereotypical regurgitation of previous publications with little if any new research. This to my mind is a terrible crime, as the archives of Europe, and of Britain particularly, are teeming with fascinating documents that are gathering dust, and the ink is fading with time and the paper crumbling, and the material is virtually ignored by many self-acclaimed historians and experts of this campaign.

The reader might think that perhaps the story has already been told and there is simply nothing new to tell but each letter and journal I discover proves this to be a fallacy; they all have something new to say; they challenge preconceptions; they disprove theories; they destroy myths; in fact, they prove beyond doubt that our 'accepted' history of the battle and campaign is wrong in so very many aspects and a complete rewrite of many episodes in the campaign will eventually be required.

However, this cannot happen until all of this buried material is exposed to public scrutiny, allowing various aspects of the campaign to be fully re-interpreted. My aim is to challenge that situation and to provide the evidence for all: complete, without sensationalism, without attempting to brainwash or to peddle implausible conspiracy theories. It is better surely to provide the unadulterated evidence, letting every person make their own judgement on the probable course of events and the reasons they occurred based on good solid primary evidence.

The British texts strangely have one noticeable and significant characteristic compared with the records being unearthed in the archives of other countries that participated in the campaign. The texts from Europe are very largely based upon official reports and returns, written to other military men and therefore often bereft of the human touch. They are factual, very dry and often cold; they rarely give an insight into the psyche of the soldiers and the suffering borne by them. Personal letters written home seem to be strangely rare; perhaps these are still hidden within families or unfortunately destroyed by the ravages of subsequent wars.

In contrast the British archives are brimming with personal letters to family and friends or journals that record their innermost thoughts, written only for themselves and close family. These teem with life; we can share the agonies of those who lost someone, the pain and suffering inflicted on the thousands of wounded is described in sometimes ghastly detail; the horrors of war are laid bare, but so also is the relief and happiness of survival. The human aspect of war and military campaigning comes to the fore: the humour and exhilaration, the fears and miseries, the starvation and exhaustion, the horror and the joy. All emotions are described and subsequently absorbed by the reader as they become embroiled in their personal challenges; a bond is formed, their happiness is shared along with their pain. As an example, I only have to point to the final poignant letter of Ensign Samuel Barrington of the 1st Foot Guards, who was struck down at Quatre Bras at the age of only nineteen, and the subsequent correspondence of those in the regiment who clearly were devastated by his loss

It will be found that a number of the correspondents within this volume are simple men in the ranks. It is usually accepted that very few common soldiers of this period could read or write and that the few letters and journals that do exist emanate from more senior non-commissioned officers, who were required to be able to write to perform their duties. The first volume in this series proved this to be a fallacy, containing as it did no fewer than six accounts from ordinary privates; this volume continues with a further three. Their style of writing can be idiosyncratic, their language blunt, but their honest, forthright ways are refreshing and show how the ordinary man in the ranks saw things, giving a different aspect to our studies.

It is particularly fitting that this volume contains a foreword by Joanna Hill, a renowned historian in her own right, as well as being a direct descendant of Lord Rowland Hill, as this volume contains the memoirs of two of his aides de camp that day: Captain Digby Mackworth and Captain the Honourable Orlando Bridgeman, who make clear Hill's invaluable role that day, which is largely overlooked by most histories of the battle. As a fascinating aside that seems to have been ignored by historians, we might note that Digby Mackworth, in his letter home rushed off at 11 p.m. on the very evening of the battle, includes the immortal phrase, '*La Garde meurt mais ne se rend pas.*' (The Guard dies but does not surrender.) It is not attributed to anyone (it was certainly not said by Cambronne, who had been captured by Halkett and was snug and warm at the inn in Waterloo village at the time) and is mentioned as if it was a well known phrase from a play, although the editor has failed to find any such source. This at least puts paid to the recent theory that it was invented by a French journalist at Paris some years later.

Mackworth's journal is also very interesting in a number of other respects: he shows that Hill held a poor opinion of the Prince of Orange's military skills. He makes some disparaging remarks on the border defences and Belgian troops prior to the campaign; he admits that Wellington was surprised and caught flat-footed by Napoleon's invasion of Belgium; and makes interesting comments regarding the difficulties of the communications with the reserve troops at Hal from Waterloo. However, both he and Orlando Bridgeman show a clear affection for Sir Rowland Hill as a man and great admiration of him as a general.

Some other highlights from this crop of letters and memoirs worth mentioning are those of Colonel Sir Colin Campbell, who reiterates that the Earl of Uxbridge was indeed very unhappy with the performance of much of the cavalry at Waterloo, despite his later more diplomatic assertions to the contrary.

The journal of Private Thomas Playford of the 2nd Life Guards provides a fascinating and honest account of the famous charge of the heavy cavalry against D'Erlon's attack and their subsequent decimation by French cavalry reserves. He tells of the utter confusion, with small pockets of cavalry in mortal combat in all directions, and his own failure, despite riding back and forth across the field, to cross swords with anybody! He also provides much valuable information regarding the death of Corporal Shaw, that most famous of Life Guardsmen, who appears to have succumbed to numerous wounds that eventually defeated the great man as his life's blood ebbed away.

Sir Hussey Vivian, the arch self-publicist, concludes that Wellington was taken by surprise at the commencement of the campaign and candidly admits that initially, when he received orders to move to the centre of the field, he thought it was so that his cavalry could shield the withdrawal of the army from the field.

As an antidote to all this gore, the early letters of Captain Arthur Kennedy of the 18th Hussars are filled with details of the fancy balls, horse races and cricket matches that filled the weeks before war broke out so suddenly. Lieutenant George Packe, 13th Light Dragoons, on the other hand, interestingly writes home on 14 June that they are expecting to be attacked by Napoleon, that he will strike against the Prussians initially and that orders are expected shortly for Wellington to assemble his force so as to strike Napoleon's left flank. Later in Paris he admits that the British troops did not compare well on parade with the gorgeous uniforms displayed by the Russian and Prussian Guards; however, as he states, 'We came to fight not to be reviewed.'

Miraculous escapes abound. First Lieutenant Samuel Phelps of the Royal Artillery describes a cannon ball smashing into the body of his horse, killing it instantly, while he was actually in the process of mounting it – yet he received no injury whatsoever. Captain George Barlow of the 69th Foot was caught by French cavalry with his company formed in line at Quatre Bras and was ridden over; he escaped unharmed by simply playing dead! As a very interesting aside, Barlow was also the officer of the guard of a small detachment on the border a few weeks earlier when King Louis XVIII and his entourage arrived in his flight from Paris.

Private Jeremiah of the 23rd Foot describes a looting expedition before the battle and describes how he returned, and presumably fought throughout the Battle of Waterloo, plastered from head to foot in flour!

First Lieutenant George Simmons of the 95th Rifles also left a fascinating account of his actions at the Battles of Quatre Bras and Waterloo, which surprisingly was not utilised by Willoughby Verner when he published his famous memoir. It honestly describes men who were weary of war and were, perhaps understandably, a little more cautious than they had been in Spain in an attempt to preserve their lives.

But the consequences of war should not be overlooked or forgotten; a series of letters written by staff surgeons treating the mass of wounded housed in every available building in Brussels and Ghent, now turned into temporary hospitals, tells of the human cost. The letters are quite matter-of-fact, being factual updates on patients, doctor to doctor; but they also describe in detail the horrific injuries suffered and the primitive treatments and horrendous pain endured by the wounded. Indeed, it should be noted that the surgeons were given little time to prepare for this campaign: many senior posts were only filled days before the fighting commenced. This led to errors, mismanagement and undoubtedly unnecessary suffering, but the surgeons did everything possible to surmount these problems. However, despite their best endeavours, their valiant efforts could not make up for shortfalls in the organisation and it must be candidly stated that the survival rate of the wounded following the Battle of Waterloo was markedly worse than that achieved by a thoroughly professional organisation working at its most efficient only a year earlier at the Battle of Toulouse.

A few reports from military experts soon after the battle throw up some fascinating issues; for example, the renowned Royal Engineer, Colonel Burgoyne, states that detachments of sappers used at La Haye Sainte the night prior to the battle may well have made it virtually impregnable and that earthworks along the crest of the ridge would have preserved many lives from the cannon fire and could have caused serious disruption to the massed cavalry attacks. However, as we know hindsight is a wonderful thing!

A civilian visitor to the field of war only four weeks after the battle completes this selection, which I trust will engage and fascinate the reader.

They all combine to bring the story of the Battle of Waterloo and the surrounding military campaign to life: you march with them, you fight with them, you die with them!

Note on transcription: as in other volumes, the letters are reproduced as closely to the original as possible, with only small changes to punctuation and spelling to aid the reader. French words are shown in italics and with appropriate accentuation for the same reason; other italics represent the correspondents' own emphasis, and it is generally clear when this is intended.

THE STAFF OF THE ARMY

**No. 1   Unsigned Return of Numbers of British Rank and File
under the command of the Duke of Wellington
in January 1814 and in June 1815, including KGL**

*By kind permission of Sir Michael Bunbury Bt, KCVO, DL, and
Suffolk Record Office, Bury St Edmunds, ref. E18/740/4*

Corps		January 1814		June 1815		
Comparative view deducting sick from both returns						
Cavalry &		8,594			9,243	Excess in 1815
Wagon Train	*419*	9,013	*50*		9,018	649
Infantry		34,443	30,016			Diminution in 1815
	13,186	47,529	*1,600*	31,616		4,427
Artillery &		5,549	5,690			Excess in 1815
Sappers &c.	*539*	6,088	*120*	5,810		141

Sick denoted in *italics*.

No. 2   Colonel Colin Campbell, Commandant at Headquarters

*By kind permission of Sir Michael Bunbury Bt, KCVO, DL, and
Suffolk Record Office, Bury St Edmunds, ref. E18/740/4*

To Major General Sir Henry Torrens[*]

Waterloo, 3 leagues in front of Brussels, 19 June 1815

My dear Torrens,
We have gained a great and most glorious victory yesterday evening and
totally defeated Bonaparte's army and taken all his cannon, baggage &c.

---

[*]   Chief Secretary to the Commander-in-Chief.

&c. the Duke has done all this; it was the severest and most bloody action ever fought and the British infantry has surpassed anything ever before known. The action began about eleven o'clock and lasted till nearly the same hour at night when the British troops were halted and the Prussians who having then come up, were sent in pursuit and Marshal Blücher has pursued them till the Sambre. Our headquarters will be today at Nivelles, this victory has saved Europe, it was frequently *all* but lost; but the Duke alone, by his extraordinary perseverance and example, saved the day. We have already taken upwards of one hundred pieces of cannon and immense numbers of ammunition wagons, &c. Marshal Blücher has since then sent word that the road is choked up with artillery, baggage &c. The rout was most complete; there are several thousand prisoners and many generals killed and taken of the enemy. Our loss is alas most severe and it grieves me beyond measure to enumerate the names of those heroes who have fallen. Picton is killed, Gordon & Canning the Duke's ADC's killed; Delancey killed; Lord Uxbridge lost his leg; Lord Fitzroy Somerset his right arm; and Colonel Ponsonby I fear will die as both his arms are broken; Barnes severely wounded. I cannot mention any more but must refer you to the Duke's dispatch for all the details, &c. which are extraordinary.

I fear our runaways, of whom there were not a few, spread an alarm over the country; recollect our army, how it is composed; not one of the British infantry were seen in the rear; our cavalry made several brilliant charges; the Household Brigade has particularly distinguished themselves and also General Vivian's; but Lord Uxbridge is by no means satisfied with them,[*] his conduct throughout the day was most unremitting and he unfortunately received his wound nearly at the conclusion when the enemy were in full retreat.

No language of mine can do justice to the extraordinary mind and talents the Duke displayed during the whole of the action, our infantry were mostly formed in squares and the enemy's cavalry were five or six or even ten times during the day *upon our ground* and round our squares, but no one of which they ever penetrated.

I never have seen or heard of a field of battle so covered with dead and wounded. The Duke was all day everywhere in the thickest of it and his place of refuge was in one of the squares when the enemy's cavalry charged.

At six in the evening the Duke ordered the attack; we had till then been

---

[*] There is much evidence from letters written immediately after the battle that Uxbridge was dissatisfied with the conduct of the cavalry during the battle. However, such a stunning victory led to all criticism being silenced and soon Uxbridge was extolling the efforts of the cavalry; a diplomatic U-turn?

on the defensive and in less than half an hour we routed their first line and threw them on their second and then the rout became general.

The Guards, Adam's, Pack's, Kempt and indeed the whole of the British and Old German Legion behave nobly. The Duke I pray to God will be saved to us as without him we can do nothing.

Our loss since the 16th I calculate at 7 or 8,000, it may be more or even less, but I have never seen so many British killed and wounded. The fire of artillery and musquetry [*sic*] was terrible.

I hope you will be enabled to reinforce us; the Duke proposes moving immediately and to enter France. The French officers say that Bonaparte put himself at the head of the Imperial Guards during the last charge and charged with them up the hill. It is believed that Jerome Bonaparte is killed. I have just learned that there is fair hopes of Colonel Ponsonby's doing well;* General Ponsonby is taken prisoner;† General Cooke has lost an arm. How truly fortunate I am in having escaped this day, I had my horse killed and several shot through my clothes. I wish that you may be enabled to read this as I have written in great haste. Captain Hay‡ a relation of Lady Delancey's has gone to Antwerp to see her sent off to England.

Be so good as to show this to Shawe§ in case I have not leisure to write. I am &c., &c.,

C. Campbell

No. 3   Lieutenant Colonel Lord Greenock,¶
Assistant Quartermaster General to Sir Thomas Graham
By kind permission of the National Library of Scotland, ref. 3615, 46–49

Cavalry Headquarters
Chateau de Roissy# near Paris, 1 July 1815
#Formerly belonging to the Comte de Caraman**

My dear General,
Since the battle of the 18th the details of which you will already have been made acquainted with by the public despatches, we have been continually on the move so that I have been too much occupied during the day and

---

* Colonel Frederick Ponsonby did survive his wounds and left a very interesting account of his adventures. See letter 20 in this volume for an expanded version of his famous account.
† Major General the Honourable Sir William Ponsonby was killed, in fact.
‡ Captain Lord James Hay, 1st Foot Guards and ADC to Lieutenant General Colville.
§ Lieutenant Colonel Merrick Shawe was Assistant Secretary under Torrens.
¶ See his other letters in the editor's *Letters from Waterloo* (letter nos 5–10).
** Francis Joseph Philippe de Riquet Caraman (1771–1843), Comte de Caraman.

fatigued at night, that I have not had a moment to inform you of my safety. I certainly would, however, have found time for this had not Stanhope* told me that he had mentioned his having seen me since the battle to you in one of his letters. The oldest soldiers declare that they never saw so hard a fought battle and I should think it scarce possible to be exceeded. The very lowest estimate of the enemy's force on that day I have heard made puts it at 95,000 men; ours until the arrival of the Prussians was probably one-third less and composed of a great mixture of nations & many of the troops had scarcely ever seen a shot fired. The battle may be said to have commenced on the 16th as Bonaparte attacked our position at Quatre Bras about 3 o'clock in the afternoon of that day, where he was repulsed with loss. Our troops remained masters of the field after a very sanguinary conflict in which the Duke of Brunswick was unfortunately killed whilst gallantly heading his infantry. Blücher was attacked at the same time and maintained his ground very well until night; the enemy suddenly, however, came on again about nine o'clock with a large force of cavalry and succeeded in forcing their position. The Prussian loss in the different affairs they had at this time is estimated at 14,000 men. In consequence of this partial success of the enemy, as well as to operate his junction with Bülow's Corps, Blücher fell back upon Wavre.

On the 17th our left flank being uncovered by the retreat of the Prussians we were forced to retire also upon Waterloo, and to occupy a position in advance of that place covering Brussels. The enemy pressed our rear guard a good deal on the 17th during the great part of which day the cavalry were exposed to a very heavy cannonade and a sharp affair of cavalry took place near the village of Genappe in which the 1st Life Guards had an opportunity of charging some lancers in which they gained credit. Our friend Kelly† was particularly distinguished on this occasion and was not a little proud of his own performance, having cut down the first Frenchman; poor fellow, he has since been severely wounded, but I hope is doing well.

The morning of the 18th the enemy remained quiet but towards the middle of the day their movements plainly indicated an intention of attacking, which they accordingly did and gave the Duke an opportunity of gaining the most splendid and important victory that has almost ever been recorded in the annals of history. Napoleon and the Duke were

---

* Lieutenant Colonel the Honourable James Stanhope, 1st Foot Guards, whose letters and journals of the Peninsular War and Waterloo Campaign have been published by the editor as *Eyewitness to the Peninsular War*. However, Stanhope did not mention Greenock in his letter to the Duke of York following the battle.
† Captain Edward Kelly of the 1st Life Guards, see his letters in *Waterloo Archive*, vol. 6.

for the first time fairly opposed to each other and the superiority of the latter as a general and of the troops under his command were most conspicuously deployed. The enemy made the most desperate efforts before the position and made great use of his cavalry in which he was much superior; the steadiness and gallantry of our infantry were quite wonderful, and the cavalry had their full share in the business of the day. Poor Lord Uxbridge is a great loss; nothing could be more brilliant than his conduct throughout the day and, with a little more experience, which was the only thing he wanted, he is beyond all doubt the most fit person to command the cavalry. The more I saw of him both as a man and an officer, the more I had occasion to like him and I cannot describe to you how much I felt at seeing him wounded so near the close of the battle. At the moment I was going to his assistance, the horse I was riding was wounded by a grape shot which broke his leg and I was for the time of course dismounted; we, however, got Lord Uxbridge off his horse and put him in a blanket & carried him a little way to the rear until we could get hold of some infantry to carry him on to Waterloo. I returned to Waterloo at night and was present when the amputation was performed. Poor Frederick Ponsonby was desperately wounded and was in great danger for some time. I am happy, however, to hear that he is now pronounced out of danger, although it will be some time before he entirely recovers. With the exception of the horse I mentioned which was a trooper, my own having been rode to a standstill, I have not the slightest graze. George[*] had two horses killed under him, viz. the brown mare and bay hackney mare, the two bought off Hodgkinson;[†] he was not touched himself. We have been constantly moving on since the 18th, through a very fine country without seeing an enemy. The people all remaining in their houses and everything going on as if in a state of profound peace. Hither this day or two, however, we have come into the march of the Prussians, who have plundered and laid waste the country in a most shameful manner and this is the time we have found any difficulty in getting supplies; however, we have a good name, and the people, finding the British instead of the Prussians, are beginning to return to their habitations. Today our army occupies a position having its right at Pierrefitte[-sur-Sesne] on the high road from Chantilly to Paris, and extending in rear of Bourget on the Senlis Road by [Le] Blanc Mesnil and Aulnay [Sous Bois] to the Forest of Bondy on which our left rests. Head quarters are at Gonesse; the Prussians occupied this ground yesterday

---

[*] His younger brother, Lieutenant the Honourable George Cathcart, 6th Dragoon Guards, was an Extra Aide de Camp to Wellington at Waterloo.
[†] Probably Lieutenant William Hodgkinson of 62nd Foot, who exchanged into 7th West India Regiment on 22 December 1814.

but upon being relieved by us have moved off to the right. It is impossible to say how the war will be terminated as yet. Paris in a great ferment, but as yet they appear determined to make their resistance. St Denis is fortified and the position of Montmartre is occupied; the Prussians took the village of Aubervilliers yesterday morning which we occupy today. A deputation visited on the Duke of Wellington at St Martin Longeau the day before yesterday composed of Andreossy,[*] Lautour-Maubourg,[†] the Duke of Valence[‡] and others, but of course the proposals could not be listened to whilst the government is carried on in the name of any of the Bonaparte family. It is now reported here Napoleon has resumed the command of the army. I hope if the French make any resistance they will not be let off to carry on but fear some terrible example should be made of the city of Paris and of all those who have returned to Bonaparte. The cavalry is commanded as previously by Sir John Vandeleur but we expect Lord Combermere[§] out immediately.

If we enter Paris soon I hope you may be induced to come out and meet us. Believe me my dear general, ever most affectionately yours,

Greenock

No. 4 Lieutenant Colonel John George Woodford, 1st Foot Guards, Extra Aide de Camp to Lord Wellington[¶]

By kind permission of Warwickshire County Record Office
ref. Newdgate of Arbury CR764/240

Lembeek in front of Halle, 8 a.m., 19 June

My dearest A[lexander][**]
I take the opportunity of a short rest to write a few lines. I cannot help beginning by expressing my gratitude for your escape[††] yesterday, which I was too overjoyed to say anything adequate about last night when we met.

Knowing as I did where you were posted judge of my anxiety, & afterwards of my joy! I trust proper notice will be taken &c., &c.

---

[*] General Antoine Francois Andreossy (1761–1828).
[†] General de Division Marie Victor Nicolas de Fay, Marquis de Latour-Maubourg (1768–1850).
[‡] General Jean Baptiste Cyrus Marie Adélaide de Timbrune de Thiembronne, Comte de Valence.
[§] Lieutenant General Sir Stapleton Cotton, Lord Combermere, was sent to France to command the cavalry as Uxbridge had been severely wounded.
[¶] Actually attached to General Colville's Division but sent on the evening of 17th June to Wellington from Hal (or Halle). He reached Waterloo a few hours before the battle commenced and remained throughout the action as an extra ADC to Wellington.
[**] His elder brother Colonel Alexander George Woodford, Coldstream Guards.
[††] He refers to his brothers' survival from the defence of Hougoumont.

We move on Nivelles by Braine le Chateau [Comte], I hope we shall meet in the neighbourhood of Nivelles for I conceive a little repose will soon be necessary for the army.

I hope Carter will join you today, remember our old system of pleasant communication; 'I am well & a date' can give no information to the enemy if he nabs it.

What a glorious day was yesterday, my imagination is still full of squares & cavalry & charging & melees. I hope you have not the advanced guard today, as you had so much yesterday. I keep this in my pocket for an opportunity [of sending].

[Unsigned]

No. 5 Diary* of Captain Digby Mackworth 7th Foot, Aide de Camp to General Hill

By kind permission of The Army Quarterly, *1937, pp.123–31; 1938 pp. 320–7*

30 March, Downs
We embarked this morning at ½ past 12 on board the *Rosario*, Captain Peake,[†] in number four, viz. Lord Hill, his brother Clement,[‡] Hillier[§] & myself, without a single horse, or a single servant, except Lord Hill's valet. On getting under sail the ship saluted his lordship with nineteen guns, and away we went bound for Ostend.

31st, Ostend
We arrived here this evening at 5 o'clock after a very pleasant though long passage. The whole town was in confusion from the number of English troops lately disembarked, all of whom, true to their English nature, were wandering about with their hands in their pockets, and their eyes and mouths wide open, staring at the wonderful sight of a few dozen heavy stupid Flemings. I was so much occupied in procuring horses, etc., for the continuation of our journey to Brussels that I had no opportunity of viewing the fortifications: Lord Hill, who visited them, says they are tolerably strong. We met here Colonel Colin Campbell, the officer who had been staying so long with Napoleon in Elba; he passed through the Prussian army on the Rhine, who were in full preparation for opening

---

* Although described as a diary, they appear to be extracts from a series of letters.
† HMS *Rosario*, 10 guns, Captain Thomas L. Peake.
‡ At this time Captain Clement Hill was an ADC to Lord Hill and is often quoted as having served in the same capacity at Waterloo. His own letter (see Siborne's *Waterloo Letters*, p.55) confirms that he actually served with his regiment, the Horse Guards, at the battle and Orlando Bridgeman was given the post of extra ADC to Lord Hill (see letter 7 in this volume).
§ Captain George Hillier 74th Foot, Deputy Assistant Quartermaster General.

the campaign. He told us that Murat was beginning to stir, but it did not appear certain. The King of France had left this place two days ago for Gand,* where he now is with not above 200 soldiers who have remained faithful to him. Marmont is the only marshal who has not left him, and he *dare* not.

Memo: the first specimen I have met with of Flemish honesty, was the being cheated soon after landing to a considerable amount in the exchange of English money for Flemish; though to give the devil his due, I must say that they offered me a glass of wine and some bread and cheese to make amends.

1 April, Gand
Reached this to breakfast at nine o'clock, its fortifications are no longer worthy of mention, but it is a large handsome town. I had the *pleasure* of seeing the King of France breakfast here in public. Poor man! It must be dreadful for him in the present state of his affairs to be obliged to wear a face dressed in smiles and good humour. Kings are more to be pitied than envied, though there are few men, I believe, even of those who say so, who would refuse the offer of a kingdom, such is human nature. We have received official information that no French troops have as yet set foot on the Belgian territories, but the videttes on both sides are posted opposite each other just as if hostilities had commenced. Not a shot, however, has as yet been fired.

2nd, Brussels, Sunday
Our journey to this place terminated last night at about 8 o'clock, and I immediately accompanied Lord Hill to the palace of the Prince of Orange, where, after waiting a considerable time the prince arrived, and had an interview with his lordship which lasted till past eleven. It appears that the prince has made himself unpopular in our army, and that the present situation has a little turned his head, nor have flatterers been wanting to make him believe that he is as great a general as some of the ancient princes of his house; which, judging from the present state of the army under his command, and from the mode in which everything is carried on by him, does not appear to be the case. He received Lord Hill with much cordiality in appearance but his lordship was not much satisfied with the interview he had with him. Delays and excuses were found where immediate action was required; and the only point in which Lord Hill succeeded with the prince, was the inducing him to withdraw the troops from the advanced position which they occupied between Tournai and

---

* Ghent.

Ath,* to Enghien, where they are to remain at present, but from whence they will probably be further removed, should the enemy appear to threaten the country in any force. While at the prince's palace I heard an anecdote concerning Marshal Ney which is worth preserving. It is on good authority, having been told me by Sir Edward Barnes,† who heard it from the Duc de Berri,‡ who was personally present on the occasion. It has been reported in the public papers that this marshal had asked the king for a command, and that he had expressed the strongest feelings of devotion to his cause, which is so far true; but could anyone imagine that he carried his dissimulation so far as to fall on his knees before the good old king, to take his majesty's hands between his own, and cover them with his tears, and to swear that his majesty had no one subject who more truly loved him with his own heart and soul! When he first asked for a command, the king told him he should be most glad to avail himself of his services, but that he really had no command worthy of him to offer. Ney replied that even at the head of a single regiment he was impatient to give the strongest proofs of his zeal and fidelity; upon which the king told him he had collected 6,000 men which he felt assured he could not trust in better hands. The marshal took his leave, put himself at the head of these troops and marched without delay to join Bonaparte.

3rd

The whole of yesterday was employed in looking out for a house for Lord Hill, in which we were not successful. His lordship dined with the Prince of Orange and we had a snug party by ourselves at the Hotel d'Angleterre, and went to the play in the evening, which was so bad that I mentally vowed not to go to it again unless on duty as ADC walking stick to my good little man, who likes going there, though he does not understand two words of what is said.

4th

Had I not been obliged to quit England, this evening would not have been spent in the solitary manner in which I am now spending it. At this moment I should perhaps have been dancing at our Farnham Ball, and enjoying all the delights which for many days I had promised myself at it; but '*Tempora mutantur, nos et mutamur in illis*';§ and I must be content with imagination, where I might have enjoyed the reality, I do think that

---

* The prince had originally prepared to advance and secure Valenciennes.
† Major General Sir Edward Barnes Adjutant General.
‡ Charles Ferdinand d'Artois, Duke de Berri, the younger son of the king's brother, eventually succeeded to the throne as Charles X. He was assassinated in 1820.
§ 'Times change and we change with them' a Latin saying.

the greatest drawback on the pleasure of a military life is that a man is so continually liable, just as he has formed connexions and acquaintances the most delightful to him, to receive an order, without the slightest previous notice, to quit them, to go to heaven knows where, and perhaps never to see them again. This, however, will not, I confidently hope, be my case; for my only comfort under present privation and hard self denial is that one firm hope that a time will come, which shall amply repay me with tenfold interest, and reposing in that hope I will endeavour to submit patiently to whatever fate may yet have in store for me. Were I satisfied as to one point, I should be content; but it may not be.

6th

We have got into our new house which was one lately occupied by Lord Waterpark,* and which has the advantage of fronting the Parc Royal, and of being but a short distance from the King's and Prince's palaces, otherwise the house is far from comfortable. Yesterday I was on duty as walking stick to Lord Hill, and accompanied him to a party at Lady Charlotte Greville's,† where as I knew no one of the ladies, and did not feel then disposed to take the trouble of becoming acquainted with them, I amused myself by observing what everybody did, and in fancying myself a 'Thinks-I-to-myself'. And indeed there was ample field for observation. Some, the greater part, were bowing to the Duke of Wellington who arrived yesterday; others were charitably endeavouring to make our hostess pleased with herself by admiring her rooms, etc., etc; others were much better employed in eating and drinking as much cakes and tea as they could lay hands on. (This by the by was my own principle employment when not on observation.) One young lady was sitting on a sofa surrounded by three or four military beaux, whose manners and attitudes strongly showed that they were seeking the admiration of the company in general rather than of her who was the apparent object of their attention. But above all, a young lady, a Miss C—l,‡ quite astonished me by a display of manners more highly fashionable, I conclude, than I was before at all aware of. I am almost ashamed to say that she appeared to be absolutely making love to a handsome general on whose arm she was hanging, and who, I am told, is not the first, second, or third, who has been equally honoured. Even my good-natured little man observed it, and remarked to me, 'It is quite a shame for young ladies to be so forward.'

---

* Sir Henry Cavendish, 2nd Baron Waterpark in the Irish peerage.

† Lady Charlotte (née Cavendish - Bentinck) was the wife of Colonel the Honourable Charles Greville 38th Foot.

‡ One of the Capel daughters. Probably Louisa Capel who made a tilt for Major General Sir Edward Barnes.

What a contrast! I could go on but I think my dose of scandal has already been sufficiently large, even to please some certain young ladies who have the honour of being my sisters, and that is saying a great deal.

8th.
I have just returned from a ride to Enghien, where I went to pay a visit to some friends of mine in the Guards. Close to the town is a very pleasant and tolerably extensive park belonging to the family d'Arenberg,* and some of the officers were amusing themselves by playing at cricket there: I joined the party, and spent a pleasant day, and returned to Brussels this morning after breakfast.

9th
Lord Hill, accompanied by all his Staff went yesterday to a grand fete, given by the City of Brussels to the king, queen and court. All the wigs in the place were there, it was very magnificent, but as I was not in cue to enjoy it: I slipped away before supper. It commenced with music and verses written in honour of their majesties, and ended with a ball, which was opened by the Prince of Orange, and a young lady of the court, whom the English, I know not why, have named 'Bang up'. The king looks like a gentleman, and has a sensible countenance; the queen is the very image of Queen Bess on her death bed, and the ladies of the court are, I hope, very *rich*, as their portion of *beauty* is small indeed. In all my life I never saw anything so tiresome as these court ceremonies. I am pretty sure they will not again catch me at them in the land of 'Bosses' as our people call the Pay Bas. The society was so select that I found among them a *lady* and her daughter, with whom a few mornings ago I had been bargaining about a house for Lord Hill; the lady is by trade a lace-maker. She appears however just as well dressed and genteel as any of the rest of them.

12th
I returned last night from Enghien where the Guards are quartered, and where I had been to join in a cricket match. There is nothing in the place at all remarkable, except a tolerably handsome park belonging to the Duc d'Arenberg, His chateau had been converted into a hospital by the original French revolutionists, but not content with that, they have since pulled it down altogether.

16th
I am so heartily sick of this life of inaction at Brussels, that it was with

---

* Prosper-Louis, 7th Duke of Arenberg (1785–1861), who was married to Stéphanie Tascher de La Pagerie, a niece of Joséphine de Beauharnais.

no small joy I read orders this morning to prepare for our removal, and I don't recollect having ever in my life used more diligence to get things in order. Surely want of employment can never be a so truly miserable state, as when one has just quitted one's friends, for how long a period heaven alone knows. The mind is in no condition to enjoy what is usually called pleasure and dissipation. It appears rather, though I scarcely know why, as a sort of mockery and insult, and one feels a constant misanthropical inclination to compare the present with the past, and in truth the comparison is sadly to the disadvantage of the former. In a word one views every occurrence through the unfair, disagreeable, self-tormenting medium of *discontent*.

17th, Monday, Grammont
Lord Hill, having determined to fix his headquarters at this place, sent me forward yesterday to have them arranged, and I was far from being sorry to leave that odious Brussels. We came by Aalst, which is much round, but it is the only carriage road, and we were not certain that the other routes were as yet practicable even for our horses; we stopped at Aalst to dine. It seemed a pleasant town, and was occupied by the cavalry of the King of France's army, amounting to about 200 men and 160 officers. The infantry of this army consists of 600 men!!! Louis's court appears to have sanguine hopes of his being shortly reinstated, and I trust it will be so. I have a high respect for *him*, though but little for the people about him, particularly that silly man the Duc de Berri, who was foolish enough to lift his hands some time ago in order to strike a French officer. The officer very properly desired him to beware, as he had a sword by his side, and the duke took the hint. The cause of the quarrel was that the officer had not dressed himself according to regulation.

20th, Ath
This is the first place we have arrived at on a tour which Lord Hill is about to make round the cantonments of his corps in order to see in what state of improvement they are. The Duke of Wellington and his lordship reviewed today the 2nd Division under the orders of Sir Henry Clinton. They were all in excellent order except the artillery, which the great man found fault with. All the wigs dined together in the evening, and the Duke was exceedingly communicative. He declared, to my no small astonishment, that there was not one syllable of truth in the newspaper account of the insulting slights put upon him, and quarrels he got into during his embassy in Paris: on the contrary he everywhere met with the greatest respect and deference. So much for the public journals; it is quite provoking to read such groundless mischievous falsehoods.

21st, Tournai
If our quarters last night were but indifferent these of today make ample amends for them. Tournai has been a magnificent, and is still a very handsome town with about 23,000 inhabitants. It is surrounded with strong works, but as its *enceinte** is 5,000 yards in length it would take at least 40,000 men to defend it properly. Our engineers are therefore turning their principal attention to the works of the citadel, which is a regular pentagon erected on the highest spot of ground in the place, commanding it entirely. The work is nearly complete and I should imagine it would require a siege in form to take, though *if* attacked in form; it could not stand many days of open trenches. Two thousand men would be a sufficient garrison. There we saw for the first time 4 battalions of Hanoverian Landwehr, they looked well.

22nd, Oudenarde
We passed through Courtrai this morning and came to this town to sleep. The works at Courtrai are trifling, and here they are too near some heights on the right bank of the Escaut to resist long. 2,000 men are daily employed in putting them in a state of defence. Tomorrow morning we shall review the 54th Regiment and return to Grammont to dinner. The 54th are commanded by Lord Waldegrave,† who has greatly distressed his family by a very imprudent marriage. Many people think the marriage has not actually taken place, though he introduces the lady wherever as Lady Waldegrave.‡ I know nothing of him but his appearance and manner are not those of a sensible man, and I am sure his conduct might make even a fool blush to be guilty of it.

27th, Brussels
After spending a few days quietly and soberly at Grammont, I have accompanied Lord Hill once more to this Flemish Babel; he is to attend a grand fete which the Duke of Wellington is about to give to all the *Beau monde* of the place, and I to commence a tour which I am anxious of making round Antwerp and Bergen op Zoom. I mean to travel incog[nito], and by the diligence, which will give me a better opportunity of seeing the ways and manners of the people than if I went '*en Grand Seigneur*'. A malicious person might hint that if I went as a *grand seigneur* I should

---

* French, curtain wall.
† Lieutenant Colonel John James Waldegrave, 6th Earl Waldegrave, commanded the 54th Foot.
‡ The marriage of Earl Waldegrave and his long-time lover Anne King did not actually take place until October 1815; however the couple had already borne an illegitimate son, John James Henry Waldegrave, born in 1802.

be still more incognito as I should not be *reconnaisable*;* but I can tell him that as ADC of the Right Honourable Lord Hill (he ought to have taken the title of Lord *Mountain* because he is a *great hill*) is not to be accounted as small beer in a country where the true value and importance of an officer is better known than in that odious England. Here we can give ourselves airs, there – alas! – we should only be laughed at. Tonight I am to sleep at this little public house (be it known to posterity that it is at the 'sign of the green tree') and shall start at 5 in the morning for Antwerp. The room below mine is filled with countrymen, women, soldiers, etc., etc., drinking, singing, swearing and fighting; while my good landlady is wasting her time and breath in assuring me there is not a more respectable house in all Brussels *'credat Judaeus'*† paugh! What a smell of tobacco is just come across my nose! But, if I mind that, I shall justly be accused of being as dainty a soldier as my Lord 'Ever and Anon' with his pouncet-box in Henry the Fourth.‡ So *coucher* and *dormir*§ and a 'good night' to all my dear good friends in England.

28th, Antwerp
My companions in the diligence consisted of a French captain belonging to Louis the 18th and two young cubs to whom he appeared to be a sort of leader, and who were all, like myself, taking a trip to see the lions¶ at Antwerp. We had a good deal of conversation about the state of their king's affairs; but the captain's gasconades were so out of all decency and measure, that there was no depending on a syllable he uttered. He had, however, the grace to acknowledge that the king's best hope lay in the friendship of England; and that was allowing a great deal for a Frenchman.

The works of this place are in a formidable state of defence, particularly the castle; but they are destroying the dock yards gradually, as no ships of war are in future to be built in them: this I conclude is caused by the never ceasing jealousy of the English government on that head. The celebrated Bason did not strike me in so strong a light as perhaps it deserved. It is certainly a very secure place for shipping against the weather, but might I think easily be bombarded and shelled by an enemy from the land side. I dined tonight for the first time at a French ordinary, and an *ordinary*

---

* Recognisable.
† A quote from Horace (*Satires* I.5, l.100), meaning, 'The Jew may believe it,' . . . but he does not; he refers to a supposedly miraculous sight that he was cynical about.
‡ He compares the foppish knight's aversion to the smell of the dead to his own aversion to tobacco.
§ French, to bed and to sleep.
¶ Lions: the sights

dinner it was. The company, male and female, was far from being select, but I cared little about that, as one of my chief present objects is to spy out the ways of the *Goths* and *Griffins.* Heavens! How they did eat! My knife and fork almost dropped from my hands when I saw a great huge burgomaster's wife send for the fourth time, and have her plate literally covered with a '*petit peu de poisson, Monsieurs, s'il vous plait'*.* In order to enjoy the pleasure of their *unreserved* conversation, I, as usual, did not understand more French than just enough to ask for bread etc (I always take good care to understand enough for that) and I was consequently treated *sans ménagement* and, *grâce à mon pensive physionomie,*† I was voted a stupid dull-looking Englishman, who[m] they concluded was coming to gape at the wonders of their great city. I tried to keep the muscles immovable, but I fear this flattering compliment must have produced something very like a 'Big-fiddle face'. I am just on the point (2 p.m.) of continuing my route to Breda.

1 May, Bergen op Zoom

My journey from Antwerp to Breda was far from being agreeable as some Dutch officers and merchants were smoking all the way inside the coach, and compassion obliged me to give up my place on the outside to a countryman and fellow traveller whom their tobacco had made quite sick. The country on each side of the road has a miserable appearance; being one continued marshy flat, with only an occasional spot of cultivation and a great part altogether under water. This is the case all round Breda, which in the event of a siege could only be approached by the dykes on which the roads run and I think on the whole it is by far the strongest place I have ever seen; its fortifications, excepting some parts of the palisade of the *chemin couvert*,‡ are perfect, but it does not appear to be at present well provided with artillery. The castle is strongly situated but not very strong in itself. It is a large square brick building, surrounded by a very broad (about 90 feet) and deep moat, which separates it from the rest of the works. The town is neat and clean and the inhabitants appear respectable in general; French is not much spoken here. From Breda to Bergen op Zoom the road is of a very deep sand, and consequently tedious, and nothing can be more frightful than the barren waste which borders it. About two-thirds of the way is a well-built large village called Roosendaal, where I could not find a soul who spoke French, but my profound knowledge of German extricated me from the difficulty, and I arrived safe here last night. Of course I have

---

* 'A little bit of fish, Monsieur, please.'
† 'Without caution' and 'thanks to my thoughtful countenance'.
‡ Covered way.

been to see the works here, and particularly those parts where the English entered by surprise under Sir T[homas] Graham.* Contrary to my former opinion I am now inclined to believe that the general was justified in making the attempt, and that had our troops, when entered, behaved well, we must have held the place; we were masters of 11 bastions out of 15, but, instead of keeping on the ramparts, and turning the cannon on the town, we sent small detachments into the streets one after the other, which were surrounded and either taken or cut to pieces immediately: whereas nothing could have prevented our holding the ramparts had we remained in one body, and the garrison would easily have been forced to surrender. The inhabitants speak with admiration of the attempt, and so has Bonaparte; only one cannot place much confidence in what he says. Bergen may, like Breda, be surrounded with water by opening sluices. It is abundantly provided with cannon.

3 May, Grammont

l have once more returned here without any particular accident, except the being made prisoner at Antwerp because my passport had not been '*visé*'.† I was, however, speedily released on making my name and situation known to the English commandant, Memo: in future it will always be better to travel on the Continent in regimentals. An officer may act almost as he pleases. Blush, England!

11 May

Prince Frederic of Orange,‡ accompanied by several Dutch Officers, breakfasted with us, and, after remaining a few hours, set off for Zottegem, where his headquarters will be established for the present. He is a very young man but I like his appearance and manners much. He appears rather timid and shy, which for a prince is certainly an error on the right side, it is not at any rate a common one. Lord Hill was much pleased with him; his Staff, particularly a Baron d'Iroy,§ were more gentlemanly men than I should have expected. I supped this evening with my hostess and family, but found them rather dull folks, and as dirty in their persons as they are clean in their house.

---

* A force under Sir Thomas Graham launched a daring surprise assault on the fortress of Bergen op Zoom in March 1814. Having gained entry and capturing most of the town, a counter-attack by the French defenders drove them back and led to much of the assaulting force having to accede to a humiliating surrender.
† 'Referred'.
‡ Prince Frederick was the brother of William Prince of Orange and commanded a reserve force in the Waterloo campaign.
§ Colonel Baron d'Ivry was 1st ADC to Frederick Prince of Orange.

13th
Yesterday we reviewed the 71st Regiment near Liège. It was in good order, and about 700 strong. After the review Lord Hill was repeatedly cheered by the men, who had served under him in Spain, and appeared much pleased with this mark of their gratitude and good opinion.

17th
Rode over this morning to Zottegem in order to arrange with Prince Frederic some day on which Lord Hill might review his division, and it was accordingly fixed for the 19th. The more I see of the young prince, the more I am inclined to think well of him. Yesterday we did not forget to celebrate the bloody battle of Albuera. Certainly I never saw before or since any one at all equal to it.

20th
Prince Frederic's Corps, upwards of 10,000 bayonets was paraded yesterday for our inspection. We found it in better order than had been supposed likely, particularly the 'Brigade of the Indies', which was composed of really fine troops. After the review Lord Hill and his Staff dined with Prince Frederic, and returned to Grammont in the evening. Of the Prince's Staff two men pleased me particularly: the Baron d'Iroy, his first aide de camp, and Colonel Count St Aldegonde,* QMG. The former has passed many years in England, and speaks the language exceedingly well.

28th
Lord Wellington gave a grand ball yesterday, at which all the principal people in Brussels were present. A most magnificent supper was prepared, and the gardens so well illuminated as almost to resemble day. The Duke himself danced, and always with the same person, a Lady Caroline Webster,† to whom he paid so much attention that scandal, who is become goddess here, began to whisper all sorts of stories, but we are not bound to believe all she says; not but that the well-known bad private character of His Grace would warrant any suspicions whatever. There must have been something essentially bad in the education of the Wellesley family: on the score of gallantry not one of its members, male or female, is *sans reproche*.‡ When the Duke of Wellington, after Lord Uxbridge's appointment to the command of the British cavalry, was asked whether he would not feel it

---

* Lieutenant Quarter-maître General Colonel Comte L. A. B van Sainte Aldegonde.
† Mackworth is in error here, he actually refers to Lady Frances Webster. The affair led to a great scandal a few years later.
‡ 'Without reproach'.

unpleasant to meet with the man who had run off with his sister?* 'Why?' said he, 'Damn him, he won't run off with me, too.' They did meet and even appeared to be on the best possible terms.

2 June, Brussels
Expecting, as I had always done, to find the inhabitants of Belgium an exact counterpart of their French masters, I have been agreeably surprised at perceiving, on nearer acquaintance, that their language and dress are the only points of resemblance between them. There is an air of frankness and welcome in the reception that a Belgian gives which is not to be found in the most winning politeness of the most *amiable* Frenchman; beside which, and surely it is the groundwork of almost every other good quality, the Belgian is still in fact religious. However mistaken his notions of religion may be, he reverences and regards its ministers and statutes. He is not ashamed of being seen at church; he does not admit of buying and selling on the day of rest; he is credulous, bigoted, and priest-ridden; but he is, and means to be, really religious, and as such must be infinitely more respected than the amiable, brilliant, highly polished French *'habitudinarian'* (that is the fashionable name for *deist*). The ladies in Belgium have not yet learned to contract marriages readily with persons who are totally indifferent to them, merely that they may enjoy a habitude of conduct when married which custom, not principle, denies them when single. While unmarried no one is more reserved and modest apparently than a young French lady; but what an astonishing change is produced in her conduct, not in her sentiments, by the solemn sacred oath to be forever faithful during life to one and only one; one would imagine she bound herself to do exactly the contrary, yet such things are.

4 June
The intelligence which we have received within these few days has worn a much more favourable aspect than ever. Not only do Murat's affairs seem desperate in Italy,† but the insurrections in La Vendée‡ appear to be of a most serious nature. Many people imagine that we ought in consequence

---

* Henry William Paget, Earl of Uxbridge had eloped with Lady Charlotte Wellesley (née Cadogan), Wellington's sister-in-law, being married to his brother Henry.

† Joachim Murat, made king of Naples, sought to second Napoleon, but launched his attack on Austrian Italy too early. He was defeated at the Battle of Tolentino on 2–3 May 1815 and fled; eventually captured he was executed by firing squad.

‡ The area of La Vendée was traditionally royalist and had risen before only to be brutally repressed. The royalist faction rose again on Napoleon's return, but it was easily quelled; however, the troops, including some Imperial Guard units, that were sent there were not available to Napoleon in the Waterloo campaign.

to advance immediately, and take advantage of the state of confusion in which France now is; but it may be alleged, on the other hand, that these insurrections may be more easily suppressed than is supposed, and that we shall settle the affair with more certain prospects of success when all our force is assembled, than if we were to advance without waiting for the Russians. In fact it does not appear that Bonaparte reaps an equal advantage from delay with us; we are increasing by thousands, and he by hundreds. In a short time not only will the Russians have joined, but the Austrians employed against Murat will become disposable, and our masses will then indeed be enormous. Still I think Lord Castlereagh* must have over-rated the force of the allies when he talks of 1,011,000 men. For instance he talks of 225,000 Prussians, and Colonel Hardinge,† who is the British officer employed at their Headquarters, told me the other day that they had at present only 120,000 in the field, and he thought they might be increased to 140,000. With regard to the British, I shall be much surprised if ever they amount to 40, much less 50,000, He also states that several of the Belgian frontier towns are already in a state to stand a siege; this is not exactly true. They are safe from a coup-de-main, but that is all. The castle of Tournai would demand some days, but all the other works are of small importance; though certainly very great progress has been made, indeed as much as could be, in placing them in a respectable state of defence. In fact our object in fortifying these places is not to enable them to stand a siege, but to repress the incursion of the French garrisons when we shall have left their strong towns behind us on our march towards Paris, and to prevent their laying the country under contribution and such object they will effectually fulfil. In the mean time the spirit of this country is becoming rapidly better. All our officers have been surprised at the gaiety with which the Belgian conscripts march to join their corps: they really seem like volunteers and they have not as yet attempted to desert. I wish I could say as much for some of our German cavalry. On the whole the prospect is bright and cheering; and I trust, if God permit, that we shall ere long pour upon these execrable followers of a more execrable chief some of the miseries which they have for a long series of years been heaping on oppressed and insulted Europe. Only let us loose, and I don't think all the Frenchmen on earth can stop us.

7th
Yesterday we had a grand cricket match at Enghien and the Duke of

---

* Robert Stewart, 2nd Marquess of Londonderry (1769–1822) was Foreign Secretary.
† Colonel Sir Henry Hardinge, 1st Foot Guards, was attached to the Prussian headquarters in 1815.

Richmond* was one of the players. I dined after the match was over at General Maitland's, and met there a Lady Mountnorris† and her daughter; the latter is rather good looking, but far from being in danger of setting the Thames on fire. Perhaps I injure them, but I cannot help thinking there is a little design formed against the heart of the handsome general. Lady M. is a noted old matchmaker, and the young lady certainly appeared to set her cap at him in a very decided manner; I'm sure no one else at least could, get a smile out of her; indeed she lavished so many on him that it was not to be expected in common convenience that she could have many to bestow on other less happy mortals, but had I better not put a stop to all this scandal? Will not people say that envy and malice have given rise to it?

9th

Yesterday there was a grand review of the whole of the British cavalry in the plains near this place.‡ They were about 6,000 strong and in magnificent order. Blücher and a great number of foreign generals and princes came over from Namur on purpose to see it; they all breakfasted with Lord Hill. A great number of ladies from Brussels and from all the country round were there, and the weather was exceedingly favourable, so that on the whole it was a most brilliant sight, and will certainly give the foreigners present an advantageous idea of our cavalry. Sir Sidney Smith§ came to see it, and does us the honour of being our guest for a day or two. He appears to be a very pleasant man, fond of talking of his own exploits, sometimes making some use of the long bow, and apparently altogether a man of more brilliancy than sound sense; more talent than judgement. When once he gets into the campaigns in Egypt, it is quite a hopeless case to attempt to get him out of them, but it must be confessed his histories and anecdotes are highly entertaining, to those who have not heard them too often before.

11th

We have just been having some races here which were very numerously

---

* Charles Lennox, 4th Duke of Richmond and Lennox (1764–1819) was in Belgium with his family in 1815, his wife holding the famous ball on 15 June. He was a keen cricketer and helped to set up the Marylebone Cricket Club in 1787.

† Lady Mountnorris (née Cavendish) had three daughters, but Lady Juliana was the only one not married. Lady Mountnorris hoped to marry Juliana to General Maitland but he had eyes only for Lady Sarah Lennox, with whom he eloped. They were married in Paris in August 1815. For details of this affair see the editor's *Recollections of the Scenes . . .*

‡ This appears to refer to the 'Grand Review' which occurred on 29 May.

§ Vice-Admiral Sir Sidney Smith, famous for the defence of Acre against Napoleon in 1799, was residing at Brussels with his family during the campaign.

attended. My little horse, Vestris, won three times, but Miss Fidget ran herself out of breath in the first half-mile and lagged sadly behind the second. I offered to run Vestris against any horse on the course, that, like him was not in training, but could not get a match for him. I am quite vain of his prowess, and so I think he is too, for he never was so spirited or saucy before since I have had him. As for Miss Fidget, she ought to be quite ashamed of herself, but like many other voting ladies, she will have her own way, cost what it may.

16th Enghien
The greater part of our staff went yesterday evening to a ball given by the Duchess of Richmond, which was of course attended by 'Everybody' at Brussels. We had heard during the day that the French had begun to advance and we knew that Bonaparte had joined them; still it was thought that, as the Prussian army was nearer to them than we were, we should have quite sufficient notice of their approach to make the necessary preparations to give them a warm and hearty reception. About 11 o'clock, however, while the dancing was yet going with great spirit, we learned from the Duke that the Prussians had suffered severely that same evening, and that our Belgian outposts had given notice that the enemy was in sight of them: it was consequently necessary to start immediately and rejoin as quick as possible our several corps. In vain did the charms of music, the persuasions, and even in some instances the *tears*, of beauty tempt us to remain; in vain did the *afflicted* Duchess of Richmond, placing herself at the entrance of the hall room, pray and entreat that we would not 'go before supper'; that we would wait 'one little hour more' and 'not spoil her ball'.* Ungentle hard-hearted cavaliers, we resisted all and departed, 'Ladies beware of all fair young knights, they dance and ride away,' In our ball costumes, brilliant with gold lace and embroidery, exulting in the assurance that our long tiresome days of inactivity were at an end, and that we were on the point of meeting this celebrated *loup-garou*† Bonaparte, so long our anxious wish, we spurred our chargers and soon covered the thirty miles which separated us from our corps, Some had already marched, and the whole arrived this evening at Enghien, where it now is. The firing towards our left is at present heavy, and we

---

* This is an interesting version of events at the ball; traditionally the dance continued into the small hours uninterrupted by the news (perhaps another invention of the Victorians to show off British stoicism in adversity?). Mackworth's version of the officers leaving in haste despite the pleas of the Duchess of Richmond has more the ring of truth.
† The *loup-garou* is a French legend of a human who changes into a wolf at his/her own will.

are just going to mount fresh horses and start off to see what it is. '*Vive la guerre.*'[*]

17th, Braine l'Alleud.

We are now able to make a few minutes repose after the sharp affairs of yesterday evening; and this morning. We have certainly been in some degree surprised, and ought to have assembled the army a day, or perhaps two days sooner. Yesterday the Belgian outposts and two brigades of Perponcher's infantry with some cavalry were driven by Marshal Ney on this side of four Bras, and were retiring in confusion until successively supported by Picton's Division and the Brigade of Guards under Maitland; which after suffering a severe loss regained the position of four Bras,[†] and retained it, until night put an end to the contest. Among others who fell on this occasion we have to regret particularly the Duke of Brunswick Oels,[‡] who fell gallantly fighting at the head of his own infantry, and died the death of a soldier. His troops outrageous at his loss *gave*, and swear they *will* give no quarter to the French who fall into their hands, and I have no doubt they will keep their word. Our army retired, with the exception of the 2nd Division which formed the rear guard, during the night, and took up a position near this place, where they now are, and where it is said Lord Wellington is determined to fight for the preservation of Brussels. Some cavalry skirmishes were the only affairs which took place during this retreat; the enemy advancing very cautiously, and I should think from their undecided movements not aware that we actually were in retreat. Whenever they did press us a little closely our cavalry charged and drove them back, in which the Life Guards much distinguished themselves, after the 7th Hussars had been unsuccessful. The infantry did not fire a shot. It was about 4 o'clock that the retreat terminated, and the troops are now getting a little rest, of which they are in the greatest need; having been marching almost ever since they set out at daybreak yesterday, with little or nothing to eat, by bad roads, and in torrents of rain. Of Lord Hill's Corps, the 4th Division, excepting Mitchell's Brigade, and the whole of Prince Frederic's Belgians are ordered to take up a position at Hal [or Halle], about five miles on our right, in order to cover that road to Brussels: the country between this

---

[*] 'Long live the war.'

[†] The crossroads at Quatre Bras were actually never lost, but the arrival of the Guards and other units in the evening allowed Wellington to launch a counter-attack using his now superior forces to regain the forward positions originally held by the Belgian troops in the morning.

[‡] Prince Frederick William, Duke of Brunswick-Wolfenbüttel led a force of Brunswick troops in the campaign and was shot dead leading them at Quatre Bras.

place and them is absolutely impracticable for any large body excepting the road by which we communicate, and even that is none of the best, part of the way it is made of felled trees.

11 p.m. 18 June 1815
Harassed and fatigued as I am, it requires a strong and a powerful incentive to sit down and write an account of the dreadful battle in which we have this day been engaged. But while the great events are yet so fresh in my memory, I should not like to miss the opportunity of committing them to paper. Indeed they have been so very extraordinary that the hand of providence alone could have brought them to bear; it is well for us that we were engaged in a good cause.

We retired yesterday from Quatre Bras to this place without any serious loss, and took up a moderately strong position across the two high roads from Nivelles and Genappe to Brussels, about two miles from Waterloo where these roads unite. Our right flank rested on Braine l'Alleud, which was occupied by a Flemish battalion, and the ground between it and the Nivelles road was held by Mitchell's Brigade of the 4th Division. Close to the high road in front of our right was a small road and chateau called Hougoumont, which were at the foot of Mont St Jean, the height on which we were posted, and were occupied by a strong detachment from the Guards. Along the summit of Mont St Jean to the high road from Genappe was placed the greater part of our artillery supported by the infantry of the 2nd Division; the Guards, some Dutch and Belgian troops, the Brunswick Oels contingent, and the greater part of our light cavalry were in the rear of these and in reserve. The remainder of the 1st corps, supported by the heavy cavalry, extended on still farther to the left, and a little beyond the high road to Genappe; in this front and close to the road was the little farm of La Haye Sainte. Our infantry was concealed from the view of the enemy, being posted a little behind the summit of the ridge, and was formed in small squares of battalions, having only the artillery and a few small parties of cavalry visible. Our troops remained in this situation with but little variation during nearly the whole of this bloody day. The French cavalry frequently charged in masses under cover of a tremendous fire from 240 pieces of artillery. Four times were our guns in possession of their cavalry, and as often did the bayonets of our infantry rescue them. For upwards of an hour our little squares were surrounded by the elite of the French cavaliers; there they gallantly stood within 40 paces of us, unable to leap over the bristling line of bayonets, unwilling to retire, and determined never to surrender: hundreds of them were dropping in all directions from our murderous fire, yet as fast as they dropped others came up to supply their place; finding at last that it was in vain to attempt to break our determined ranks, they swept round our rear and, rushing into the Nivelles road, attempted to cut their way back to their own lines. But the whole road was lined with our infantry on both sides, and at the advanced part of it was an almost impassable barricade of felled trees. Here fell the remainder of these brave cuirassiers, of whom not one was taken without a wound.

The cannonade continued without intermission, and about 6 o'clock we saw heavy columns of infantry supported by dragoons forming for a fresh attack, it was evident it would be a desperate and, we thought, probably a decisive one; everyone felt how much depended on this terrible moment. A black mass of the grenadiers of the Imperial Guard with music playing and the great Napoleon at their head came rolling onward from the farm of 'La Belle Alliance'; with rapid pace they descended the opposite heights, all scattered firing ceased on both sides, our little army seemed to collect within itself, the infantry deployed into line, and the artillery, charged to the muzzle with grape and canister, waited for the moment when the enemy's columns should commence the ascent of our heights; those spaces in our lines which death had opened and left vacant were covered in appearance by bodies of cavalry.

The point at which the enemy aimed was now evident; it was a re-entering angle formed by a brigade of Guards, and the light brigade of Lord Hill's corps, Lord Hill was there in person. The French moved on with arms sloped '*au pas de charge*';[*] they began to ascend the hill, in a few seconds they were within a hundred paces of us, and as yet not a shot had been fired. The awful moment was now at hand, a peal of ten thousand thunders burst at once on their devoted heads, the storm swept them down as a whirlwind which rushes over the ripe corn, they paused, their advance ceased, they commenced firing from the head of their columns and attempted to extend their front; but death had already caused too much confusion among them, they crowded instinctively behind each other to avoid a fire which was intolerably dreadful; still they stood firm, '*La Garde meurt mais ne se rend pas.*'[†] For half an hour this horrible butchery continued, at last seeing all their efforts vain, all their courage useless, deserted by their emperor, who had already flown, unsupported by their comrades, who were already beaten, the hitherto invincible Old Guard gave way and fled in every direction. One spontaneous and almost

---

[*] 'At the charge.'

[†] 'The Guard dies but does not surrender.' This is an extremely interesting use of this famous phrase, often attributed to General Cambronne, General Michel or cited as the invention of a French journalist in later years, but this appears to be in letter written on the very night of the battle! However, without the ability to view the original it cannot be established beyond doubt that it is not a later addition.

painfully animated 'Hurra' burst from the victorious ranks of England, the line at once advanced; general officers, soldiers all partaking of one common enthusiasm. The battle was over, guns, prisoners, ammunition wagons, baggage, horses successively fell into our hands; night and fatigue compelled us to halt, we halted on each side of the Genappe road, and in a short time we saw numerous columns of Prussians advancing along in pursuit of the enemy, each column cheered us in passing, the officers saluted, and many embraced us; never was witnessed a more enthusiastic moment; we felt amply rewarded for the exertions of the day. We retired to take a little most welcome repose while the Prussians continued the pursuit without intermission, and thus ended this ever memorable day.

Lord Hill and Staff returned to a small cottage, where we now are; we have but one room between nine of us, including him; all but myself are now asleep. Good night.

No. 6   Captain the Honourable Orlando Henry Bridgeman, 1st Foot Guards, Aide de Camp* to Sir Rowland Hill
By kind permission of Staffordshire Record Office, ref. D1287

Brussels, 21 June 1815

On Thursday the 15th I left Grammont to come to a ball given at this place by the Duchess of Richmond, about six o'clock that evening; when walking in the park, I heard that we were going to move immediately, but on enquiry I found that everybody meant to stay out the ball, I therefore determined to do so myself. About half past eleven it was said that the French Army was advancing & I found that orders were immediately going off to Lord Hill to move his corps, I therefore determined to stay no longer, & consequently I went off to Grammont, & reached it on Friday morning [16th], the head quarters of our corps were that day at Enghien, the troops marched on all night halting only for a short time, that evening we heard a very heavy cannonade, & found afterwards that the French had attacked the Prince of Orange's position, & that though they had not succeeded in driving us off, yet that we had suffered very severely, & that it was not thought safe to remain in the position. It was therefore determined that we should retire to a position in front of Waterloo, Braine l'Alleud & Hal, which was done on Saturday the 17th. Our corps kept marching on through Braine le Comte, Nivelles & arrived at the position late on that night, having had no rations at all. The whole army was

---

* Dalton mistakenly shows him as an 'extra' aide de camp, but wrongly shows Hill's brother Clement serving at Waterloo as his first ADC whereas he definitely served at the battle with his regiment the Royal Horse Guards. See the editor's *Letters from Waterloo* (letter no. 3).

concentrated there, but the greatest part of the Fourth Division, with the whole of the Dutch & Belgian troops under Prince Frederick of Orange, were on the right at Hal, & never were engaged. Our army bivouacked that night, many of them with empty stomachs, from the utter impossibility of getting up the stores; it rained the whole night through. Our staff got into houses near Waterloo, & laid down about eleven. On Sunday the 18th we were all on our horses at twenty minutes before three in the morning & everything was quiet; we rode all round the position; & returned to eat something about ten. We then went out again, about half past eleven; the enemy showed some columns of cavalry & infantry upon which our guns opened, from that time the action increased till two when it was at its height, & it lasted till ½ past nine at night. No troops could fight more desperately or with greater courage than the French. As for our troops, it is impossible to say enough for them; they were determined not to give way & nothing but that, & the personal exertions of the Duke of Wellington, who himself saved the day several times, & the rest of the officers under him, could have procured us the victory we gained. The French army consisted of eighty odd thousand infantry, twenty odd thousand cavalry, & upwards of two hundred pieces of artillery, commanded by Bonaparte in person with all his best generals; Bon[aparte] himself directed the different attacks, the last & most desperate one was by the Old Imperial Guards.* Napoleon harangued them before they advanced, & promised them this town to plunder; very luckily the Prussians came up to pursue the enemy; our poor fellows were too much exhausted to have gone so far; the loss of the enemy has been immense, ours too; I fear, very great. All Napoleon's baggage is taken, in his carriage are found many bulletins, & proclamations dated from his Imperial Palace at Brussels, so confident was he of success; this town is filled with our wounded, the kindness & attention of the inhabitants to them all [is] most striking. It is a singular thing that just as the action commenced, a report was set about the camp that the French had beaten the Prussians, & were in our rear, there was no sort of foundation for it, & it must have been set a going by some of Napoleon's friends. The Duke of Wellington's staff suffered most cruelly, & it is a miracle how he escaped, for he was in the hottest of the fire the whole day. Our Staff were very fortunate; none but poor Colonel Currie,[†] who was shot through the head by a grape shot, & myself were touched, six horses of our staff were shot. Lord Hill had one killed under him, & had several shots through his cloak; I was hit on the left side, just up on the heart, by a grape shot at the close of the day; if it had entered it must have killed me. Lord Hill insisted on my coming here the following day,

---

* It was actually made by the Middle Guard.
† Brevet Lieutenant Colonel Edward Currie, 90th Foot Assistant Adjutant General.

but I trust very soon to be able to join him. I rode the same horse all day & had the enemy beat us I must have been taken for my horse was quite smashed up.

No. 7   From the Same

Brussels, 23 June 1815

I yesterday morning put my letter no. 10* into the post office, & in the evening I got your no. 1 dated, I believe, May 22nd. Accept my most heartfelt thanks for it my ever dear ever kind mother; I gave you some account of the battle in my last, & I trust soon after you receive it you will get the Gazette from England, when we meet I will give you as long an account of it as you please. Such a battle I believe never was fought before, on both sides with such obstinacy & determination to conquer. I thank the Almighty, for giving us the victory; my wound is of no consequence, & tomorrow morning I set out to rejoin Lord Hill. Had I heard of poor George Gunning's death when I wrote last? Poor fellow, he did not suffer much for he was shot through the body, fell from his horse & never moved again.† I have written to his poor father, & as soon as I join the army I will get such things of his as I can to take home to his father; it is melancholy, very, very melancholy, the number of friends we have lost; in my regiment alone there are thirty-four officers killed & wounded; the French fought with the greatest possible courage, no troops could behave better, ours it is needless to speak of, the event speaks for that, but I assure you, my dear mother, I do not forget that it was the lord of providence that gave us the victory: it is you, my kind parent who has taught me to look there for everything. Lord Wellington was exposed as much as any soldier in the field, & his escape as well as that of my dear general's is a miracle, I was with them both the whole day, I never saw either of them in action before, & it is impossible to say which is the coolest, the greater the danger the more they rise. Sir Robert & Lady Lumley are here on their road to Geneva, & to them I shall entrust this letter to be forwarded to you by the best opportunity. You acknowledge my letters no. 6 & 7, have you received all those I have regularly numbered previous to them? I always think it is wrong to dwell too much on oneself; but yet I feel sure you will not be satisfied if you do not get an account of my wound, it was quite at the end of the day about eight o'clock in the evening, I was next to Lord Hill when I was smacked

---

* Clearly Orlando wrote a series of letters from Belgium before the fighting commenced but unfortunately these are missing. He adds the letter number on some letters.
† Lieutenant George Orlando Gunning was killed serving with the 10th Hussars at Waterloo. Dalton omits to show his death.

off my horse by a grape shot that struck me directly on my back; it did not enter, if it had, of course it must have killed me. I was carried to the rear; the next day Lord Hill insisted on my coming here. Thank God I am now tolerably well again, & start tomorrow morning to join the army. I like Ian who I took from Henry very much; the horse I rode in action was the one Whitman gave me you remember it; I was on her back at ½ past two in the morning, & did not get off again till half past nine at night, having ridden her hard the whole of the day before, for we have not seen our servants or baggage since Friday, & the battle was on Sunday; what a way to pass the Sabbath! The rest of the horses I have are very good. You ask me, my dear mother, how I felt on leaving certain persons in England, I did not see them a long time, my feelings are the same as ever, I venture to say no more, indeed I know no more & nothing more has ever passed on the subject.* I received a letter not long ago, saying that Charles† was gone to the East Indies; of him I know no more; I have had one letter from my father‡ since he went, the accounts of dear [George?]§ were very satisfactory. I am expecting to see Henry¶ here on his road to you, I wish he would come; this is so fine an opportunity of seeing the armies. Adieu my beloved mother with my dearest love to Lucy & whomever, believe me your very affectionate & dutiful son,
    O. H. B.

No. 8   From the Same

Villiers la Bel,** 3 July 1815

No. 12
I wrote to you from Brussels my ever dear mother, two letters, one I sent by the common post, the other Lord Conyngham†† kindly undertook to get conveyed by a courier, I trust one of them at least reached you as soon as you heard anything of our battle. I have two letters to thank you for since, no. 2 dated May 31st & no. 3 dated June 9th from my heart, &c. I thank you for them both, no. 3 reached me first, no. 2 only yesterday. I

---

* This almost certainly refers to Selina Needham, daughter of the 5th Earl of Kilmorey, whom he eventually married in 1817.
† His brother the Honourable Charles Orlando Bridgeman was an officer in the Royal Navy and eventually rose to the rank of Vice Admiral (1791–1860).
‡ Orlando Bridgeman, 1st Earl of Bradford, (1762–1825).
§ His elder brother, George Augustus Frederick Henry Bridgeman, who became 2nd Earl of Bradford (1789–1865).
¶ His younger brother, Reverend the Honourable Henry Edmund Bridgeman (1795–1872).
** This is now virtually an outer suburb of northern Paris on the N16.
†† Henry Conyngham, 1st Marques of Conyngham.

left Brussels on the 24th & after a very tedious journey I joined the Duke
of Wellington's headquarters at Nesle on the 27th proceeded to Lord Hill
the following day; I came up in the rear of the army, all the commissariat
horses, heavy baggage, spare ammunition &c. being on the road a great
deal of ours fell, and made it terrible. However, I got a most kind reception
from Lord H[ill] and all his Staff & this soon made me forget all my
troubles. Our army is now in position in front of Montmartre about five
miles from Paris; the Prussians were on the position which we relieved
them, & they have all crossed the Seine, & are in position on our right.
Montmartre is very strong & must be turned; this is what the Prussians
are now doing, they attacked yesterday evening, we have not yet heard
the particulars, but they advanced considerably, & now must be very
near to Paris; the British headquarters are at Gonesse. The headquarters
of our corps here about two miles in rear of our position. Yesterday
morning three French officers came over to us; they say that Napoleon
quitted Paris on Friday, that Davout commands, that they have collected
about seventy thousand men besides the National Guard; the latter are
in favour of the king but can do nothing against the regulars who still
stick to the other order, negotiations are going on for the surrender of
Paris, if they succeed well & good, if not & Paris is attacked, it certainly
will be destroyed. I defy the power of man to stop the Prussians, every
place they have been at is plundered, what they cannot carry away they
break & the inhabitants all fly. Since we have been here most of them
have returned; what a state has Napoleon reduced this country to. The
Prussians are expected daily, till they come we shall attempt nothing &
with them the job will be easy. I am writing in very great haste; we are on
horseback from sunrise to sunset, but I have begged half an hour to write
this to you; you must therefore excuse the hurry in which it is written,
my wound is quite well, though my side of course is still rather tender.
Before this you will have heard from my father how delighted I am with
my present situation; I am very sorry you have worried yourself with
thinking that I was not pleased with it, & more so as it was my own
fault; from the moment I joined Lord H[ill] to the present moment my
situation has become pleasanter, & I do assure you I would not change it
for any other; the Hills you must know are all very cold mannered men, &
I did not know the Staff at all, but now that I [am] acquainted with them
I like them all very much; & as for the general; I adore him; he is just the
sort of man you would delight in, but you must be some time acquainted
first, he is very shy; his conduct in the battle the other day was perfect, I
never saw, nor could I have conceived such coolness. Though in your last
letter you say that you were to move to Lucca, at the end of this month,
yet I shall direct this to Florence as of course you will leave orders about

your letters being forwarded. If after we have been round our corps all is quiet, I mean to go over to poor G[eorge] Gunning's regiment & try what things I can get of his to take care of for his poor father; I literally have not had time to do this before; I have, however, ascertained that his body was found the day after the battle, & buried; this will be a satisfaction to his family, to know poor fellow. I had become very well acquainted with him lately & liked him very much. I must conclude my beloved mother with my most affectionate love to Lucy & Wolryche,* believe me your affectionate & dutiful son,

O. H. B.

No. 9   From the Same

Headquarters, Gonesse, 4 July 1815

Paris has surrendered & all is over; I have just come in here with Lord Hill, & have got this letter to open it, imagining the comfort it would be to you. The terms are that the French troops retire beyond the Loire, we get possessed of the villages all round Paris today, tomorrow we take possession of Montmartre & the next day ours & the Prussian army march through Paris to encamp on the Bois de Boulogne; our headquarters will probably be in Paris, adieu again my ever dear mother, I have time for no more.

No. 10   From the Same

Paris, 17 July 1815

A thousand thanks my ever dear mother for your letter no. 3 dated the 9th ult. brought by the Duke of Bedford† to Brussels & from thence forwarded me. I wrote two letters to you from Brussels on the 21st & 23rd ult. & once hence I again joined the army of the 3rd of this month; I grieve to think what you must have suffered about me; for I fear the accounts of the battle must have reached you some time before you could have heard of my safety; my expression is inadequate & whenever I look at the place where my wound was I think that I have a mother whose prayers were heard by the Almighty, all is now over; & we may look forward to meeting all together at dear Weston‡ next spring. How well shall we then be repaid for our separation; the headquarters of Lord Hill are at Boulogne about

---

* His youngest sister Lucy had married William Wolryche-Whitmore of Dudmaston in 1810.

† Lord John Russell, had succeeded to the title of sixth Duke of Bedford (1766–1839). His third son was the distinguished politician known as Lord John Russell.

‡ The family seat was at Weston in Staffordshire. It is now a luxury hotel.

three miles from hence the town from which the Bois de Boulogne takes its name; we have all houses in town, & have been here the last week; the emperors & kings are all here & have held dances; the general officers & their Staff have all attended; & been presented by the Duke of W[ellington]. Lord Hill talks of going back to Boulogne soon; I rather wish he may, for I prefer it much to being here. Lord Clancarty* arrived here a few days ago & R[obert] Gunning† with him; I have not seen the latter since I left England to go to Cadiz; Lord Clancarty tells me he [Gunning] felt his brother's death very much. I had a letter from my uncle a few days ago written in very low spirits & now dear Henry I must address a few lines to you, to thank you for your letter from Brussels, of the 3rd, you mention having sent the seal by Wildman,‡ but he is arrived, & says you did not send it to his house; I am therefore at a loss to guess what is become of it. I cannot tell you how surprised & disappointed I was that you did not come here, it would have been so little out of your way, & you never can have such an opportunity of seeing two armies; besides which H. G.§ has never been here; so sure did I feel that you would come that I had everything ready, beds, &c.; you may suppose therefore my disappointment in reading your letter; the letters you brought out all reached me safe; the reason I did not leave a letter for you at Brussels, is that I did not get your letter mentioning the day you were to start till I joined the army. I have no more to [say to] you so adieu, & now my dear mother, to return to you, I had a letter from George this morning dated the 13th, there had been a nasty easterly wind for a day or two which had made him cough, but he wrote in excellent spirits; was to leave London on the 17th for Horton¶ & meant to reach Weston on the 20th. Everybody seems to think that we are likely to remain here some time; the King of France will keep us if he can, for our army behaves itself; & the Prussians plunder & destroy everything they lay their hands upon. I shall take this letter to Lord Clancarty & beg him to forward, give my kind love to Lucy, Whitmore & H. Simpson** & believe me my dear mother, your very affectionate & dutiful son,

    O. H. B.

---

* Richard Le Poer Trench, 2nd Earl of Clancarty diplomat, was credited with resolving various border disputes in Holland, Germany and Italy at the Congress of Vienna 1814–15, and in his role as Ambassador to the Netherlands.

† Lieutenant George Gunning 1st Dragoons was severely wounded at Waterloo.

‡ Almost certainly Captain Thomas Wildman, who was an ADC to Uxbridge and was wounded at Waterloo; his younger brother Edward, a captain, was also wounded and his younger brother John a lieutenant survived; all served in the 7th Hussars.

§ Almost certainly the initials HG stand for Henry John Gunning who became a clergyman.

¶ Horton House, Northamptonshire, was the seat of the Gunnings.

** Henry Bridgeman Simpson.

THE CAVALRY

1st Brigade of Major General Lord Edward Somerset
1st Life Guards

No. 11   Captain John Whale
By kind permission of Warwickshire Record Office CR2900/35,
box CR2900/PtII, shelf C.20.34

This is an intriguing narrative of the battle by Sir John Whale, as recorded by his daughter Augusta many years after the battle. By a careful comparison of this memoir, it is clear that it follows the 'Circumstantial Detail of the Waterloo Campaign' which starts on page 1 of volume 1 of a *The Battle of Waterloo by Near Observer*, which, although published anonymously, has been clearly shown to have been compiled by Charlotte Eaton, author of a *Narrative of a Residence in Belgium during the campaign of 1815; and of a Visit to the Field of Waterloo*, published in London 1817.

I believe that John Whale, who remained at Brussels after the battle having lost two horses beneath him and being wounded, gave his version of the battle to Charlotte and that she incorporated it within her narrative. I have omitted below those parts of the narrative that clearly relate to Charlotte's own statement of occurrences at Brussels during the fighting as John Whale was then with the army.

In the evening of Thursday the 15th June a courier arrived at Brussels from Marshal Blücher to announce that hostilities had commenced. The Duke of Wellington was sitting after dinner with a party of officers, papa among the number over the dessert and wine, when he received the despatches containing the unexpected news that Marshal Blücher had been attacked that day by the French but he seemed to consider it as a mere affair of outposts which was not likely to proceed much further at present, though it might probably prove the prelude to a more important engagement. It was the opinion of most military men in Brussels that it was the plan of the enemy by a false alarm to induce the allies to concentrate their chief military force in that quarter in order that he might more successfully make a serious attack upon some other point and that it was against Brussels & the English army that the blow would be aimed. The troops were ordered to be in readiness to march at a moment's notice but no immediate movement was expected and everything appeared so perfectly quiet that the Duchess of Richmond gave a ball to which all the world was invited. Rumours were circulated through the room in whispers but no credit was given to them till the general officers whose corps were in advance began to move and when orders were given for persons to repose to their regiments matters began to be considered in a different light.

The drums beat to arms and the trumpets loud call was heard from every part of the city. It is impossible to describe the effect of those sounds, heard in the silence of the night, the men not long left in doubt of the [cause?]. A second courier had arrived from Blücher, the attack had become serious, the enemy were in considerable force, they had taken Charleroi and had gained some advantage over the Prussians and our troops were ordered to march immediately to support them. Instantly every place resounded with martial preparations. There was not a house in which military were not quartered and consequently the whole town was one scene of bustle. The soldiers were assembling from all parts in the Place Royale with their knapsacks on their backs, some taking leave of their wives and children, others sitting waiting for their comrades, others sleeping upon packs of straw, surrounded by all the din of war, while baggage wagons were loading, artillery trains tramping, officers riding in all directions, carts clattering, chargers neighing, bugles sounding, drums beating and colours flying. A most laughable contrast to this initial scene was presented by a long procession of carts coming quietly in as usual to market filled with old Flemish women seated among their piles of cabbage, peas & strawberries, totally ignorant of the cause of all these warlike preparations and gazing at the scene around them with many a look of gaping wonder . . .

. . . All the inhabitants [of Mont St Jean] had fled from this village previous to the action & even Waterloo was deserted. In a farmhouse at the end of the village nearest the field, one solitary woman remained shut up in a garret from which she could see nothing while they were fighting at the very door, while shells were bursting in all the windows & while cannon balls were breaking through the wooden gates into the farm yard and striking against the walls of the house. This farmer's wife was asked by Captain Whale of the Life Guards her motive for this extraordinary conduct replied 'that all she had in the world was there ... poultry, cows, calves & pigs and that if she did not stay to take care of them they would all be destroyed or carried off ... ' The three lower rooms were filled with the wounded British officers ...

... Captain Whale had 2 horses shot under him but returned & remounted to his charge ...

2nd Life Guards

No. 12   Private Thomas Playford
From the editor's edition of Playford's memoirs

The departure of Bonaparte and his armed followers from the island of Elba in the spring of 1815, with their sudden appearance in France, followed by the flight of Louis XVIII to the Netherlands, and the resumption of the Imperial throne by Napoleon, were events more wonderful than the fictions of romance; and all Europe looked on with astonishment. But the nations soon resolved that Bonaparte should not reign in France, for his restless ambition was not to be trusted: and nearly every European state prepared an army to assist in removing the emperor of France from his throne; and a dreadful struggle was expected to ensue.

The English Life Guards were among the troops selected to take part in this gigantic contest which was to decide the dynasty of France and probably the destiny of the world: and in the month of June 1815 I was in quarters in Flanders, awaiting to take an individual part in the great enterprise.

The entire French nation did not espouse the cause of the Emperor with all the zeal he had hoped to see manifest; yet he had a body of veteran troops, full[y] devoted to his interest, which he believed was more than a match for any one of the armies preparing to attack him: but not capable of contending with the whole united. He therefore resolved to attack them in detail and to destroy them one at a time, and he determined to commence with the Prussians and English, who were nearest the frontiers, that he might destroy them before the Austrians and Russians could come up. And to enable him to take them by surprise, he sent his army forward by forced secret marches; at the same time he called a public meeting near Paris, to induce a belief that he was meditating pacific measures.

In this he so far succeeded that the commanders of the allied armies appeared satisfied that no hostile movement would take place for some time. The Prussians reposed in quarters; and the Duke of Wellington and many of his officers attended a ball at Brussels: not thinking that the French legions were coming down upon them with astonishing rapidity.

When Bonaparte had finished his speech at the public meeting he galloped off to join the army: and he made a bold attempt to surprise and destroy the Prussians.

I was in quarters among the Flemish peasantry: we had been grinding our swords and putting new flints to our carbines and pistols, that we might be ready at a moment's notice. About two or three o'clock in the morning of the 16th of June I happened to be awake and heard the notes of an English bugle at a distance breaking in upon the silence of the night; I called to some of the soldiers sleeping in the same apartment, and the bugle was again heard. Some said the light dragoons in the next villages were going out to exercise; but it was too early for that. We therefore concluded there was some cause for that unusual call to horse, and although the call did not concern us, we got up and dressed ourselves.* Presently our own trumpet sounded the 'Alarm' followed by 'To horse', when we saddled our horses and proceeded to the point of assembly. We waited some time for the other regiments of the brigade to come up, and then advanced along the road leading to Nivelles. But no one could assign any reason for this movement; nor was it for a moment suspected that Bonaparte had made a desperate attack on the Prussians, and a body of French troops had advanced against the British post at Quatre Bras.

After we had been a few hours on the march, we heard the noise of a cannonade at a distance, and we then began to understand the reason of this sudden march. Towards evening we entered Nivelles and saw women seated at their cottage doors scraping old linen into lint, and this showed us that they expected many wounded soldiers to arrive. A little further we saw an English surgeon dressing the wounds of French prisoners: we hurried forward but before we arrived at the field of battle darkness had put an end to the contest. We passed the night in a corn field, in ignorance of what had taken place during the day, beyond that there had been some fighting and the French had been repulsed at this point.

On the following morning all was quiet: our horses ate the green corn in the field. We had a little food which we had brought with us ourselves; and we stood in line dismounted and looking around us. Presently we saw infantry regiments march one after another past us along the road to Brussels. They were followed by artillery and cavalry, and our brigade seemed to be left alone: and in time we learned that the Prussians had been driven from their position on the preceding day and had retreated; and that the Duke of Wellington had resolved to retire to keep up his communications with the Prussians.

---

* It is interesting to note that at even this late hour on the 16 June, that some regiments of cavalry were still unaware of the call to arms and march towards Quatre Bras.

In the eventful times alluded to, I was acquainted with a singular character among the guards of the royal person: his name was Shaw, and he was afterwards celebrated for his heroic conduct at the sanguinary field of Waterloo. Shaw was six feet high, and possessed a powerful athletic frame. His features were large and rather coarse, his countenance indicated a measure of good nature as well as of determined purpose. His broad chest, muscular arms, and large bony hands, denoted a powerful antagonist to be encountered in close combat. He was not only well versed in the use of the broad sword and could use the shining blade with a speed of a flash of light, but he also knew the science of pugilism, and few men could stand before him. A blow from his sword would have been dangerous and disabling if not fatal to an armed man and a stroke from his clenched fist dreadful to a weak man.

Looking back into the treasures of memory, I have a clear recollection that on the morning of the 17th of June 1815 the troops of our regiment were reposing in a cornfield near the Brussels road, ready to take part in covering the retreat from Quatre Bras to Waterloo, when Shawe laid down among the corn and fell asleep. From this slumber he suddenly aroused himself, and springing on his feet with agitated countenance said, 'I have just dreamed that a Frenchman shot me.' He was, however, as little addicted to superstitious fears as any man on earth, and instantly shaking off the unpleasant feeling his dream had produced, he joked about the alarming apparition he had seen in his sleep.

After a short time we saw large bodies of French troops in front of us, and we were ordered to retire. When we turned round, a very imposing and pleasing spectacle burst upon our view; it was the whole British cavalry and artillery, skilfully put in array, to cover the retreat of the British army, by the Earl of Uxbridge; and each brigade was so placed as to be seen to the best advantage. And there was need for a good force to do this; for Bonaparte, having driven the Prussians from Ligny with great loss, and sent a French corps in pursuit of them, was directing the main body of his army against the English, hoping to crush them at one blow before the assembly of their army could be completed. But the retreat towards Brussels was skilfully conducted.

This day's work was more noise and sham than otherwise; each brigade retired in succession and the front had always a formidable appearance. The use of fire arms on horseback had not attained much perfection. For on one occasion I watched the mounted skirmishers of the French and English armies, firing at each other for more than twenty minutes, and not one man or horse fell on either side. The French artillery occasionally hurried forward and fired a few cannon balls at us; I saw the flash and the smoke, and heard the sound, but no harm was done; the gunners must therefore have been bad marksmen. Our guns opened a heavy fire in return; and now and then a Congreve rocket* went hissing through the air; but I suppose little damage was done. And a heavy fall of rain cooled human ardour on both sides.

Some fighting took place in the village of Genappe and the Seventh Hussars were at one time in some danger, but a very gallant charge of the First Life Guards turned the tide of affairs, and the rear guard quitted the village without much loss.

On arriving at the rising ground in front of the village of Waterloo, the British infantry and artillery stood prepared to repel any further advances of the French who halted on the opposite heights, called Mont St Jean; and the two armies passed the night without molesting each other.

Although midsummer was near, we passed an uncomfortable night exposed to a cold wind and to heavy rain. There we stood on soaked ploughed ground, shivering, wet, and hungry; for there was neither food for man nor horse. Some soldiers complained of the hardship, some jested at their sufferings, and others tried to guess at what would take place on the morrow; and some hinted at the probability that not many of us would see the 19th of June. But no one believed in gloomy prognostications. We pulled down a fence and made a fire, but we gained little good by standing round it, for while one side was warming the other was cold and wet.

The morning was clear, the rain gradually abated and Shaw,† myself and several others were sent in search of food for our regiment. We found a wagon loaded with bread abandoned by the driver and horses. We each took a sack full of loaves, and then went to a large farm house in search for cheese, butter, or bacon, to be eaten with the bread;‡ but at that moment a cannon shot gave indication of the approaching battle. 'The work is beginning', exclaimed one of our company (Shaw), 'Come lads, let us hasten to our regiment; we have each our share of duty to perform today' and we hastened to our regiment with our bread; but the firing had become very brisk before we joined the ranks.

---

* William Congreve had developed a rocket system during the war and in 1809 two troops of horse artillery had been converted to 'rocket troops'. These weapons had been used with some success, such as at the crossing of the Adour, but were extremely unpredictable and Wellington was clearly not a fan. One rocket troop commanded by Captain Edward Whinyates was in Belgium in 1815, but Wellington ordered them to be fitted out with conventional cannon. Whinyates retained the rockets as well and they were used to some effect on both the 17 and 18 June.

† Shaw was a corporal-of-horse (equivalent to a sergeant) and apparently led the foraging party.

‡ Another interesting example, showing that plundering dwellings for food clearly did occur within the British army at Waterloo, where because of the speed of movement, the commissariat supply system had temporarily broken down.

The occurrences of the 18th of June have a place in my memory like a dreadful dream; like some fearful vision of the night when gloomy horrors brood over the [mind?]. Scenes of frightful destructions flit before my mind as shadows and yet I know that they represent awful realities. I have a confused, disjointed recollection of many things; yet no clear, comprehensive idea of them as a whole. I recollect our brigade (consisting of the 1st Life Guards, 2nd Life Guards, Royal Horse Guards, 1st Dragoon Guards) being formed in regimental columns of squadrons under the brow of a hill near the centre of the British army and dismounted. The field of battle was in front of us, but it was hid from our view by the rising ground. We heard a thunder of cannon, the fire of musketry, and the shouts of combatants near us; and we saw many wounded men passing towards the rear: some were carried in blankets, others walked slowly along, and several fell and died. It was dangerous to pass the ground behind us, for the shot and shell which passed over our heads struck the ground behind us in great numbers.

Sometimes the turmoil of battle appeared greatest on our right; at other times on our left; and at length there was a tremend*ous thunder of cannon which drowned every other sound, immediately* in front of us; but the rising ground before us concealed from our view what was taking place; yet we naturally concluded a powerful attempt was being made to force the centre of the British army; and as there were no troops in our rear, we viewed ourselves as a last resource to defeat this project. The conflict was raging violently beyond the rising ground in front of us, and the roar of artillery with the report of small arms was incessant, yet we could not see what was taking place; but the commander of the cavalry, the Earl of Uxbridge, rode forward to gain a full view of the conflict and to watch the progress of events, that he might bring our brigade of a thousand powerful swordsmen into action under the most favourable circumstances, and at a moment when a charge of heavy cavalry was particularly wanted.

After a time I saw the Earl of Uxbridge, who had been in front watching the progress of events, gallop towards us, when a slight murmur of gladness passed along the ranks. The word 'Mount' was given, and the trumpet sounded 'Draw swords': and the command followed, 'Form line on the leading squadron of the 2nd Life Guards.' This done the word 'Advance' was given, and the trumpet sounded 'Walk'. But we saw no enemy; yet there was a strange medley of shouts, musket shots, and the roar of cannon, beyond the rising ground in front of us.

Presently we met a number of English foot soldiers running for their lives: they passed between our horses, or through squadron intervals, formed behind us, and followed us. They were succeeded by a confused mixture of artillery and rifle men, hastening to get out of our way and form behind us. At the same time I noticed the soldiers of a battalion of Belgian infantry, formed under the brow of the hill, run away: and I supposed they were very young soldiers, for no veterans would have done so.*

So great was the impetuosity of the various attacks, that our first line was somewhat shaken, and a body of cuirassiers was ascending the crest of our position. The First Cavalry Brigade deployed and advanced; halted a few minutes between the first and second lines [of infantry], (not one hundred yards from the enemy's ranks) and then charged in line! It was a magnificent sight. The charge of the Life Guards was tremendous! They rushed with overwhelming fury on the ranks of the enemy, and hurled them back in confusion.

The French cuirassiers came on in the pride of assumed superiority, and with all that martial bearing and daring audacity so remarkably evinced by that arm throughout the day; their advance was therefore singularly imposing; but being met in mid-onset by the British Household Cavalry, although in every respect the elite of the French army, and like the mailed warriors of chivalry, 'locked up in steel', they were completely overthrown, cut down, and driven back, *l'épée dans les reins.*† In the pursuit the Second Regiment of Life Guards# passed some columns of French infantry, and captured several pieces of cannon; but being pressed on all sides by superior numbers, and the regiment having to fight its way back, it was unable to retain possession of the guns, which were consequently dismounted and abandoned. Before the regiment could regain the position of the allies it was closely pressed by a corps of lancers, of more than treble its own strength, and was exposed to the fire of two columns of French infantry.

Note by Playford: The first cuirassier corps encountered by the Second Life Guards was the Carabiniers a Cheval, the elite of the French army.‡

Our troop formed the right half of the left squadron of the brigade. In the centre of the squadron troop quarter master Beamond (who was killed) was stationed. On his right hand was Shaw, riding a very powerful

---

* Although some undoubtedly fled, most of these British soldiers had dispersed to allow the cavalry to pass and reformed in their rear. The Dutch/Belgian troops mentioned as fleeing, although some undoubtedly re-formed, were those of Bijlandt's Brigade, which had already suffered heavily at Quatre Bras.

† Literally, 'a sword in the kidneys'.

‡ Playford is in error here. The cuirassiers they faced were not the Carabiniers a Cheval who were stationed near Hougoumont. The 2nd Life Guards initially crossed swords with the 1st Cuirassier Regiment of Dubois' Brigade.

horse and grasping a recently ground broad sword. Next to Shaw rode a trooper named Adamson (who was killed); on Adamson's right was seen Hilton (who was also numbered with the slain). On Hilton's right hand I was stationed; and on my right hand rode a powerful Yorkshireman named Youeson:[*] but memory fails to retain the names of the other brave men who fought near us; they were, however, nearly all killed through penetrating too far into the French lines.

We were advancing in line at a slow pace with horses well reined in; for they were excited by the dreadful din of battle in our front; but we saw no enemy, for the scene of combat was still hidden from us by the rising ground.

The trumpet sounded 'Trot', yet we saw no enemy. The Earl of Uxbridge was in front watching for the best moment to bring us into action; and he regulated the pace we should move at accordingly. Meanwhile a few cannon shots took effect in our ranks and Shaw was hit, as we rode slowly forward Youeson gave me a nudge with his elbow and said 'Shaw is hit!'. I instantly looked to my left and noticed Shaw's head had fallen from its erect position, his right hand was raised in the air, and his sword had fallen from his grasp but was held by a strap fastened to his wrist: and as his person was not injured I concluded that he had been struck by a spent ball which had knocked the breath out of him. A few moments afterwards Youeson nudged me again and said 'There goes Shaw's horse without a rider; what a splendid creature he is!' I then noticed that Shaw's horse had galloped through the squadron and was sporting in front; and with head raised and tail extended he galloped first one way and then another. I, like Youeson, thought him a magnificent beast.[†]

The Earl of Uxbridge again approached us; he took off his hat, waved it round his head, and then passed his hat forward over his horse's head. It was a signal, and the trumpets sounded 'Charge'. Hurrah! Shouted the soldiers; Hurrah! Responded the infantry behind us; and there appeared to be a pause in the battle to look at us. And at that moment a line of French horsemen in bright armour appeared in front of us; they were shouting, waving their swords and sabring the English infantry and artillerymen who had not got out of our way. Our shouts had arrested their attention, and looking up they saw fearful ranks of red-horsemen coming galloping forward, shouting and brandishing their swords. The cuirassiers paused

---

[*] Private John Youeson received a Waterloo medal but did not claim a General Service Medal when issued later in 1848.

[†] Playford is pretty certain he saw Corporal John Shaw fall, struck by a spent ball, but he agrees that all the evidence seems to show that Shaw was able to remount and take part in the charge where he did kill and injure a number of the enemy before succumbing himself.

and looked at us as likely to prove an easy conquest. Their bearing had all the bravado and audacity of veterans accustomed to triumph and they appeared to look upon us as victims given to their superior swords. They met us in mid-onset near the brow of the hill as men confident of victory, but the shock of battle overthrew many of them; for the weight and power of our men and horses was too great for their less powerful men and weaker horses. They gave way, some fell back: but returning to the attack, hand to hand and sword to sword the work of death went on; but our weight and strength of our men and horses again proved too much for them. Many fell; others fled, and were pursued towards their own lines. British valour had triumphed so far; but the French cuirassiers were also brave men and good swordsmen; only we fell upon them when their line was a little deranged, otherwise they would, doubtless, have stood their ground longer; yet I think that our charge was irresistible. As the cuirassiers fell back, and the English troopers pressed forward a melee took place in which lancers and infantry musketeers mingled in the fray.

From the moment that Shaw fell from his horse I never saw him alive afterwards; but presuming that the heroic conduct ascribed to him by journalists and historians was founded on facts witnessed by some of his companions in arms (although, perhaps, a little heightened in print), it would appear that he speedily revived from the effects produced by the spent cannon ball, regained his horse, and dashing into the thickest of the hand to hand fight, when cuirassiers, lancers, and musketeers fell beneath the broad sword wielded by his powerful arm. For he was a very strong man of impulsive temperament and determined purpose, and it is affirmed in history that he wrought wonderful execution among the opposing combatants. According to the accounts published at the time the glittering blade of this heroic swordsman was seen descending with fatal violence first upon one enemy and then upon another until his strength was exhausted, when he received a fatal wound which terminated his victorious career. In the printed records he is compared with some of Homer's heroes. And while it may be truly said that many brave men fell at Waterloo, it may be added that Shaw was one of the bravest of the brave.

I have a painful recollection of the pursuit, of shots, of clashing swords, of mangled bodies and groaning men; yet, strange to say, no enemy confronted me. Those who first looked me in the face rode off before we crossed swords, not I suppose, from the fear of a personal conflict, but from noticing that it was impossible for them to maintain their ground against our numbers.

I pursued; my progress was arrested by a hedge, and I looked over the fence, when I saw dreadful deeds taking place in a paddock a little to my right: my blood was hot and I went to a gap in the fence, but it was choked up with horses struggling in the agonies of death. I turned to my left and saw fearful carnage taking place on the main road to Brussels; but my recollection of what I saw is confused like a frightful dream. Under a hot impulse I hurried to the scene, but the fighting there soon ceased; and all I could do was to ride after some cuirassiers who, however, contrived to escape. As I rode on I saw our soldiers destroying the men and horses of some French artillery. But in whatever direction I turned every Frenchman got out of my way, excepting one cuirassier who fell completely into my power. He was unhorsed, his helmet was knocked off, and I raised my hand to cleave his skull; but at that moment compassion sprung up within me, I checked the blow and let the conquered cuirassier escape with a wound on the side of his head.

We pursued the French too far, and when we returned we sustained some loss. We had galloped through wet ploughed ground, and many of our horses panted for breath; at the same time a number of fresh enemies rode down upon us, and a few single combats occurred in which Frenchmen generally had the advantage. Yet I rode among conflict and slaughter and every enemy avoided me. Those of my companions who fell at this time generally lost their lives from rash bravado; for they rode singly out of their way to attack two or three enemies, and when a greater number came against them, their horses were blown and they could not escape. They could only sell their lives as dear as possible.

I saw a comrade (Joseph Hindley[*]) whose horse had been killed, running to catch a French horse and I rode between him and his pursuers, for my horse was comparatively fresh. I helped him to catch the French horse, and stood by to defend him while he mounted; and, although musket and pistol balls passed near us, we remained uninjured.

As we rode back towards our lines, a body of French infantry intercepted us; a regiment of the King's German Legion menaced the infantry with a charge, when the French formed two squares; between these squares we had to pass, and as we approached both squares opened an oblique fire upon us; but not a single man and only one horse fell. I therefore concluded that these French soldiers were not good marksmen; for as we were not much above two hundred yards from them, I considered that the greater half of our number ought to have fallen, but their balls must have struck the ground before they reached us or have passed over our heads.[†]

---

[*] Private Joseph Hindley (incorrectly named James in the Waterloo Roll) later rose to the rank of sergeant and claimed a GSM with bars for Vitoria and Toulouse.

[†] Playford seems to indicate that he returned via a route to the west of the Brussels chaussee and would have passed the troops of Charlet's Brigade returning from their failed attack on La Haye Sainte. This would also tie in with his memory of KGL troops in the vicinity.

During the engagement his grace came to the head of the First Regiment of Life Guards, and thanked the squadrons for their distinguished bravery.#

Note by Playford: After the return of the army to England, the Duke of Wellington came to the barracks of the Second Life Guards, in King Street, Portman Square; and, the regiment being on parade, it was formed into a close column, when his Grace again expressed, in the strongest terms, his admiration of its conduct during the whole of the periods it had served under his command, in the Peninsula and on the Continent, particularly at the Battle of Waterloo; and observed to Earl Cathcart, the Colonel of the regiment, who was present on this occasion, that its conduct had repeatedly produced in the breast of his Grace the most lively feelings of exultation; when his Lordship replied 'I have known the regiment more than twenty years, and have always had reason to feel proud of its conduct.'

When our regiment was again formed, I looked round to see who was there, and I found that about three out of four were not present. Many were killed, some were only wounded, and others had lost their horses; but our loss altogether was a dreadful. We were only a small remnant of what we were in the morning; and some of that remnant were bleeding.

The battle was still raging and we again occupied a position under the brow of the hill, but much nearer the combatants; and in this instance many cannon shots took effect, so that officers, soldiers, and horses fell one after another: and I noticed the same taking place in other regiments of our brigade. This is, perhaps, one of the most painful situations a human being can be placed in; to sit still and be shot at, and to see men and horses falling on each side of you, and yet you are not allowed to move. When men are fully engaged in the hot work of war, their animal nature becomes fired, and their blood appears to boil within them; and they are too busy to think or to fear: but when a man has to sit still and be shot at; with nothing to think about but that the next shot will probably deprive him of life or of a limb; and that in a moment or two he shall be weltering in his blood in the agonies of death or under the [surgeon, his blood?] appears to run cold. At the same time his thoughts are apt to wander home to a father, mother, wife, or child; particularly if the individual is not given to thinking on such subjects. And I felt glad that my mother did not know the danger her son was in. Generally, however, men, under such circumstances, sit motionless and dumb; if they survive, you may learn from conversation afterwards what was passing in their minds at the time.

[Towards the end of the day] We again advanced and I have a confused idea of lancers, cuirassiers, and infantry retiring before us; and it appeared to me that the work of destruction was partly stayed. There was, however, a solid mass of French horsemen, consisting of light cavalry and lancers in the centre and cuirassiers on the outside, and for sometime this body of men remained immovable. I saw a corps of heavy horse belonging to the King of the Netherlands charge that mass without effect; indeed the low country horsemen never came within some 4 or 5 yards of the French, but when they saw that the cuirassiers stood firm the Hollanders faced about and retired. We were also directed to charge that mass in column. The First Life Guards, being at the head of the column, rode boldly up to the heads of the horses of the French and made cuts and [thrusts?] at the men. Hand to hand the contending horsemen fought, but the cuirassiers were in armour and stood their ground. Yet it was a noble spectacle and I admired the heroic conduct of the 1st Life Guards who fought with determined bravery. This close combat producing no important consequence, we retired about fifty paces, and facing about confronted that formidable body of horsemen, ready to take advantage of the first movement. Meanwhile a troop of horse artillery had arrived and unlimbered behind us unseen by the French; the word 'Open out' was quietly passed along, and we formed a lane along which cannon balls were fired against that mass of French horsemen with terrible effect, men and horses falling in rapid succession. In an instant the whole column broke and fled in some disorder pursued by the English cavalry.* Our regiment sustained serious loss on the 18th of June. A number of our horses, whose riders had been killed were straying about in search of food; at the same time men, whose horses had been shot, were looking for horses.

Here my memory fails to identify particulars in which a melee of all arms were mingled in close combat. The French were driven from the field; the Prussians arrived and pursued the broken fragments of the French army. I became separated from my regiment, and passed the night in a barn near the road to Brussels together with three or four other men of our regiment.

On the following morning we went in search of the surviving fragments of our regiment, and found a few officers and men; perhaps twenty in all including ourselves. In this search I rode across one part

---

* This advance at the end of the battle is not mentioned by any other witness from the Household Brigade; however, it does appear that the small remnant of the heavy cavalry left at the 'crisis' attached itself to Vivian's light cavalry and presumably charged with them, being too few to attempt anything on their own. This is confirmed by the account of Major Dorville, 1st Royal Dragoons, in the editor's *Letters from Waterloo* (letter no. 28), where he states 'The heavy cavalry being at that period of the day so much reduced, the light under General Vandeleur and Vivian were brought forward and formed up with the heavy . . .'

of the field of battle, and Corporal Webster* pointed out to me the dead body of Shaw, pointing to a spot where several dead French soldiers lay, said 'There lies Shaw'. I replied 'I rode over that ground this morning, and noticed that one of our regiment was among the slain, but his face was concealed'. Webster said 'I examined the countenance and recognised Shaw. He appears to have received a fatal injury in his body, for there is a deep wound in his side, near the heart, which appears to have been inflicted with either a bayonet or a lance'. This Shaw was only two file from me in the ranks; he was a powerful brave man and fell early. I think I saw him fall but it is possible he revived again. As I did not witness the exploits of Shaw in close combat, nor yet inquire of the wounded French soldiers near his corpse, by whose hand the dead lying roundabout had fallen, I can neither add to, nor take away from the published accounts; but from the position in which Shaw's remains were found among dead adversaries, with only one or two killed Englishmen near, this seems to favour what has been said concerning the havoc he produced among the French troopers before he fell. What I knew of him would favour this: for he was the strongest and most resolute man I ever knew, and had such great confidence in his own prowess that he would not hesitate to attack as many foes as could stand opposed to him.†

When the remnant of our regiment was collected together we looked a strange medley, some on French horses and some on foot, and from time to time we found one of our own horses whose rider had been killed. We followed the army a few miles and then halted for the night.

When I had cut green forage for my horse, and sat down on the ground looking at him eat, I reflected on the preceding day's work. I wondered at the fact that I had gone through such dreadful scenes and had appeared as an actor in such dreadful carnage without ever having slain one human being!

I contemplated the occurrences of the 18th of June and recollected that some men of our regiment, of impulsive natures, had become decidedly insane during the hot work of war. They shouted, raved, and rushed recklessly into battle where several of them perished. One man, Samuel Godley, had his horse shot and his helmet knocked off, and he raved about the field of battle on foot until he met a cuirassier, whom he slew

---

* Corporal William Webster received a Waterloo medal and claimed a GSM with bars for Vitoria and Toulouse. Interestingly the GSM records show him ranked as a private.
† The actual death of Corporal of Horse Shaw is shrouded in mystery. Major Knollys argues that Shaw survived till late in the day and that he died near a village, presumably La Belle Alliance. Playford's description discounts this, indicating that Shaw's body was on the slope in open ground where the original charge had passed.

and rode off with his horse to new scenes of conflict. I saw Godley[*] perform that daring exploit which is recorded of him by his regiment. He lived some years afterwards and when he died I made a drawing for the device on his tombstone, which may be seen in the burial ground St John's Wood, London.

Other men of the regiment distinguished themselves; and mention is made in the Historical Records of The Life Guards of John Johnson, who triumphed over three cuirassiers. I knew Johnson well; he was a quiet man of few words, but a brave soldier.[†]

Other men, naturally of nervous infirmity, became almost helpless; I saw one man about forty yards from me, drop his own sword, and seize the sword of his opponent.

Some men, not naturally hard hearted, became so brutalised by the conflict that they were ready for any act of barbarity. I saw one soldier, who had always before appeared to be of a humane disposition, slay a grey-haired French officer, who had surrendered, in a most savage manner. Some men appeared anxious to shed blood whether there was any occasion for it or not.

I had conversed in the morning with several who were killed during the day; and they had expressed a conviction that they should fall in the conflict, and they did fall; but I never had any such impression: nor had any of those who were alive at the close of the day any presentiment that they were to be killed that day. On the 17th of June, when we were halted in a cornfield and were dismounted, several men lied [*sic*] down; and one soldier (Shaw) started suddenly up saying 'I have just dreamt that a Frenchman shot me': and he fell about the same hour on the next day. I have noticed on several occasions that strong presentiments often prove true (but not always); and if the presentiment produced a dream the dream may also prove true.

As we followed the French army in its flight towards Paris, I noticed that the cruel propensities called into development by hand to hand struggles and combats, did not subside when all danger was past. One evening, when cutting forage, the troopers found a French soldier concealed among the corn, and brought him prisoner to the bivouac, where he was told to sit down under a tree. Presently a farrier coming that way, saw the Frenchman, and said 'That fellow shot at me yesterday, and now I will have my revenge'. The farrier's countenance manifested a determined purpose; he drew a sword, and muttering 'I'll cut him to pieces' walked deliberately towards the trembling captive. I thought it

---

[*] Private Samuel Godley, famous by besting three cuirassiers while dismounted.
[†] It is unclear if he refers to Private John Johnson Senior or Junior as there were two of this name in the regiment.

wrong to kill a prisoner, and stepping between the farrier and his victim, I induced the former to desist. He threw down the sword with an oath, and walked away cursing me for interfering. And several men hinted their disappointment of my conduct; and yet these men had formerly been as kind and humane as the generality of mankind. But shedding blood had deadened their sensibilities, and it required time for them to regain their former principles and tenderness.

At the close of another day's march I was affected by noticing a soldier grieving over his dead horse. The faithful animal had been wounded on the 18th of June, but had travelled several days without appearing to be seriously injured. The horse, however, died suddenly at the end of the fourth day, and the soldier shed tears: I listened with deep attention to the afflicted soldier as he spoke of the excellent qualities of his steed, and told how that faithful beast had carried him through Spain and France; and had borne him triumphant through the dreadful scenes at Waterloo. The soldier told how the horse would eat out of his hand, lick his face and hands, and give evident signs of attachment to his master. And I felt gratified at these signs of sympathy and tenderness in one of my companions in arms. I, however, knew that many soldiers are attached to their horses: and some horses evince attachment to the man who gives them food.

The flight of Bonaparte from France, his surrender to a British ship of war and his subsequent exile in St Helena are events which followed in succession. The allies entered Paris; Louis XVIII was restored to the throne of France, and the British army occupied quarters near the French capital. I was stationed at the village of Nanterre,* near Paris, for several months, and I was employed as an assistant clerk to the regiment, which was a duty agreeable to my disposition: for to keep books, preserve records, and enter correspondence, was an employment to which I had no objection.

The war was terminated, but some time was occupied in settling the conditions of peace and in arranging the affairs of Europe, during which period the small remains of our regiment was stationed at Nanterre. During these negotiations, a number of reviews took place, at which the Emperor of Russia, the King of Prussia, and other great personages were present.

While I was at Nanterre I noticed some of the customs of the people, and particularly that in several families the wife conducted the business, while the husband loitered about or went to the wine house. At the house where we had our regimental office the mother and her two sons, who were quite youths, carried on a large business as wholesale pork butchers. The woman went to market twice a week, purchased pigs, superintended

---

* This is now part of Paris, near La Défense.

the killing and dressing, and sent the pork to Paris. She also sold the meat in the wholesale markets at Paris: while her husband loitered at the wine houses. I think there is no country where females are so kindly treated as in England. I have seen French women filling manure drays, driving teams, and performing work which in England is supposed to require masculine powers.

The French placed confidence in English soldiers, and treated them with kindness. The Portuguese and Spaniards looked upon us as heretics, and although we appeared as their deliverers from foreign oppression, they manifested nothing beyond a cold political friendship, and never forgot our religion. But the French had less bigotry; they appeared to lose sight of religious differences; and they treated us with warm-hearted kindness, although we had come as enemies to force upon them a king whom they spoke of with ridicule and contempt.

My hostess would often, after returning from market, empty her cash purses upon the table before me, gold, silver and copper all mixed, and request me to count it up while she was busy in household affairs. I was to fold it in papers, the copper ten penny lots by themselves; the silver in twenty franc lots by themselves; and the gold in twenty Napoleon (20 s) lots; and she put each lot into a separate purse ready to be taken to market. I also mingled with several family circles, and was invited as a guest to weddings and entertainments. And it seemed strange to me that English soldiers, who were foreign enemies, just arrived with a victorious army to impose an objectionable yoke upon them, should be treated as brothers. But it was understood that the Russian, Prussian and Austrian soldiers treated the French peasantry where they were quartered with some cruelty: and the more civil behaviour of the English was appreciated. At Nanterre I was promoted to the rank of non-commissioned officer [corporal].

The French appeared to regard Sunday as a day of merriment. A few persons attended public worship in the forenoon; and the afternoon and evening were generally devoted, at least by great numbers, to card-playing, to billiards, and other games, and more especially to dancing. The dancing rooms at the wine houses were generally crowded on Sunday evenings. The Spaniards also formed dancing parties on Sunday afternoons in the streets of Logrono.

It seemed to me right to observe Sunday as the Lord's Day, but French and Spaniards looked upon it as a day for amusement.

After reposing in comfortable quarters near Paris for several months, we received directions to return to England, where we arrived in February 1816 and resumed our former duties in London.

1st or King's Dragoon Guards

No. 13   Captain William Elton
By kind permission of Wiltshire & Swindon Archives, ref. 413/382

Ruille near Paris, 15 July 1815

Dear Sir,

I was honoured with your letter only this morning & lose no time in sending you the particulars of the action, so painful to the feelings of those who are destined to survive their best friends. I lived constantly with Major Bringhurst[*] for six weeks, till the sudden order arrived on the morning of the 16th to move with the greatest expedition.

The first day, this brigade marched near 50 miles and did not arrive in presence of the enemy till eleven o'clock at night. The second day during that retreat, this regiment was not engaged except a few men in skirmishing and notwithstanding the bivouac that night in such weather, they were next day quite fit for service.

At ten o'clock the regiment began to suffer before they were mounted & in columns, from the shot which missed the English batteries 200 yards in our front. Major Bringhurst recommended the colonel to move nearer to the battery, which was done with good effect; the shot passing over us & killing the Belgian cavalry who took our ground during the time they staid [*sic*] in the field; and previous to their running away and plundering our baggage.[†]

Lord E. Somerset thinking we were still too much in line of the batteries, deployed into line on one side & in rear of the infantry. Major Graham, Bringhurst, Battersby, Brooke and Bernard[‡] were the officers of the right squadron. As mine was next, I could see them the whole time we were in position and under the cannonade, which still did us considerable mischief, the more in horses than men.

The enemy after several attacks upon the Duke's position, the brow of a hill wherein he was repulsed, seemed likely to succeed opposite our brigade by the increased fire of artillery and musquestry [*sic*], 200 yards in our front. The infantry suddenly broke out of their line into solid squares[§] & we saw the crests of the cuirassiers.

---

[*]   Captain John Dorset Bringhurst was a major in the army, killed at Waterloo.
[†]   This actually refers to the Hanoverian Duke of Cumberland's Hussars, whose commander, Colonel Hake, was cashiered after the battle.
[‡]   Captain Henry Graham, a major in the army, Captain's Bringhurst and George Battersby, Lieutenant Francis Brooke and Cornet the Honourable Henry Boyle Bernard (son of the Earl of Bandon) were all killed.
[§]   The troops fell into a solid square as a rapid means of defence against cavalry.

The line without waiting for any particular orders, drew swords & set off at full speed. Every squadron took the interval of our infantry which was next to them and there the right squadron & mine paired off & I never saw them more.

What particular resistance they met with at first, I never could ascertain, but every officer belonging to them was killed. Owing perhaps to their going faster than the Life Guards who were, or ought to have been upon their right flank , the enemy flying & drawing them on without order & afterwards surrounding them with their very superior numbers of cuirassiers & lancers. The squadron I had the honour to command fortunately met with resistance early & ground which could not be traversed at that pace. The enemy stood very well till we came within 20 yards. They had every appearance of being picked men, extremely large & well mounted; which I believe was the case, as they were cuirassiers of the Imperial Guard.* Our men setting up a general shout, many of them went about immediately. Those who could escape lost no time; the others were blocked up in a corner, a large fence on one side & a broad ravine on the other, these were all killed by our people, but their cuirass secured them to such a degree, that not one blow told out of five.

Here Lord Uxbridge had a round with one of their officers & though two of our men charged him & gave him plenty of cuts & thrusts on both sides, the man escaped into the lane where he was killed by the others. Lord E. Somerset who charged with us, crossed the ravine & was followed by all of us whose horses could leap in such slippery ground. Many dragoons lost their lives by falling in, others went round. The lane leading from the Duke of Wellington's position into the plain was quite choked up with cuirassiers & our men mixed & engaged with each other. At length it was tolerably well cleared & Lord Edward having heard that the greater part of the K[ing's] D[ragoon] G[uards] were broke & gone away without order into the enemy's lines, ordered me to rally & halt as many as possible, which was done, but too late, as no one seemed to know what was become of the right squadron and other broken troops & the ground in the plain where they had so far advanced was covered with immense columns of the enemy. Scarcely a man belonging to the right of the regiment has returned. Colonel Fuller went with them at least a mile in advance of the Duke's position, behind the whole French army. Part of the left squadrons did the same, but the resistance there was not so great. The colonel & all the men with him were entirely surrounded & cut to pieces. He was heard calling to his men to advance, without any support

---

* The British were not used to fighting the cuirassiers, the terrain of Spain being impracticable for heavy cavalry, and they often erroneously describe them as pertaining to the Imperial Guard.

& not a squadron of the regiment together. Poor Bringhurst was seen lying dead on the side of the hill between the English & French position. It is reported that he killed four of the enemy's lancers, who seem to have attacked him [from] behind. He had a wound in the side near the loins from a lance or sword, which from the man's report who examined his body, must have been instantly mortal. Not a man has returned who can give positive account of the precise manner in which he received his wound and the French occupied the ground afterwards; belonging to their army rather than ours; the English being a defensive position. He was buried in the same grave with Battersby & Graham. Every other regiment of heavy cavalry engaged that day seem to have shown equal gallantry with as little judgement.

But it is easy to be wise behindhand and nothing but a house or stone wall 50 feet high would have stopped either of those brigades. Had the enemy been desired to select every officer for whom we had the greatest esteem & regard, he could not have done better than the chance of war that day. And most of us who remained in the field till the evening, had canon shots through our horses & lost all our baggage, trifles in such circumstances.

Excuse dear Sir, this imperfect account of these affairs, wherein the honour acquired by the regiment is but a small consolation for the loss of such friends. It is true that the enemy suffered much more; but the sacrifice of all the Frenchmen that ever existed would not console me for Bringhurst alone. Believe me dear Sir, sensible of being honoured by your remembrance & your most obedient servant,

William Elton

2nd Brigade of Major General Sir William Ponsonby

No. 14 Major General Sir William Ponsonby
Permission kindly granted by the Borthwick Institute for Archives,
University of York, ref. Halifax A1/2/4

To his mother Lady Louisa Ponsonby.

Denderhoutem, 11 June 1815

My dearest mother,
I have to thank you for your very kind & comfortable letter, which was a great pleasure to me. I am always delighted to hear you like & approve of our little girls & do hope they will grow up what we could wish. Little love in a letter which I received from her yesterday gave me an account of the visit of Grandmama and Aunt Mary.* I am very happy to hear that

---

* His younger sister the Honourable Mary Elizabeth Ponsonby.

Charles spoke so very well (though I should consider his doing it but a matter of course). There seems to be in England a decided feeling for war & perfect confidence as to the successful result. How far this confidence is well founded a few months will show. Bonaparte will certainly have need of all his extraordinary abilities to resist the immense force about to attack him & I should think it impossible for him to do so, unless he is backed by the cordial & nearly general support of the population of France. Upon this point, it is impossible to obtain any information to be depended upon. The accounts given by the people about Louis 18th certainly do not come under this description. He [Napoleon] is said to be now at Maubeuge, which is not very far from here & as you know absolutely upon the frontier. His *game* would appear to be (& it is certainly his *manner*) to endeavour to strike a decisive blow on this side, before the Russians and Austrians come into play & if he finds himself strong enough to give him any rational prospect of success, I have little doubt he will try it. The Duke of Wellington, however, considers himself very strong & is *very confident*. My brother George* had written me word (as well as Richard's†) of Lord Fitzwilliam's‡ most kind & handsome proceeding, respecting the arrears, I quite agree with you that he is a person quite by himself, but I must consider Lady Fitz§ *a part of himself*. I have not heard what or whether *any* arrangement has since been made respecting the principal of the annuities. It was very good of you to give me so comfortable account of Georgiana, I am glad she has gone to town now & then, & to two or three parties, her life at Hampstead must be very solitary & dull & stands much in need of some relief. I hope John¶ has got safe away from France by this time, the state of the country is such as to render the residence of an Englishman there, by no means comfortable. How particularly unfortunate he has been, I wish he had fixed upon some town in Germany rather than France, as he certainly cannot afford the expense of travelling from place to place. We are told here that the insurrection in the Vendée is very extensive & formidable & I believe it is so, but there is too much reason to apprehend that Bonaparte will be able to crush it, before the ground attack commences. It is understood here that he was at Maubeuge yesterday & has been at Valenciennes; his *game* would appear to be (& certainly it is his *manner*) to think a blow

---

* The Honourable George Ponsonby.
† His brother the Honourable Reverend Richard Ponsonby.
‡ His father, William Ponsonby had died in 1806 and William Fitzwilliam, heir to the 3rd Earl Fitzwilliam appears to have acted as a benefactor to the family. Their mother eventually married Fitzwilliam in 1823, the year before she died.
§ Fitzwilliam was married to Lady Charlotte Ponsonby until she died in 1822.
¶ His brother John Ponsonby, 1st and last Viscount Ponsonby of Imokilly.

here before the Austrians & Russians come into play, & I am surprised at his not having already attempted it. However, we understand that the roads communicating with Belgium have been completely broken up, the bridges broken & every possible obstacle contrived, which of course must throw difficulties in the way of an attack on his part, in the same proportion as of our advance, so that one must suppose that it is not his intention to make an attack. I think your resolution will hardly hold out against Charles's attacks & indeed I should think it the best & most agreeable plan for you. I see the catholicks [*sic*] have lost ground considerably not only in the number but in the zeal & tone of their supporters, the necessary consequence of this intemperate unseasonable & most ungrateful conduct. Unless they alter very much their mode of proceeding, they never can have any chance of obtaining a decision in their favour. I enclose a little note for Frederick, give my love to Mary & her girls, Charles &c., &c. believe me my dearest mother, ever your affectionate
W. P.

I send this through Major General Charles Willoughby Gordon, Quarter Master General, who will I am sure forward to me any letter &c. you may wish at any time to send me. I conclude you know him, he is a friend of C. Grey's.*

Note by his mother: The last letter written to me by my beloved son seven days before the fatal battle.

1st or Royal Dragoons

No. 15   Sergeant Thomas Critchley†
Extract of a Letter from Sergeant Critchley, pp. 58–9 of
'The Battle of Waterloo by a Near Observer', *vol. II*

Nanterre, 24 July, 1815

... The action fought on the 18th of June, at Waterloo, was dreadful and difficult to gain, I can assure you, although we made a complete victory of it with hard fighting, by the double courage of our British heroes. The British cavalry exerted and displayed themselves gallantly. Our brigade was the first that charged, and great havoc we made; broke their lines and columns; took two stands of colours, two eagles, and made them fly before us a mile or more: but the loss of the brigade was severe; yet it

---

* Charles Grey, politician and 2nd Earl Grey, was married to William's sister Mary.
† Sergeant Thomas Critchley of Captain Phipps No. 5 Troop, 1st (Royal) Dragoons.

surprised me that so many escaped as did, for their guns and small arms were playing upon us on every side, pouring like hail, and men falling, and horses, as thick as possible. Dear Tom, I came off pretty safe, my horse shot through the leg, and myself slightly wounded with a bayonet, but nothing to signify of any consequence; in short, there were but few escaped wounds or scars. The French had the better of the day about 12 o'clock at noon, when the Belgians turned their backs to them*, and left the British infantry to the mercy of the world; and the French advanced upon that part of the line, and would have had possession of it in a few minutes, had it not been for our brigade making a rapid charge, which took such effect, and repulsed them, and drove them to confusion, which lightened the hearts of our infantry, and encouraged them to rally together, which was of great service at that point. The enemy kept up a continual firing, and the battle was equal as good upon their side as it was with us, till between seven and eight o'clock in the evening, when the victory turned glorious on our side. They began to retreat, when the Prussians, with their brave commander, von Blücher, was close after them, who never let them have any rest until they came to Paris. The day after the battle we buried our dead, and rested the following night, and then commenced our march, and got to Paris gates; and shortly the rebels yielded their capital, and evacuated, and suffered two armies to invest it. On the 24th instant, we had our British army reviewed, by the Emperor of Russia, Austria, and King of Prussia, Duke Wellington, Prince Blücher, and all the noted warriors in Europe, at the entrance of Paris gates. Dear Tom, you hear more news in England than we do here; only what we see is the real thing, which must be preferable to hearsay accounts. The Prussian army plays the devil with the country wherever they go; they made destruction in all the villages on the road from Waterloo to Paris, and beyond. I am not in the least sorry for them, for it just serves them right, and not half bad enough, for the usage they gave the Portuguese and Spaniards; it makes them feel a little of the seat of war as well as the rest of their neighbours . . .

---

* Bijlandt's Brigade broke as D'Erlon's troops closed, but some did stand on the wings of the British and helped to defeat the attack.

2nd (Royal North British) Dragoons, Scots Greys

No. 16   Major Isaac Blake Clarke,
Regarding Lieutenant James Carruthers*
By kind permission of Carlisle Record Office, ref. D Sa 3/6

Brussels 19 June 1815[†]

By the request of your son I am pained to inform you that in an attack on the enemy yesterday he received a musket shot on his right breast, which has incapacitated him from writing to you himself. I have not seen him myself but from those who have, I am led to hope that his wound is not dangerous. The number of letters I have to write prevents my adding more than my most sincere wishes that your son may speedily recover and give you a good account of himself, and that such a comfort may be yours is the fervent prayer of your most obedient servant,
  I. B. Clarke Lt Colonel 2nd Dragoons

Our regiment has suffered most dreadfully.

No. 17   Mr John Sadler Esq.
Regarding Lieutenant James Carruthers
By kind permission of Carlisle Record Office, ref. D Sa 3/6

Antwerp 24 June 1815

To James Carruthers Esq

Sir,
It is with regret I have to inform you of the melancholy event of your son James Carruthers, officer in the Scotch Greys.
  While engaged in that dreadful battle on Sunday about 5 o'clock in the evening he was killed by a cannon ball. He was the next officer that was killed after General Hamilton[‡] & was buried in the same place. I was on the field soon after, but too late to see him buried. His servant was sent in the rear on Saturday with his baggage and did not see him at [all] after. Four days before he was killed I saw him down here looking through this

---

* Lieutenant James Carruthers of Liverpool. The family seat was at Annandale.
† Unfortunately early reports informed home that he was injured and was likely to survive – the next letter would therefore have been a great shock.
‡ Colonel James Inglis Hamilton was killed, having been wounded in both arms in the attack on D'Erlon's corps, therefore it is unclear whether he met his death as late in the battle as stated here.

town, I had a long conversation with him. His servant is now gone up to the regiment with his horses & baggage.

In a few days I shall leave here again for the army. If you wish that I should see after his property I will either send it you or have it sold & sent you. Any other information you may require it will give me great pleasure to communicate to you. For the meantime, I am your most obedient servant,

John Sadler

Address me J. Sadler, care of Messrs D. Thewcet & co. Antwerp.

No. 18   Captain Edward Payne,
Regarding Lieutenant James Carruthers
By kind permission of Carlisle Record Office, ref. D Sa 3/6

To James Carruthers Esq, Mount Pleasant, Liverpool

Nanterre, France, 14 July 1815

My dear Sir,
No doubt but you will be much surprised at receiving this letter from me, which I assure you is a most severe task to me to write, indeed I really do not know in what words to express my feelings upon so melancholy an occasion to the parent of my deceased friend. Your late son, my dear sir, was a most intimate & particular friend of mine, such another I never expect to meet with. The many happy hours we have passed together will never be erased from my memory. There is one consolation & a great one, in knowing that he lost his life in bravely fighting the enemies of his native country.

I find, my dear sir, my feelings are leading me astray, as I merely took my pen to inform you that yesterday I sent a small parcel by the servant of the late Captain Barnard* (who is upon his road to England), belonging to my late friend.

I regret to have to inform you that his watch &c. was stolen as he lay on the ground previous to being discovered by our regiment. Believe me to be my dear sir, yours most respectfully,

Edward Payne, 2nd RNB Dragoons.

---

* Captain Charles Levyns Barnard Scots Greys was killed at Waterloo.

4th Brigade of Major General Sir John Vandeleur
12th Light Dragoons

No. 19   Lieutenant Colonel the Honourable
Frederick Cavendish Ponsonby
By kind permission of the British Library, Mudford papers, Add. MS 19390, ff11–13

Substance of answers given to questions respecting the Battle of Waterloo put to Lt Colonel Ponsonby by his particular friends.
[A fuller version of his well-publicised statement]

The weather cleared up at noon and the sun shone out a little, just as the battle began. The armies were within eight hundred yards of each other; the videttes before they were withdrawn, being so near as to be able to converse. At the moment I imagined that I saw Bonaparte & a considerable Staff moving rapidly along the front of our line. I was stationed with my regiment (about three hundred strong) at the extreme of the left wing, and directed to act discretionally; each of the armies was drawn up on a gentle declivity, a small valley lying between them.

At one o'clock observing as I thought, unsteadiness in a column of French infantry (50 by 20) (1000) or thereabouts) which were advancing with an irregular fire, I resolved to charge them. As we were descending in a gallop, we received from our own troops on the right, a fire much more destructive than theirs, they having began long before it could take effect, and slackening as we drew nearer; when we were within fifty paces of them they turned and much execution was done among them, as we were followed by some Belgians, who had remarked our success.

But we had no sooner passed through them than we were attacked in our turn, before we could form, by about three hundred Polish lancers, who had come down to their relief. The French artillery pouring in among us, a heavy fire of grape shot, which however for one of our men, killed three of their own. In the melee I was disabled almost instantly in both of my arms and followed by a few of my men who were presently cut down (no quarter being asked or given). I was carried on by my horse, till receiving a blow on my head from a sabre, I was thrown senseless on my face to the ground. Recovering, I raised myself a little to look around (being I believe at that time in a condition to get up, and run away) when a lancer passing by exclaimed '*Tu n'est pas mort, coquin*'* and struck his lance through my back, my head dropped, the blood gushed into my mouth, a difficulty of breathing came on and I thought all was over.

Not long afterwards (it was then impossible to measure time, but I

---

* 'You are not dead, knave.'

must have fallen in less than ten minutes after the charge) a tirailleur came up to plunder me; threatening to take my life. I told him that he might search me, directing him to a small side pocket in which he found three dollars, being all I had. He unloosed my stock and tore open my waistcoat, then leaving me in a very uneasy posture, and was no sooner gone, than another came up for the same purpose, but assuring him I had been plundered already he left me, when an officer bringing on some troops (to which probably the tirailleurs belonged) and halting where I lay, stooped down and addressed me saying, he feared I was badly wounded. I replied that I was and expressed a wish to be removed into the rear; he said it was against the order to remove even their own men; but that if they gained the day, as they probably would (for he understood the Duke of Wellington was killed and that six of our battalions had surrendered) every attention in his power should be shown me. I complained of thirst and he held his brandy bottle to my lips, directing one of his men to lay me straight on my side, and place a knapsack under my head. He then passed on into the action and I shall never know to whose generosity I was indebted, as I conceive for my life; of what rank I cannot say, he wore a blue greatcoat.* By and by another tirailleur came and knelt and fired over me, loading & firing many times and conversing with great gaiety all the while, at last he ran off saying '*vous serez bien aise d'entendre que nous allons nous retirons, bonjour, mon ami*'.†

While the battle continued in that part, several of the wounded men and dead bodies near me were hit with the balls which came very thick in that place. Towards evening when the Prussians came, the continued roar of the cannon along theirs and the British line, growing louder and louder as they drew near, was the finest thing I ever heard. It was dusk when two squadrons of Prussian cavalry, both of them two deep, passed over me in full trot; lifting me from the ground, and tumbling me about cruelly. The clatter of their approach, and the apprehensions it excited, may be easily conceived. Had a gun come that way, it would have done for me. The battle was then nearly over, or removed to a distance, the cries and groans of the wounded all around me, became every instant more and more audible, succeeding to the shouts, imprecations, outcries of '*Vive L'empereur*,'‡ the discharges of musketry and cannon, now and then intervals of perfect silence which were worse than the noise. I thought

---

* According to Captain Gronow Ponsonby did subsequently discover the identity of his saviour. When Ponsonby was governor of Malta, he met a French Waterloo veteran and as they exchanged stories, it became obvious this was the very man, one Baron de Laussat. See pp. 153–4 of *The Reminiscences of Captain Gronow* London 1964.

† 'You will definitely be relieved to hear that we withdraw, good day, my friend.'

‡ 'Long live the emperor.'

the night would never end; much about this time I found a soldier of the Royals lying across my legs, who had probably crawled thither in his agony; his weight, convulsive motions, his noises, and the air issuing through a wind in his side, distressed me greatly, the latter circumstance most of all, as the case was my own. It was not a dark night and the Prussians were wandering about to plunder, (and the scene in Ferdinand Count Fathom* came into my mind, though no women I believe were there), several of them came and looked at me, and passed on; at length one stopped to examine me, I told him as well as I could (for I could say but little in German) that I was a British officer and had been plundered already, he did not desist, however, and pulled me about roughly before he left me. About an hour before midnight, I saw a soldier in an English uniform coming towards me, he was I suspect on the same errand, he came and looked in my face, I spoke instantly telling him who I was, and assuring himself of a reward, if he would remain by me; he said that he belonged to the 40th Regiment,† but had missed it. He released me from the dying man, being unarmed, he took up a sword from the ground and stood over me, pacing backwards and forwards. At eight o'clock in the morning, some English were seen at a distance, he ran to them and a messenger was sent off to Hervey;‡ a cart came for me, I was placed in it and carried to a farm house, above a mile and a half distant, and laid in the bed from which poor Gordon§ (as I understood afterwards) had been just carried out, the jolting of the cart, and the difficulty of breathing were very painful. I had received seven wounds; a surgeon slept in my room and I was saved by continual bleeding (120 ounces in two days, besides the great loss of blood on the field).

Such probably is the story of many a brave man, yet to me it was new. The historian describing military achievements passes silently over those who go into the heat of the battle, though there as we have seen every character displays itself. The gay are still gay, the noble minded are still generous, nor has the commander in his proudest a better claim to our admiration than the meanest of his soldiers when relieving a fallen enemy in the midst of danger and death.

The lancers, from their length and weight, would have struck down my sword long before I lost it, if it had not been bound to my hand. What became of my horse I know not, it was the best I ever had. The men

---

* Tobias Smollet's *The Adventures of Ferdinand Count Fathom* appeared early in 1753.
† The 40th (2nd Somersetshire) Regiment.
‡ Colonel Felton Elwell Hervey 14th Light Dragoons.
§ Lieutenant Colonel the Honourable Sir Alexander Gordon, 3rd Foot Guards, Aide de Camp to Wellington, died following the operation to amputate his leg.

soon grow very savage from being knocked about, much inconvenience would arise from allowing the wounded to be carried off; the men being so ready on the slightest pretext, to leave the field.

The man from the Royals was still breathing when I was removed in the morning, and was soon after taken to the hospital.

Much confusion arose and many mistakes from familiarity of dress. The Belgians in particular, suffered greatly from their resemblance to the French, being still in the very same clothes they had served in under Bonaparte. Our scarlet is more distinguishable than any other colour. Horses are very unwilling to go into battle; they cower and hang down their heads, when the balls are whistling about them.

Sir Dennis Pack said the greatest risk he run the whole day was in stopping his men who were firing on me and my regiment when we began to charge. The French make a great clamour in the action the English only shout.

No. 20   Robert Hume* Deputy Inspector of Hospitals and Surgeon to the Commander of the Forces, Regarding Ponsonby's Injuries

10 August 1815

I hereby certify that Colonel the Honourable F. C. Ponsonby commanding the 12th Light Dragoons in the Battle of Waterloo on the 18th of June last, received a cut from a sabre on the outside of the fore right arm opposite the edge of the ulna which divided the integuments† and muscles longitudinally down to the bones extending from near the elbow to the wrist. He was also struck behind on the left side by a lance, which fracturing the sixth rib entered the chest and wounded the lungs. Besides these two severe wounds, he received several smaller cuts on his head, shoulder and left arm (which was also disabled) and different parts of his body; and was bruised all over in such a manner as to render his recovery very doubtful; his recovery towards convalescence has been very slow; he has still little or no use of his right arm and hand; his breathing is much affected, by the wound in his chest, which is still open, and his strength is so much impaired that it is more than probable his constitution will never recover the shock which it has received.‡

---

* John Robert Hume, Inspector of Hospitals, Drew, *Medical Officers*, number 1988. He was for many years the private physician of the Duke of Wellington.
† Skin and fat.
‡ Despite his severe wounds he lived until 1837.

6th Brigade of Major General Sir Hussey Vivian

No. 21   Major General Sir Hussey Vivian
From The Historical Memoirs of the XVIIIth Hussars, *Colonel Harold Malet,*
London 1907

Wynne Pendarves, Esq.,*
No. II, Queen Anne Street, London

St Benin,† 23 June 1815

My dear Edward,
I did not write you, not because I had no time, but because I had nothing
to write about, (or in truth the six weeks prior to our friend Napoleon's
beating up our quarters were passed in indolence and ease, not so the last
eight days, they afford plenty to write about and but little (time) to write
in. If you were in Cornwall I should refer you to a letter which my father
will receive for a full, true (that is, not many lies in it), and particular
account of the 18th and the affairs which preceded it; as it is, I will as
shortly as possible relate them.

We had heard prior to the 18th that Bonaparte had been collecting his
men near Maubeuge, and was himself about to leave Paris to attack us,
and Lord Wellington had felt persuaded he would do so, but what reason
he had to change his opinion I know not, but certain it is that on the 16th
at a ball at the Duchess of Richmond's we were all surprised to find that
the French were pressing on in great force upon Binche and Nivelles.

We all left the ball and returned to our quarters, and the following
morning at five o'clock marched upon Enghien, Braine le Comte, and
Nivelles, from thence to Quatre Bras, where we came too late to join
in a very serious affair, in which a very small part of our army had been
engaged, for to tell the honest truth our great general had committed a
sad blunder in not having before collected his force.

On the 17th, owing to the Prussians having been beaten on our left and
retreated, we were obliged to do the same to Mont St Jean, near Waterloo,
where we occupied a position, and no very strong one either. Our retreat
was considerably pressed by the enemy's cavalry, who gave us a pretty good
specimen of their boldness. They played the devil with my old regiment,
the 7th, which is not in my brigade. They did not press me much.

I covered the retreat of the left column. We had the most tremendous
rain I ever beheld, and were soaked to the skin without anything to
change, and the canopy of heaven for our covering. No very comfortable

---

* Edward William Wynne-Pendarves, MP for West Cornwall.
† Two miles south of Cateau Cambresis.

commencement of a campaign which was to take us almost without a blow to Paris.

On the morning of the 18th, about 11 o'clock, our advanced posts were driven in, and we saw the enemy's columns advancing to attack us, the firing soon began, and about one o'clock one of the most desperate attacks I ever witnessed was made on the centre and left centre of our line. This was defeated and repeated twice, the armies constantly mixed actually with each other and the French always covering each attack by the most tremendous cannonade you can possibly imagine. With respect to the particular situation in which my brigade was placed, it did not suffer much until the last attack. The ground on the left did not admit of the cavalry advancing, and I being on the left of all, consequently suffered only from the cannonade; about 6 o'clock, however, I learnt that the cavalry in the centre had suffered dreadfully and the Prussians about that time having formed to my left, I took upon myself to move off from our left, and halted directly to the centre of our line, where I arrived most opportunely at the instant that Bonaparte was making his last and most desperate effort, and never did I witness anything so terrific, the ground actually covered with dead and dying, cannon shot and shells flying thicker than I ever heard even musketry before and our troops, some of them giving way. In this state of affairs I wheeled my brigade into line, close within 10 yards in rear of our infantry, and prepared to charge the instant they had retreated through my intervals. The three squadron officers of the 10th were wounded at this instant this, however, gave them confidence, and the brigades that were literally running away, halted, on our cheering them, and again began firing. The enemy on their part began to waver, the Duke observed it, and ordered the infantry to advance. I immediately wheeled the brigade by half squadrons to the right, and in column over the dead and dying, trotted round the right of our infantry, passed the French infantry and formed lines of regiments on the first half squadrons. With the 10th I charged a body of French cuirassiers and lancers, infinitely superior to them, and completely routed them. I then went to the 18th and charged a second body that was supporting a square of the Imperial Guards, and the 18th not only defeated them, but took 14 pieces of cannon that had been firing grape at us during our movement.

I then with the 10th, having reformed them, charged a square of infantry, Imperial Guards, the men of which we cut down in the ranks, and here the last shot was fired. From this moment all was *derout*. Whether the Duke will do my brigade justice or not I know not; but Bonaparte has given them their due in his account. We are the cavalry that he alludes to where at the end he says 'At 8 o'clock, &c.' and the colonel of the 3rd Chasseurs who lodged the night before last in the house I occupied last night, told the proprietor that 'two regiments of British hussars decided the affair. The third regiment (the 1st Hussars) I kept in reserve.

Of course our loss was severe. All those returned missing are since ascertained to have been killed. I never saw such a day, nor anyone else. I expect and hope that every soldier will bear a medal with 'Mont St. Jean' on it. I would rather do so than be adorned by the brightest star that any potentate could bestow on me.

Yours most truly,

R. H. Vivian

No. 22   Sir Hussey Vivian to General Bloomfield[*]
By kind permission of Northamptonshire Record Office C(A)box 53/76

19 June 1815

. . . You will hardly expect me to detail to you the proceedings of this most extraordinary battle & most glorious victory but I will as briefly as possible state precisely the situation in which the regiment was placed. The whole of the early part of the day my brigade was on the left of the line where we were exposed to a very severe cannonade which they stood in a manner the most creditable; the 10th on the right & the most exposed. Towards the end of the battle, the whole of the cavalry on the right being almost annihilated I heard they were in want of us & the Prussians arriving on my left, I trotted along the rear of our line to the right & formed in the rear of our infantry where there was the most tremendous fire of round, grape & musketry I ever experienced; the 10th led the column beautifully. The enemy began to give way, I trotted in column of ½ squadrons from the right, round the flank of the infantry in my front & in this manner the brigade proceeded led by the 10th under the heaviest fire of grape & musketry you can possibly imagine, in as good order, intervals as well preserved & as steady, as if at a field day in England. We led for the left of the French where there were two strong bodies of French cavalry (cuirassiers & lancers in each, with a square of infantry in the centre. I directed the brigade to form lines of regiments on their front ½ squadrons, they did it to perfection; this done, with the 10th I charged the left body of cavalry; they went on in the best possible line & at full speed & entered the enemy's line which outflanked & wheeled up to receive them, but was in an instant overthrown & great numbers cut down.

I then ordered the 18th to attack the cavalry on the right of the square & the 10th to rally, which they did to perfection, when I directed Major Howard's squadron, supported by the other two, to charge the square;

---

[*]   Major General Benjamin Bloomfield Royal Artillery.

the gallantry with which they did this is not to be expressed; they were received by a most tremendous fire, but they persisted & cut down the French in their ranks. From this moment, not a shot was fired, every man of the French infantry was either sabred by the 10th or made prisoners by General Vandeleur's Brigade which came up shortly after.

Of course under circumstances such as I have related, the loss must be dreadful. Poor Major Howard[*] & Lieutenant Gunning[†] are I lament to say killed; Lieutenant Arnold[‡] is I fear mortally wounded. Colonel Quentin[§] was early wounded in the ankle, I never saw a cooler man under fire or an officer more zealous, or who had his regiment in better order. Never either did I see a finer corps of young officers, more gallant or more anxious to do their duty or men more steady & well behaved.

I cannot close this letter without stating in justice to the 18th that in the advance & attack they most handsomely imitated the example of steadiness & gallantry that had been set them by HRH's Regiment[¶] & the conduct of the 1st Hussars [KGL] was highly creditable to that distinguished corps.

Major Howard & Lieutenant Gunning killed
Lieutenant Arnold wounded
Captain's Wood,[**] Gurwood[††] & Grey[‡‡] also wounded but not dangerously & also Lieutenant Bacon.[§§]

---

[*] Major the Honourable Frederick Howard.
[†] Lieutenant George Orlando Gunning. Dalton fails to show him as killed.
[‡] Lieutenant Robert Arnold, 10th Hussars, is not shown as wounded by Dalton but is in *A Near Observer*. However, the wound did not prove fatal as he lived until 1839.
[§] Lieutenant Colonel George Quentin led the 10th Hussars and was wounded at Waterloo.
[¶] The Prince of Wales was regimental colonel of the 10th Hussars which were titled 'The Prince of Wales' Own'.
[**] Captain Charles Wood is not shown as wounded by Dalton but is listed as wounded in the London Gazette.
[††] Captain John Gurwood was actually serving as aide de camp to Lieutenant General Clinton.
[‡‡] Captain John Grey.
[§§] Lieutenant Anthony Bacon

No. 23   From Sir Hussey Vivian to William Siborne[*]
By kind permission of the British Library Add Ms 34706 ff235–237

14 February 1837

My dear Siborne,

It affords me great pleasure to find that all I have stated has been so fully corroborated by the information you have obtained from others on the subject of the Battle of Waterloo. I do not know how or why it was but I felt on that day so perfectly cool & collected that I have the most exact recollection of everything that occurred immediately about where I was placed & most especially as to what occurred to those under my orders as far as it came under my observation. In a brigade of three regiments & 6 guns[†] at times some portion must have [been] out of my sight from the confusion & smoke in which the field lay.

In reply to your first question as to any sudden attack on Smohain. I should say that when the advanced body of the Prussians was driven back (as I have said in a former letter without making much resistance), I think the French followed them & occupied Smohain. There was a good deal of firing out the hedges & lanes where I stood & on my left as I faced the French position, & I have little doubt that the French then pushed into Smohain. I did not observe any other attack in which they could have done so & I feel confident it could not have occurred *after* I had quitted the left for shortly after that the Prussians must have been arriving there in force. The answer I have now given to your first question in part answers your second, viz whether any part of Ziethen's Corps had reached our left before I quitted it. I have already referred to an advanced body of Prussian infantry that arrived very early. Whether they belonged to Ziethen or not, I cannot say. It was some time after this that patrols I had sent to the left to look out came & informed me that the Prussians were advancing on the road from Ohain in force & their advanced cavalry had come on so that I saw them from a point on the left of our position & rather to the rear of the little lane. To that point I rode purposely to look out on hearing that they were coming. On seeing that there could be no longer any apprehension of our left being turned & hearing from Colonel Delancey Barclay[‡] that cavalry were wanted in the centre that I proposed to Sir O. Vandeleur[§] to move with his brigade and mine, he was the senior

---

[*] This letter has not previously been published by either Siborne or this editor.
[†] This refers to Gardiner's Troop of Royal Horse Artillery, which was attached to the brigade and moved with it to the centre of the position.
[‡] Lieutenant Colonel Delancey Barclay, 1st Foot Guards, Assistant Adjutant General.
[§] Major General Sir John Ormsby Vandeleur, commanding the 4th Cavalry Brigade.

officer, although we acted separately, towards the centre where we might be of service. Sir O. V. objected to moving without orders & I then put my own brigade in motion & passed along the rear of Sir O. V.'s Brigade & soon after having commenced my march I met Lord Anglesey* who was much pleased at what I had done & sending orders to Vandeleur to follow, proceeded to accompany my brigade towards the centre, passing immediately at the bottom of the slope behind the position in which stood Sir T. Picton's Division. On the march in consequence of a mistake on the part of Captain Horace Seymour[†] who (Lord Anglesey had left me to proceed towards the centre in order to see where I could be of most use) brought me an order from Lord Anglesey I understood to form line. I wheeled my brigade into line immediately before reaching the high road and with my right touching on it. I remained there some few moments until Lord Anglesey discovering the mistake came & moved me on. I have mentioned this because it enables me to speak to what was then occurring in the position on the left of the road where there was much firing, but I should not say any determined attack. On the right of the road & in front of the ground to which I afterwards moved after passing the road there appeared to be [a] more serious attack & there was some shouting but I saw no sudden & confused retreat such as you speak of. I must tell you, however, that during the whole of my movement from the left to the right & especially when halted & formed line, the impression on my mind was that our troops were getting the worst of it in our position & that Vandeleur and I should have to cover the retreat & when I got the orders as I understood to form line in the plain before the slope at the back of our position I was persuaded it was for this purpose. There was a retreat & a very hurried one a considerable time before the advance of the Imperial Guard immediately on the left of the road but this was in the attack of the French columns on Picton. Then our advanced troops were driven back at a great rate, I have heard from those who saw it but this could refer to the retreat spoken of by our Staff officers.

The foreign hussars that attached themselves to me were Dutch. I am persuaded there was a strong squadron. I think the officer in command told me his name was Mellin but I am not certain.[‡] They remained & charged I believe on the flank of the 18th Hussars & after we had halted & rallied I told him I would make a report of this good conduct & saw no more of them.

---

* An anachronism, Anglesey was still Earl of Uxbridge at Waterloo.
† Captain Horace Seymour, 18th Hussars was one of Uxbridge's aides de camp.
‡ This could possibly be Major General Merlen who commanded the 2nd Netherland Light Cavalry Brigade and was killed at Waterloo.

Sir R. Gardiner's* battery followed me from the left, they had suffered much but after I crossed the road I cannot speak with certainty as to what became of them, I was so much occupied with the regiments & in their front, but I do not think Gardiner came into action in the position *at once*, but I know that he did before the day closed, open a fire from it.

I have no doubt the position of the guns on my sketch may have been incorrect in fact I gave it merely to show as far as I could then observe what appeared to me to be the relative bearings of the different objects without at all meaning that I was exact in my view of their bearings. Sincerely yours,

H. Vivian.

18th Hussars

No. 24   Lieutenant Colonel the Honourable Henry Murray[†]
From The Historical Memoirs of the XVIIIth Hussars, *Colonel Harold Malet, London 1907.*

We saw several columns of the enemy advancing to the attack, and our pickets were again attacked by the French cavalry, who repulsed us a short distance from the position we had taken up in brigade on the extreme left. The skirmishing lasted till nearly eleven o'clock, at which hour the battle of Mont St Jean or Waterloo began, and it lasted eight hours in the midst of the most terrible bloodshed. The Adjutant[‡] having detached during last night a party under the command of Lieutenant Coote[§] towards the road to Brussels, returned in time for the men and horses to be refreshed with what the party brought, namely, oats, bread, and some hollands. The 18th were, at this time, posted on the extreme left of the British army, where they remained some time exposed to a severe cannonade from the enemy's batteries.

It had been noticed during our retreat yesterday that the French horses, so little, could hardly struggle over the fields so deep and heavy, so they preferred to follow the 7th Hussars on the main road. During the day Vivian rode forward, to observe the progress of the action. He saw more than his officers. Major Harris[¶] (late of the regiment) and Keane[**],

---

* Lieutenant Colonel Sir Robert Gardiner's Troop of Horse Artillery.
† This is not the same version as his letter published by Siborne.
‡ Lieutenant Henry Duperier.
§ Lieutenant Robert Coote.
¶ Captain Thomas Noel Harris, Major of Brigade to Sir Hussey Vivian.
** Captain Edward Keane 7th Hussars Aide de Camp to Vivian.

and Mr. Fitzroy*, were, I believe, with him. It was not until half-past seven o'clock and just as the Prussians were arriving on the right from the left of the position where we had been in line with the 10th, in rear of the Wavre road, and withdrawn a little from the crest of the ridge, the right of the 10th Hussars resting on a lane leading up from Smohain, crossing over the position and descending along the reverse slope; that we proceeded in the direction of Verd-Coucou,† with the 1st Hussars in reserve. The roar was now so great that though close together we could not make ourselves understood except by hollering. The smoke was very thick, and only allowed the enemy's heads to be seen; all at once we burst from the darkness of a London fog into a bright sunshine.

From the time we came up to where Lord Edward Somerset's brigade was, very little was to be seen, except as in a fog, that was immediately near you. It was one of the annoyances of the moment that we were so completely in the dark as to what was going on of great importance. After Ponsonby's and Picton's Brigades had charged (when both these gallant officers fell), Sir Hussey Vivian ordered the 10th and the regiment to move through the hollow way to their right, with orders to the 1st Hussars to keep a look out on their left, our new position being on the right of the lane leading to Verd-Coucou. The Brunswickers were in the centre of the British position, and on the Duke of Wellington rallying them on their wavering, and reforming them, the regiment came up in brigade and formed line with the 10th (the 1st Hussars being still in rear), relieving the exhausted remains of the Scots Greys and the 3rd Hussars German Legion. In consequence of a mistake in the transmission of orders, we had been halted on the high road about midway between the front line and the farm of Mont St Jean, whence, however, it was speedily brought forward and posted as above. The air of ruin and destruction that met our view in the centre of the line was calculated to inspire us with thoughts by no means akin to anticipations of victory, and many thought that they had been brought from the left to cover another retreat, yet no despondency was visible, and the feeling of reliance on the oft proved skill of our chief cherished the hope that by persevering a little longer our repeated heroic exertions would yet be crowned with success. This feeling was aptly expressed by Sir Felton Hervey, of the Duke's staff, who, as he rode to the regiment to change his wounded charger, exclaimed, as he was about to mount a trooper, 'The Duke of Wellington has won the battle if we could but get the damned devils to advance.' The

---

* Lieutenant Charles Augustus Fitzroy, Royal Horse Guards, extra aide de camp to Vivian.

† Verd Coucou is a village just beyond Mont St Jean in the direction of Waterloo itself.

regiment now followed in brigade in support of the Brunswickers and Nassauers, and by its proximity to these troops, on whom a fire most close and unremitting was maintained, was placed in a trying situation for cavalry, and suffered in much consequence. It was now that the Duke found himself at last, owing to the failure of Napoleon's last charge, able to become the assailant. As soon as our infantry had rallied and got into line in their former position, Vivian withdrew his brigade under the crest of the ridge thirty yards off to place his hussars out of fire. On the Duke of Wellington seeing the success of the charge of Adam's Brigade, he ordered fresh cavalry to check the probable advance of the enemy and to attack the French themselves in front of La Belle Alliance. Lieutenant Colonel Lord Greenock, AQMG of the cavalry, was sent to Vivian with orders for him to move his brigade to its right from its position in the rear of Alten's Division, so as to get clear of the infantry, and then to advance directly to the front by the right of Maitland's Brigade of Guards. A trot now sounded, and our brigade advanced against the cavalry reserves near La Belle Alliance by half squadrons to the right, the regiment following the 10th, the 1st Hussars in rear. Proceeding a short distance in rear of the infantry and parallel to the crest of the position, part of the time over fine standing corn, we approached Maitland's brigade, and here the leading half squadron was ordered to wheel to the left through Napier's battery and to lead perpendicularly to the front, and the manner in which Sir H. Vivian led the brigade down, always keeping under the cover of the hill where the ground allowed it, was excellent.

On the occasion just mentioned, the officer commanding this leading half squadron, not correctly catching the word of command, in consequence probably of the noise created by Napier's guns, as also from the shouts of Adam's brigade, which was following up its triumph, wheeled up to the right instead of to the left. This was rectified by General Vivian in person galloping to the flank of the leading half-squadron, and, with emphasis and a good hearty damn, called out that it was 'towards' and not 'from the enemy' they were to wheel. He took the flank officer's place, and led the column down the hill in the direction he wished to move, and the column thus advanced across the ridge in left front of Vandeleur's Light Cavalry Brigade. We were saluted by the latter with cheers of encouragement, and in a similar manner by Maitland's Brigade, as we passed their flank. As soon as the smoke allowed General Vivian to see the disposition of the enemy's troops in his front, he formed line with the regiment and the 10th, with the 1st Hussars in support. The moment of the arrival of our brigade was also the moment of Napoleon's last advance, and the fire to which we were exposed, both of cannon and musketry, was very severe. General Vivian, after seeing the attack by the 10th that he ordered, was returning to the regiment, when he was attacked by a cuirassier; his right hand was in a sling in consequence of the wound he had received at Croix-d'Orade.* Taking the reins in this hand, which was barely capable of holding them, be contrived to give the cuirassier a thrust with the left. At this moment his German orderly joined him, who cut the man down. Lord Uxbridge, when on his way to the regiment at this time, was shot in the right leg, and amputation was performed afterwards. After the gallant charge of the 10th General Vivian then, as stated, galloped to the regiment which he found in line and in perfect order. On the front stood two squares of the Grenadiers of the Old Guard, on its left front and much nearer to it were posted artillery and cavalry in advance of the proper right of these squares. This cavalry consisted principally of cuirassiers, the wrecks of entire brigades; nearer to, and partly in rear of the squares stood the chasseurs and grenadiers-à-cheval of the Imperial Guard, greatly diminished in numbers. It was immediately evident to Vivian that the attack must in the first instance be directed against the advanced artillery and cavalry, and having put the regiment in motion, he placed himself in front of the centre, beside Colonel Murray, for the purpose of putting us into the required direction. He on this said to the regiment '18th, you will follow me,' on which the Sergeant Major Jeffs† (afterwards Adjutant of the 7th Hussars) and several exclaimed, 'By Jagus, general, anywhere, to hell, if you will lead us.' He then ordered the charge to sound, when the regiment dashed forward with the greatest impetuosity, and at the same time with as much steadiness and regularity as if they had been at field day exercise on Hounslow Heath. Thus the direction of the charge by the regiment diverged as much to the left as that of the 10th had inclined to the right. Just as our charge commenced, some French artillery coming from their right, and slanting towards the regiment, made a bold push to cross our front at a gallop, but the attempt failed, and we were in an instant among them, cutting down the artillerymen and the drivers and securing the guns. In the next moment we fell upon the advanced cavalry, which we completely dispersed, and then bringing forward our left shoulders we attacked the cavalry and guns that stood more to our right front and near to the right square which was now retiring. This cavalry appeared at first determined to make a stand, and an officer in its front dashed forward and fired at Colonel Murray, but in another moment the regiment was fiercely and dexterously plying their sabres amongst them, and we next charged the Imperial Guard, their cuirassiers and lancers, a regular

---

* In this action in Southern France on the 8 April 1814, Vivian made a bold attack with the 18th Hussars and captured a vital bridge.
† Regimental Sergeant Major Thomas Jeffs.

medley of them all, including infantry and guns, etc., such a scene! The infantry threw themselves down except two squares, which stood firm, but did no good. The sneaking prisoners we had taken hollered '*Vive le Roi.*' The Duke said, who saw the brigade charge, 'Well done 10th and 18th.' The Guards, too, who saw us coming down had cheered us in high style. On charging, not only did the infantry throw themselves down, but the cavalry also from off their horses, all roaring 'pardon,' many of them on their knees. We came to a deep hollow, and on the opposite side was a steep knoll, with a square of infantry very well formed on it. Down this hollow dashed a party of the regiment and up the hill at the square in most gallant style, but were checked and turned by their fire.

But for our charge, I am convinced in ten minutes there would have been a good lot of cavalry rallied and squares formed.

No. 25   Captain Arthur Kennedy
From the letters from Captain Arthur Kennedy 18th Hussars by Lieutenant Colonel E. E. Hunt, May 1998 (unpublished). By kind permission of the Regimental Museum 13th/18th Royal Hussars and the Light Dragoons

Grammont, 1 June 1815

My dearest Grace,[*]
I am quite at a loss to account for the silence of you *all.* Mail after mail comes in without a line from anyone. I wrote you a short bulletin from Brussels which Mr. James undertook to forward. I saw Lady Emily who looks very well and I think will *very* soon increase the illustrious house of Stewart[†], she mentioned having had a letter from you. We had a magnificent ball at the Duke of Wellington's, quantities of grandees foreign princes etc. A few days after we had a most superb review of all the British cavalry at present in Flanders. Old Blücher came over from Liège to see such a sight as I believe he nor anyone else has ever witnessed. 46 of the finest squadrons of cavalry ever seen were drawn up in a place in their lines, with 6 troops of horse artillery and a brigade of rockets, in all about 6,500 men. The day was remarkably favourable for all the *haut ton* of Brussels to come and see the review, the crowd in consequence was as great as if it had been at Hounslow Heath. Blücher and all the foreign princes were highly delighted and the most handsome orders were issued by the D[uke] of W[ellington] expressing his high approbation of the excellent appearance

---

[*]   His sister in law Grace Dorothea Kennedy (née Hughes) who had married his brother Hugh in 1799.
[†]   Lady Emily Jane Stewart, daughter of the Marquess of Londonderry, was married to Mr John James, who was Sir Charles Stuart's Secretary of Embassy.

of both men and horses which certainly exceeded anything I ever saw. You would have thought the sky would have been rent with the shouts of the people on the approach of Blücher and Wellington who were received with a royal salute from the artillery. After the review they all went to dine with Lord Uxbridge at Ninove.

We have established a very good race course and have had some excellent races, so you see we contrive to amuse ourselves as long as we can. I should think, however, our stay here will not be of much longer duration. The news from France continues favourable. I saw some deserters with the white cockade pass here yesterday; they bring favourable intelligence, if it can be relied upon. The army on the frontiers have not received pay for a fortnight and the French people are becoming as one may suppose very anxious to get rid of their guests, who are of course living on them at free quarters. They will now begin to feel the effects of war in their own country. I hear they are longing for our advance to finish the business. In the meantime the Russians and the Austrians are not sufficiently near the Rhine to warrant our advance on this side. Yesterday the colonel of the 7th French Hussars deserted to us from the outposts. I have not heard what he says but matters must be in rather an unpromising aspect when such men are deserting the *Bonaparte standard.*

I went over to Ghent a few days ago to dine with Lord Portarlington* who commands the 23rd Dragoons there. Old Louis and his household are still there. I believe he already musters about 4 or 5,000 followers but the moment we pass the frontiers no doubt thousands more will flock to his standard. We are to be brigaded with the 10th Hussars and 1st Regiment of Germans and report says a squadron of each regiment will move immediately to the advanced posts. I shall I suppose go being the senior squadron. I trust we shall finish the matter before another month by hanging Bonaparte, Ney and a few more of his attendants. We hear today a courier has been sent to Paris from Vienna offering to permit him to abdicate again. But I should think he will not be very likely to accept the offer, I rather think he will have a fight for it. If so he will soon be gratified, for such a beating as his army will get I think never had any unfortunate set of wretches yet had if the accounts are correct of the force in march against him.

I have just had a letter from my mother. I am glad to hear you have had a loose drop in old Greer. It is almost time some of the old gentry took their departure. If you could persuade some of the tough ones to

---

* Lieutenant Colonel John Dawson, 2nd Earl of Portalington. He was at Brussels on the morning of 18 June and failed to get back in time to command his regiment during the battle and charged with the 18th Hussars instead. Unfortunately the stigma remained and he was forced to resign soon after.

come out here perhaps we might dispose of some of them for you. Lady Londonderry has very kindly volunteered to be my post mistress so you have only to send your communications to her in future and I shall in return endeavour to convey mine to Mr James. Write often as our stay in this part of the world is at present very precarious according to Forbes life is short. Pray remember me to everyone, your mother, Di, etc. etc. and believe me my dear Grace, always most sincerely yours,

A. K.

Tell Hugh[*] he ought to visit the Pays to see fine crops; I never saw such corn 9 or 10 feet high in some fields and such quantities of it. I only wonder how half of it is ever consumed. Where is the governor. He never writes. Tell him I have been in expectation of a line from him for some time. Alick I hear is become a Benedict,[†] Harriet acted as bridesmaid I hear. I see by the Brussels paper the Emperor left Vienna the 26th so I suppose the guns will soon commence.

No. 26   From the Same

Enghien, 17 June

My dear Sir,[‡]

I take this earliest opportunity of informing you of our campaign having at length commenced in this quarter. In consequence of the French having moved forward to attack the Prussians at Charleroi near Namur. The whole of our army broke up yesterday morning for the neighbourhood of Mons where I suppose we shall have a very large force collected by tomorrow. I think it not unlikely but that a very great battle may be fought in the vicinity of Maubeuge possibly Malplaquet which was formerly the scene of one of Marlborough's feats. You are indebted for this early communication of our movement very much to my horse who *unintentionally* so much injured me yesterday as to oblige me to lay up here today. I hope, however, to be well enough tomorrow or the day after to move up after the regiment. I don't recollect ever having had a much more narrow escape of being seriously hurt or rather I may say killed. We had halted between Grammont and Enghien and to avoid the heat of the sun I jumped over a ditch behind a hedge, and whilst sitting in the shade holding the bridle of my horse that was in very high spirits, he thought he might as well be in the shade as well as his master and accordingly

---

[*] His youngest brother Hugh Kennedy.
[†] A Benedict was a long-time bachelor who is newly married, from the character in *As You Like It*.
[‡] Written to his father John Kennedy.

sprang over the hedge ditch and all *on* me, most fortunately his feet came so lightly on my legs *only* as to bruise them severely and cause them a good deal of pain and consequent lameness which I hope I shall soon get rid of. Had his forefeet come on my stomach or breast laying as I was, the consequence must have been much worse. Indeed as it was, everyone who saw the accident stared when they saw I was still alive. I am resolved at all events on pushing on tomorrow in a carriage or cart as I should not like to be absent should a general battle take place.

I can give you no certain information of the business at Charleroi having heard nothing to be depended on as yet but the noise of the cannon which we could hear distinctly yesterday evening it being only 11 or 12 leagues off. A peasant from the neighbourhood passed here today and his news is that the French at first drove out the Prussians but that they were reinforced and in their turn drove the French back so that they are now in full retreat. From the movement we are making I shall not be surprised to find that the whole of the Charleroi gentlemen have fallen into our hands at least. If I can judge from the situation of affairs on the map I think they must be surrounded if they were not very quick in their movements. It seems pretty clear that the grand scene of our operations will be the banks of the Sambre and the Meuse and the country between these two rivers which run in a parallel line some way into France. From the immense columns of troops English, Hanoverian, Dutch and Belgian that have passed here all last night and today almost without interruption, I should think our modern Marlborough will have a pretty respectable force gathered on the frontiers tomorrow. I don't think, however, that it is our policy to fight a battle for several days until the Russians come nearer, at it is inferred so from Lord Wellington having intended to give a ball Monday next at Brussels. I wrote you a line by Captain Ellis* who returned sick a few days ago. When you receive this will you have the goodness to forward it to Dublin. I will save writing and do as well.

Ever my dear sir, sincerely yours,
A. Kennedy

Yesterday we had very fine weather, but today the rain has recommenced most violently which will be bad for troops in bivouacks.
18th my bruises are better today, excuse scrawl & hurry. French in complete rout. I hobble after them.
20th Glorious and decisive victory.

---

* Captain Richard Ellis, 18th Hussars was not present at Waterloo.

No. 27   From the Same

Nivelles, 20 June

My dearest Mother,[*]

If you have received as I conclude you have, a letter I wrote to father it will inform you of the accident I met with on the march the *first* day. We broke up to proceed to the frontiers which unfortunately (or as I suppose you will rather say *fortunately)* prevented my sharing in the glories of the most glorious but bloody day that England or France ever knew. Glorious indeed for England but purchased dearly with some of her most precious blood. I am in such a hurry at present getting on after the remains of the regiment which is today beyond Mons in full pursuit, that I have scarcely a moment to write, all I can say at present that history neither ancient or modern furnishes us with any battle at all to bear a comparison to that of Sunday last near Genappe. It almost exceeds credibility that so immense a carnage should have been made in so few hours and it is quite impossible that *my description* can give you an idea of the field of battle I have passed over. Of course the Gazette long before this can reach you has announced the glorious intelligence I need only therefore at present tell you that we have begun and *terminated* (I think) the war completely and Mr Napoleon may go back if he can and improve his island of Elba for the game on the continent is up with him. The flower of his army, almost all his Guards, his cavalry in particular (the finest men without exception I ever saw) are strewed in thousands over the field at Genappe. His cuirassiers (certainly the most beautiful regiments in the world) are literally cut to pieces by our cavalry and the road strewed with their armour and coats of mail. Of course you know that Jerome Bonaparte is dead[†] and today they report that Napoleon is wounded and taken himself but I don't believe it. Such a scene as the road exhibited by which he fled (for a retreat it cannot be called) I had no idea of. It equalled Vitoria in everything but riches, but the French officers who have been at Leipzig and Austerlitz say that the battles there were but skirmishes compared to this and the retreat from Moscow nothing in comparison. Our regiment behaved most gallantly and indeed all the cavalry have immortalised themselves for the great brunt of the battle fell on them. We had not more than 7,000 British cavalry which with Belgians and Dutch might amount to 10,000 against 22,000 of the elite French dragoons. Judge therefore the disparity. The French army estimate at 85,000 in all against our British, Belgian and Dutch only 55,000 strong. It was a fair trial of strength. The two first captains in the world against

---

[*] His mother was Elizabeth Kennedy (née Cole)
[†] This false rumour was very prevalent after the battle.

each other on an open plain where neither party had any advantage of position and our communication with Blücher's army cut off previously by the French at Fleurus left Lord Wellington to his own resources. What a wonderful man this has proved him to be. I can't tell you how vexed I am not to have witnessed the battle. No one had an idea of being engaged so soon not even the Great Duke himself.

Adieu I am so hurried I scarce know what I write. We expect to be at Maubeuge in a day or two but you may be assured that the business is over and I should not be surprised if my next is from Paris.

Love to all Ever affectionately,

A. K.

You may communicate this to your tea-table friends, etc. I am getting much better and shall endeavour to catch the regiment at Mons today if possible. Already we count 200 pieces of cannon and more than 10,000 prisoners, Count Lobau, Vandamme* and many others.

No. 28   From the Same

Le Bourget a village distant six miles from Paris, 2 July 1815

My dearest Mother,

I take the opportunity of the first halt day we have had since the battle to inform you of our proceedings during the last eventful fortnight, eventful indeed for Europe and which will give more employment to the pen of the future historians than probably any 14 days ever did since the commencement of the world.† Posterity ought to be much obliged to the British army of the present day for having terminated in so short a space of time what all Europe have been fighting for these 20 years. They will not have much more war I should think for the next 100 years at least if the cause of it is now (as he, I hope will be) put completely hors de combat and rendered for ever incapable of again disturbing the peace of civilised Society. I thought myself almost awake from a dream when at sun rise yesterday I saw the dome of the Invalides and Mont Pantheon of Paris, Montmartre distant only 3 miles. I could scarcely help exclaiming 'How are the mighty fallen' when I found it was not a dream but that the man who this day fortnight advanced with so much confidence at the head of 150,000 of the finest looking troops in the world, apparently certain of entering Brussels triumphant, should on this day be himself hunted to his usurped capital and like a fox after a hard day's chase completely run to earth, from which I trust we shall dig him out before many days elapse

---

* Again false rumours.

† Never a truer word has been spoken.

and thus finish the business as well as it has begun.

I hope you received my last letter from Nivelles in which I believe I told you that my next would probably be from Paris. You see I have not been far out in my calculation. I think it most likely before tomorrow we shall enter the city. The heights on this hill are very strongly fortified with upwards of 300 pieces of cannon and Montmartre appears quite a second Gibraltar. Old Blücher, however, has crossed the Seine in two places with his Prussians who have been cannonading all yesterday evening very heavily in the direction of Versailles. The British army are closing fast round this side of Paris and by tomorrow we expect 40,000 Bavarians up from the Rhine so that the 80,000 gentlemen who are said to be enclosed in the walls of Paris must shortly surrender or be destroyed with their capital, which the Prussians have resolved on pillaging should they attempt to hold out. Lord Wellington's head quarters are about four miles from this at Gonesse and flags of truce are continually passing through here from the enemy with proposals but I believe none will be accepted but the unconditional surrender of Bonaparte's person; should he escape with his life I don't think the French nation will be in a hurry to receive him again as they have already paid pretty dearly for their iniquities. It is impossible to give you an idea of that part of our march which the Prussians have already passed through; the inhabitants almost everywhere fled and their houses and villages converted into complete deserts. If all the other allied troops follow the same system there must be a famine here next year, thousands of people along our line of march must be completely ruined and one would be inclined to pity them did we not reflect that the French army have done the same thing wherever they have yet been. In short Bonaparte after having scourged the rest of the world has been reserved to be the scourge of the French nation. You may rely on it they will not be anxious for revolutions or wars in this country for some years to come, they will have had enough of it before we leave the country.

But to relate the late wonderful occurrences. I may commence with supposing you are made acquainted with the principal part of them through the medium of the newspapers in which Lord Wellington's lame account appeared, which by the bye seems to have given offence to the whole army by its coldness, will have given you some idea of our movements. Bonaparte's bulletins do much more justice to the British army than the despatch of His Grace, who is also, entre nous, not *a little accused for his want of information of the enemy's movements previous to the attack; from the scattered* manner in which our troops were dispersed over the country we did not seem the least aware of the intended attack. It was on the morning of the 12th of June Bonaparte left Paris to take command of his army 150,000 strong, which he had been collecting from various points to the vicinity of Maubeuge from whence he marched direct to Charleroi drove in the Prussians and brought them to a general battle on the plains of Fleurus on the 15th [16th], the anniversary of his victory at Marengo and Friedland of which by the way he took care to remind his troops in his harangue to them previous to the battle. It is also extraordinary that the French had gained at the same place a great victory over the Austrians on the same day 21 years before.

By way of exasperating his men against the English he desired those among them who had been prisoners in England to recollect the hulks in which they had been confined and finished with promising them as it is said with the plunder of Brussels. After this you may suppose the desperate manner in which they fought and the various anecdotes of barbarity that have been related on the part of the French during the battle almost exceeds belief; in short they never were known to fight so desperately nor with half so much impetuosity. The Prussians after an obstinate battle were completely defeated and having thus cut off the communication between them and our army he made sure of beating the English whom he conceived justly to be only a handful compared to the victorious force which he commanded. As soon as he had succeeded in cutting Blücher off from us, Marshal Ney with two divisions of the French was pushed forward to the Quatre Bras, a large house situated on the road to Brussels where four roads cross each other viz that from Nivelles to Namur and that from Brussels to Charleroi. On the evening of the 15th or morning of the 16th it appears that the information of the French advance was known at Brussels, but it was not until the 17th (they say) that the Duke knew of Blücher having been beat and the communication interrupted. The troops nearest to the spot viz the Quatre Bras happened to be the garrison of Brussels, the gallant brigade of highlanders and the Foot Guards from Enghien; the cavalry were so distant and so dispersed over the country they could not be collected in time and the highlanders, the guards and some Belgians and Brunswickers under the Prince of Orange sustained the attack of Ney, and, after suffering most severely from the circumstance I hear of their not having cavalry to support them, they succeeded in driving back the enemy to some distance until Lord W[ellington] arrived with the remainder of the infantry and Lord Uxbridge with the cavalry.

On the morning of Saturday the 17th the British army had concentrated at Quatre Bras and it was then discovered, I believe for the first time owing to a mistake of Blücher's, that our communication with Blücher had been cut off which left the Duke no alternative but a retreat as the French were now about to advance again reinforced with all their army except that corps under Grouchy who had been left to follow Blücher's retrograde movements and the force opposed to the British was computed at 85,000 men of which 23,000 was the elite of the French cavalry. This was rather a formidable disparity compared to 55,000 of which we had not more than 10 or 11,000 cavalry in all, 5,000 only of which were British the others, of course not worth much, of Belgians and Dutch many of whom by running off to Brussels during the battle did much more harm than good and excited such alarm and confusion especially among the baggage as I believe was never before known on any similar occasion: the mob of Brussels of course took advantage of the confusion and were not sparing of helping themselves. Hundreds of officers have lost all their baggage and a great deal of money etc. Fortunately mine is saved in consequence of my having it on mules instead of carts which could not get out of the way when the reign of terror commenced among the wagoners. On the morning of the 17th our retreat commenced towards the Forest of Soignes through which the two great roads pass to Brussels, one from Nivelles and the other from Charleroi. Our cavalry had come up after a dreadful wet night's march and during the retreat, which was only for two leagues and was most admirably conducted, the movement was covered by our brigades of hussars viz Vivian's and Grant's and suffered severely from the immense numbers of the enemy's lancers and cuirassiers who pressed them on all sides. The French cavalry were never before known to have fought so well nor were their artillery ever so well served in short they were almost all composed of the Imperial Guard, the picked troops of France. During this short retreat the 18th did not suffer much but the 7th did severely. After having retreated about two leagues it is said Lord W[ellington] received a dispatch from Blücher to say he had been obliged to fall back but would contrive to join him the next day at a certain hour. This I believe decided the Duke to form up on the skirts of the forest and give battle and most fortunate it was he did so as there is no knowing the injurious consequence that would have followed the abandonment of Brussels which must have been the case had he retreated further than the entrance of the forest. So certain does Bonaparte seem to have been of our retreat to Antwerp that he had already sent off Vandamme's Corps to intercept us and his own carriage baggage etc. were close up with his army which would not have been the case had he not been pretty certain of the victory. In the battle and victory of Quatre Bras the Duke of Brunswick was killed and one or two of our highland regiments nearly annihilated by the lancers and by their having most unfortunately mistaken these worthy allies the Belgian for the French and expended much ammunition on them before they discovered their mistake. This was what I always thought would be the case from the similarity of their costumes; the fine brigade of Foot Guards also suffered dreadfully on the same day. Many of the officers had been at our races a few days before, amongst the rest poor Lord Hay* and your friend Adair of Clifton, both of whom fell, the latter since dead.† Severe, however, as was the engagement on the 17th it was but a skirmish to that of the following day; the French officers who have been at Austerlitz, Marengo and everywhere else allow that nothing was ever to be compared to it nor indeed do I believe that history can afford any parallel to the sanguinary day of the 18th June. It was about ten in the morning of Sunday (as usual the fighting day) when Bonaparte finding we had retreated, advanced with his immense masses of infantry and cavalry supported by nearly 300 pieces of cannon. The attack commenced immediately most furiously on our right and centre which he wished to turn in order to gain possession of the road to Brussels the ground was so level that neither party could derive any mutual advantage of position; of the two the French appeared to have the best. Consequently it was a fair trial of strength or rather an unequal one on our part being so inferior in numbers to them especially in cavalry. It is very probable owing in great measure to the excessive impetuosity of the cavalry at the beginning that the enemy finally lost the battle for their cuirassiers bore down almost like an irresistible torrent for some until Lord Uxbridge charged and defeated them with the our own heavy brigade of cavalry, Lord E. Somerset's consisting of the Blues, Life Guards and King's Dragoon Guards all of whom suffered most severely. In the leading squadron of the latter regiment poor Bringhurst was killed‡ and scarcely an individual of the squadron was left alive having got through the enemy's line of cavalry and found themselves opposed to a square of infantry in the rear. Young Brooke§ also I believe belonged to the same squadron, he also fell.

In short the battle lasted with the utmost degree of fury on both sides till about 6 in the evening, our army in fact acting more on the defensive than otherwise and affairs were beginning to wear a rather gloomy appearance when the head of General Bülow's column made their appearance on the right flank of the enemy and amidst the cheers of our whole line came up in the finest style ever seen and at full gallop instantly attacked on their right; this decided the Duke to act on the offensive and a general attack of the whole line was the almost immediate consequence. The battle raged still for some hours and never was any cannonade known so heavy nor their guns better directed. Cannon were taken and re-taken several times, charges of infantry and cavalry were made in rapid succession, and it was

* Ensign James, Lord Hay 1st Foot Guards.
† Lieutenant & Captain Robert Adair 1st Foot Guards
‡ Captain John Dorset Bringhurst
§ Lieutenant Francis Brooke.

not until nearly dusk when the fate of the day still hung in the balance that our brigades of light cavalry which had been but little engaged as yet (in consequence of their having had so much to do the previous day) were brought up from the left flank of our line as a *bon[ne] bouche** in a column of squadrons, our brigade leading and most admirably led by Sir Hussey Vivian. This it was, it is said, that decided the day although not a word of it is mentioned in the Duke's dispatch but by referring to the French account you there see it mentioned our regiment advanced to the attack amidst cries of 'No quarter'. The Young Guard of the French in squares were immediately charged and having been mistaken by the French for the Old Guard[†] on seeing them run off a general panic seems to have overtaken the command and pervaded the whole of the enemy's line and '*Sauve qui peut*'[‡] was the universal shout, infantry, cavalry and artillery now mixed through each other in the utmost confusion and this fine army became in a moment a confused mob scampering in every direction over a most open country and the remains of them saved only by the night. The ground was so wet owing to the almost incessant rain for two days that almost all their cannon fell into our hands before they had retreated half a league: ammunition wagons, tumbrels, coaches, and carriages all stuck fast in the mud before they reached the village of Genappe which was only a league from the field, and Bonaparte disguised in a grey frock and round hat with some difficulty got so far in his coach and six English horses, when he was obliged to get out and fly on horseback, leaving his coach behind him. Some of the Prussians were lucky in finding quantities of snuffboxes set in diamonds and a good deal of plunder in the carriages. The Prussians pursued by the road to Cambrai, and 16 regiments of our cavalry by that of Mons, and our brigade being the advanced guard and never having a day's halt till we reached Cateau [Cambresis] near Cambrai. Poor Heyland[§] fell leading on the 40th to a charge of bayonets, I am told, in the most gallant style; a musket shot hit him in the throat and he was killed instantly. Our loss has been immense, especially in officers, I hear 13,000 men in all including the German Legion, and every officer I asked for was either dead or severely wounded. But for everyone we lost the enemy must have lost two or three. Such a scene of carnage I could have no idea of on so small a space of ground and the work of destruction seems to have made such rapid strides in so short a space of time as to nearly exceed belief. The dead and wounded of every nation were lying

---

* 'A tasty morsel.'
† It was actually the Middle Guard that was defeated by Wellington's troops, whose dress resembled closely that of the Old Guard.
‡ 'Save yourselves if you can!'
§ Major Arthur Rowley Heyland, see his last letter (no. 98) in *Waterloo Archive*, vol. 3.

indiscriminately as they fell absolutely in heaps all over the field. Horses by half squadrons laying on each other as if the whole squadron had fallen by one discharge of grape shot so exactly did they lie in rows, the ground literally strewed with arms and armour of every description, in short never was there seen such a field of battle before. No description can give you any idea of the scene. Never was there a butcher's stall more completely drenched with blood than the whole of the field and the wounded French were so numerous that it must have been totally impossible to have carried them all off the ground for several days. Thus you may say, had one day commenced and ended the war.

I am happy to say the 18th behaved most admirably. Sir H. Vivian after the battle told the regiment they had even exceeded his expectations and he issued the most flattering orders in consequence. Several regiments have been nearly destroyed. Our loss is about 100 killed and wounded two officers only wounded. The Scots Greys have buried 8 officers in the field and of the King's Dragoon Guards three squadrons out of four have been totally annihilated. The Life Guards and Blues have lost many likewise.[*]

For some days after the battle the rain continued. We were obliged to halt a day at Cateau until Valenciennes, Cambrai and Maubeuge were invested and on the 25th we reached St Quentin, the 27th Compiegne, the 29th Senlis where we overtook old Blücher's army. He pushed on by St Denis and crossed the Seine near Versailles where he now is so that we have Paris now nearly invested. I hear the Prussians have totally destroyed the finest porcelain manufactory in the world at Sèvres near Versailles.[†] This will be good news for the English manufacturers, in short they have spared nothing wherever they have been. The crops of corn, all nearly ripe, have of course suffered in no small degree and in short France is ruined and not impossible but the coup de grace will be the burning of Paris.

1 July
I had got so far when the news of an armistice arrived, the abdication of Bonaparte you of course know of, he has I believe made his escape to America and the Provisional Government of Paris have agreed to march their army which is about 80,000 strong behind the Loire, there to take the oath of allegiance to Louis the 18th, but the report today is that the

---

[*] Siborne in his *History of the Waterloo Campaign* records the number of killed, wounded and missing for the 18th Hussars was 102 officers and men. The Scots Greys did lose 8 officers killed; Siborne records the King's Dragoon Guards losing 275 officers and men (*A Near Observer* seems to give a later, more correct, figure, 246) and 228 horses, half their number. The Life Guards and Blues lost 341 officers and men out of a total effective force of 698.

[†] I can find no evidence for the Sèvres factory being destroyed or damaged.

army in Paris have refused to move so I don't know how the business will end. I suppose they will be all shot as soon as we can get at them.

The weather is now delightful but so warm. I am today at the outposts with my squadron close under the heights of Montmartre and Aubervilliers near the Forest of Bondey famous for the *Dog of Montargis*[*] where the enemy's advanced picquets are also placed. The inhabitants of Paris are most anxious to receive the British troops. I am on picquet in a most splendid chateau, sans windows, doors or furniture like the rest of the chateau of this devastated country, literally sans everything that could be carried away or destroyed; for what the Prussians left undone the Belgians have finished. What a just judgement on the French nation for all their enormities and crimes before and since the revolution. I am in hopes before I send this to inform you of our arrival in the capital at present the head quarters of infamy perjury and treason. Meantime adieu.

5 July

The business is nearly over, a capitulation has been signed and we expect orders every hour to enter Paris. The troops have orders to make clean for the occasion and to put green boughs in our caps; we are to pass the Duke in review, I believe, on the famous Champs de Mars so that we shall have a Champs de July instead of de Mai![†] The town of St Denis is given up to our troops and by the day after tomorrow all the scattered remnants of their army will be on the Loire where I dare say they will be ordered to ground their arms, as their services will no longer be required. I have just been to see the Mausoleum of the French Kings[‡] together with Bonaparte's tomb he intended for himself. I saw the place where Robespierre had the bones of 36 kings burnt in the revolution. Since the Bourbons have returned they have erected a small tomb which is now covered with the fleur de lys. You cannot think how high the English rank among the few inhabitants we have yet met. On entering the town of Senlis, where the Prussians had

---

[*] *The Dog of Montargis, or Murder in the Wood* was a nineteenth-century melodrama first performed in Paris in 1814, but an English version was soon being performed at Covent Garden. The legend of the Dog of Montargis has a courtier of King Charles V of France murdered around 1400 in a forest near Montargis by an envious knight. The dead man's dog showed a remarkable hostility to his killer and the king decreed a trial by combat between them. The dog won, and the killer confessed and was hanged.

[†] A play of words on the great assembly known as the Champ de Mai (although held on 1 June 1815) on the Champ de Mars in Paris, when Napoleon brought forward the 'Act Additionel' which amended the French constitution. It was passed virtually unanimously.

[‡] The Basilica of St Denis contains the bodies of the French monarchs from the tenth century to the eighteenth century. During the Revolution the graves were opened and the remains thrown into a mass grave.

been the day before, their shops and houses close shut but on finding we were English, instantly the town crier went about desiring everyone to open their houses to receive the English, the white flag was displayed and numbers of well dressed ladies distributed fleur de lys to all the troops hailing us as their liberators. We expect a fine scene on entering Paris & I hope in a few days shall proceed to decapitate a few of the principals and ringleaders of the mutiny. That, with the hanging of the Bonaparte family is all that is wanting to make the Prince Regent and his government stand higher in the estimation of the world than any other government that ever ruled England or any other nation.

No. 29   From the Same

Château de Sausne near St Cloud, 8 July

We have just arrived here a most delightful village on the Seine close to St. Cloud and a league from Paris. I am in hopes we shall remain some time as I was never put up more to my satisfaction. I occupy the country house of the Princess Montmorency Laval,* a most excellent establishment of servants and famous feeds, the finest view of Paris St Cloud and all the course of the Seine for many miles, you can imagine. My hostess lives in Paris at present, I hear entertains Lord Castlereagh and Talleyrand today, whilst she entertains in the country the *next greatest personage!* Lord Castlereagh passed through Bourget yesterday and he and the Duke entered Paris today. The French army they say are disbanding themselves as fast as they can and in a short time will scarcely leave a wrack behind. What astonishing consequences have resulted from our victory. You may direct to Paris where we shall arrive some time.

9th. Louis entered yesterday amidst cries of '*Vive le Roi*', the tricoloured cockade was universally worn in Paris at 11 o'clock, at 3 the white had universally replaced it, what an extraordinary weather cock nation. I have only now to hope you may decipher the above scrawl. Written in much haste on Brussels paper. Farewell,
     A. K.

No. 30   From the Same

Paris, 12 July 1815

My dearest Grace,
Our movements have been of late so rapid and since our arrival here we

---

* Catherine Jeanne Tavernier de Boullongne the wife of Mathieu-Jean-Félicité Vicomte Montmorency-Laval, a politician who was created a Viscount on his return with Louis XVIII from Ghent.

have been so much taken up with one show or another that you must excuse my not having sooner given you a line on the subject of our operations. I have written my mother some account of our movements and must refer you to her. If she can decipher a scrawl on very bad paper and written at hurried intervals on the march. I know you are fond of military bulletins.

Lord Castlereagh arrived in very good time just as we were taking possession of Paris he passed through Bourget a village where we were the evening before. I have called and left my name at his hotel, but he is so busy as you may suppose there is no seeing him. The Emperors of Russia and Austria and the King of Prussia are also come and I think we only want your majesty to complete the congress of crowned heads. They have all got hotels close to Wellington who seems to be the polar star among them. We expect a grand review of our cavalry in a day or two by these aforesaid big wigs, who testified a wish to that effect I hear. Well they may wish to look at the British troops for they have saved them many broken heads and have accomplished in one day what they have been all trying to do this 20 years. Never was a nation so completely humbled as this. It appears almost incredible and I often almost imagine myself awoke from a dream. You can't think how their tone is altered and how completely abased the rascals all appear whilst on the other hand the high admiration they hold the English in is not to be told. The Prussians they hold in abhorrence and I think they will have some reason for doing so before all is over with them. At present they are levying immense contributions on them, and the soldiers live on the inhabitants at free quarters.

I am most comfortably fixed at a beautiful village near St Cloud in the country chateau of the Princess Vaudimet. She has a house in Paris also, and servants and establishments at each. She is too happy to have me there to prevent the Prussians pillaging her house and I live in the most splendid style you can possibly imagine. Two courses every day and nothing but the finest Madeira and claret, so that I don't care if the war lasts a little longer at this rate. She and her friend the Countess of Jarnac (Chabot's mother dines with me there today and I have some idea as she is a widow of proposing for her highness! I don't know how it is I am always stumbling over a princess somehow. It would really make you fat [?] to see the style I keep up. As a particular mark of my esteem I have room in *my stable* today for her coach horses. This was being more civil than the Prussians who carried off her cows the day before we came and about 300 bottles of her wine.

Tomorrow we march into the Tuilleries to do duty for the day, we take it by regiments turn about. I wish you could come over here; you never saw anything more beautiful than the neighbourhood of my chateau. [Issy-les-]Moulineaux (where Bonaparte was the day before he went off) is beautiful and the paintings at St Cloud are magnificent. I saw Blücher a few days ago. Old Louis arrived on Saturday and on Sunday I saw him go in state from the Tuilleries to Notre Dame to say his prayers. I think the business completely ended now. The miserable remains of the French army can do but little if they were even inclined. We have just heard that our friend Boney has been taken at sea but I hardly believe it.* I rather think Louis means to pardon them all. If so he deserves anything he may afterwards meet with. Bonaparte would not have been so lenient to him if he had been in his power.

I am very anxious to hear some further intelligence of poor unfortunate Tom. What an extraordinary unaccountable proceeding. I have had only [one] letter from you on the subject which I received on the march at Cateau. I saw Lowry Cole yesterday who was speaking to me about it but knew nothing more certain than he was supposed to be going to America with some woman that he was ashamed of. It was really a melancholy business and shows in the strongest light the dreadful effects of a young man getting into low and bad company without anyone to direct him. I trust it may not turn out worse than it at present appears. But I confess I have many apprehensions on the subject.

Pray write soon. Love to your mother, Dr Hughes, Johnny† and all the young ones, ever my dearest Grace in haste Sincerely yours,

A. K.

Excuse hurry as I am just going to dine with my hostess. Don't be surprised if I become a prince ere long, more unlikely things have happened I can tell you.

No. 31   From the Same

Beauvais in Picardy, 3 August 1815

My dearest mother,

We left Paris last Sunday and are so far on our way God knows where, but most likely to Calais where we may turn our horses' heads where they please as our business on the continent is pretty well over. I rather think, however, we shall remain here some time until everything is arranged. The Guards only are to occupy Paris in conjunction with the Guards of Prussia, Austria and Russia. We were sent away in consequence of the forage getting scarce in the vicinity of the metropolis and most sorry I

---

* Napoleon surrendered himself to the British aboard HMS *Bellerophon* at Rochefort on 15 July.

† His nephew, John Hughes Kennedy.

was to go. It was quite a tender separation between the princess and her guest, I assure you, and I have promised to correspond with her. The day before we marched she had Prince Metternich the Austrian Ambassador, The Duke d'Alberg the French minister, Prince Louis of Austria and the last not least in roguery the famous or rather infamous Minister of Police Fouche, Duke of Otranto, to dine with me! The latter is again very high in favour at court having been the president of the provisional government and the principal person in making Bonaparte abdicate; in short they attribute the salvation of Paris to him and he is now as great a man with Louis as he was formerly with Bonaparte. My curiosity to see a man who has acted so conspicuous a part in the great drama of the revolution was as you may suppose rather great and it was highly gratifying to meet two such opposite characters as Fouche and Metternich. The latter is a very gentlemanlike man not unlike Lord Castlereagh, where as the former is the most villainous looking fellow you ever saw but at the same time contains something in his ugly visage denoting great talent. You of course know his character, he is the most complete spy in France and as such may, if he is faithful, be of great use to the king. I had a good deal of conversation with Metternich and after dinner by way of amusement he got a pen & ink & was quizzing Fouche about Bonaparte. He drew up a sort of ridiculous form of abdication for the ex Emperor which he made Fouche sign and as a witness I put my name to it which I daresay he will show Lord Castlereagh the first time they meet. I think they will be rather surprised to find my name to a paper under those of the two greatest men in Europe. It amused the princess extremely. I believe I told you in my last that Lord Castlereagh and Stewart* dined there some days before. We were all to have had a grand dinner at Stewart's to meet the Duke of Wellington and Blücher but for our sudden departure.

I suppose you have seen the account of our famous review. We had scarcely 70,000 men under arms and about 7,000 British cavalry. We were drawn upon the road from Paris to Neuilly and passed by the sovereigns by half squadrons, in the Place Louis Quinze,† on the spot where Louis 16th was guillotined! It was one of the finest sights ever beheld at Paris I believe and you have no idea of the crowd that came over to see it; rather a novel sight for the Parisians so large an English army reviewed under the walls! The Emperors all wore the Order of the Garter on the occasion. But by far the most splendid as you may suppose amongst the rich dresses was his lordship of Stewart, absolutely one sheet of stars and lace. The Prince of Orange came up from Brussels for it. He marched past

---

* Charles William Stewart, Castlereagh's half brother, was the British ambassador in Vienna. He eventually became 3rd Marquess of Londonderry.
† Now known as the Place de la Concorde.

and saluted with his arm in a sling as he has not yet recovered [from] his wound.

I had a letter yesterday from Maria. I find they are gone to Swansea for the benefit of the sea breeze, symptomatic of augmentation to the family I think! I wrote to you by Doyne who left Paris last week. I saw the [Vigogues?] there. I was sitting in the Palais Royal when he came up and asked if my name was K[ennedy]. I said yes, and so we went in search of her ladyship whom I discovered with a quantity of her progeny at his father's house. They talk of staying some time in Paris. I saw the Duchess d'Angoulême make her first appearance in public on Sunday last, an immense crowd gathered round the Tuilleries to see her and the king who came to the window and bowed to the mob. '*Vive le Roi*' was of course shouted in all directions.

Let me hear from you soon. Love to Betsy[*] and all about you. Ever my dearest Mother, sincerely yours
A. K.

If you have an opportunity you may enclose this to Grace. It will inform her of our movements as the heat of the weather makes it rather troublesome to write much at present. Direct as above. Remember me to Harry Cole if you are there just now. This is a very nice town and very cheap. I think it would amuse you well suppose you came over, we are likely to remain I think some time although everything is very quiet.

Verner[†] has got the brevet. Lord Wellington gave it to *one* captain in each regiment, in general the senior present. In the 18th Hussars he gave it to the *second* eldest in the field viz. Grant,[‡] passing over Croker[§] who was the eldest so that I suppose had I been there I should have gained nothing by it. Grant had been in India with him which I believe was his reason for recommending him. Croker has memorialised and in the event of Croker 's success I have also sent a memorial stating the accident that prevented my being on the field and requesting to be included also. He is such a positive man in everything he does that I fear neither of us have any chance of success. I must therefore rely upon Lord Castlereagh or Stewart doing something for me with the D[uke] of York privately. I have given Stewart a copy of my memorial on the subject and he has promised to do what he can. I think nothing but Lord Castlereagh's mentioning to the Duke of York the circumstance of the unfortunate accident that

---

[*] His sister Elizabeth Kennedy.
[†] Captain William Verner 7th Hussars.
[‡] Captain James Grant was made a brevet lieutenant colonel for Waterloo.
[§] It would appear that Captain Richard Croker was successful as he was made a brevet major for Waterloo.

prevented my being present will be of any use. If anything can add to the extreme mortification I experienced on reaching the field just as the battle was over it would be that of having two junior captains promoted above me in the regiment merely because they were luckily the two eldest in the field.

You need not say anything of this to anyone, I mean of my having memorialised, till you hear further from me on the subject. Colonel Murray* and General Vivian have backed my memorial, the latter in very handsome terms but I know it will have no effect on the Duke of Wellington whatever, it may have on the Duke of York if Castlereagh presents the memorial. One would suppose that those officers who have got the brevet did something wonderful to obtain it but the fact is they did no more than anyone else. They were merely recommended as having been the senior of their rank in some instances and others were recommended through the caprice of the Great Duke. Grant who has got it has, however, some claim having been 20 years in the army and seen an immensity of service in India. Should Croker, however, get it, I shall try hard for it as he is junior to me in the army.

No. 32   From the Same

A château near Neufchâtel,† Normandy, 11 December 1815

My dearest mother,
I can't conceive what you are about as it is an age since I have heard from you. I should have written sooner but every day for this month past we have been in a state of uncertainty over whether we should not go back to England. It is at last, however, settled that we remain to watch these restless people for some years, some say three others five.‡ I rather think the former. We go to Gournay§ and in a short time I believe to our final destination near Cambrai.

Since I last wrote to you I sent another memorial to the Duke of Wellington by the princess at whose house he dined. He read it, put it in his pocket and told her he should attend to it. However, in a few days after I had a letter from his secretary saying it was not in his Grace's power to comply with my wish having recommended two already. Indeed I thought as much. At the same time he gave the princess every assurance

---

* Lieutenant Colonel the Honourable Henry Murray commanded the 18th Hussars at Waterloo.
† Neufchâtel en- ray
‡ The agreement was for five years, but the troops actually went home after three years once French reparations had been paid in full.
§ Gournay en Bray

and she said she would take every opportunity during the winter of reminding him of his promise but it is evident there are no hopes in that quarter. I have therefore resolved on a memorial to the Duke of York which I have this day enclosed to Castlereagh in London with an appropriate letter asking him to forward it to Sir H. Torrens.* Now I wish you would on receipt of this write him (Castlereagh) also a stave on the subject which I think would have the desired effect. It is the only possible chance I have now of promotion for years as the termination of the war totally excludes all hope of advancement. You may commence with complimenting him on the distinguished part he has taken in public affairs and hoping he will now have leisure to attend to his old friends etc. I have stated to him that no less than 5 captains all originally junior to me [in] the regiment have been by chance or interest promoted above me in the army and for no meritorious act whatever. This in itself is rather annoying you must allow. As we are to remain on the continent it is of the utmost importance my obtaining the rank as the allowances are so much more handsome to a brevet major than captain, independent of other considerations. This you might state to him. I don't think Lady Londonderry's letter ever reached him or Lord Stewart. Perhaps it would be well if she wrote to him also. If Torrens is in Dublin his writing to his brother might be of use and perhaps Maria would speak to him on the subject. In short no time should be lost making every interest possible. Then if we don't succeed it will not be our fault. It is so easily procured that one word from Lord Castlereagh would obtain it from Torrens. I shall rely on your exertions with his lordship on the occasion. You can mention my commission having cost so much money, my misfortune in losing a troop which I ought to have had for nothing by waiting another year, and having now the mortification to see the *very same* captain who got this troop for nothing get above me.

Tell Maria and Betsy I received their letter and shall reply to it when we get settled and that I can bring my thoughts to any other subject than this cursed promotion which at present engrosses my attention. I am sure Lady L[ondonderry] and your writing to his lordship with the letter I send him today must have the desired effect.† Tell John I have written to have my memorial relative to Curtis forwarded. It is too bad if I don't get justice done me from my memorials in some quarter or other. I shall be very anxious to hear from you. I am at present in a large chateau near this town which, notwithstanding the aid of immense wood fires, is so cold owing to the intense frost that I can scarcely hold the pen. You must therefore excuse the shortness of this and with *mille choses* [a thousand

---

* Major General Sir Henry Torrens was Military Secretary to the Duke of York.

† He did gain his promotion to brevet major on 4 December 1815.

loves] to Maria and Betsy, etc. Believe me ever my dearest mother, yours sincerely *jusqu'a la mort*,*

A. K.

I expect to get leave to go to Paris next week. I shall probably write to you from thence. Ney's death has struck the Bonapartists with terror in this country. They did not expect that Old Louis would have displayed such firmness.

Don't lose any time in writing to Castlereagh so that he may get your letter and mine nearly together.

I received a letter from William, the first for 13 years. He was going to Calcutta with his regiment last April and talks of coming home on his promotion next year.†

No. 33   Sergeant Matthew Colgan‡
From The Historical Memoirs of the XVIIIth Hussars Colonel Harold Malet,
London 1907

His stepfather was in the 1st KGH.§ It appears that he had been sent on duty from Sint Maria Lierde to Brussels early on the morning of the 15th, in charge of the sick of the regiment. Knowing that his stepfather was quartered somewhere near Brussels he volunteered for this duty. On his arrival there to his astonishment he found nothing but a baggage guard at three o'clock in the morning, and on asking what the meaning of all this sudden march at so early an hour was, he was unable to be informed except that a sudden route to march had arrived, but for what place his informant could not say.

The following morning, after much difficulty, he heard the regiment was ordered for Nivelles, and on meeting a brother sergeant also on the look-out for the regiment, they both proceeded together.

I had not been mistaken, for in the course of half an hour or so I observed the blue bags,¶ and all then was right; I soon came up with the regiment my stepfather was in, who gave me a welcome salutation, without dismounting, and slipped a few gold pieces into my hand, and gave me his

---

* 'Until death.'
† His brother William held a number of appointments in India, eventually becoming Deputy Military Auditor General of Bengal.
‡ Of Captain George Luard's troop.
§ 1st King's German Hussars.
¶ The colour of the 18th's fur cap bags.

blessing. I put spurs to the old grey, showed Mainwaring[*] the position the regiment lay in, and desired him to make all speed and report his arrival. A few minutes brought me to them, and I reported my arrival to Colonel Murray and fell in, being told off as the centre sergeant of the centre squadron, under the command of Captain Luard. We then dismounted, and in a few minutes the enemy's cavalry made their appearance, debouching in the[ir] masterly and splendid style from a wood which bordered an adjoining field. Never have I seen movement executed in so daring and correct a manner, they formed into divisions, wheeled into line, and instantly opened a cannonade. The first shot they fired knocked over a man on my right in the squadron I belonged to, and killed him on the spot. We on our side were formed up in a similar manner, and for some time returned the fire with interest. Skirmishers were thrown out, but in a short time the retreat was ordered, and we fell back on Waterloo in one of the most severe tempests and thunderstorms it has ever been my lot to behold. So bad was the weather that on arriving at the position we were to take up for the night, approached as it was by bye and cross roads choked by mud, we resembled drowned rats more than anything else. Our guide, who was with Sir Hussey Vivian, did not like it at all, when the latter made him mount and proceed there with us in the pouring rain,

The situation our regiment was encamped on was a declivity, covered with a young shrubbery or nursery of young trees, in the vicinity of corn fields, and to the left of the village of Waterloo, as far as I can remember, after the many windings we took during our brief retreat. Not having seen the ground before or since, I cannot be certain as to the exact spot.

The men were ordered to cut green forage for the horses, and take what rest they could, as well as circumstances would permit, without unsaddling. The poor fellows huddled together as well as possible, rolling themselves in their wet cloaks, the only comfort which was then possible for them, many of them without breaking their fast at the time, for if they had had anything to cook, it was impossible to do so, placed as they were.

In casting my eye round I observed the troop sergeant-major's[†] man making a nest for his master among a few of the young striplings, planting his sheepskin on the grass, so I requested a share of this, the only dry spot, especially as it was in front of my horse and gave me a sort of claim to it, and we both lay down in one another's arms with both cloaks over us. When we awakened in the morning we found ourselves a few yards lower down, owing to the current that passed under our cot, and which had completely wetted every article of clothing as if it had been dragged

---

[*] The only Mainwarings in the regiment I can find are two privates (John and William) in Captain Lloyd's troop.
[†] Troop Sergeant Major William Black.

through the mire of mud and water which was floating around us.

In that condition we rose and endeavoured to dry our clothing by the sun, hanging it on the branches of the young trees, when a sudden order was given to mount and fall in. I hastened to put on the only dry shirt I possessed, and bridling my horse I bundled up all my kit before me on my horse, put on my overalls, mounted, finishing my dressing there and crying out to those I had charge of to mount also.

Pray reader, do not smile at my open confession of the picture I must have cut, though I can never look back on it myself without doing so.

We formed up, were told off in squadron, and marched to our position on the left of the British line, as near as I can judge, the only other troops on our left being some artillery.

We had not been many minutes in this position when the French guns opened on us, but they were harmless owing to the manner the general, Sir H. Vivian, who had taken up his position on a headland with his Staff and black trumpeter, manoeuvred us, having no effect further than dashing the earth in our faces, some falling short and others over-reaching us. In that position we remained for some time, going threes right, left, forming division, half squadron, mounting and dismounting, according to the general's fancy, as he had one eye on the enemy's guns and the other on our regiment, which was then under his especial care.

Little aware at that time of the carnage that was going on in other quarters of the field, and which I was to witness before eve, I was in tolerably good spirits, with a silent and searching eye towards the spot the general occupied, experience having taught me to have much confidence in him; at least my spirits at that time were not at the freezing point, or if you please the sticking point, to which they were shortly afterwards brought.

During the period we were posted in that position, many aide de camps, Prussian and English, passed to and fro, especially at a most rapid pace to my left. I did not then know the treasure they were about to discover and bring to light, a treasure which at length made its appearance, for if I was astonished by the sudden and very splendid appearance of the French cavalry emerging from the wood on the day before, the reader may imagine the agreeable surprise with which I now beheld one of the grandest sights I ever beheld, when all of a sudden, and as if by magic, the Prussians threw out their columns at a distance on our extreme left.

What a delightful sight; nothing ever appeared to me to equal it, grand and imposing as it really was. Grand and imposing was the sight, and what a spirit did it infuse into our minds on beholding their formation, and on seeing them open their fire on the enemy, although I thought they were not within range at the time, or can I suppose it possible, from the turn the action took at that period, that their troops could come into immediate contact with the enemy on their arrival on the ground they had diverged on to.

At the above period of the day our regiment made a movement to the right, which brought us, as I think, to about the centre of the line, and for a short time we remained in the rear of the Belgian troops (infantry), with our horse's heads almost resting on their rear ranks, during a most dreadful peal of musketry, which, had we not been thrown into open column at the time, would have placed us in a most destructive situation. However, the balls passed through the intervals, and the summit of the rising ground on which our pivots rested sheltered us in a great degree. Otherwise no cavalry could have remained motionless for any time under such a torrent of small arm fire as played on us at the time.

These were trying moments indeed. Who can describe the change of feelings that now take place after viewing the havoc around in breasts that but for an hour before were swelling with enthusiasm at the prospect before them? Sitting as we were, motionless on our horses, each awaiting the fate of his companion, expecting every instant to be swept off without the liberty to make any exertion, with the deafening thunder of small arms, coming, as it seemed, from a shower bath, strained and loosened our nerves. A few of the men and many of the horses had been wounded at this period, among the latter being Captain Luard, our squadron officer, who then popped down the ranks, eyeing which horse he would select and dismount the rider; he selected a mare ridden by the corporal who covered me (Woolley).* What will the reader think now of all the boasted gallantry of the writer of this narrative on that day, who was on the eve of saying to the captain, 'Take mine,' as I was known to be the best mounted man on the field of Waterloo as a trooper.

It was painfully apparent, from the groans which escaped from some, and the agonised expressions on the countenances of others, how greatly we were tried, waiting so long for the striking point, and how much our courage was taxed. A man's temperament is indeed changeable, one moment drooping in spirits and the next acting with savage bravery, yet a man does not really know himself until he has experienced these things. He is an animal that requires to be thrown on its mettle, as will hereafter be seen. While undergoing these painful sensations, we were at last released by the sight of Brigade Major Harris,† who galloped up with a 'brief' to us, with these or similar words, 'Eighteenth, you are about to

---

* Corporal John Woolley.

† Captain Thomas Noel Harris. In later years Colgan seems to have become devoted to Harris, and Harris appears to have helped him financially at a difficult time. Before he died, the sergeant sent Harris his Waterloo Medal. See *Military Illustrated*, no. 9 (October/November 1987).

charge; the general trusts to past experience that you will act as soldiers, and I know you will, Eighteenth.' What a relief to our feelings to be taken thus from the scaffold (as I must term the position we were then in) to fight our way to death or glory, which henceforth was to be the motto for all. The elements, the thundering of cannon and small arms on all quarters, proclaimed the necessity of a desperate effort at this moment. Here I may well pause for a moment to repeat the following lines, though they fall far short as descriptive of the scene:

> Man, courser, all were mingled in the fray,
> While liquid flames from thundering cannon play
> To hang black horrors on that bloody day,

But all description would be a mere mockery. A complete insult to the minds of the heroes that day. No borrowed language, pen, pencil, canvas, or representation can convey any adequate idea of the convulsed field of battle, such as Waterloo was at the moment we charged, enveloped in clouds of smoke, emitted by small and great guns as it was. I will leave the reader to depict it to his own vivid imagination, and proceed with the detail of my own experiences. At the moment when we reached the summit of the hill, which commanded the view of all before us. I was so blinded by the dust and smoke as not to be able to see the flanks of the squadron I belonged to, a duty which I should especially have attended to, being, as I was, the centre sergeant of the squadron, by whom the movements of the squadron and regiment had to be regulated. The gallop sounded and we increased our pace, the colonel and the captain immediately in front of me.

Acting as the compass or needle which was to direct me, my right arm extended as a direction for those on both flanks. The first regiment I saw during our rapid advance was the 10th Hussars, many of them were stretched out, killed and wounded by our own guns, whose front they must have crossed, on the ground we passed over. They soon disappeared from my view, and my attention was next attracted by a line of cuirassiers, and from the reflection of the sun that was then almost setting, shining on their cuirasses, and the unconcerned manner they displayed on our approach, it struck us that they were our own Life Guards, and consequently I felt no apprehension from them, and when within reach I called out to them to go threes right and to make way. They did not move, and all at once I found myself disconnected from the right half squadron, colonel and squadron leader, and left with a little more than the division (the left centre) I commanded. I passed the cuirassiers, and on my left I observed a column of the enemy's infantry, to all appearance broken, and on our approaching them they threw themselves down.

We did not wait to take them prisoners, however, but galloped on, myself and the few men with me, until we were stopped by about a company (I cannot say the exact number) of the enemy's artillery crossing our front, and so absolutely cemented together as not to present any chance of our getting through. I galloped up to the outrider or driver on the foremost horse of one of the guns in my front, and, as he was only a boy, I knocked him off his horse with the flat of my sword and held the reins of his horse until my party had made the gap secure.

The share of prize money for Waterloo and the capture of Paris was as follows:

Field Officers	£433 2s 4d
Captains	£90 7s 3d
Subalterns	£34 14s 9d
Sergeants	£19 4s 4d
Rank and File	£2 11s 4d

7th Brigade of Colonel Sir Frederick Arenschildt
13th Light Dragoons

No. 34 Lieutenant George Hussey Packe
By kind permission of Leicester Record Office, ref. DE1672/4 and DE1672/3/1 (and DE 1749/113, incomplete copy of previous) combined

Timetable of Journey to Waterloo 1815
Embarked at Ramsgate, Saturday May 13th,
Landed at Ostend Sunday 14th 1815

May	20th	Marched to Bruges
	21st	Eeklo
	22nd	Drongen (Near Ghent)
	26th	Nieuwerkerken
	27th	Haute Croix [Heikruis?]
	29th	Review at Schendelbeke
June	16th	Plains of Fleurus
	17th	Mont St Jean
	18th	Brussels
	23rd	Nivelles
	24th	Bavay
	25th	Le Cateau Cambresis
	26th	Maison de Grand Prise
	27th	Armancourt [near Compiègne]

	28th	[Space left blank]
	29th	Pont [Pont St Maxence]
	30th	Roissy
July	2nd	Ville Pinte
	5th	Genevilliers
	30th	Luzarches
	31st	[Space left blank – around Clermont?]
August	1st	Breteuil
	2nd	Amiens
	3rd	Flixecourt
	4th	Abbeville
Dec	3rd	Frevent
	4th	Hernicourt [St Pol sur Ternoise]

1816

Jan	12th	Lille
	13th	Steenvoorde
	19th	Hazebrouck

No. 35   From the Same

To Charles James Packe Esq
6 Hinde Street
Manchester Square
London

Ostend, 16 May 1815

My dear father,

Having an hour to spare, I cannot employ myself better, than giving you the details of my journey so far. I hope you received a letter from me, dated Ramsgate, it must have contained not one word of sense, as I fell fast asleep over it twice. I embarked on board a transport at 2 o'clock on Sunday morning and having a good wind we came in sight of this place, at 10 o'clock in the forenoon, where we were obliged to anchor in consequence of the tide being out, and we arrived here, and disembarked, at 4 o'clock on Sunday afternoon. I got my horses safe. It is a very bad coast to disembark [on] as you are obliged to swim the horses for 30 or 40 yards, there was an officer of the artillery lost a horse that he gave an hundred & fifty guineas for the day before. The inhabitants of this town have removed all the furniture etc into the interior, expecting Bonaparte will besiege this place the first thing he does. There is a garrison of 5,000 soldiers here, Hanoverians, Belgians, Germans & English, a thousand of whom are working every day to fortify the place. It looks a most tremendous sight, canons, balls, etc., etc., fill the streets as you enter the town in every direction. The inhabitants talk a language which you cannot understand at all, it is a mixture of Dutch, German & French, but by speaking French you can be pretty well understood. I expect to leave this place tomorrow, or next day, but it will all depend upon the arrival of my regiment, which they told us at Ramsgate it had. Half a troop arrived yesterday, they came straight from Cork, and there are some more vessels in sight, which will come in next tide, which look like transports. This is like all foreign towns, dirty, and the inhabitants are not so civil as they ought to be. There are a great many different hotels, you breakfast at one, dine at another & so on, you cannot have two comfortable meals at the same hotel. Four of our officers dined together yesterday & for dinner and two bottles of Bordeaux wine, we paid in all (with the waiter) a pound, which is cheap for England, but very dear for this place. Captain Goulburn* is staying here with me and another officer, we are all billeted in the same house; the people are pretty civil, but nothing to boast of.

My bed consists of two cloaks in a great coat, which I begin to find is not very comfortable, I wish I had brought a bed instead of a stretcher but I shall grow older & wiser. You can buy almost everything here, but at an exorbitant rate & the people try to cheat you in every manner they can. From hence we shall go to Bruges & from there to Ghent, where we shall remain two days and then join the army. Pray when you write, tell all the political news; as we are quite ignorant how the world is moving.

As it has happened, it was a very lucky circumstance that I came over when I did, for if I had waited at Ramsgate for the arrival of the 13th, it would have been an amazing expense, and [I] had to come in the packet at last because they will [probably?] not touch at Ramsgate, for they charged us a guinea a night for my three horses; which is dearer than London & everything is in the same proportion. Gin here is so cheap that we are obliged to keep a very sharp look out, to keep our men; what they charge in England 1/- you get here for a penny; my man has got drunk once since he has been here and I think myself pretty lucky he is not drunk day & night. I bought some soap and salt at Ramsgate, but they stole it before I got here, there is no soap to be had here; excepting soft soap which the people use to wash with. It is with the greatest difficulty they are able to fill up the tenth, that is the reason I suppose John Trollope was put in, they call them here the Prince's Mixture† having I think related everything

---

* Captain Frederick Goulburn.
† There had been a very embarrassing case involving the 10th Hussars. Colonel Quentin had been accused by his fellow officers and tried but acquitted. The officers of the regiment were packed off to other units and the tenth was filled from other units whilst Colonel Quentin retained his command. John Trollope was gazetted to

that has happened since we parted, with kindest remembrances to all my relations & friends. I remain your ever affectionate son,

G. H. Packe

PS Should Captain Edwards[*] be coming soon, I will thank you to send me some soap, tell him if you see him I shall write in a day or two. Direct to me 13th Light Dragoons, British Army, Netherlands.

No. 36   From the Same

Haute Croix [Heikruis?], 1 June 1815

My dear Father,

I should have written to you before had I had any time to fill up my letter. Before I proceed any farther I will thank you for your kind letter, which I received on Sunday; and now I will give you an account of my proceedings, since I last wrote. Colonel Doherty[†] with a detachment of the 13th arrived at Ostend on the 20th and I marched with them up to Bruges that evening, which is 14 good miles, with a canal on one side the road & a fen ditch on the other. I began to fancy myself in Lincolnshire again, but when we came within a mile of the town, the scene changed to one of the most beautiful views I ever saw; the town is about as large as Leicester and one of the cleanest towns I have seen since I have been in this country, but I did not see much of it, as I arrived at 6 o'clock in the evening & marched at 6 o'clock the next morning. The next day we marched to Eeklo which is 18 or 19 miles from Bruges, the road was beautiful, as it was one continued avenue of trees, but the country we could not see much of, as it [is] either low wood, or very high rye fields. The town of Eeklo is very small, equal to one of our country villages, the people were remarkably civil and would make us dine with them, for which we did not want *much pressing*; the next day (22nd) we marched to Drongen which is 12 miles from Eeklo; the road was precisely the same as the day before, here we found all the 13th that had arrived in this country and were dispersed about in every direction, some were three miles from Drongen. We were quartered about 2 miles from Drongen, the country was beautiful and at the end of every field was a house of some sort or another. We were billeted in a house close to a gentleman's house, where we took all the strawberries, cherries etc, in short we just began to enjoy ourselves, when we were ordered to march up here. Drongen is three short miles north west of Ghent, which is a very fine dirty town, there is one

join the 10th Hussars as a cornet on 27 April 1815.
[*] Captain R. Bidwell Edwards, was on half pay.
[†] Lieutenant Colonel Patrick Doherty.

square which is very fine; I think it is as big, or larger than Birmingham. It is bigger than Paris they say, but not having seen Paris I cannot say. I saw the King of France, who made a most gracious bow, the town is full of French and as we marched through the town they pulled off their hats to us. Victor was there and Marmont* but I think they will not be long before we see some of them, where we shall the least expect them. We left Drongen on Friday the 26th and marched to Nieuwerkerken which is about 25 miles from Drongen. We did not arrive until 10 o'clock at night, that was the first night we experienced any service, our horses went without any sort of forage and we got our suppers and lodging at the first house we could scramble into. I got very well off but was obliged to threaten destruction and by that means got everything I wanted. The next day we marched to this place which is 21 miles; the country was beautiful but the road was so sandy, and of course so dusty, that we could see very little.

On Monday 29th we marched from here 4 leagues (12 English leagues) to be reviewed on an immense plain at Schendelbeke, it was the finest sight I ever saw; there were 15 regiments (in short all the British cavalry & artillery) in this country. Lord Uxbridge took the command, the line extended 3 miles, the Duke of Wellington was there; Old Blücher, and in short all the great people about here. They afterwards dined with Lord Uxbridge at Ninove (where he is staying) and they drank Blücher's health & in return he gave 'The good people of England, the friends of the world'.

I saw Robert Packe† at the review & went and spoke to him, he was *particularly civil*. We marched back that night and got home about 9 o'clock; we left this place at 4 o'clock in the morning, so that we had a pretty good day's work. I think they ought at least to have given us a dinner, but we provided ourselves, by instead of carrying pistols, we took half a chicken in each holster.

Yesterday I rode over to Brussels which is about 12 miles from here, it was a very wet day, so that I saw very little of the town, but happened to meet Robert Packe, he was coming to call upon me in his way here, he is 12 miles from here and I have appointed to dine with him at Brussels tomorrow. He asked me to come and see him and he said he would give me a bed & a stall for my horse, which in this country is rather a good offer, as my horses are at present in a barn without a door and great holes in all parts of it, they are all very well. Robert Packe talked of everything but Leicestershire & when I mentioned any person in the county he

---

* Marshals Victor and Marmont had remained loyal to Louis XVIII.

† Major Robert Christopher Packe, Horse Guards, was his uncle. He was killed at Waterloo.

turned the subject. This place where I am now is a very small village, I am billeted upon the mayor who is a farmer and Captain Doherty* is billeted at the priest's, where Acton† and myself dine every day, the headquarters are at Castre [Kester] which is about a mile & half from here. We are the only officers here, the priest is very stingy, we are obliged to buy everything & it is no small matter to make them understand what you want, for they speak nothing but low Dutch. We expect to leave this place (to march to the front) every day. I heard yesterday in Brussels that the Prussians had begun skirmishing but don't give it much credit. As to the desertions from the French, they make a great deal more of them in the London papers than they really are. We have only a post once a week here, I believe, but shall take this letter with me tomorrow to Brussels. This country is very unhealthy, we have a great many men ill, with the ague, our colonel at their head; but the common people recommend a glass of gin every morning which keeps it off.

Our wine here is very *dear* and very *bad*, we had some wine at Drongen which was an inferior kind of hock, for which they charged 4 franks [*sic*] a bottle (a frank is ten pence). They give you for a Bank of England note here 14 franks & that with a little grumbling. I am very happy to find Edwards is coming out again, but I am afraid he will not get appointed. I think we shall wait for the Russians coming up before we begin in earnest, we have began popping at one another but only two or three men have been killed on both sides, through mistake. We are all of different opinions here as to the war, but I believe the majority think that we shall embark again at Ostend and that Boney must fly, but I am very sanguine as a second reduction would not be so pleasant. The country about here is full of soldiers, you don't pass through the smallest village, without seeing an hundred or more. The 13th are brigaded with the First & Second German Light Dragoons, which are particular fine regiments.

I suppose you have begun to taste the grapes before this time, there is no such thing as a hot house in this country or we should have certainly have plundered it a little. Wherever we can pick up anything to eat or drink, it stands very little chance. All the villages I have mentioned you will find in Faden's map of the Netherlands,‡ my maps that I brought out are very bad ones & have none of the small towns in.

Having pretty near exhausted this sheet of paper, I must bid adieu. I shall write again the next post day & give you an account of Brussels.

---

* Captain Joseph Doherty.
† Lieutenant Henry Acton.
‡ *A Map of the Seven United Provinces, with the Land of Drent and the Generality Lands* by William Faden, originally published in 1789. The 'Generality Lands' were parts of Catholic Flanders captured and controlled by the United Provinces.

With kindest love to all my relations & friends in England, I remain your ever affectionate son,

G. H. Packe

No. 37   From the Same

Haut Croix [Heikruis?], 11 June 1815

My dear mother,

As I dedicated my last letter to my father, I shall direct this to you, we still remain in the same situation & I rather think we shall remain here another fortnight, as the Duke of Wellington has contracted with a man to feed us for that time. I went to Brussels according to appointment and met Robert Packe. Brussels is a large town, but very dirty and the streets very narrow; just where the Prince of Orange, Duke of Wellington & a few more of those great people live, in the upper part of the town is beautiful, but I don't think it is so fine a town as Ghent. The shops are very good and the articles very dear, the lace shops are magnificent but very near as dear as in England. I engaged to go and stay a day with Robert Packe at Liedekerke, which is about 11 or 12 miles from hence, but we had such wet days I have just put it off until next Thursday; he is gone today to Antwerp & stays till Wednesday. We went again yesterday to Schendelbeke to be reviewed by Lord Uxbridge; all the 5 regiments of light cavalry were there, but the ground being so wet he could not employ us all at the same time & he told us that he should have us all out together some time to practise his command and to make us act altogether, he thinks that we shall begin immediately & he gave a dinner to all the captains, at which he announced to them that Bonaparte had arrived on the frontiers, though through what channel he had heard the news I know not.

We had so long a day yesterday, I am very much afraid I shall not be able to mount my mare for a month or more, she has got two very bad setfasts,* one on each side her shoulder, which will be obliged to be cut, in a day or two. This country I hear is almost equal to a preserve in England for game, but have seen none until this morning, when the master of the house where I am billeted, presented me with a fine young leveret, which we are going to feast upon today. Three of us mess together, we are now almost reduced to a fraction and have no hopes of getting a farthing of our pay for three or 4 months (we must not talk of the French army being paid, when our army will be just as bad). The only consolation we have is that we are all alike in the respect. I heard of Edwards by an officer who joined us yesterday, who told me they saw him and he did not mention

---

* A setfast is the area of superficial skin gangrene that develops on an acute saddle-pressure sore on a horse's back.

that he was coming out and am afraid from that, he is not coming. I shall be much obliged to you to remember me particularly to Mrs Pauncefort* & tell her I will make use of my pen & write to her when you leave London, as you communicate all the news, I should not be able to fill a letter. The Guards are quartered within 3 miles of this place. Their headquarters are at Enghien, which is just a league from here. I went over there & saw Captain Chaplin,† who you may perhaps remember, was wounded so bad leading the forlorn hope at San Sebastian, his wounds have just broke out again and he won't be well of some time I am afraid.‡ The rides about the town of Enghien are beautiful, the town itself is nothing to boast of, like the generality of towns in this country. Having I believe giving [*sic*] you an account of everything that I have heard & seen since I last wrote, with kindest remembrances to all my friends & relations in England. I remain your ever affectionate son G. H. Packe.

No. 38   From the Same

Haut Croix [Heilkruis?] 14 June 1815

My dear Charles,§

I received your letter the day before yesterday, for which accept my best of thanks and I now sit down to answer it as I may perhaps not have so good an opportunity, at another time. We are still in this village but expect the route every hour, as the headquarters are going to be removed from Brussels to Grammont, or somewhere nearer the frontiers. I was at Brussels yesterday and everything is preparing there for a general move, the pontoon brigade had just arrived, which shows we shall not remain long before we open the ball, as they are the forerunners of a route. We are all in high spirits and ready to be attacked. I am happy to see by your letter, you are going to take a tour this summer, instead of remaining in Oxford, but if I might be allowed to give an opinion, I would recommend your going to Holland, for two reasons, the one is that you cannot come every year, the other is, that there are some English travelling round this year & wherever they go they raise the price of every one article & for that reason you would find it much cheaper this year. In this country you may live for about 8 franks a day, which is eight *10 pennies*. I saw more Englishmen at Brussels yesterday than ever, there are balls given every

---

* Lady Alicia Margaretta Hockmore Pauncefort Duncombe (née Lambart) wife of Philip Duncome Pauncefort-Duncombe of Great Brickhill and Witham in Lincolnshire. She had a residence at 15 Welbeck Street, London.

† Lieutenant & Captain Thomas Chaplin, Coldstream Guards.

‡ The wound was severe enough to earn him a pension of £50 per annum.

§ His brother, Charles William Packe.

night by some of them. Mrs Mullens is one of the most dashing characters there. I have not heard of any order being issued out respecting amateurs approaching the army, it is merely to frighten people if such an order was given, as it is impossible it ever could be put in force, for we shall have something else to do with our men, than placing them as videttes to keep off the English, besides they won't like the smell of powder, which will keep them at a distance. Will you be so good should you see or hear anything of Coke to tell him I shall be very happy to see him & perhaps I may be of some service to him, as the dragoons generally know all movements long before any other regiments. Should you feel inclined to become a spectator, if you will bring a horse out with you & a bed you will be able to live as comfortable as possible & see all the fun. But I am very much afraid we shall reap our harvest in England again, for yesterday a troop of French artillery deserted, with 6 guns and marched to join the royal army. Since my mother wrote I have two more lieutenants gazetted under me and shall in the course of 2 or 3 months have two more under, which will nearly bring me out of the break. I was very sorry to see in one of our English papers the other day the death of poor Mrs Weld of Lulworth Castle.* She was the most agreeable, pleasant, agreeable [*sic*] woman I ever met. Bonaparte is determined to make an attack upon the Prussians first;† and his army made a movement to the left the day before yesterday, consequently we shall move to the right & surprise him, which movement we are now hourly expecting. I am to go and see Robert Packe tomorrow, should we not march. We have had a great deal of wet weather and all the amusement we could find was going to sleep, as the house we are in affords no amusement of any sort and the priest was amusing himself by praying for fair weather. We begin to get quite tired of these quarters, the only thing that keeps us in humour is a cheerful glass of champagne, which we get very good (& cheap for England, but dear for this country) for 4 franks a bottle. Having given enough of my awkward scrawl, I must conclude with kindest love to my father, mother & all the rest of my relations. I remain yours very affectionately,

G. H. Packe

PS My mare is a great deal better since I last wrote & am in hopes she will be well in a short time.

---

* The wife of Thomas Weld, younger brother of Joseph Weld the Squire of Lulworth died in 1815.

† A very interesting comment given what happened; Wellington did not come to the same conclusion.

No. 39   From the Same

Brussels, 20 June 1815

My dear Father,

As I know you will be very anxious to hear from me and suppose you will see my name in the newspapers amongst the wounded, makes me particularly desirous of writing to you as soon as possible, to say that I shall be quite well in a few days. Now I will give you an account of what has happened since I last wrote; on Friday morning [16th] at 5 o'clock we received an order to march and leave all our baggage behind us. We marched 11 leagues and arrived in a wheat field at 1 o'clock the next morning, where we lay down until daylight. Then we mounted our horses and advanced in front of the enemies [*sic*] lines, which we covered until the infantry had retired and then retired (in the heaviest thunder storm I ever was in). The French charged us twice, which we repulsed, we got into a field of rye, which from the wet we had was about to snipe shooting at Crowland* but I got into an empty house. At 3 o'clock the next morning, Sunday, we mounted our horses with everything wet, which was not very agreeable and I had not had any one thing to eat since Friday, excepting a small piece of sour bread, which was as good as the most delicate fricassee. We took up a position on the right of the line and at about 10 o'clock I looked on the top of the hill and saw amazing columns of French coming on. The action commenced at 11 o'clock and in good earnest, at about 3 o'clock when we had been under the fire of the enemy about 2 or 3 hours, (for they did not begin by cannonading us) a piece of shell hit me in the left groin and knocked me off my horse. I was carried to the rear and into this town at night, where I have remained since and shall join the regiment again in a day or two.

I have omitted to tell you of the action, which took place on the Friday. We marched up, the infantry were cut up in all directions, the cavalry were so far in the rear, we could not get up before the bloodshed was over. If we had been 3 or 4 hours sooner, we should have saved above 200 lives. Our officers who were all the time in the peninsula, say that those battles were merely field days in comparison to Sunday. I should think there never was a harder contested battle. The Duke of Wellington led two regiments to charge the Imperial Guard, which they cut up and put to flight in all directions. Bonaparte commanded at the beginning, but directly he found he was going to be cut off by the Prussians he fled. All his baggage is taken and he had dated several dispatches 3 or 4 leagues in rear of this place. I saw poor Robert Packe about ½ an hour before he was killed, the Blues had made one charge then. The news we hear here is that

---

* Crowland is six miles north-east of Peterborough.

Bonaparte is going to make another grand push, but from officers who were taken prisoners at the beginning, we learn that this army was all the old soldiers he had & consisted of from 100,000 to 200,000 men, but we cannot credit anything that is published in this town now, as about one third are disaffected. I believe I saw Bonaparte on Saturday evening, but could not distinguish him out of all his Staff. Captain Jebb* of the Blues requested me to say that he saw Robert Packe buried, as that may be some satisfaction to his relations, he is universally lamented in the Blues. The Scotch [*sic*] Greys buried seven officers yesterday, but it is useless for me to give an account of the loss of officers as you will see a list that will surprise you. The Russians are coming up, they were at Aix la Chapelle on Sunday, we hear the royalists have risen and marched to Paris. You shall hear from me soon again, with kindest love to all who inquire after me. I remain your ever affectionate son,

    G. H. Packe

The Prussians are to the right of us and cross the frontiers today with sixty thousand men, the Belgians ran away as fast as they could.

No. 40 From the Same

Near Pont [Pont St Maxence], 11 leagues from Paris, 29 June 1815

My dear father,

I take the earliest opportunity of writing to you, according to my promise. I am afraid you were a long time before you received my last, as no post went from Brussels after the headquarters were removed, but I fortunately found Captain Jebb of the Blues going to England and he said he would deliver it. I am now nearly recovered from my wound, so as to enable me to do duty again with my regiment, which I joined the day before yesterday, after marching by forced marches to catch them, for five days. We came 9 leagues today and expect to reach Paris tomorrow. We always march at daybreak (which is at ½ past 2 o'clock) and hope tomorrow will conclude as it is not so agreeable turning out at that hour. I often think you are going to bed *in London* when we are going to march. At present I have been very much disappointed with France, as I have not seen a house at all equal to your farmhouses at Caythorpe.† The country in some parts is beautiful, but not in my opinion at all equal to England. The Prussians plunder beyond any description; in the village we are in now, the Prussians went through two days ago and not a single inhabitant is to be seen, not a window, door, or anything else [unbroken],

---

* Captain John Jebb.
† Caythorpe is seven miles north of Grantham.

they say they will have their revenge, which they have. In truth it serves the French perfectly right, they will now know what it is to go to war, which they never knew before, because their armies always were paid by the plunder of other nations.

We met a flag of truce today going to the Duke of Wellington, with proposals of peace from Boney, but of course he would not accede to them, we have heard no particulars at present. The day before I left Brussels I saw Mr Lucas & Colonel Pierrepont,* the former said he saw you well about a week before, he said he should follow the army but have not seen him since. If I can procure anything for you at Paris, be so good as to let me know, when you next write. We don't at all know at present how much longer we shall remain in this country. I think we shall annihilate the army before we leave them, as we have began it so well. I suppose you are now getting tired of London and you will not be long before you go down to Hanthorpe.† I will thank you to leave the key of my trunk with Williams and Whyte, as I think we shall reap our harvest in England. Charles I suppose will have started on his tour before this reaches you. I wish he had come to this country, as he may not have so good an opportunity again.

We are all very anxious to see the English papers, as we know not until we see Lord Wellington's dispatch, what victory we gained, as we have so many different reports. We have seen Bonaparte's account which is more correct than any one he ever before published, he has paid the British cavalry the highest compliment possible, as he lays all his misfortunes to them. In coming here we came over the field of battle, which was completely a burying ground for miles. In all history you will not find so hard contested a battle. As we are to march again tomorrow morning again and it is getting late, fearing I shall not be able to send it if I delay another day, I must conclude with kindest remembrances to all my relations & friends. I remain your ever affectionate son,

G. H. Packe

I will write again soon.

---

* Lieutenant Colonel Michael Pierrepoint, Major Commandant of the Rutlandshire Militia. The militia unit was deemed too small for a lieutenant colonel hence his peculiar rank. I must thank Ron McGuigan and Philip Haythornthwaite for this information.
† Hanthorpe House, near Bourne in Lincolnshire.

No. 41   From the Same

Genevilliers, one mile from Argenteuil, 11 July 1815

My dearest mother,

I received a packet of letters from Edwards yesterday and also some soap, for which except [sic] my kindest thanks and not being able to fill letters to all of you, I write to you as I believe I wrote to my father last. We are now reaping the fruits of our labour, which has been hard, but of short duration. We are now in tolerable good quarters, within 3 miles of Paris, the person who we lodge with sends us fish, wine & meat from Paris every day, he lives in Paris but comes to his country house occasionally, he is remarkably civil and in short everywhere where we have found inhabitants in France, they have been remarkably civil as the English do not plunder, and every one of our allies do, to the greatest extent. We are now in one of the finest countries in the world, nothing can be more beautiful than where we are now, vineyards for miles all round us and the land which is not made use of for the culture of the vine, is just like a garden. I don't know how long we shall stay here, but I think as long as matters remain as they do and an army of 100,000 men, only the other side of the Loire, they will not think of removing us out of this country. I was yesterday in Paris for the first time. I think Paris would be thought nothing of if it was not composed of the most beautiful things of every nation. The buildings in my opinion, are not to be compared to Bath, certainly there are a few exceptions, but I had no time to look at much of the exterior as we went to see the Louvre (the first thing). It is an immense building, there are about 6 very large rooms on the ground floor, containing all the most beautiful sculpture, we saw the real Venus de Medici, Gladiator, and many other originals, our sculpture is not to be mentioned in the same year. After seeing the ground floor, we went upstairs and saw above one thousand paintings, which Bonaparte had picked up in his various travels, it took us 6 hours in looking them over and as we returned to dinner, you may suppose we had not much time to see the exterior, but being so near, I can ride in any leisure day. I wish Charles would come here, because as I am here and likely to stay in the neighbourhood of Paris for some time, I could be of great assistance to him as he might live with me, the same as Edwards does, and at one third the expense that it would otherwise cost him and he certainly should see Paris. I know you have a great deal of influence with him and if you can turn his course & make him go south, instead of north, it would be very advantageous. The English are returning to Paris very fast, we have once more prepared the road for them. I suppose you have laid hold of the grapes by this time, [I] am sorry to hear they are the same as last year, the vineyards are very forward and will be ripe in another 6 weeks.

There is a beautiful garden belonging to this house, the apricots are [torn- ripe?] the rest of the wall fruit very forward. I think from what little I have seen of the French that Louis will never be placed upon the throne, they hollow out '*Vive le Roi*' but the reason is, that the allies are so near them. There was a great deal of hissing in the opera the other night. The Emperors of Russia and Austria were to enter Paris yesterday, our Household Brigade went as an escort to bring them in. One corps of the Prussian army are gone to watch the French army the other side of the Loire. The exchange with England is getting better every day, they now will give nineteen franks and an half for a pound note. The reports in Paris are very numerous, we heard yesterday that Bonaparte had been taken with all his friends near Bordeaux, but I don't credit it, if that is true I am afraid I shall remain a lieutenant for some years to come. If it was for any other person than Mrs Pochin I could buy her a beautiful repeater, but as she is so particular I do not wish to have the commission, as there is so much choice she might see one she liked better and I should never hear the end of it. With kindest love to you and my father & brothers. Your ever affectionate son

   G. H. Packe.

Edwards desires me to remember him kindly to you & my father.

No. 42   From the Same

Genevilliers, 23 July 1815

My dear father,

If I had been in your situation and you in mine, I should have been much alarmed for your safety, as I have not received a letter from you since Edward's arrived with a large packet, until today when I received one from you dated the 8th & another from Charles of the same date. You mention in your letter, that my mother had written to me but I have not received it and I conceive from your letter you have not received two or three of my letters, as I have written 5 or 6 times since I wrote from Brussels. We are now living on the fat of the land but are obliged to pay very dear for it, as the French try to impose upon the English in every manner they can. I have been into Paris about every day and have seen pretty near all that is to be seen. I hope to give you a description when we meet, as it would be impossible to give you an account in writing. Yesterday I saw the Prussian Guard reviewed in Paris, which consisted of 14,000 men not one less than 6 feet in height, certainly the finest sight I ever can see. The Emperors of Russia and Austria command two regiments and they marched at the head of them and saluted the King of Prussia, Blücher, Schwarzenberg* and Wellington were there & in short all the great generals of all nations were there. The whole of the British army are to be reviewed tomorrow, we cannot look so well as we have left all our fine things at home, *we came* here to fight, not to be *reviewed*. Paris is in a sad gloomy state, half the people crying for Boney and the other half lamenting the losses they have sustained by the Cossacks. Paris is at present full of Prussians, Austrians, Russians, Cossacks and a few English. Lodgings are not to be had under exorbitant prices. Lord Combermere† is come out and taken the command of the cavalry, he occupies the house which Madame Josephine used to reside in at Malmaison. Lord Castlereagh told some officers yesterday that the British army would be in England by the 25th of August, if we are, we shall be in France again before that time year, as the English will be the only means of restoring the Bourbons to the throne. I wish Charles was out here now, as Paris will not be worth seeing in a short time, for the emperors and kings seem to be casting lots & a great many beautiful things are at present taken. An express was sent yesterday to request the honour of the Prince Regent's company here, will you allow him to come? I have no doubt he would be delighted. We have had a great many different stories here, concerning what government intend to give us, to commemorate the Battle of Waterloo, some of the Duke's Staff told us that all the officers would have gold medals, the non-commissioned silver and the privates would be made out of the cannon that was taken on that day,‡ but we have heard nothing more since, this was ten days ago. Reports are prevalent amongst the light dragoons that Quentin shot by his own hand, but I don't conceive it can be true; the tenth are quite silent about it.§

I have heard of Henry Packe and John Hanbury¶ but have not seen them, it was my intention never to have so much as given him a look. The Blues very much lament poor Robert; Heathcote** is just come out here with a remount of the Blues, I have not seen him.

John Hanbury is about 5 miles from here. I have this instant received

---

* Field Marshal Charles Philip, Prince of Schwarzenberg, commanded the Austrian troops.
† Lieutenant General Sir Stapleton Cotton, 1st Baron Combermere.
‡ The Waterloo Medal was the first issued by the British Army to all ranks. Everyone actually received a solid silver medal; it is interesting to note from this letter that it may originally have been suggested that it was cast in three metals for differing ranks.
§ See footnote on p. 98 regarding the background to this story. Quentin was wounded in the ankle.
¶ Both were captains and lieutenant colonels in the 1st Foot Guards.
** Cornet Lionel Edward Heathcote, Horse Guards.

Plate 1 Entrance to the Forest of Soignes where the two roads from Brussels meet. Note the lack of undergrowth in the forest

Plate 2 The interior of the chapel at Waterloo showing wall plaques commemorating those killed at the Battle of Waterloo

Plate 3 The scene along the skirt of the wood at Hougoumont

Plate 4 The ruins of Château Hougoumont

Plate 5 The ruins of the village of Ligny

Plate 6 Photograph of Private Thomas Playford in later life. He served at Waterloo with the 2nd Life Guards, but never actually crossed swords with anybody; and a drawing of a Life Guard, about 1815, by Playford. With the kind permission of Andrew Prince

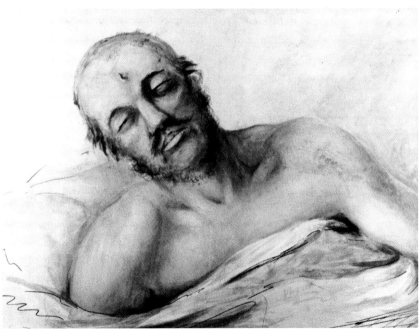

Plate 7 Drawings made by Sir Charles Bell of Private Wanstell of 10th Hussars and Samuel Pritchard of the 4th Foot. With the kind permission of the Wellcome Trust

Plate 8 Sketch of Napoleon on board HMS *Bellerophon*
from George Tighe's letter, courtesy of Eunice Shanahan

a letter from you dated the 15th and am much obliged to you for paying 40 pounds into Greenwood's hands,* as it will be very acceptable here. My [horses?] are I may say pretty well, my mare I have not been able to ride since the 6th of June in consequence of a sore back, but shall ride her tomorrow at the review. I don't know at present how I stand for the next reduction, but I think we shall be one of the last regiments that cross the water, as we have not lost our old character on the 18th. We are very comfortably put up in this village, the master of our house is a rich grocer in Paris, but we cannot get much forage, as we are not allowed to cut the corn and take it where we can find it, as we were in all the villages before we arrived here. We get our letters and newspapers very regularly now, before last week all our packets came by Brussels and the Belgians took about half. I am going to write to Charles by this post to request if he has any intention of coming to Paris, to come soon. Our posts go from here Mondays & Thursdays, so you may guess when to receive letters. I shall write again on *Thursday*. With kindest love from me, remembrance from Edwards to you & my mother. I remain your ever affectionate son,

    G. H. Packe

No. 43   From the Same

Genevilliers, 26 July 1815

My dear father,

According to my promise, I now take up my pen to give you a few lines, not that I have any news to communicate, but as you wish to hear from me, I will give you all that I am able. We were on Monday last reviewed by all the allies, our line extended two miles. There were about 80,000 men seen, the Belgians I understand cut a very bad appearance as they marched by, immediately after our brigade of Guards, which was completely putting the beggar upon the gentleman, but I understand the Emperor of Russia was very much pleased. We expect an order every day to move from here and to march into Normandy and to remain there for some time, to be in readiness in case the revolutionists should rise. The Prussians are *noble allies* for if ever an Englishman gets into a row with a Frenchman right or wrong, they always take the part of the English. Blücher put no less than eight bankers in Paris under arrest, for not supplying money enough to pay one of his corps; had Blücher been in Paris himself, he would have paid his army very well, but the great people, I am sorry to say, stopt [*sic*] his hand; if the Parisians could they certainly would murder him. Everybody in Paris now are afraid of their heads, as the king is going

---

* Greenwood, Cox and Hammersley, Army Agents, Craig's Court, London.

to try all those people who took up arms against him. Carnot* is to be the first and if they are *acquitted* by the court, they are to sell all their possessions in France and leave the country, the time allowed them (to sell up) is one year, this is the latest news we have from Paris.

The harvest is nearly all over here, one week more will completely finish it, I suppose you have hardly got the hay in [in] Lincolnshire. I rode some days ago to see the fortifications at Montmartre. It certainly is very strongly fortified but *English soldiers* would have taken it in two days, without any considerable loss, if Boney had had about 6 months longer to have worked at it, we should have found it rather a difficult matter to have got into Paris on this side. The Duke of Wellington rides a good deal about incognito, what he is going to do I know not, but you seldom if ever go into Paris without meeting him, if we move into Normandy he will of course remain in his present quarters and I should think he will keep his own regiment to guard him. John Bull will be very much mistaken if he comes over to Paris to save money, it is not like last year, for when you dine in Paris you cannot (at the lowest rate) get away under 19 or 20 franks and you pay 6 franks a day for merely a bedroom and think yourself lucky you get it. I have seen a friend of mine who came over here, thinking to live for almost nothing and is going to return again already as he can live cheaper he says in London. I wish the revolutionists would pick up a dust now, just to send the English back again and I am sure the first shot that is fired they will set off for Calais, for there are so many coming over every day, they raise the prices of everything. We want to enjoy it for a little time and when we move, I will allow them to come. Captain Edwards is still here, he don't know whether to proceed into Switzerland or not, for if he happens to meet with the Prussians he will not have a rag left, as they strip everyone they suppose to be French, so he would stand a bad chance should he fall in with them. I hope by this time Charles has started for Paris, as the Prussians, Russians etc are packing up the statuary and pictures every day. I never thought Bonaparte would have given himself up in the manner he has, how can he expect mercy? I should think this time he is pretty safe in the Tower. I suppose all England will go to London to see him, only don't let him go, as we don't want another 18th June to be spent in the same manner that [the] last was.

I have enquired for several of my friends since and almost everyone is killed or wounded. Fearing I shall be too late for this post if I delay any longer I must finish by giving my kindest love to my mother, brothers & yourself. I remain your ever affectionate son,

G. H. Packe

---

* Lazare Nicholas Marguerite Carnot, Napoleon's ex-minister of war was banished and he wandered across Europe, eventually dying in Magdeburg in 1823.

No. 44　From the Same

Genevilliers, 26 July 1815

To Charles W. Packe Esq, Maxstoke Castle,* Coleshill, Warwickshire

Dear Charles,

I received your letter of the 8th instant two days ago and have made every enquiry I can for you concerning your tour in this country. Posting is as dear in this country as in England and that would be the only way for you to travel without you come out by yourself and bring nothing but a pair of saddle bags & come up to me, I could then put you in a right method. I am now situated within two miles of Paris, at a very pleasant village but I don't think we shall remain here above 4 days longer. A soldier never knows one day where he will be the next. I believe we shall go into Normandy, to remain there a short time previous to our going to England. I recommend you to come out here and the sooner the better, as the allies are claiming everything valuable and several of the best pictures & statuary are at present taken; as to what it will cost you, it is impossible to give a guess as you may live at the rate of 10 shillings or 5 guineas merely dining by yourself, but at a rough guess from the tract of country you intend to go, I should think 60 pounds would pay it out of England, but I by all means recommend you to come to me first wherever I am, as I shall be able to tell you several things which is impossible I can mention in a letter and by seeing you I might be able to make out a better plan for you. We were reviewed on Monday last by the allied sovereigns, the British & Belgians and Hanoverians extended for above 3 miles. I understand it was a very fine sight but as I only saw the part of cavalry where I was standing I cannot give any opinion, the Emperor of Russia was very much delighted. He always dresses himself in the dress of one of the Prussian regiments as he is colonel of one of the King of Prussia's Guard. The King of France has now began the sport, he has confined Carnot & several others who took up arms against him and is going to try them by a court martial and if acquitted they will be obliged to sell all their possessions in France and quit the country in a year, that is the only way to clear France of such a set of rascals. I believe the day after we quit this country, there will be another revolution as Bonaparte has left a great many friends behind him. Paris is now the most gloomy place in the world, everyone is hanging down his face for fear of being brought before the court and being beheaded. I have seen almost all that is to be seen in Paris but have a great deal to see yet in its vicinity. Montmartre is very strongly fortified, but *British* soldiers

---

* Maxstoke Castle remains a fine example of a fourteenth-century moated castle.

would have taken it in a very short time, but at a good deal of expense. I suppose you are enjoying yourself very much, the only thing we want here is society, as the French women are all risen from a mere nothing and have as much manners as a pig. I suppose you have got Bonaparte pretty safe in England, of course you have been up to London to see him,* as I suppose you are all in a state of madness to see him, only don't let him go as we don't wish to pass another 18th of June in the same manner as last and I have not the least doubt, we shall if he does make his escape. We hear that government are going to give us all medals for the Battle of La Belle Alliance, I don't think they will. Blücher has raised plenty of money for his army and any person who refuses to give what he requires, he immediately confines, but the emperors have now stopped him. Edwards sends his congratulations on the recovery of your knee & desires to be remembered to you, he is between two minds whether to proceed to Switzerland or not. I wish you had come out with him, as your living would not have cost you more than about 3 or 4 shillings a day at most, as you would have lived and lodged with me. I shall be much obliged to you to make a thousand pretty speeches for me, and give my love to all my Warwickshire relations. I have not met Henry Packe,† if I do I shall cut him as my father desired. I hope as soon as you receive this letter, you will make preparations for starting to this country, if you want any more information write to me, as now a letter is only 4 days coming over. Believe my dear Charles your ever affectionate brother,
    G. H. Packe

No. 45   From the Same

Abbeville, 17 August 1815

To Charles William Packe Esq, 6 Hinde Street, Manchester Square, London

My dear Charles,
I received your letter yesterday, dated the 9th instant, by which I am very happy to find you are coming out to this country with William Dilke.‡ I have written a letter to you at Blyth§ but should think you would hardly

---

* Napoleon was in fact not allowed to land from ship in Plymouth sound and was eventually sent directly to St Helena on board *HMS Northumberland*.
† Captain & Lieutenant Colonel Henry Packe, 1st Foot Guards, was another uncle, but it is unclear why he was being cut by the family.
‡ The Dilkes lived at Maxstoke Castle.
§ Blyth is in Northumberland.

receive it as my last letter was so long in finding you. We are likely to remain in this place for some time & hope as you pass through this place you will take up your abode here for at least *3 days*. You must be careful as there are two great roads from Calais to Paris, the one goes through here & the other through Amiens, this is the best road by far. I by all means recommend you not to buy guineas to come out to this country as they give you a fair price for pound notes, if you can get them for 21 shillings by all means bring them. It all depends upon yourselves, the time you take to see Paris, for one week would see the whole if you do not employ yourselves in any other way and when you are here I think you should go & see Brussels, Antwerp & so home, as it would not make 5 days difference and that when you are out here is nothing at all. I shall be much obliged to you to bring out for me 2 pounds of gunpowder, as it is impossible to get that article good here and a few flints. If by chance you should be able to prig a dog do, as they are bad & scarce here. When you arrive in this town enquire for me at Mr Forceville, No. 24 in the same street where the Tête de Boeuf is where all the diligences stop.

Bring a French dictionary out with you, you will find it very useful, one that you can put in your pocket. I will settle everything for you as to sleeping, etc, so enquire for me when you arrive. If you write home after receiving this letter, tell my father I will answer his letter in a day or two, having no time to finish this letter, I must conclude with kindest love and hoping to me you soon in a conquered land, I remain yours very affectionately,

    G. H. Packe

No. 46   From the Same

Abbeville, 20 October 1815

To Charles W Packe Esquire, Oriel College, Oxford
My dear Charles,
I received your portion of a letter with much pleasure, but am sorry to find that two letters which I wrote to you were not received, the one directed Brussels, the other to the Military Post Office, Paris. We still remain here, but from the articles of the treaty, should suppose we shall be removed into the neighbourhood of some of the fortified towns which are to be given up to us. If they don't send us there we shall be sent to England or Ireland, the latter place there seems to be great disturbances at this time. The people here are very much dissatisfied with the peace & say that it will be impossible for France to perform it. I think we have let them off very easy, if I had been a party concerned, they should not have had Lille as that is the key to France. Edwards has got an appointment

upon General Conran's Staff* at Gibraltar, he left us in a great hurry about 3 weeks since. I have been out shooting 3 times since you were here, I found plenty of birds, but so wild it was impossible to get a shot, there are plenty of woodcocks in the market. I shall try my luck [again] in a day or two, they are not so plentiful as other years. We have had very sporting races here and we gave the people a *déjeuner*† which very much delighted them. I believe if we remain here another month we shall give a ball and supper. We have been afraid of riots in this town more than once, Old Arenschildt (our general) had a squadron mounted and two guns one night but they were not wanted, we have had 15,000 of the Army of the Loire in this town since you were here and I should not be surprised if we had a good row with them as they are very impudent. You requested me to get you some gloves, but in your hurry you neither mentioned quantity, quality or colour. You may depend upon my bringing you some eau de cologne, let me know when you write whether you were able to take any silk stockings, as I understand marked or not, they seize them at Dover. Maclean and Acton‡ are now removed into town, the former has had two classes since you were here, they both desire to be remembered to you and Dilke. Old Greasy Guts is very well, his daughters (who if you remember were not bad looking) have fallen victims to Maclean & me, we go & dine with him and give his daughters *supper*. Maclean will be returned fit for *duty* I think, in another day or two at farthest. The Prussians are come within 4 leagues of us, I don't think we shall have them any nearer, as we are on the borders of Picardy, which province they are ordered not to enter. If we have any disturbances here, we will send for them, as they are allowed to shoot as many French as they please, but we poor devils are obliged to act only on the defensive. I have written to Sir R[owland] Hill to try & procure Edmund§ 4 months leave as it would be a great advantage to him coming from Eton. I have not great hopes as we have had a very strong [document is torn: order?] against leave of absence, but there is nothing like trying. We are going to have our Half Yearly Inspection on Monday in consequence of which, we have had field days every day this week. I have now not a minute longer left for me to finish my letter, with kindest love to yourself & Dilke, I remain yours very affectionately,

G. H. Packe

---

* Captain Edwards became Aide de Camp to Major General Henry Conran at Gibraltar.
† Lunch
‡ Lieutenants Allan Maclean and Henry Acton 13th Light Dragoons.
§ His younger brother who had joined the Royal Horse Guards.

No. 47   From the Same

Abbeville, 1 December 1815

My dear Charles,

I have delayed answering your letter for a week thinking I should be able to send it to London by Captain Doherty* who applied for leave of absence about ten days ago & cannot receive it until we are in settled quarters. We leave this town on Sunday the 3rd instant, our present destination is St Pol which is 12 leagues from here, whether we remain there or not, we do not know, but we are certain of remaining in the country for 3 or perhaps 5 years according as the French behave themselves. The troops which do not remain in the country commence their march tomorrow & they are obliged to be out of the country by the 12th instant according to the treaty. All the Germans and Hanoverians excepting 5,000 are to go back to Hanover to be reduced immediately, which they do not like at all. We have heard nothing about a reduction, but if they reduce the troops of the dragoon regiments in England, we shall share the same fate as our remaining here is to be taken the same as the Irish duty. I am afraid it would be useless for me to apply for more leave for Edmund for this reason. The Blues are now on their way home and of course there are many officers who will want leave of absence and they would put in their claims, so that I think it would be troubling Sir R. Hill for no good, as he must send in their claims prior to Edmund's. I will not forget to write to Captain Jebb who I know will do everything he can for him. We have ordered our mess plate and band [from England], and the colonel has ordered us to get all our dress appointments, but I shall defer that until March, when I shall if possible come to England, as I shall want a great many things and we shall know by that time, whether we are to be reduced or not. I am going to get Captain Doherty to bring me a good many things out of my trunk, which is in Hinde Street.† I have given him every instruction where to find keys &c. & ordered him to seal up again everything he finds sealed. I am not very sorry we are going to leave this place, as the inhabitants have had quite enough of us; they begin to be impudent, though I am sure the place we are going to we shall not be near so comfortable as it is not one third so large as this place and will scarce hold our brigade of artillery, so that we shall be scattered about in different villages which will be very bad at this time of year. I am sorry to say the Prussians have bought up every drop of good wine that was left at Paris and its vicinity, so that the London wine merchants must begin in their own defence to play Old Gooseberry with you. The Tenth are still

---

* Captain George Doherty, the son of Lieutenant Colonel Patrick Doherty.

† Hinde Street runs off Manchester Square in London.

in the neighbourhood, they have received an order to go to Ireland, but the Duke of Wellington has applied for them to remain here. I perceive by the papers they have put my father down to be nominated for Sherriff, but of course he will not be for this, or the next and I should think he would be in Leicestershire the year after. Being now rather pressed for time I must conclude with kindest to my father, mother & brothers. I remain your ever affectionate brother,

    G. H. Packe

No. 48   From the Same

Hernicourt, 1 January 1816

My dear Charles,

I have to acknowledge your letter which I received yesterday and I ought to have received it about a week since, but owing to the dispersed state of the allied troops at present we have nothing regular and having nothing particular to do at this time I sit down with my pen, to try and fill up a sheet of paper; which I assure you I think I shall not be able to accomplish. I was not a little surprised at your intelligence about the rings. I am particularly obliged to you for putting my name in so well; as I am sure I could not have written half so fine a letter and so much to the purpose & shall be much obliged to you to send my ring by James,* to Hinde Street as Captain Doherty is now in London and should this letter reach you in time, I think, he will not have left London. If my box of things, which he has directions to bring out, is gone to Hinde Street, Captain Doherty is to be found at no. 3 St James Street or 14 St James Square (Mrs Boehm's), he will leave London on or about the 15th instant and any letters &c. you had better send by the same conveyance. I have applied with the other officers who were wounded at Waterloo, for a Medical Board to try and get a year's pay for our wounds. I don't think I shall succeed, but nothing hazard, nothing have; and I am determined not to lose it for want of asking. If I succeed in getting it I shall come and spend it in London; but if not I think I shall not come to England this year, as in the first place it will be so very expensive and in the second place, I have given directions to Captain Doherty to bring me out everything, sufficient to last me a year, which would be my chief reason for coming. I thought after so much was said in England, of the French cuirassiers & lancers, we could not help following their example, his royal highness is going to order 2 regiments of light dragoons to be made lancers, 2 hussars & all the heavy dragoons cuirassiers, then we shall be correct, & to complete the thing properly, he had better order us,

---

* His brother, James Packe.

to *fight like the French*. This news came from the Marquess of Anglesey. The French government want to give the officers instead of meat &c. 2 franks a day, as it is inconvenient to them to distribute it, but our noble allies the Prussians objected and said if they would give 3 franks, they would take it. I am rather afraid they have overshot their market as I am sure one frank would pay for everything we get, but if they succeed so much the better. Should you not be able to get lodgings in Lincoln Inn and have nothing better to employ yourself, I recommend your coming out here, for if you come by *yourself* I can always make a Frenchman give you a bed and it would be little or no expense to you, you might pick up a good deal of the language, which hereafter you might find very useful. I have your gun very safe and hope you are not in want of it, at this time we have no shooting at all. I am rather afraid of sending it to England for fear they should seize it, but I will bring it when I come, if you are in want of it. I think by your last letter, I have the laugh against you now, I leave you to guess what for, recollect me before you left Abbeville. I am sorry to find my grandmother has not been so well as usual, as every little thing at her time of life might be reckoned serious, pray in your next letter, let me know how she is. Having now done a great deal more than I conceived I was able, by filling this sheet up with writing, for I can call it nothing else, I must conclude with wishing mother, father, aunt & brothers a happy New Year and kindest love to all. I remain yours affectionately,

G. H. Packe.

No. 49   From the Same

Hazebrouck, 13 March 1816

Charles William Packe, 23 Lower Brook Street, Grosvenor Street, London

My dear Charles,
As I have now an opportunity of sending a letter free to London, I will not let slip so good a chance, though I believe I am not a letter in your debt. The bearer is Lieutenant Bowers,* who has got a month's leave and what will perhaps more astonish you is, that I think you will see me in London about Wednesday the 28th instant. I am going to send off, the day after tomorrow, my application for leave which will take a week or more before I receive the answer, of course I shall start immediately I receive it (if I can get my leave which I do not much doubt). It will therefore be impossible for me to write again, as I shall travel faster than the letter. Captain Doherty is going to apply at the same time, of course

---

* Lieutenant Charles Robert Bowers, 13th Light Dragoons.

we shall come over together. I have not time to write by this conveyance to Hanthorpe,* therefore will thank you to write & let them know that I am coming, that they may have a bed aired. I cannot say for certain the day I shall be in England as there is the uncertainty of water, winds & the headquarters of the British army, but conclude it will be about that time. I don't know where I shall put up, as in the first place I know not where you are; who is in London, or anything about it, but will be much obliged to you, to settle me a lodging somewhere for two nights, either with uncles, aunt or an hotel near you. Now for another bore, I must trouble you to send for my things, which remain in Hinde Street, as I shall come over without a single thing, in fact I have nothing here. Having I think laid enough burden on your shoulders, I must finish by requesting you will send me a letter, to know where to find you and the arrangements you have made (addressed Post Office, Dover). Should I not succeed in procuring leave of absence I shall certainly write to you as soon as possible. Not being allowed time to finish my paper, I must conclude requesting you to remember me to all relations and friends & I remain my dear Charles, your affectionate brother

    G. H. Packe

---

* Hanthorpe House in the village of Hanthorpe, two miles north of Bourne in Lincolnshire.

THE ARTILLERY

The Staff

No. 50   Lieutenant Colonel Sir Augustus Frazer, Commanding the Horse Artillery

JSAHR, vol. XLII, no. 171, September 1964, reprinted with kind permission.

To Lieutenant Colonel Robe RA

Waterloo, 19 June 3 a.m.

My dear Robe,

We have gained a great but bloody day, having completely repulsed in our position of Braine l'Alleud the repeated attacks of Napoleon. The fruits of the day I yet hardly know, but the enemy has received a severe & complete defeat. Of artillery I think I have seen 50 guns & we hope to find 50 more[*] but the action (which was decided at last by the total failure of the attack by the infantry of the Imperial Guard) was not over till 10 p.m. and the pursuit was in the dark.

The greater part of the action may be called an action of artillery. We had 108 British and 16 Belgic guns in play, the enemy more than 200. The enemy's cavalry behaved nobly, herding [? charging] us to the very mouth; all our guns were repeatedly abandoned but our gallant infantry formed into squares, never budged, & after each repulse we returned to our guns again.

Foiled in attacks of cavalry on our right, our left, & through our centre, Napoleon made before dusk a desperate effort with the whole of his infantry chiefly of the Imperial Guard, but they could make do impression on our infantry, & after the most determined bravery were driven off the field. The affair was now decided but the darkness prevented one's seeing more than hosts in pursuit, or hearing more than the loud & continued shouts of the victors.

---

[*]   Clearly an early estimate.

Our own arm, I speak of the horse artillery, has suffered, but has suffered with honour. I had it in my power to employ it in masses, & it has well repaid the confidence placed in its exertions. Bull's Howitzer Troop was brought up against a Wood (*Frazer's side note*: With obvious and acknowledged good effects) which placed to the right of our centre, (indeed almost to the right of our line) was three times taken & retaken by the enemy. A part of it was never abandoned by the British Guards though the building in which they were posted was burnt in the action.

The accompanying memorandum will show the killed & wounded.

It is underrated & imperfect; but early intelligence is valuable, & you shall have regular and more correct returns.

William* you will observe among the wounded, a musket ball is in the groin, but there is no danger I hope and he is free from pain, has had surgical assistance & is in the very house in which I write, he shall be well attended to. Mr Ambrose† is the medical officer who has seen him.

Every exertion is now making to refit the troops and when the mounts & equipments on the field of battle shall have been picked up I conclude we shall do well, but men & horses especially the former are much wanted & surely will be sent. Now must be our struggle to follow up the blow without intermission. The morale of the enemy is believed to have received a shock which it must be our struggle to increase.

Adieu. I write to you as our lieutenant colonel though I know I have to wish you joy of a step & I do so with all my heart.‡

Adieu. Private feelings will have to cut. Poor Bean,§ Cairnes¶ & Ram[say].** The last I had the mournful consolation of burying during the action, when his whole troop paid the tribute of sorrow for his loss. Bean & Cairnes fell without speaking, but they fell as we must all be ready to do. Yours sincerely,

Augustus S. Frazer

---

* Lieutenant William Robe of H Troop who actually succumbed to his wound on 19 June. He was the son of Lieutenant Colonel Robe.
† Assistant Surgeon James Ambrose of the Ordnance Medical Department (Drew, *Medical Officers*, number 2522).
‡ Robe had been promoted to colonel on 16 May 1815.
§ Major George Bean commanding D Troop was killed.
¶ Major Robert Cairnes of I Troop was killed.
** Major William Norman Ramsay of H Troop was killed.

RETURN OF CASUALTIES IN THE EIGHT TROOPS
[Figures in square brackets indicate figures from the official returns]

I Troop
Major Bull* 450 rounds of 5" inch howitzer
Major Bull slightly wounded
Major Cairnes killed
Lieutenant Smith† slightly wounded
Men killed 2 wounded 9 [13]
Horses killed 16 [15]
2 nine pounder wheels disabled

F Troop
Lieutenant Colonel Smith‡ 670 rounds of light 6-pounder
Lieutenant Craufurd§ wounded slightly
Lieutenant Forster¶ severely
Men killed 9 [4] wounded 1 sergeant major
  [8 men, no sergeant major mentioned]
Horses killed 24 [20]

G Troop
Captain Mercer** 700 rounds
  [Mercer states 700 per gun, an impossibility]
Lieutenant Hincks†† wounded slightly (begs not to be included)
Men killed 18 [5] wounded not known [16]
Horses killed 40 [69]

D Troop
Major Bean's
Major Bean killed
Captain Webber‡‡ wounded slightly
Lieutenant Cromie§§ ditto severely
Men killed 8 [7] wounded 1 sergeant 9 men

---

* Major Robert Bull.
† First Lieutenant William Smith.
‡ Lieutenant Colonel James Webber Smith.
§ First Lieutenant Donald Craufurd.
¶ First Lieutenant Henry Forster was wounded in the foot by grape shot.
** Second Captain Alexander Cavalie Mercer.
†† First Lieutenant John Hincks.
‡‡ Second Captain William Webber.
§§ First Lieutenant Michael Cromie was hit in the legs by a round shot and died two days later.

Horses killed 19 [24]
Ammunition Wagon blown up

A Troop
Lieutenant Colonel Ross* 2 guns only
Major Parker wounded severely left leg amputated
Men killed 1 [5] wounded 5 [9]
Horses killed 7 [21]
The rest of the guns with Lieutenant Day†

E Troop
Lieutenant Colonel Gardiner's‡
Men killed – 1 sergeant 1gunner – wounded – 2 [10] men
Horses killed 6 [9]
One limber destroyed

H Troop
Major Ramsay 660 rounds
Major Ramsay killed
Captain A[lexander] Macdonald wounded severely
Lieutenant Brereton ditto
Lieutenant Robe§ ditto
Men killed 5 [2] wounded 9 [13]
Horses killed 12
1 Gun disabled, not with the troop
1 Wagon ditto

[Rocket Troop]
Captain Whinyates's
Captain Whinyates wounded slightly¶
Captain Dansey** slightly
Lieutenant Strangways†† slightly
Men killed 7 – Uncertain in the report if the only officer left

* Lieutenant Colonel Sir Hew Ross.
† First Lieutenant James Day, towards the end of the battle only a few guns could be moved due to lack of horses, Ross must have given command of the stationary guns to Day.
‡ Lieutenant Colonel Sir Robert Gardiner
§ Lieutenant William Robe, son of Colonel Sir William Robe.
¶ Captain Edward Whinyates had three horses shot underneath him, was wounded in the leg and then severely wounded in the left arm near the close of the battle.
** Captain Charles Dansey
†† First Lieutenant Thomas Strangways was dangerously wounded

with a part of the troop which has been detached
[29 wounded and 24 horses killed]
Rockets all well.
Augustus S. Frazer Lieutenant Colonel

[*On the back of the letter appears a summary as follows:*]
Officers, killed 3 captains 1 sergeant major, 51 rank & file
Wounded 6 captains, 8 subs, 1 sergeant major, 1 sergeant,
60 [men]
& probably 20 men 124 horses killed.

No. 51   Lieutenant Colonel Sir John May, Royal Artillery, Assistant Adjutant General

By kind permission of Sir Michael Bunbury Bt, KCVO, DL, and Suffolk Record Office, Bury St Edmunds, ref. E18/740/4

Headquarters, Cateau, 23 June 1815[*]

My dear colonel,[†]
I have not written to you because my time has been and is so taken up, that I can hardly call half an hour my own.

In the battle of the 16th and 18th instant the Duke of Wellington has even exceeded himself and adorned his brows with that one laurel more that was wanting to complete his fame and glory, in the entire defeat of Bonaparte. The battle of the 18th was one of the most gigantic struggles it is almost possible for the mind to form an idea of. The returns of the killed and wounded and the immense number of dead bodies strewed about the field, sufficiently attest its effects.

The Duke indeed was too much exposed and it is difficult to understand how he escaped unhurt; he lost, however, two aides de camp, Gordon and Canning, and Lord Fitzroy Somerset has had his right arm amputated, but is doing well. Our loss in artillery is the severest as to officers ever known; and several of our best have fallen.

The battle of the 18th was a complete lesson in the art of war and accounts for, most satisfactorily to my mind, of the cause why Bonaparte had such brilliant and decisive success over the allies, until they were beaten into the same system.

---

[*] Another copy of this letter was recently sold by an American Auction house, who provided a copy of the letter on the internet. From this it was confirmed that the two are identical.

[†] It is uncertain as to the identity of the recipient, could it be to Chapman? See Letter 52.

The cannonade from perhaps more than double the number of guns we possessed was tremendous and destructive; the charges of cavalry, principally of the Imperial Guards and cuirassiers were terrific and would probably have shaken the nerves and solid squares of any other infantry but our own; and their infantry was led on with great spirit and determination.

Bonaparte crossing the Sambre at Maubeuge with his left and his right marching from Beaumont, found himself early in the morning of the 16th before the Duke of Wellington at a place called Quatre Bras, where four great roads divide, the one to Brussels, another to Charleroi, a third to Namur and the fourth to Nivelles. The Prussians were concentrated near Fleurus, a distance of about ten miles from us, though in communication. The Duke was attacked it is said by Marshal Ney with two corps. His Grace had in the first part of the day only the 5th Division commanded by Sir Thomas Picton;[*] but towards the evening the Prince of Orange's corps, composed of the first and part of the 3rd Divisions, arrived. This battle had no very particular features except some desperate charges of cavalry in which they gained no advantages and the firing ceased with daylight, we preserving in every respect the ground originally taken up. But it did not fare quite so well with the Prussians against which Bonaparte was opposed with the principal part of his force. At 8 o'clock in the evening the French cavalry broke through their centre, swept off 16 pieces of cannon with most of the reserve ammunition of their army together with a number of prisoners, which caused Blücher to retire to a more secure position at Wavre. This compelled the Duke to do the same, in order to put himself in more close communication with him, by which undoubtedly he mended greatly his position.

The British army therefore moved at 9 a.m. to the rear on the 17th; in its retreat it was greatly pressed by the enemy's cavalry. The position taken up in the afternoon was with the right on the Chateau de Hougoumont and the left in the rear of a wood (which we occupied) at Ohain.

On the 18th at about 12 o'clock at noon, the cannonade of the French commenced, which was tremendously heavy, particularly always just before the attacks of cavalry and infantry; and had not the ground had several small vallies [sic] running parallel to the position, our loss must have been much more severe even than we experienced. The cannonade thus continued for two hours, when a charge of cavalry was made with great bravery on the left and centre of the line; this was received by the infantry in squares and by a reciprocal charge on the part of our cavalry, when the enemy without making any impression retreated with

---

[*] This completely ignores the brave defence carried out by Perponcher's Dutch troops.

precipitation, pursued close to their infantry. A second charge of cavalry throughout the line was also made without success, supported by infantry and repulsed in the same manner.

Bonaparte finding the cavalry had not had the desired effect he expected, redoubled his efforts with his artillery, cannonading our line for a length of time and as his artillery was full double of what ours was, occasioned great loss; the more particularly as the Duke ordered our guns only to fire upon infantry and cavalry and not upon artillery.

In his last effort he is said to have assembled 20,000 infantry of his Guards, 96 pieces of canon and with cavalry on the flanks, advanced to pierce our centre. In this, however, after a desperate struggle, he failed, and the charges of several regiments of infantry, particularly the 52nd in the front and others that had been ordered by the Duke in squares and lines on the flank, the whole was put in complete confusion retreating with the greatest precipitation. About this time the Prussian army under Blücher made its appearance on the right of the enemy's line which together with the rapid manner in which they were pushed back to the main road on which their cannon was before retiring, obliged them to abandon there, and on the field of battle, 122 pieces and near 300 ammunition and other wagons. In short no victory could be more complete.

The Duke had about 70,000 infantry, 10,000 cavalry and about 150 pieces of cannon; but the enemy's force very much greater. The Prussians were not attacked, but all the weight of the French on us. I remain &c., &c.

J. May.

No. 52   Lieutenant Colonel Sir Alexander Dickson, Battering Train
By kind permission of the National Library of Scotland, reference Acc 9742 and Sir Michael Bunbury Bt, KCVO, DL, and Suffolk Record Office, Bury St Edmunds, ref. E18/740/4

To Lieutenant Colonel Chapman[*]
Secretary to the Master General of The Ordnance

Brussels, 20 June 1815

My dear Chapman,
I wrote you a hasty letter on the 16th which would inform you of my arrival here and that the enemy being in motion I was just going to the front with Sir George.[†] The same day a general action took place, the Prussians being attacked near Fleurus and we at *Les Quatre Bras* where

---

[*] Lieutenant Colonel Stephen R. Chapman RE.
[†] Colonel Sir George Adam Wood commanding the artillery.

the roads to Namur and Charleroi separate in front of Genappe. We repulsed the enemy in a handsome manner, but the Prussians although they held their ground for the moment were obliged to fall back in the night to Wavre which compelled us to do the same next day to Waterloo where we took up a position. On the 18th Bonaparte attacked us with immense force with a determination to conquer, but after a battle as obstinate as I believe ever took place, which lasted for 12 hours without intermission, his army was totally beaten and the Prussians having in the mean time attacked his flank he was obliged to fly with the loss of all his artillery. The destruction of men in these two battles has been immense, and our artillery was most conspicuous and inimitably handled by Sir George. I attended him throughout both the days and of course assisted as much as in my power. Our casualty [list] has been great and is the best explanation of the heaviness of the fire, which on the part of the enemy was general and incessant. You know I have seen a good deal of works, but such a day as this of close fighting and duration I never witnessed. The conduct of the French cavalry was brilliant, and no one but the Duke of Wellington could have resisted such impetuosity. Our infantry manoeuvred in the most admirable manner, and fully corresponded with the beautiful disposition made by their commander.

You will oblige me by showing these few lines to General Macleod[*] to whom I will write in a day or two but have no time to do so now.

I am going to equip the Battering Train forthwith in readiness for movement. Ever &c., &c., &c.

A. Dickson.

The Foot Artillery
Major Lloyd's Battery, Royal Artillery

No. 53   First Lieutenant Samuel Phelps, RA[†]
By kind permission of The National Library of Wales, ref. MSS 12173E[‡]

To John Phelps[§] Esq, Ely, Cambridge.

Bois de Boulogne Comy near Paris, 18 July 1815

My dear John,

---

[*]   Lieutenant General John Macleod, Colonel Commandant RA.
[†]   1st Lieutenant Samuel Phelps RA (Major Lloyd's Battery).
[‡]   This letter is in a very poor condition and very difficult to read fully. I have therefore been forced to make conjectures on many words which are indicated as usual by square brackets.
[§]   Brother of Samuel Phelps.

I felt much gratified by receiving a letter from you, not having heard from you for such a length of time and am much astonished in not having heard from Withybush* for nearly five weeks, and I have written four or five letters since the late engagements. I must, therefore suppose that my letters that were sent must have miscarried. I shall now give you, (as far as lies in my favour) the particulars of the late operations and how we are getting on in this country; from the newspapers you will get more news and information than from any other channel as it is through them we often hear of things that happen in this army, therefore (in the first place) I must tell you that the brigade of guns to which I belong had been quartered in a beautiful village in the neighbourhood of Ghent where we had been some time prior to the battles of the 16th and 18th June.

On the 14th instant we received an order to march,† when after two days hard marching we arrived at the scene of action at about 3 o'clock in the evening of the 16th, our guns were immediately brought into action. We began by commencing a heavy fire upon the enemy's position which was kept up until late in the evening. We lost a great many horses killed but did not suffer much in men, the troops of the line suffered considerably especially the highlanders, we, however, drove the enemy back and our right troops occupied the ground he stood upon! You are of course aware that there was only a third of the army engaged, the rest not having come up. I was mounting my horse, one foot in the stirrup, when a cannon shot struck him dead having gone through him. We lay all this night in the rear of the field of battle repairing our damages as well as possible and at about twelve o'clock on the 17th we were ordered to retire as the Prussians on our left had been obliged to retreat, the enemy being too superior to them, our brigade took a position on the heights of Genappe famous for a battle that had been gained in former wars, from that we retreated to the heights of Mt St John [*sic*]. The weather was dreadful, it rained in torrents with much thunder and lightning, the enemy came on at a brisk rate, afterwards our [cavalry made?] some beautiful charges, however, they continued [to push?] on and it was not until we put a fear[some fire?] into their columns that they decided for the [suspension of arms as?] this was the most uncomfortable night. I was [soaked to?] the skin, no shelter, nor anything to eat the whole day! On the morning of the 18th at [10 o'clock?] I went to the rear to bring up some ammunition [caissons when?] about twelve o'clock the enemy commenced [a heavy fire?] upon our lines. I did not return to the fighting until two o'clock; we had hard work with our guns [sinking?] it being so

---

* Withybush House near Haverfordwest in West Wales, owned by the Phelps family.
† They were ordered from Ghent to Brussels on 14 June and marched with the 3rd Division on 16 June for Quatre Bras.

wet that it was with difficulty [that we could?] work them, we kept up a warm fire upon the enemy when of a sudden an immense body of cavalry came out of some corn in our front and charged through our guns, it was with difficulty that we got to the squares of infantry in our rear, the line fired volleys into them, they retired and we got to our guns and peppered them finely; they charged us again four times following but we killed such a number of them that they were glad to retire at last. Our losses was considerable, two officers out of five are severely wounded,[*] a great number of our men and horses killed.

After that memorable day we had incessant marching for a fortnight until we arrived before Paris, where at first the enemy intended to make a stand, but at last capitulated, so ended this campaign. I have been into Paris several times and have seen all that is worth looking at, the houses are better than in London but it is not near so fine a city.

I do not know how long we shall stay in this country but hope to meet you at Withybush next Christmas, remember me kindly to my Aunt Griffiths. I hope some day to see them, as I shall take the first opportunity of visiting in that part of the country again. I remain your affectionate brother,

Samuel Phelps

PS Excuse this scrawl as have not the convenience for writing.

---

[*] Captain William Lloyd died of wounds received on 29 July 1815. Second Lieutenant William H. Harvey lost his right arm and was awarded a pension of £70 per annum.

THE INFANTRY

First Division of Major General George Cooke
1st Brigade of Major General Peregrine Maitland

No. 54 Major General Peregrine Maitland
By kind permission of Sir Michael Bunbury Bt, KCVO, DL, and
Suffolk Record Office, Bury St Edmunds, ref. E18/740/4

To HRH The Duke of York

Nivelles, 19 June 1815

Sir,

I have the honour to make your Royal Highness acquainted with the movements and conduct of the 1st Brigade of Guards in the late glorious operations.

It was at Quatre Bras that the brigade first came in contact with the enemy. Here they arrived very fortunately after a march of about twenty six miles. At that moment the French with two battalions had occupied a wood which extends from the road leading from Nivelles to Quatre Bras, about a mile and a half to the right. Had the enemy maintained himself here, he would have cut off the communication between Lord Hill and the corps of the Prince of Orange. The brigade formed across the wood, advanced with the bayonet cheering and drove the enemy entirely from his post. He, however, with a reserve of three battalions on the right of the wood, which is long but not broad, and two pieces of artillery at the extremity, continued to harass us and to make frequent attempts to regain the wood. He also pushed on a corps on our left which attempted to cut us off from the high road, but all his efforts were rendered vain by the spirited resistance of the brigade. I caused part of the brigade to advance frequently against the last mentioned corps of the enemy and as frequently drove him back. Nothing could exceed the gallantry both of the officers and men. In one of these last mentioned attacks poor Lord

Hay,* my aide de camp, was killed by my side. Our loss on this day as your Royal Highness will have perceived by the Returns was very severe both in men and in valuable officers.

In the last glorious action, the two brigades of Guards bore a most conspicuous share; and never was praise more unqualified than that which was bestowed upon them by the Duke of Wellington. An artillery officer on our right assured me that he heard the Duke say during the action 'Guards, you shall be rewarded for this.'

The cannonade which began the action was very heavy and we suffered in our squares from this with the greatest steadiness. Afterwards the French cavalry advanced against us in immense masses, one after another attempting with the greatest gallantry to break our squares. They halted at a certain distance, sent forward some of their men to fire their pistols at us, but ours were too steady to return their fire and preserved it for their charge which was continually fruitless. They then assailed the third battalion square (in which I was and which was the most advanced) with a square of infantry. Finding their fire galling and relying on the steadiness of the men, I pushed forward against them in spite of the cavalry and drove them down the hill. Here the third battalion halted still in square in front of the whole line. The enemy poured on us a heavy fire of his artillery, mowed a passage two or three times through the faces of our square, while the cavalry were prepared on our right to take advantage of the least disorder. The coolness and rapidity with which our ranks were closed, left him no opportunity of which he thought proper to avail himself.

Finding the fire too deadly to be long maintained and that I was too far in front of the line, I caused the square to retreat up the hill about forty yards, which it did with the greatest good order. It was at this period that Napoleon made his last effort against our centre and advanced with masses of infantry supported by cavalry and a blaze of artillery. At the command of the Duke of Wellington our two squares formed into a line four deep. Napoleon himself led his Imperial Guards against us, to the bottom of the hill (or rather the small acclivity). The moment they appeared and began to form about twenty yards in our front, we poured in the most deadly fire that perhaps ever was witnessed, as the field of battle abundantly testified the following day. The Imperial Guard retreated; the whole of our line advanced and the rest on the part of the enemy was all flight. The two light companies were detached with the other brigade.

Of the conduct of Lord Saltoun† and of all their officers and men, General Byng speaks in the highest terms. After the report I have had

---

* Ensign James Lord Hay, 1st Foot Guards.
† Captain and Lieutenant Colonel Alexander Lord Saltoun, 1st Foot Guards, commanded the light companies of the brigade.

the honour to make to your Royal Highness which is an accurate detail of all that occurred. The square of the second battalion through the day continually supporting that of the third and repelling the cavalry with the same unshakable perseverance. I need hardly comment on the splendid conduct of the officers and men. Your Royal Highness has lost many valuable officers, I, many dear and excellent friends. May I beg you Sir, to excuse any inaccuracies which are incidental enough to the hurry of such a moment and may I beg your Royal Highness to believe me &c. &c.

Peregrine Maitland, Major General

2nd Battalion 1st Foot Guards

No. 55   Ensign the Honourable Samuel S. Barrington[*]
By kind permission of Staffordshire Record Office Reference D1778V1034

Ath, 29 March 1815

My dear mother,[†]
I wrote to you by the last post from here and thought upon the whole I had done my duty on that head; but as I only got your 2 letters of the 17th and 23rd both together last night, upon my return from the field where the Battle of Jemappes[‡] was fought, it was too late to send a letter off then, and therefore this must wait till the next post. Having little to do here and being obliged to keep two horses, I rode out yesterday with 2 others, to view the different positions of the French and Austrians at the famous battle. The best information that we could obtain we did upon the field and could make it all out very well. But if ever we get back to England I will give you some account of it and hope also to tell you of the fine style we will knock the French about, if we can but get up our reinforcements from England before they advance against us. We are all in the highest spirits here and anxious to try our strength with the first who dare oppose us. If we do but get the Duke of Wellington we are sure to lick them. Of course all sorts of reports fly about here as in other places, but nothing very certain is known or at least published. I believe Bonaparte's chief plan, will be the old one of setting the allied powers together by the ears and then coming off best of all himself. I think, however, if we should have the good fortune to take him, he will not be alive many moments. I hope my father has received my letter about the £50 for which I was

---

[*] Ensign the Honourable Samuel S. Percy Barrington, 1st Foot Guards, killed at Quatre Bras.
[†] Elizabeth Barrington (née Adair), spouse of the Reverend George, 5th Viscount Barrington.
[‡] Fought on 6 November 1792.

obliged to draw and I trust that I shall not abuse any sum that he may think right should be applied to my use. I have nothing to say for myself, but that I am as well and as happy as ever I was in my life and if I escape with a whole skin, shall think myself well off and be thankful. If on the contrary some unlucky ball finished me, I trust I shall not be wholly unprepared to face danger & death. Buckley* is very well and I fancy that before this time some of the Seymour's are safe in England if not all as the two sons and I believe Lord George left Brussels before our army.†
If anything goes on here, I will take care to write in good time. I am just going to ride, if I meet with any adventure I will tell you.

I went to see a curious grotto called [Gommiro?]‡ 5 miles from hence, but I have no room to describe it at present. There are two reports in circulation at the moment, one that we march tomorrow, the other that Napoleon is assassinated by Marshal Mortier, neither of which do I believe,§ although I should not be sorry to hear both confirmed. Barry is safe in England, or at the bottom of the sea by this time. I live just opposite the church, the bells of which are never permitted to rest quiet 5 minutes in the 24 hours and the din of course is seldom or ever out of my ears, though I fancy we shall hear more inharmonious music soon. Give my love to all that care about me, or I about them and to my father, Mr Gamlin, Miss Chaytor and Thomas Fry. Ever your affectionate son,
S. S. P. Barrington

Direct as usual as head quarters are still at Brussels and as long as they remain Mrs Glynn need not be alarmed.

No. 56   From the Same

Enghien, 15 June 1815

My dear mother,

I have just this moment heard that Captain Perceval¶ is coming out very shortly. I wish you could contrive to send my gun out by him, as I trust it is in a state fit for immediate service under the care of Thomas and superintended by his master in Mortimer Street. It is said now that we shall not stir a step in this business until the advance of the Prussians, when I suppose we shall come upon the French like hail. The weather

---

* Lieutenant Edward Pery Buckley, 1st Foot Guards.
† Lord and Lady George and the Miss Seymour were still in Brussels and attended the Duchess of Richmond's Ball.
‡ Probably the 80-foot hillock at the Chateau d'Attre, Ath, with its artificial grottoes.
§ Both completely false.
¶ Lieutenant & Captain Philip Joshua Perceval, 1st Foot Guards.

here is at present very unfavourable for campaigning and indeed for all manner of field sports as it rains at all times of the day and night and has done for the last fortnight and promises fair to do the same for another fortnight. I wonder whether Saint Swithin has anything to do with the state of the weather in this country as in England. Captain Chaplin[*] (the brother of the man who married Miss Fane), who was so badly wounded at San Sebastian is suffering from it again as it has broke out worse than ever. Tell William that I got every quill out of my bow with the Boyses,[†] by quietly and deliberately kicking one of them downstairs, he went to the major who reported it to the general and I got off without any further trouble. In future I shall begin with fists first and words after, if they choose to wait, in fact we have found out, there is no eloquence like force and no sauce so good for one impudent fellow as thrashing. My love to all at home, ever your affectionate son,
S. S. P. Barrington

No. 57   Lieutenant Colonel Alexander Lord Saltoun, Regarding Ensign Barrington

Camp Comini,[‡] 23 June 1815

To the Right Honourable Lord Barrington

My Lord,
The command of the 2nd Battalion 1st Regiment of Guards having devolved upon me, the very painful duty of acquainting your lordship with the particulars of the fate of the Honourable S. S. P. Barrington has fallen to my lot. He fell in action, in the Bois de Bossu on the 16th instant in the most gallant execution of his duty and even under these melancholy circumstances, it must be some consolation to his friends to know that his death was instantaneous and not attended with the slightest suffering and that his body was the next morning buried on the field of battle. From the circumstances of the ground on which he fell being immediately afterwards in momentary possession of the enemy, I regret to say that on our regaining it, they had taken possession of his sash and sword and what other things he had about him which I should

---

[*] Lieutenant and Captain Thomas Chaplin, 1st Foot Guards. His brother Charles Chaplin married Caroline Fane in 1812.
[†] There were only two officers named Boyse with the army, Major Shapland Boyse 13th Light Dragoons and Captain Jaques Boyse, 32nd Foot who was killed at Waterloo. Presumably therefore it was the latter who was kicked down the stairs!
[‡] Other officers of the regiment record it as Gourmignies, but I have been unable to find this village in the vicinity of Cateau Cambresis, where they were that day.

have wished to save to send them to your lordship. I have the honour to be my lord, your most obedient servant.

Saltoun, Lieutenant Colonel Commanding 2nd Battalion 1st Guards

No. 58   Major Henry Askew, Regarding Ensign Barrington

Antwerp, 4 July 1815

My Lord,[*]

It would have been my duty to have communicated to you the first and painful intelligence of your son's death, but being obliged to leave the field in consequence of a severe wound, I was not aware of the melancholy fate of my young friend until some days after my arrival in this place. At this period I ought to apologise in intruding upon your affliction but it may be some consolation to a father and I do feel it is a tribute so justly due to the son to say how exemplary his conduct with his regiment had been. As an officer I ever found him intelligent, attentive and conscientious in the discharge of his duty. As a gentleman he was only to be known to increase the list of his numerous friends.

Believe me my dear lord, when the memory recurs to the events of that glorious day, the name of Barrington will long, long live in a corps in whose ranks he so nobly fought and fell. With my sincerest participation in your grief, for so irreparable a loss. I have the honour to be your lordships most obedient very humble servant.

H. J. Askew Colonel Commandant[†] 2nd Battalion 1st Regiment of Guards

No. 59   Lieutenant Colonel Henry Dawkins,[‡]
Regarding Ensign Barrington

Paris, 8 July 1815

My dear mother,

The enclosed will tell you all the news and our proceedings since my last letter and I shall confine this paper to the information reflecting poor Barrington.

It is with much satisfaction I am able to acquaint you that his writing desk is now safe at Brussels and his sash is now here in Buckley's[§] possession and we will endeavour between us to have these things with

---

[*] Samuel was the third son of George 5th Viscount Barrington, prebendary of Durham Cathedral and Elizabeth (née Adair).
[†] 2nd Major Henry Askew was a colonel in the army.
[‡] Dawkins served with the Coldstream Guards.
[§] Lieutenant & Captain Edward Pery Buckley

any others we may be able to collect, sent home by an early opportunity. It must I feel confident be gratifying to poor Lady Barrington to know that her son was universally liked by all the officers of the brigade and that his death was instantaneous owing to a musket shot in the head on the evening of the 16th. He was buried on the 17th in the most regular way that circumstances would allow.

Acquaintance commenced in the regiment from Dover to Calais last January when he gave me a letter of introduction from Mrs H. Calvert.* He joined our party to Brussels and as I believe I wrote you word at the time, both Dashwood† and myself were particularly struck with his fine and gentlemanly manners and conduct, and since that time I always endeavoured to improve acquaintance and have every reason to regret his unfortunate fate, and the only consolation (and which I really think is great) I am able to afford, is that I feel sure he was quite well and happy until his death which was instantaneous, whilst several of my other friends lingered in great agony for two or three days. I shall let you know when and by whom these things are sent home and had I not imagined that some officers of the 1st Regiment had sent home these particulars, I should certainly have done so to Mrs Calvert before. I have my dear mother written more fully than I meant on the subject of wounds &c. in order to show that some consolation is certainly to be derived from poor Barrington's fate, in comparison with some of our other friends and as you are now fully aware all war is at an end, I do not think it necessary to alter it. In case you see any of the friends of the wounded officers of the Guards, I am happy to tell you that the last accounts from Brussels mention all going on well. Hesketh‡ and Bowater§ to drive out in a buggy, the former was wounded in the neck. I must now conclude this disagreeable subject and believe me my dear mother, your very affectionate son,

Henry Dawkins junior.

No. 60   Unknown Officer, Regarding Ensign Barrington

The fate of poor Barrington is very distressing and his friends feel it most acutely at least I do, for never was there a better officer, a kinder friend or a more gallant soldier. I wish his parents could have seen him at the head of his company, cheering his men forward, with his sword in the air, it would have made their hearts proud as it did mine, to see that I had a friend like him. [Unsigned]

---

* Wife of Lieutenant General Sir Harry Calvert, Adjutant General.
† Ensign Augustus Dashwood was not at Waterloo.
‡ Lieutenant & Captain Robert Bamford Hesketh 3rd Foot Guards.
§ Captain & Lieutenant Colonel Edward Bowater 3rd Foot Guards.

No. 61   Mr Ulysses Price, Regarding Ensign Barrington

Extract of a letter from Mr Ulysses Price to the Bishop of Durham,
dated 24 September 1818

I very lately paid a visit to Dr Baillie,* we went to the churchyard to see a magnificent yew tree, when it was proposed to extend our walk I declined and the Dr said to a young man of the party, you had better return also, lest it should be too much for your foot. As we walked I asked him, what was the matter, he answered he had received a shot through his foot. I said 'at Waterloo?' 'Yes'.

'Then' said I 'Were you the friend of my relation Sam Barrington?'

He said 'Yes' and then began the highest praises of him and said he was killed instantly by a shot through the head having his hat off cheering his men. He said he had asked him in the morning if he had said his prayers? 'Yes' 'Did you pray to be saved?'

'No I did not care whether I should be killed or not, but I prayed to be saved after death.'

He then proposed to his friend retiring into the wood to pray.

No. 62   Mrs Sophia Baillie,† Regarding Ensign Barrington

Lower Grosvenor Street, 27 July 1815

My Lord,

I enclose a packet which my nephew‡ has brought with him from Brussels and am desired to inform your lordship, that your son's heavy baggage is at Ostend, from which it will be forwarded to England. His writing desk is in my possession and I shall keep it till I receive further directions. His watch was taken by some British officer upon the field of battle, I do not at present know his name, but Colonel d'Oyly§ has undertaken to make every enquiry to find him out if possible.

Permit me my lord to add that all I hear from my nephew increases my admiration of your son and my deep concern for the loss you have sustained. Even his noble courage could not exceed the excellence of his principles and his strong religious feeling. Upon this subject I have an incident to relate, which considered as almost the last action of his

---

* Dr Matthew Baillie who was physician to King George III throughout his long illness.

† The wife of Dr Baillie, her maiden name was Denman.

‡ Her nephew was Ensign Thomas Elmsley Croft of 1st Foot Guards who was severely wounded at Quatre Bras. Sir Richard Croft 6th Bart. had married her sister Margaret; Thomas was their first son.

§ Captain & Lieutenant Colonel Sir Francis d'Oyly.

life acquires a peculiar degree of interest and must be cherished by his friends with a most dear and tender recollection. As the Guards were passing through the wood on the 16th where they were much scattered in different directions, they heard heavy firing around them and met a number of Belgian troops returning wounded. Your gallant son said to his companion 'Croft we are likely to have warm work, suppose you and I say our prayers.' And these two young men said their prayers together in a corner of the field, and then rushed on with undaunted courage to the attack, where one fell gloriously and the other was carried off severely wounded. I am sure your lordship will hear with satisfaction, that my nephew is better than we could have expected and has not suffered from his removal. His wound is going on so favourably that we are encouraged to hope his recovery will ultimately be complete, but the ball is not yet extracted and we must prepare ourselves for a very tedious confinement and occasionally great suffering. But he is very good and very patient and I think he will be the better all his life, for having begun the world with such a friend. I have the honour to remain my lord, your lordship's most obedient servant.

Sophia Baillie

No. 63 By An Unknown Officer

20 and 22 June, extract of a letter from a young officer of the 1st Guards to his father[*]

. . . I will give you some account as well as I can of all our movements since we left Enghien on the 16th Friday morning by an order from the Prince of Orange about 2 o'clock in the morning very suddenly, as we heard the Prussians had been attacked and been licked and that we were to go to Braine le Comte, headquarters of the prince. We arrived there about ½ past 7, we staid [*sic*] there four hours whilst we were getting our rations and marched to Nivelles, where we understood we were to bivouack for the night, but after we had been there about an hour, Colonel Hervey Q.M.G.[†] came riding up, saying that the French were advancing and we were immediately to move up to the front, being at that time about 12 miles from the enemy. We set out about twelve and arrived where the enemy were about six, having heard a tremendous cannonade all the way. The Belgians only had been engaged and had run away not having behaved so well as they ought. However, we came then to their support and put ourselves into a wood (the 1st Brigade) where we marched along some time under a very heavy fire of artillery and musketry. The wood being very thick, we could not deploy and the corn in the fields very

---

[*] Not quoted in *A Near Observer*.

[†] Assistant Quartermaster General Colonel Felton E. Hervey 14th Light Dragoons.

high, to say nothing of the men having marched from Enghien to Quatre Bras, about thirty miles. When we were in the wood everything was in confusion, we advanced as well as we were able into the fields and fired away at one another, though they had nothing but skirmishers and a small body of cavalry, but were very close to one another, we remained there and kept the ground till dark. Barrington was killed at dark. We put out our picquets which the Coldstream and Third did having relieved us, we were so much cut up in the morning. We retired a little and slept in the rear of the wood that night, *we* having done very well. The Prussians I fancy had lost a great quantity of men who were on our left and had no more ammunition when the French cavalry attacked them and beat them back. We staid where we were till about 8 o'clock the next morning, when in consequence of the Prussians retiring, we were obliged to retire also. We marched to a place called Waterloo where we took up a position and bivouacked on the hills. The French followed us very closely, but halted that night, there being only skirmishes with picquets. We passed a most unpleasant night in a ploughed field running [with water] all night. Next day (having heard we were to be attacked) the French advanced in great force.

22 June

We are now in a wood about 6 miles from Bavay, you will have heard of 'Our complete victory'. But to continue, they attacked us at one point, which if they had carried, they would have been at Brussels now; but they met with such strong opposition, that they gave that up, though not for some time, after repeated attempts of cavalry to charge our main body, but we formed squares and were under a hill so that they could not see us till they came close. It was very pretty to see the cavalry so often repulsed, our squares stood so firm, that nothing could break them. The cavalry withdrew. They brought up large columns of infantry, the line lay down, and put one regiment to skirmish in front. They, seeing so few men, thought they had beat us and advanced very rapidly, when all of a sudden we stood up, and poured in such a volley they could not stand and they retired in great disorder, leaving the field covered with dead. We were opposed to the Imperial Guard, who said Bonaparte led them on, and had promised them the plunder of Brussels, which they expected to have got, but I am happy to say that they were disappointed. We followed them up with our cavalry till 10 o'clock at night when we halted, but have been marching ever since. This is the fourth day, the Duke wished to have halted, but Blücher will push on. We hear the Austrians are at Lyons. [Unsigned]

3rd Battalion 1st Foot Guards

No. 64   Account of Private Henry Swan*
By kind permission of Surrey History Centre, ref. G70/33/5

The history of Henry Swan a Waterloo pensioner who enlisted at Guilford and was sworn in on the 2nd October 1810 in the Second Royal Surrey Militia and went to Ireland 1811. And in 1812 volunteered into the First Foot Guards.†

. . . And in March 1815 we were ordered out again, when all the strong and active young men were picked out to fill up the other two battalions, when we marched out of London with the Duke of York at our head to the Greenwich College yard and went onboard there and landed at Ostend and marched to Ghent from hence to Enghien. There the 3rd Battalion laid in barns and the others in the town. We lay there until the 16th of June in the morning at about 3 o'clock when we marched about 35 miles, where we arrived at about 6 o'clock. And the first job that we had was to drive the French out of the wood. In drawing the wood we lost our sections, the under wood being so very thick, when the lancers charged us. When I received a ball through my knapsack and blanket and grazed my shoulder and it knocked me down. We then drove the lancers away, when our officers ran out and took up the ground, when we ran to them. When Colonel Miller‡ received his death wound at my side, I being the left hand man of the company, the bravest soldier ever drawed [sic] a sword. At nightfall we had orders to lay down and not to unbutton anything.

On the 17th we retreated back to the plains of Fleurus where we halted for the night. The 18th being on Sunday about 10 o'clock a.m., we commenced and almost directly formed squares when the cavalry charged us ten times in succession and they could not break us. Then we formed line and was engaged so for several hours until the Duke of Wellington come to us and told us that we was agoing [sic] to be exposed against Guards, the first time that ever we was in our lives. When he said 'Now Guards, for your honour you must stand, form four deep and every man to load and lay down, and when I orders you up, you will fire a volley into them, come to the port and charge.' When he ordered us up with 'Up Guards and at them',§ which we did with a Huzza and the French turned

---

* Served in Lieutenant Colonel Miller's Company
† Swan was with the 1st Battalion at this time.
‡ Captain and Lieutenant Colonel William Miller died of his wounds at Brussels on 19 June 1815.
§ This famous phrase is very unlike something Wellington would normally say. It is possible that Swan, writing so many years later, has simply repeated what by then had

round and run for a little way, that being the close of the battle.

On the 19th we halted for a day's rest and on the 20th we went on the march for Paris, when Sir Sidney Smith came to us on the road when our commander formed into line and told us that was Sir Sidney Smith, Admiral of the Red,* when we gave him 3 times 3, which he returned, then on we went. When we arrived at Paris I was one that went with General Byng with a flag of truce. When we lied [*sic*] in Paris until after Captain Hutchinson my captain,† Mr Bruce & General Wilson was tried.‡ and then we came down to Cambrai, there we lay until the latter end of 1818, then we came to Calais and embarked for Dover where we landed and marched on our way for London, when our route was countermanded for Windsor to bury the Queen.§ After that was over, we went to Chatham where I was discharged on the 4th May 1819 with a good character, they wanting me to stop, promising me to make me a N. C. officer which I declined. I having two medals in my possession,¶ I came to Guildford and they knew me again and I was engaged on the Militia Staff where I served upwards of thirty years as a N. C. officer, a sergeant. I was discharged on the 28th October 1862 with a good character, with a pension of 1 shilling a day that being the highest pension that a militia man can get. Born 29th October 1791.

---

made the transformation from myth to fact.

* Vice Admiral Sir Sidney Smith, had been travelling home when at Brussels, the Waterloo campaign started. He visited the field of battle during the fighting and followed the army to Paris.

† Hutchinson who was not at Waterloo but is listed as being in the Netherlands during the campaign by *A Near Observer*, took command of the company on the death of Miller.

‡ Captain John Hely Hutchinson 1st Foot Guards, Mr Michael Bruce and General Sir Robert Wilson were tried by a French court for assisting in the escape of the Count de Lavalette. They were found guilty and imprisoned for 3 months. Hutchinson then re-joined the regiment at Cambrai and the others returned to London.

§ Queen Charlotte of Mecklenburg Strelitz, wife of King George III, died on 17 November 1818.

¶ He is not recorded as having received a Military General Service Medal for Nivelle and the Nive but the medal roll is not perfect.

2nd Brigade of Major General Sir John Byng

No. 65   Major General John Byng
By kind permission of Sir Michael Bunbury Bt, KCVO, DL, and
Suffolk Record Office, Bury St Edmunds, ref. E18/740/4

Nivelles, 19 June 1815

To His Royal Highness the Duke of York

Sir,

Your Royal Highness I am sure will wish to be informed of the conduct of the brigades of Guards and unfortunately that duty has devolved upon me from my respectable friend General Cooke[*] being severely wounded, having lost his left arm. In the brilliant affair of yesterday both brigades have suffered severely, but I have the authority of the Duke of Wellington to say that they highly distinguished themselves; that, from the commencement to the end of the action their conduct was most excellent. It happened that both had important duties to perform, which they most gallantly executed. At the commencement of the action my brigade which was on the extreme right, had to occupy a house and wood which it was of the utmost consequence we should keep. Lieutenant Colonel Macdonell[†] of the Coldstream with the two light companies occupied the house and the wood by the light companies of the 1st Brigade and some battalion companies of the battalion of the Coldstream, the whole under Lieutenant Colonel Lord Saltoun's[‡] command. Against this post the first attack of the enemy was made and was successfully resisted; as were the numerous efforts made to the close of the day by the enemy to get possession. The Duke of Wellington himself in the early part of the day gave his particular attention to that point and when called to the left by a serious attack on that point, he confided it to my care with directions to keep the house to the last moment, relieving the troops as they required it and the whole of the brigade, except two companies were required before the action ceased. Colonel Hepburn[§] and Woodford[¶] affording me every assistance and giving a fine example to their battalions. The conduct of Lieutenant Colonel Macdonell in defending the house even

---

[*]   Major General George Cooke commanded the First Division.
[†]   Captain and Lieutenant Colonel James Macdonell, Coldstream Guards.
[‡]   Captain & Lieutenant Colonel Alexander Lord Saltoun, First Foot Guards. His letters to his wife have been published by the editor as *Waterloo Campaign Letters, Written by Lieutenant Colonel Alexander, Lord Saltoun, 1st Foot Guards 1815* Godmanchester 2010.
[§]   Second Major, Colonel Francis Hepburn, 3rd Foot Guards.
[¶]   Second Major, Colonel Alexander George Woodford, Coldstream Guards.

when it was on fire and maintaining it as ordered, has I have no doubt been particularly noticed to you by the commander of the forces. It was admirable; as was that of Lieutenant Colonel Lord Saltoun. About four o'clock the command of the division devolved upon me; and having rode over to see the first brigade just at the time the attack was made by the enemy's cavalry, I had an opportunity of witnessing the steady manner in which they received the several charges made to their front. I had also to witness the gallantry with which they met the last attack made by the Grenadiers of the Imperial Guard ordered on by Bonaparte himself. The destructive fire they poured in and the subsequent charge which together completely routed the enemy. A second attempt met with a similar reception and the loss they caused to the French of the finest troops I ever saw was immense. I beg you Sir to understand that my presence or advice to General Maitland* never was required, I merely staid [*sic*] with him as an humble individual, when the assistance of every one was required. His judgement and gallantry directed everything was necessary. I cannot say too much in his praise or in that of the several commanders his battalions had. The conduct Sir of every officer and man of both brigades was everything I could wish, the officers on every occasion being conspicuous for their gallantry. Sincerely do I regret the loss of so many valuable officers, such excellent men. I hope I have not trespassed too far on your Royal Highness in my wish to do justice to my gallant friends and soldiers. I believe everyone who witnessed their conduct will confirm my statement. The Staff of the division afforded me every assistance, Lieutenant Colonel Sir Henry Bradford Assistant Quarter Master [General] was wounded, my Brigade Major Captain Stothert[†] has lost an arm and my Aide de camp Captain Dumaresque[‡] was shot through the body. I propose recommending to the Duke of Wellington, Lieutenant Colonel Stanhope[§] of the First Guards to do duty for Sir Henry Bradford and Captain Walton[¶] Adjutant of the Coldstream to succeed Captain Stothert as Brigade Major. Should I obtain His Grace's assent, I hope the appointments will meet your approval. I have &c. &c.,

John Byng, Major General.

---

* Major General Peregrine Maitland commanded the 1st Brigade of Guards.
† Captain William Stothert, 3rd Foot Guards was actually killed.
‡ Captain Henry Dumaresque 9th Foot.
§ Captain & Lieutenant Colonel the Honourable James Stanhope, 1st Foot Guards did temporarily stand in for Bradford.
¶ Lieutenant & Captain William Lovelace Walton, Adjutant.

2nd Battalion Coldstream Guards

No. 66   Lieutenant Colonel Daniel Mackinnon
The original is in possession of the Coldstream Guards. JSAHR, *vol. XLIII,
no.174, June 1965, republished by kind permission*

Brussels, 23 June 1815

Our division broke up from their cantonments in and about Enghien on the 16th instant. Made a forced march through Steenkerque, Braine le Comte, Nivelles, and formed on the right of the Prussians at Quatre Bras, they had been fighting all day; by nine in the evening the enemy was repulsed at all points, during the night their cavalry got into Blücher's position, taking fourteen guns and putting hors de combat 15,000 men, the consequence of which was the Prussians were obliged to fall back on Wavre.

The next morning the Duke of Wellington retired through Genappe and took up a position on the right of the Prussians covering the two great roads to Brussels, his headquarters at Waterloo. The right resting on Braine l'Alleud and extending to the Forest of Soignes, the left joining the Prussians. Our division, &c., &c., formed the centre a little above a large farm house (La Belle Alliance)[Hougoumont] which was the point attacked and occupied by the light company of the division &c., &c. The grenadiers and three other companies of the Coldstreams under my command were ordered to charge the enemy who had surrounded the house. I was wounded in the act, also had a beautiful grey horse shot, however, I did the best that lay in my power and succeeded in repulsing them till relieved by the remainder of the battalion; the whole were then obliged to fortify ourselves in the farm yard which we were ordered to defend, let what would oppose us; in short, we remained in it till night against repeated attacks of the French Army; at last it was demolished and burnt to the ground by the enemy's cannon. My poor dun horse has been almost burnt to death, he lost an eye &c., &c. My servant says he must be shot. The day preceding I also lost a horse, so you will see I have lost all three of my English horses. The ball struck me exactly on the cap of the knee so you may suppose the pain is most excruciating . . . Lord Hay was killed on the 16th . . .

PS Since writing this letter I am much better and have passed a good night and feel in great spirits. Adieu.

No. 67   Ensign Charles Short

Monday 19 June, Nivelles.

My dear mother,
I hope you will excuse my not writing to you before, but since we left Enghien on Friday morning at 3 o'clock, I have not had the least opportunity. We received orders to march at one in the morning, in consequence of Bonaparte's having crossed the Frontiers and attacked the Prussians. Colonel Woodford* was at a Ball with Lord Wellington at Brussels when the news came and they all set off directly for their different posts and arrived at them about the time we were ordered to start, in their Ball dresses. We marched at 3 o'clock (the 16th) through Braine-le-Comte, where we halted for about 4 hours and then towards Nivelles and were going to bivouac, when we heard cannon firing on the other side of Nivelles. We then marched forward and reached the place of action at Quatre Bras at about half past 7, having marched 25 miles since 3 in the morning, the men were very much fagged indeed. The 1st Brigade of Guards being in the front, went into action immediately, and in a very little time lost 500 men and nearly 30 officers killed and wounded between the 2 battalions. (Promotion for Greville† at least 10 steps or perhaps 15) our brigade was drawn up in a road on the left of a thick wood (Bois de Bossu), to be ready to relieve the 1st Brigade and about half past 8 we received orders to march through the wood in line and charge the French on the other side. However, they retired, beat throughout the day by the English, Brunswickers and Dutch though not half our army had arrived. The Belgians ran at the 1st shot. We then retired to our position and I being first for duty went on the outlying piquet it being the first time I was on this duty and nobody to direct me. I kept a sharp look out and did the best I could by placing my sentries to give the alarm in case any attack should be made. The night, however, passed off very well, though the groaning of the wounded was rather disagreeable or so, for the first time. I was very hungry the next morning having had nothing to eat since 10 o'clock the day before, but a ship biscuit. I was called in about 4 o'clock. I then went to sleep and awoke about half past 5, when I found Whittaker‡ had sent me some bread and meat and a bottle of brandy, which I assure you was a great comfort, not being able to draw rations, Lord Wellington who had not pulled off his ball dress commanded and we found it necessary to

---

*   Colonel Alexander George Woodford.
†   Ensign Algernon Greville 1st Foot Guards.
‡   This could refer to Private Kendall Whittaker who presumably served as his servant, but if so he would have fallen into the battle line; alternatively some civilian sutler or purveyor.

make a retrograde movement, rather to the left to communicate with the Prussians, who had been also attacked and beat the French back, but they made an attack in the middle of the night with the whole of the cavalry and broke the Prussians who retreated in consequence. We also retreated (the 17th) to a position about 8 miles to the other side of Genappe in the direct road to Brussels. The name of the place I do not know, you will see it in the Gazette, and it will be remembered by Europe as long as Europe is Europe. We had just arrived and pitched our blankets etc. and the men began to make themselves comfortable, when cannonading was heard and the rear guard was engaged with the French. The rear guard was composed of cavalry who came up in the night. The French took up a position opposite ours. Our right rested on a wood in which the light infantry of our division was posted it being most likely that we'd be the point the French would make their attack on. Our brigade was on the right of the first line, on a hill above the wood. We were under arms the whole night expecting an attack and it rained to that degree that the field where we were was halfway up our legs in the mud.

Nobody of course could lie down and the ague got hold of some of the men. I with another officer had a blanket, and with a little more gin, we kept up very well. We had only one fire and you cannot conceive of the state we were in. We formed a hollow square and prepared to receive cavalry twice but found it was a false alarm both times. Soon after daylight, the commissary sent up with the greatest difficulty some gin and we found an old cask full of wet rye loaves which we breakfasted upon. Everybody was in high spirits. We broke up the cask and got some dry wood and made some fine fires, got some straw and I went to sleep for a couple of hours. About ten we were formed, finding that the French were advancing to the attack in very large columns. We opened some artillery and checked them a little by shells, but soon after the light troopers commenced the attack on the wood in which our light infantry were posted and the firing commenced in prime style some Belgian light troops were in the wood and when one man was wounded, at least a dozen would carry him out so that the chief of the work was left for our men. The French were too strong for us and after about a couple of hours, they succeeded in driving us back to a large farmhouse in the wood (Hougoumont) and the rest of our battalion moved on to support the light infantry when the 2 rear companies were ordered to remain with the colours. General Byng thinking that the battalion would be too much cut to pieces, as the firing was so very rapid. The 7th and 8th companies stopped with the colours and 2 companies of each battalion of our division (I believe I told you in my last of my being recently appointed to the 7th company) we were ordered to lie down in the road, the musket shots flying over us like peas. An officer next to me was hit on the cap but not hurt as it went through, and another next to him was also hit on the plate of the cap, but it went through also without hurting him. Two sergeants that lay near me were hit in the knapsacks, and were not hurt, besides several other shots passing as near us as possible. I never saw such luck as we had. The brigade major* was wounded by a cannon ball which killed his horse and broke his arm and General Byng was wounded slightly while standing opposite to me about 5 paces. General Byng did not leave the field. Lord Wellington with his ball dress was very active indeed, as well as Lord Uxbridge and the Prince of Orange both severely wounded, the former having lost his leg, and the latter being hit in the body. General Cooke commanding our division lost his arm. The battle kept up all day in this wood where our brigade was stationed. The farmhouse was set on fire by shells; however, we kept possession of it, and several wounded men were actually roasted alive. The cavalry came on about 5 o'clock and attacked the rest of the line, when the Horse Guards and the other regiments (except a few) behaved most gallantly. The French charged our hollow squares and were repulsed several times.

The Imperial Guards, with Napoleon at their head, charged the 1st Guards, and the number of killed and wounded is extraordinary, they lie as thick as possible one on top of the other. They were repulsed in every attack and about 7 o'clock the whole French army made a general attack for their last effort and we should have had very hard work to have repulsed them when 25,000 Prussians came on, and we soon drove them like chaff before the wind, 20,000 getting into the midst of them played the very devil with them and they took to flight in the greatest possible hurry. The baggage of Bonaparte was taken by the Prussians and the last report that has been heard of the French says that they have re-passed the frontiers and gone by Charleroi hard pressed by the Prussians. The French say that this battle beats Leipzig hollow in the number of killed and wounded. Our division suffered exceedingly. We are to follow on Thursday. Today we bivouac near Nivelles. Lord Wellington has thanked our Division through General Byng and says that he never saw such gallant conduct in his life. The 7th Hussars behaved very badly on Saturday, they were ordered to charge the Polish Lancers, and when they got to them (the lancers remaining steady) they turned about and away they went, the lancers then charged them and the Horse Guards and Blues charging the lancers overthrew them and cut them nearly all to pieces. The Horse Guards and Blues have behaved famously. Lord Uxbridge would have been taken only for our infantry, in consequence of some of the cavalry running away and he rode up to the company and said he

---

* Captain Sothert was killed.

owed his life to them and that the French were beyond the frontier before 12 o'clock. There never was such a glorious day. Everybody agrees. Send me the Gazette. It will tell you more than I can. You must excuse the mistakes I have made I am in such a hurry. I will give a fuller account of some little things relative to myself, the narrow escapes we had and so on when I have time. I had my horse killed. It was very beautiful to see the engagement though horrid afterwards. The French killed a great number of our wounded soldiers. We have taken 120 pieces of cannon. The Prussians are coming up every hour and cheer us as they pass. I have a great deal more to say, but I have not time as I must be back at the camp by 8 o'clock. All the baggage was sent to Antwerp in case we should have been defeated yesterday. The number of prisoners is immense. I must conclude. God grant that I may live to see you again. We have only 2 officers killed but several severely wounded. My love to you. I have heard nothing of Major Hodge*. I remain your dutiful and affectionate son,

C. W. Short

No. 68   Ensign James Hervey

By kind Permission of the National Library of Wales, Reference Aston Hall (2) 3991

To Mrs Lloyd,† Hotel de Flandre‡

Genappe, 10 a.m. 16 June

My dear Mrs Lloyd,
The enemy attacked both the Duke & Blücher without making the slightest impression on either, indeed both are rather more advanced than in the morning.

Adieu, yours sincerely,
J. M. Hervey

---

* Major Edward Hodge 7th Hussars was captured at Genappe and lanced to death when it appeared that he might escape or be freed on 17 June .
† The Lloyds of Aston Hall Shropshire.
‡ The Hotel de Flandre was situated on the Grand Place at Brussels.

Third Division of Lieutenant General Baron Alten
5th Brigade of Major General Sir Colin Halkett
2nd Battalion 33rd Foot

No. 69   Ensign William Thain
By kind Permission of Hertfordshire Archives and Local Studies, ref. DE/MI/86379

J. Thain Esq., Newcastle upon Tyne, England*

Brussels, 19 June 1815

My dear father,

I have arrived here after one of the hardest fought and bloodiest battles that has yet been recorded. The French having crossed the frontier, we marched from Soignies & we attacked them on the 16th and remained masters of the field, but about noon next day retired pursued by the enemy and took up a position on some heights near the village of Waterloo about 9 miles from this place where we bivouacked and were again attacked about noon yesterday. We carried all before us until about 7 o'clock in the evening when fortunes appeared to change against us, it was about that hour that the squares were ordered to advance against the enemy's artillery, the 33rd forming half of the front and the whole of the left face, that I received a musket ball through the left arm a little below the shoulder, but as the bone is not fractured I hope to be soon well again. We all thought from the strength of the enemy and the manner in which their artillery mowed us down in the evening that we had lost the day, but I am happy to inform you that the French are retiring in all directions. The Belgic cavalry refused to charge but a square of some Dutch infantry repulsed a charge of cavalry very gallantly. Our division which was 7,400 new is now only 1,500. Feats of personal courage were shown by every individual and the British have placed the ball at the feet of the northern allies who will find no difficulty in kicking it on to Paris. French Imperial eagles have been paraded through the streets by a party of our dragoons and columns of prisoners are marching through continually for Antwerp to be embarked for England. Never was [there] a more glorious day for our dear country. I have spoken with the Paymaster General just returned from the advanced posts who says that the French are entirely destroyed and the number of cannon which we have taken cannot yet be counted. Bonaparte's private second carriage with all his baggage has just come in escorted by Prussians who have continued the pursuit. Our whole army has been engaged, our little brigade took twelve pieces of cannon themselves and General Halkett

---

* His father, Mr James Thain of Newcastle.

with his own hand made a French general officer prisoner.*

My arm is very painful, I shall therefore only request you to write to Sophia† to tell her I shall soon recover and to remember me most affectionately to all my friends. Yours affectionately,

William Thain.

When we attacked the French on the 16th they occupied the famous Austrian position on the heights of Jemappes. I had a horse killed under me that day.

2nd Battalion 69th Foot

No. 70   Captain George Ulric Barlow
By kind permission of The British Library, ref. F176/55

To G. H. Barlow,‡ Bart & KB, Streatham, Surrey

Ypres, 25 February 1815

My dearest father,

An officer of the regiment being on the point of leaving us for England tomorrow, I avail myself of the opportunity of enclosing a few lines for Fanny. I have nothing particular to tell you except that I leave this place on the 1st March for Brussels on an excursion of pleasure & shall positively return by the 10th of the month & then hope to receive some accounts of you all, my last are of the 24th & 26th December. I have taken the liberty of drawing a bill on you at *Glyn's* dated the 24th instant & payable to our Paymaster Mr Vyvian§ on his order for thirty pounds if you will have the goodness to accept it, my Uncle William will refund you the amount; I draw on you as my uncle may be at a distance from town, the bill is payable soon after sight.

Give my dearest love to my mother & accept the same my dearest father of your most affectionate son,

G. U. Barlow

---

* His brother Colonel Hugh Halkett captured General Cambronne, therefore likely making the story of this officer's famous outcry during the final stand of the Old Guard to be a myth.

† His sister Sophia Thain.

‡ His father Sir George Hilaro Barlow (1763–1846), Governor of Fort William, Madras.

§ Paymaster Philip Vyvian.

No. 71   From The Same

Menin, 24 March 1815

My dearest father,
We do indeed live in an extraordinary age, each succeeding year teems
with fresh wonders, more outstanding even than those that are just gone
by, and which have yet scarcely ceased to excite amazement; surely we
are awaking from some long dream in which a Louis on the throne of
France was a mien agreatly beguiling the imagination, but the dream
scene having now flitted past, we arise alive to the painful reality of
finding a Napoleon in his place, scarcely will our senses allow of believing
that this usurper has taken possession of a throne with as much ease
& rapidity, as a lawful owner enters upon the enjoyment of his estate,
did not the events of yesterday, afford too melancholy and irresistible a
proof of what would otherwise stagger credulity and of which I myself
was a painful witness.

It will be necessary to tell you that Menin stands precisely on the
boundary line dividing Flanders from France & is situated upon the little
River Lys, here about thirty yards in breadth & over which is thrown
a small bridge; the frontiers following the course of its stream. I had
just returned express from Courtrai, having been sent thither with the
Moniteur of the 21st containing the news of Bonaparte's first entry into
Paris & his proclamations. Having been thoroughly drenched to the skin
by the way & almost in the act of changing a rare hubbub on a sudden ran
through the town and a French general came galloping in; he announced
that Louis the eighteenth was close at hand escorted by a party of
cuirassiers. We had scarcely time to stand to our arms when the cavalcade
appeared & stopped at the bridge. Upon arriving the king desired his
escort would return into Lisle, which they I am told were very unwilling
to do; but his majesty insisted & their parting was very affecting; many
of the soldiers rode up to the window & kissed his hand, whilst several
in the most determined manner declared they would accompany him;
whether he would allow them or not & a few are therefore permitted to
enter.

The 69th were drawn up in the main street and received the cavalcade
with all due honours. It was composed of but four carriages, that of the
king leading, drawn by six very indifferent post horses, the traces being
of rope. Upon arriving at the colours, close to where I stood, it stopped
and he let down the window. The commanding officer desired me to
step up to the carriage and enquire what were His Majesty's wishes and
which I accordingly did. There were no post horses in the town, and as he
expressed a desire to proceed to Bruges I offered to go on in advance and

prepare the requisite number [at] Roussclaere which he thanked me to do. The commanding officer, however, thought proper to send forward two dragoons and thus I was saved some hard riding, in addition to that of the morning. The remaining carriages were filled with his suite, consisting of different noblemen, among whom was the Prince of Neufchatel & Wagram, Marshal Berthier, the old friend & companion of Bonaparte, whom he has attended throughout all his campaigns & of whose success he is supposed to have been one of the most efficient causes.

I will leave you to conjecture my dearest father, what were my feelings on beholding this unfortunate monarch again rejected from the bosom of his ungrateful country, to seek an asylum in a foreign land, and with what cordiality I joined in the shouts of 'Vive le Roi', which were rather more sincere than those he has of late been accustomed to hear. From the little opportunity I had of judging, he seemed very resigned, though the noblemen in his carriage were much affected at once more entering upon a state of exile & shed tears.

Ever since both by night and day carriages belonging to his suite & friends are continually passing through this town and as we are but nine miles from Lisle, everyone is obliged to undergo strict examinations, at several of which I have been present; General Drouet a notorious partisan of Bonaparte has been released from confinement & commands at Lisle a numerous garrison and we feel rather awkwardly situated, not being able to push any posts into the French territory for the purposes of observation & the people of this town are said to be unworthy of trust as spies; everyone therefore sleeps in his clothes accoutred, so as to turn out at a moment's notice.

We quitted Ypres on the 21st instant after having passed in it four very pleasant months; our departure I may say with all truth was much regretted, as the conduct of the troops throughout that period was most exemplary & good, and the sum of money put in consideration by a pretty numerous garrison was such as to keep the bourgeois in good humour, had they even been otherwise inclined. Ypres was never before so considerable a military cantonment and the good conduct of the 52nd & 69th Regiments has I believe contributed to leave rather a favourable impression [of our?] national character.

As for myself I am perfectly well & in good spirits, but shall be obliged to do my duty on horseback as *the foot* although *certainly better & stronger*, is not yet capable of active service. Could the smallest idea have been entertained of what has of late so marvellously come to pass, I should have fitted myself out rather differently, but for this there is at present no remedy, and as we are in a Christian like civilised country I trust to be able to contrive matters pretty well.

God bless you, my dearest father and all beneath your kind roof, give my very best love to everyone & accept the same of your dutiful & affectionate son,

G. U. Barlow

No. 72   From the Same

A small public house near Soignies, 22 April 1815

My dearest father,

Your kind letter of the 29th of March from Streatham came to hand whilst the regiment was in the act of marching out of Tournai on the 4th instant. In times like these and in our situation nothing affords me greater comfort & happiness than hearing from those we love and esteem. It is therefore needless to mention what kind of reception any arrival from Streatham meets with from me. As you make no particular mention I think that you continue to enjoy your usual good health & spirits, these are too constant. I think you have for ever engaged in your interests and it makes me happy, I think that they never can desert you.

In reply to your enquiries regarding my foot, I have only to repeat that it continues in much the same state, as long as we continue on a fine flat road it does very well but if our march should be across a ploughed field or difficult ground I could no longer keep pace with the rest and have therefore obtained permission to do my duty on horseback. This being the case I propose looking out for some country beast, that which I ride at present being far too good to expose to the chances of war and should any mishap befall it, I am entitled to no recompense whatever.

I thank you for accepting my bill, on our pay master, it is I presume the last of the two drawn by me upon him. It was for thirty-two pounds dated I think on the 14th February, the former was for fifty-five pounds in payment of the horse & was addressed to Frederick; should you have honoured them both in consequence of my uncle being out of town, the latter I have requested when convenient to reimburse you in their joint amount.

I am most obliged by your offer regarding an introduction to any general officer, but really am at a loss to fix upon one in the view you mean, everyone is anxious to provide for his friends and the peninsular war now brings forward a host of claimants. Brussels I am told is crowded with these gentry and the list was quickly filled up as soon as opened; in these circumstances we must lay upon our [arms and await?] the turn of events.

Since writing last from Menin we have consecutively been to Courtrai, Tournai, Ath & lately moved to the cantonments we at present occupy after having spent a few days at each of the above mentioned. I have now made an excursion to Mons, the regiment is dispersed about in the neighbourhood of Soignies, a small town nearly half way between Castries and Mons. I am quartered alone at a small ale house by the roadside such as you would probably see in England on the highway with the sign of the Leg of Mutton and Turnips. The people, however, are the civillest creatures in the world, and as they furnish me with a clean bed I require nothing further.

God bless you my dear father, and those belonging to you require my most affectionate love to everyone and believe me ever your dutiful & affectionate son,
G. U. Barlow

No. 73   From the Same

Lens, 6 May 1815

My dearest father and mother,
We shifted our quarters from Soignies yesterday afternoon to this place, a town half way between Ath and Mons on the great high road. I am as usual lodged in a town house about two miles out and riding by accident into the village where the Adjutant General resides, learn that the post for England will be despatched in the course of the afternoon. I lose therefore not a moment in giving you some account of our proceedings up to the very last opportunity of consequence, although thrown together in a very hasty manner imagining that these would be more satisfactory than nothing at all.

It is now pretty generally understood that the campaign will commence about the latter end of the present month; at least everything will be in perfect readiness for that purpose, unless pacific arrangements at Vienna or Frankfurt should settle what has now every appearance of being decided by the sword. Cavalry, infantry, artillery, commissariat are all in motion along this frontier and the country unmercifully crammed with troops. I am in a very small farm together with the two officers of my company and twenty five men lodged in the chief barn; such are the delightful consequences of an army of seventy or eighty thousand men being assembled in one's neighbourhood.

Pray offer my best remembrances to Miss Page for her very kind letter which I received near Soignies on the 25th last month; she informs me of a circumstance which till then I had never heard, namely my aunt's recent indisposition at Brighton; this in some degree accounts for my not having received any advices from my uncle or herself in answer to the letters I have severally addressed to each.

On the 24th of last month I wrote a bill on you for twenty-five pounds payable to the order of Mr Vyvian our Paymaster; I have money enough in my uncle's hands to answer this as well as all my former demands & only trust that the advances, which you have been so good as to make me from time to time will not occasion you any inconvenience. I would draw on my uncle's at Glyn's but as he is now out of town & my bills are at ten days sight, I am necessitated to trespass on your goodness, as being more immediate on the spot.

Give my kindest love to my mother as well as all the dear little girls, remember me also to Miss Page and believe me to be my dearest father, your most dutiful & affectionate son,

G.U. Barlow.

The money I have drawn is for a fit out and various expenses attending preparations for campaigning.

No. 74   From the Same

Neufville, 31 May 1815

My dearest father,

Your kind letter of the 19th instant came to hand on the 26th and imposes on me the agreeable trick of returning you my best thanks for the affectionate sentiments therein expressed; offer also my love to dear little Fanny and Anne* for their respective shares in the acceptable packet and to the latter my congratulations on her improvement in letter writing, the style and turn of which were very prettily expressed and particularly attracted my notice.

I am much concerned at your message respecting my aunts health, it is really melancholy to terminate ten long years of sickness and find one self in nearly the same state as at the commencement of the mournful period, this is sufficient to break the stoutest hearts, or the very best spirits; I am sorry at thus accounting for the long silence to the letters some time since written by me to each, but trust that a repetition of the warm sea bathing, which produced such wonderful good effect last year, will in like measure be now attended with similar beneficial consequences; I propose writing again in a few days to the same quarter.

Contrary to general expectation, you see, we have thus long remained tranquil without hostilities being committed, on either side. Report states us to be only awaiting the arrival of the hardy sons of the north, previous to finally throwing aside the scabbard. In the meanwhile the enemy remains by no means idle and is employing every method to meet the impending storm; he has put in requisition all the horses of the

---

* His younger sisters Frances and Anne.

gendarmerie throughout France to remount his cavalry & laid hands on all the carts, wagons & beasts of burthen throughout French Flanders; their peasants are therefore coming over to us daily with their vehicles in order that they may not fall within this undiscriminating seizure. Desertion alone among his soldiery are also very numerous & the only hope of success left to him is to [cause?] dissensions among the allies and raising insurrections in the country or Germany where an unfortunate sequence of events has created for him a considerable number of partisans & [particularly?] Saxony & Poland; it will be hoped, however, that [the side?] of justice will finally prevail.

In the meanwhile we are passing our time very pleasantly in the different farmhouses and cottages around the little village of Neufville; the country people are extremely hospitable and obliging throughout, nothing wanting to complete their happiness, but a continuance of that tranquillity which they have recently been enjoying some months past & which is now so lamentably about to be attacked. Already has the work of destruction commenced, 12,000 acres of fine rich land having been flooded around Mons, to secure the works of that place from a hostile attack.

And now I must conclude with desiring you to offer my very best love to my mother and all the good folks of the [?] and that God may ever bless you all is the sincerest prayer of your most dutiful & affectionate son,

G. U. Barlow

No. 75   From the Same

Field of Battle, eight miles from the [City of?] Brussels,19 June 1815

My dearest father,

I am writing a few lines in haste on my knee, it is now sunrise and I take therefore the earliest opportunity of informing you that an all kind providence has preserved me in two most sanguinary conflicts on the 16th & 18th instant. That of yesterday was perhaps one of the severest ever fought, Bonaparte commanding in person & the Imperial Guards both horse & foot having made the most desperate & repeated attacks to force the Allied army from their present ground, but all to no purpose. The enemy were the assailants and their cavalry commanded by the King of Naples,* elated by some trifling success on the 16th, made repeated charges, more especially the cuirassiers upon our infantry formed into squares, but never succeeded in breaking any one of them. These charges were made in the most daring manner up to the bayonets of the

---

*   This was untrue.

infantry & the muzzles of our cannon, but every attempt was punished with frightful loss. The artillery on both sides was very well served & numerous and that of the British particularly so, as the present scene alas too desperately bears clients; this field is strewed with helmets, cuirasses & horses. Seventeen guns are taken [on this?] part of the field & I believe many more in other directions. The combat terminated only with the night, which I believe alone saved the routed remains of the enemy as our cavalry followed in full pursuit & many prisoners have been made although their numbers I know not. The field is covered with the Imperial Guard, who were the forces chiefly employed in this direction.

As for poor George, providence saved him on two or three occasions in the affair of the 16th. A large body of cuirassiers charged the 69th before they could form into square & consequently before they could resist their attack & therefore dispersed them; the cavalry rode over George, who was incapable of running on account of his foot & therefore he lay on the ground till they passed by & then getting on his legs & he rejoined the 42nd who had not been attacked & were formed in square a short distance to the right. He is yet very lame in consequence of the exertions of yesterday.

I am sorry to inform you that I must draw a bill in consequence of the casualties of yesterday. My horse attended by my servant was in the rear of the army in a village about dusk, when a Dutch soldier whom I have not been able to discover, attacked & wounded him most severely & took the horse from him by force; my poor servant has had his arm amputated in consequence, such you see is the consequence & confusion of this general action.

God bless you, & with my love to all, believe me to be your most affectionate son,

G. U. Barlow.

No. 76   From the Same

Camp near Paris, 7 July 1815

My dear father,

It is now the 7th of July and since the few harty [*sic*] lines written to you & ever since the 19th June I have scarcely had an hour which could well be called my own. Excepting on the 23rd we have been making daily forced marches & these rapid strides brought us on the 1st of July in sight of the great city of Paris. I have moreover [been] of late pro tempore filling the situation of brigade major and undertook it at a period of no ordinary difficulty. Upon the loss of every adjutant but one, most of the sergeant majors and the absence of all the regimental books, rendered it rather a troublesome office.

So decisive was the tremendous blow struck on the 18th ultimate that tyranny has never been able to recover from its effects, which are best seen by our rapid progress this far, but for a wonderful celerity the march has resembled a triumphant progress rather than an invasion of a hostile country. Not a shot has been scarcely fired since the business of Belle Alliance, & here we are on the 7th of July encamped in the Bois de Boulogne.

To attempt a description of these wonderful events would exceed the limits both of my time & paper. I will therefore as briefly as possible recapitulate the chief circumstances which have occurred since the opening of the campaign. We left Soignies on the 16th of June, & marched to Nivelles in the direction of Fleurus; Bonaparte having concentrated his arm at Maubeuge on the 14th, entered Belgium and drove the Prussians from Charleroi on the 15th. Marshal Blücher then resolved to give him battle on the 16th notwithstanding a large corps of his army under General Bülow was not yet arrived. This took place at Fleurus and the Prussians after a most gallant resistance against very superior numbers being worsted, were obliged to retire with severe loss both in men & cannon.

As I have said before, we moved from Soignies on the same day to their succour, but on reaching Nivelles there was ample work enough for ourselves. Marshal Ney had penetrated within a league of that town. Our division (General Alten's) hastened forward & found General Picton's division with some Belgic troops engaged against very disproportionate numbers, which the arrival of our reinforcement by no means equalised. It was a fine summers evening about five o'clock when we first came into fire & we soon found ourselves under a heavy cannonade. The division was then formed into squares of regiments, a measure which the proximity of the enemy's cavalry and the total absence of that species of force on our part, rendered absolutely necessary.

The scene of action lay upon ground diversified with little dales & gently rising slopes, covered throughout with rye & wheat which here grows extremely high, between five or six feet. In the course of manoeuvring the 69th for a moment found itself at the bottom of one of these little dips & being formed in square was perfectly secure. A certain personage,* who shall be nameless, sent down an order that the 69th should deploy into line. It was obeyed & scarcely done when a strong body of French cuirassiers as if by magic showed themselves close in rear of our flank at about fifty yards. As I have before mentioned, we happened to be in a small hollow commanded on every side with high gentle hillocks & the height of the surrounding corn precluded a view of everything beyond the close distance.

---

* This refers to the Prince of Orange.

The enemy taking advantage of it, approached close to the regiment unperceived, & rushed at us from an ambuscade on the flank of the line, a situation which rendered us perfectly defenceless. An attempt was made to form square, but the proximity of the cuirassiers and the instantaneousness of their attack, rendered it impossible. In a flash they rode through & over our little battalion of 400 men. One colour was taken in the confusion which ensued, the other was preserved. Many of our unfortunate men were sabred & wounded but no prisoners made, as the neighbouring regiments taking warning from our example quickly threw themselves into square & before the cuirassiers could reform, they kept up such a terrible fire that the greater part of our gallant enemies perished on the spot.

Night falling, the whole of the French army retired into some neighbouring woods and we bivouacked upon the field of battle.

I have been thus circumstantial in my details as the event of losing a standard has been blazed in the French papers and I have therefore attempted to account for such a circumstance & presume this case to be one of misfortune rather than dishonour; perhaps almost unavoidable. This opinion formed upon minutely examining the very spot next morning; whither curiosity by the circumstance interested me to proceed & which I coolly dispassionately surveyed.

As for George, when he saw that the game was up & resistance at an end & some of these armour bearing cuirassiers at his back, he had [the] presence of mind to throw himself down on the ground and the enemy passed by & over him. He had heard before of this species of ruse & being incapable of running, no other resource was left to him; he waited a while & then getting on his legs made the best of his way to the square of the 42nd Regiment & was thereby rescued.

Towards dusk George returned to the spot where he had left his servant & horse. Upon my arrival I learnt that some Belgic, Brunswick or foreign hussars had attacked my poor servant & wounded him so desperately in the arm, that the arm was obliged to be amputated next morning, taking away at the same time my much valued horse [the?] good Barossa. Never since have I ever been able to obtain any tidings or sight of her; the thief probably went direct to Brussels & disposed of his ill acquired spoil, thus was I left destitute for the march & retreat of the ensuing day, the 17th, deprived also of my coat & cloaks to keep out the heaviest rain which it has been my lot perhaps ever to witness. Will you credit that on the 17th I walked between thirteen & fourteen miles to the position of Waterloo in country cross roads of the most execrable description. The circumstances of the occasion, however, kept me up & I was determined to hold out to the last; as towards evening the enemy's cavalry came on along the pavé

& made many prisoners of those who had straggled or stopt [*sic*] behind the march of the columns.

Night came on & with it the flood gates, it however seemed to be opened as it poured in torrents without intermission. We had no canopy but the sky, nothing to eat, thus hungry; drenched & sleepless around a fire which barely emitted heat, & would scarcely burn, did we await in a cornfield the dawning of the 18th of June.

The tendency of all our movements the preceding evening and having before witnessed the system of our great chief all conspired to make me think that a general action would ensue the following day for the possession of Brussels. The Prussians made a corresponding movement in retreat on Wavre & the whole English & Hanoverian army during the evening & night of the 17th by various routes & different columns, marched into the position of Waterloo, our force as near as I can ascertain being rather more than 80,000 men of all sorts & descriptions including the Prussian division of General Bülow, but of course not the remainder of Marshal Blücher's army.

The position of Waterloo upon which the battle for the destinies of Europe was about to be fought, was nothing more than a range or moderate rising ground, touching upon the right the pavé leading from Nivelles to Brussels & extending on the left to the high road from Genappe & conducting to the same metropolis. Here two routes formed the summit [of] an angle, meeting near Braine l'Alleud, to which the position of the British army served as the base, or third side, its flanks leaning upon & thus covering either approach. It was fine commanding open fighting ground, but traversable in all directions by cavalry & cannon. The French artillery lined the whole summit of these heights. The army was drawn up in order of battle behind them a little way down the reverse of the slope so as to be perfectly concealed from the enemy who could by no means get sight of its force or disposition and according to his own, confirm he was kept in perfect ignorance of its intentions.

To get the anxiously desired peep behind, it was necessary to come up to the muzzles of one hundred & fifty pieces of cannon placed in different directions steady troops on their rear & the French position of a corresponding order & parallel to our own. The party quitting their [position] therefore laboured under certain disadvantages, which, however the superiority of the assailants, in this case ought to have counterbalanced; one corps being left to watch the Prussians. Bonaparte brought the remaining four entire and the whole of the Imperial Guard (itself about twenty thousand men) and upwards of two hundred guns against the Duke of Wellington's army.

The day became fair about eleven & the cannonade on both sides commenced. An impetuous attack was first made against the right, where the Guard and German Legion held some loop-holed houses & a small cypress coppice; the Germans* quitted their post after making an admirable defence. The enemy having set fire to the building, the Guards were fortunate in having maintained theirs against repeated assaults & very much distinguished themselves. Abattis thrown across the road impeded the enemy much & after sending parallel efforts they directed themselves against the centre where General Alten's corps was posted.

This happened about two o'clock when our friends, the cuirassiers again showed themselves, who by the rapidity of their advance forced our artillery men to quit their guns; these last, however, galloped away with the limbers & traces so that the enemy had no means of carrying them off over the ploughed ground; those on foot took shelter in the squares of infantry, which had been formed in that order since the commencement of the attack & were a short distance in rear, all perfectly prepared. The cuirassiers & dragoons then attempted to pierce the squares but were received with such a terrible fire that they were thrown into the greatest disorder & obliged to fly with all possible speed.

Such was the result of the first attack of the cavalry which I had conceived to have been a reconnaissance on the part of the enemy, but to my great surprise, this was succeeded by a second on the left, then a third and afterwards by a variety of others, during the course of these hours till five o'clock on every part of the division & Lord Hill's corps these attacks were reiterated in the most daring manner. Their officers we saw [urging them] on in a very gallant style and their men followed up the example; but the squares stood firm throughout and not one of them was for a moment disordered. The enemy cavalry repeatedly dashed into the centre of the British centre and at each attempt were received with such destructive vollies [*sic*] from the surrounding squares to excite my astonishment at such useless destruction, nor were they discontinued till the flower of the French cavalry both in men & horses were almost wholly destroyed and the remainder could not be brought to act with any effort at a period shortly afterwards when their service were most arguably required as will be presently related.

Between six & seven o'clock Bonaparte ordered forward his infantry; several large masses were put in motion and began to ascend the British position in various directions covered by the fire of their batteries and [the] cannon were then ordered to be poured against them to retard their advance. As soon as they had arrived at the proper distance the infantry

---

* The German troops at Hougoumont were from Nassau and only those in the woods were forced to retire; those within the chateau complex fought there throughout the battle.

commenced and after a very heavy fire on both sides succeeded in making them retire. Eight o'clock came and found the battle yet undecided, for shortly afterwards four solid masses of the Imperial Guard infantry advanced and made a most formidable attack. These fellows came up with carried arms and in the most determined manner to within seventy or eighty yards of the heights along which our infantry were placed and poured a terrible fire, two pieces of cannon accompanied them and being placed affront our brigade, which was formed en masses, raked it most severely with grapeshot as did shells from some more distant howitzers. This was indeed the crisis of this eventful day, both armies were in close contact and hot action and the cannonade really tremendous along the whole line as the entire artillery of either army were in full play to support their respective parties in an effort which was to decide the fortune of the battle, an effort worthy of the great stake for which each contested.

No. 77   From the Same

Paris, 27 July 1815

My dearest father,
After an interval here of some few days I again resume my pen for the purpose of giving you a description of those objects worthy of notice which have come within my observation during that period. Paris has the character of being a city containing more for the inspection of foreigners than perhaps any other in the world and my own private opinion is much inclined to subscribe to the justice of the same remark.

From the telegraph on the top of the heights of Montmartre you have a delightful view of the surrounding country, and at one scope take in nearly the furthest limits of this great metropolis. It is said to stand on more ground than London, but I question much the accuracy of such a statement. Paris possesses, however, one advantage over its rival, namely in point of appearance. The exterior of the houses being chiefly white and as at this season of the year there are so few fires for which also fire wood is used, the clearness of the atmosphere formed a pleasing contrast to that sombre, smoky darkness which hovers over the site of our metropolis; but this latter impresses the stranger with far greater ideas of opulence and national prosperity. Here the eye ranges with delight over the variety of spires & public edifices. Uncertain how to decide the preference amid so pleasing & numerous an assemblage, here it remains fixed on two or three objects, the Hotel des Invalides, the Pantheon, the Church of Notre Dame, the only things of the kind and not equalling St Paul's, Westminster Abbey &c., &c.

Descending from thence you find yourself on the boulevards, which *are* peculiar, I believe to this city alone. Fancy an avenue of fine large trees similar to that which runs by Madame [Pirzzi's?] house but the road of which is twice the breadth, circumventing almost the whole of Paris and with the chaussee's branching off to every quarter of the kingdom planted for the post two or three miles all along their sides in the same fashion and it will give you some idea of the avenues to this capital. Previous, however, to entering, it is necessary to pass a Barrier, here your vehicle is generally met & detained by a douanier or custom house officer & here the precautions of an arbitrary government are most visible, these Barriers are in fact in many Guard houses planted at convenient distances with which to communicate between each, so that no carriage or cart driver can pass; consequently in times of trouble, Paris may be most strictly blockaded.

And now were a stranger to be blindfolded on his arrival at these gates and the bandage not removed until he was set down somewhere near the Tuilleries and if you should restrict his walks within a circumference of almost three miles of which the above palace was the centre, he would most assuredly pronounce Paris to be the first & finest city in the world, a city laid out by someone comprehensive mind which had uniformly kept a new elegance & regularity of structure throughout and had selected this spot to exhibit a *chef d'oeuf* of its taste whose completion it had superintended and witnessed. The Seine is here nearly of the same breadth as the Thames about Kensington and which with three or four bridges of very light & elegant structure, is highly ornamental. Near its banks close to the Pont de Concorde stands the magnificent palace of the Tuilleries, a habitation worthy the monarch of a great nation. Behind are three celebrated gardens, always open to the public, divided into parterres, shrubberies & walks, with fountains in the centre, the whole laid out with a regularity & care too uniform to be natural & consequently differing from our English notions of taste, but they are nevertheless very striking and correspond with the princely edifice to which they appertain. After beholding these, I no longer wonder at a foreigner's surprise on being shown St James or Carleton House as the residence of our sovereign's edifices insignificant, in comparison with that which I have already described.

On going out of the gardens of the Tuilleries you cross the Place de Louis Quinze, celebrated as being the place of execution to his unfortunate successor and then enter upon the Champs Elysees which is planted thick with fine trees & resembling Kensington Gardens & is pretty enough extending nearly to the Pont de Jena; this is a new bridge extremely beautiful, built by Bonaparte and has a delightful appearance conducting to the Champ de Mars. When the quays that are now building along either banks of the Seine are complete, the tout ensemble of all the above objects added to the House of Commons and the venerable Hotel des Invalides with its gilt dome & cupola crowning the whole will constitute to produce an admirable effect.

Hereabouts Paris is certainly beheld to the best advantage and variety of design seems to pervade every part, and what was so magnificently planned and commenced by the Louis's has with similar ability been continued by a Bonaparte, for this assuming despot neglected nothing which might contribute to pamper the Parisian vanity in seeing their city enlarged and enriched. The arbitrary imposts which have impoverished the outposts & ruined the commerce of France have in some fashion been expended on the Imperial residence, and thus whilst at Marseilles, Bordeaux & Rochefort, the character of the man appeared in its true light of an oppressor, at Paris it at least shone in the fictitious glass of a benefactor.

But step not over the prescribed limits of this pleasing circle, for beyond its boundaries the contrast is most disagreeable & unvarying. You traverse throughout narrow dirty streets, wretchedly paved & having no walk for foot passengers. The shops are neither so numerous or magnificent as in London; that pleasing bustle & hurry of business, that superabundance of population is wanting and a dull stupid mediocrity pervades the whole, partaking neither of the commercial activity of the city, or the elegance & quiet of the West end of the town. To this observation, the interior boulevards form a pleasing but the only exception; they are planted with trees precisely the same as those I have described in a former part, and present to an Englishman the singular spectacle of avenues of foliage, in the middle of a large city, with houses on either side & paved streets, a mixture which at first sight seems rather unnatural, though custom may in some degree reconcile it to the eye. Setting these aside a small region whose limits are very circumscribed, Paris cannot bear any comparison with London, in the one excellence, however great, is confined to one inconsiderable space, in the other it is more generally, though not so strikingly at first sight diffused.

In attempting thus to draw something of a parallel between these two cities, I have studiously endeavoured to avoid any undue influence or natural prejudice. The acquisition of knowledge and the enlargement of one's ideas which thereby enables us to form a more correct judgement of things by the making of comparisons, is one of the great advantages of travelling. The insular situation of Great Britain, added to a peculiar series of political events have contributed to exclude her inhabitants from the continent during the greater portion of the last fifteen years and thus doubtless you may find a greater portion of that natural lies amongst us than perhaps any other race of people. There are few who feel a greater attachment to their native soil than myself, I am desirous therefore on all occasions of counteracting in a certain measure the influence of such sentiments so that they may not attain too great a degree of sway, being assured that they will always maintain their due preponderance.

A description of the interior of all those edifices & buildings before mentioned shall be reserved for some future letter, in the meanwhile my dearest father, in answer to the latter part of yours of the 10th instant, I have to observe, that if you could contrive to get me confirmed in my present situation, an important point would be gained. I am not yet eligible for a family, this five or six weeks, but am at present pro tempore filling the situation of brigade major to this brigade & have held the same ever since three days integument to the Battle of Waterloo.

General Halkett who is wounded at Brussels recommended a friend of his own, but the appointment was not confirmed. Colonel Elphinstone commanding the 33rd Regiment & then senior officer together with the Adjutant General of this division have written to headquarters on my behalf a month since, but no notice has been taken of it; perhaps these documents have been mislaid or lost; in the meanwhile a new brigadier has superseded Colonel Elphinstone and another general succeeds to the division pro tempore, to him both I & Colonel Evans* [are] utter strangers. General Halkett is now duly expected here & will no doubt in time have some friend of his own appointed.

This General Halkett is a very anxious man, he is acquainted with my Uncle William[†] and with Mr Clarke's[‡] brother in law, notwithstanding this he has never taken any notice of me whatever for particular reasons.

I most positively request that neither you nor my Uncle William will make any representation whatever & Mr & Mrs Clarke on my behalf; sooner than this I should prefer returning to my duty in the 69th; any other channel, particularly addressed to headquarters would be acceptable.

I have drawn a bill on you for twenty seven pounds dated I think July 20th payable to the order of Major Evans 5th West India Regiment.[§] This is on account of a horse I was obliged to buy at the same time, saddle

---

* Major De Lacy Evans became a lieutenant colonel immediately after Waterloo and he would appear to mean the same man here although he refers to him as major at the end of the letter.
† William Barlow was a London merchant who lived at Chatham Place.
‡ This would appear to be Sir Simon Haughton and Mrs Catharine Clarke (née James) who were distant relatives.
§ Major De Lacey Evans was extra aide de camp to Sir William Ponsonby at Waterloo. He is associated with the so called 'Delancey Disposition' which purports to show the dispositions of Wellington's troops early on 16 June, his copy being the only version extant.

&c., as that which poor Blackwood* was bringing up to me was all lost & plundered after the battle of the 18th, the sum total of the animal & his equipage amounted to sixty seven pounds, forty of which I have given myself, it was impossible to procure anything fit for a brigade major to be seen upon at a parade as it would have looked so disreputable to see a Staff officer mounted upon a miserable animal, a country pony, and to have thus marched past Lord Wellington & all the emperors as indeed the day before yesterday & I fear that it may yet be necessary to make some farther trespass on your liberality, for as the losing of my horse has made my expenses beyond my means, but I will avoid doing so if possible. Were I confirmed in my present situation such necessity would no longer exist & until such confirmation is made I am not entitled to any pay whatever.

No. 78   From the Same

Paris, 10 August 1815
In the Bois de Boulogne

My dearest father,
I received your two kind letters of the 4th together with its enclosures on the 8th instant and have to assure you how much I feel this new proof of your kindness in addition to the many former instances which you have shown, as early as I can recollect, in my behalf. The encomiums bestowed on the little narrative of the 7th of July, are really more than such a thing can merit; it was drawn up with no particular care, as I had never imagined that the letter would have gone beyond the circle of the family, or perhaps of one or two friends; otherwise it might have received a further degree of attention, previous to falling into such high hands.

Yesterday there was a grand review of the Russian Imperial Guard and the duke of course fully occupied in the society of emperors & kings; today or tomorrow therefore I will deliver to him your letter; I shall take care also to write to Greenwood† according to your instructions.

Give my love to Richard‡ for his very nice letter, and assure Miss Page how kindly I take her half of the sheet of paper. It gives me great pleasure to hear that she is doing as well & advancing towards a perfect recovery. I will shortly send each of them answer, Mr M. shall also be remembered.

Last week we daily expected orders to quit this metropolis for the purpose of being cantoned in Picardy or Normandy to which provinces all our cavalry are already marched and are anon stationed in the

---

* Captain Robert Blackwood, 69th Foot was killed at Waterloo.
† The Army Agents, Greenwood, Cox & Hammersley of Craig's Court.
‡ His brother Richard Wellesley Barlow, then aged about eleven.

neighbourhood of Rouen. But these rumours have died away and it is reported that our stay here will be protracted for some further time, until things become a little more settled. As for any disturbance of consequence in this city, it is out of the question during the presence of our army; but what new revolutions might take place when it is once marched off, no one can conjecture. Paris is full of officers & soldiers from the disbanded army on the Loire, & after what we have already witnessed of the fickle character of this nation [we?] should be prepared for anything.

In the mean while Paris begins to swarm with English bucks & families; among them we have Sir John Malcolm;* the Duke has received him with great attention & lent him a carriage &c. to drive about this place, which piece of intelligence I gained the other day from a friend & relation of his.

I am in much haste and must conclude with desiring you to present my best love to my mother & all the school room & believe me to be, your most dutiful & affectionate son,

G. U. Barlow

No. 79   From the Same

Paris, 1 September 1815

My dearest father,

For the first time in my life do I feel under an embarrassment when sitting down to write to you, the ever ready pen seems now at a loss for a commencement, but silence any more would be criminal and be it mine to remove that veil of delicacy, which would be misapplied in sheltering any longer the enormities of guilt.

Alas my dearest father you have had but one fault, one of the most amiable, a guileless hue in too much kindness in that goodness which has led you to judge of others by yourself. Letters shown me some years back by that unpalatable woman on whom the laws of nature and the fetters of speech yet free me to impose the name of mother and acts themselves infinite in number & more powerful than words have convinced your son, who it was that alike deserved to be called the best of husbands as the best of fathers. The forward glance of iniquity shall regard the transactions of twenty-six years & seek in vain for one instance to the contrary, has it ever known a want or a wish ungratified has me frown ever obscured the ray of habitual and all melting tenderness & patience. But for you I would be ashamed of the blood that flows in my veins, of an existence derived from such demon like origin.†

---

* Colonel Sir John Malcolm had served in the East for many years; Wellington knew him from his India days and was a close friend.

† It is unclear what his mother Elizabeth (née Smith) was guilty of, but adultery

But it is done, the work of enormity is complete and nought remains but to assume that attitude which the laws of justice and our country so fully authorise. The die is cast and we must accommodate ourselves to the result. I candidly acknowledge that my own personal sufferings regarding the miserable object in question are little indeed, for alas I never knew the sound of maternal fondness, no not even the slightest whisperings from my earliest period of being able to be acquainted with them. It is for you alone (& that a great God is witness). I do really feel how sincerely I adopt your sorrows and make your situation my own.

One source of comfort still remains, may it be superabundant and perennial, may you ever find it in the midst of that family whom providence has bestowed & trust but to make amends for the conduct of their unnatural, their guilty mother; stand in the middle of us and as the church service tells us, never will you have reason to be dismayed. The world and its affairs will frequently call particular members from the united society.

They, I trust, will however never be found wanting to the present head; while those whom sex and circumstances more especially allow of being encircled around you will (God be pleased) be destined to afford constant subject for consideration & comfort; that may thus God bless you most respected & beloved of fathers will be the constant prayer of your most dutiful & affectionate son,

G. U. Barlow

No. 80   From the Same

Paris, 25 September 1815

My dearest father,
It occurred to me the other day, when on the point of writing to Mr Greenwood regarding the matters connected with your kind letter of the 29th of August, that the subject would receive more attention coming from you, than from myself, the immediate object of such a communication. Under this impression I was induced to decline entering on any correspondence with Mr G, who from his situation is no doubt fully surcharged with similar applications from every quarter and one originating with so humble an individual as myself, would gain nothing perhaps, but a civil answer. As you have therefore so kindly offered to speak on my behalf, I will thank you to do the same at a convenient opportunity. The point in question is one of great importance, and the attaining of it has always been attended with considerable difficulties, which are now doubly augmented by the present state of things, so large

---

seems likely, as his father applied for and gained a divorce in 1816.

a portion of the army being employed on actual service and the inefficient part of it now at home being so soon about to be reduced on half pay.

As for my brigade major-ship, it is already decided that I should keep it no longer; a letter from General Halkett at Brussels has just been received, stating that the nomination of the brigade major having been placed at his disposal, he had recommended a Brevet Major Love* of the 52nd regiment for that situation. With this officer I am very well acquainted, he is at present wounded & somewhere in the rear, I believe Brussels, & has previously been attached to the general in the same capacity; this does not occasion me therefore any surprise. Every man will naturally provide for his own friends & acquaintances. I shall therefore very quietly descend from the major into a minor situation whenever my successor arrives.

As for the duke, he is extremely taken up with the various important military & political arrangements now making between France & the allied powers. I paid him a visit the other day & encountered the hero with a great bundle of papers in an anteroom. He stated having a perfect remembrance of you, asked if I was not on the Staff; my reply was that I held a temporary situation. 'Let me see you to dinner at six o'clock'; with these & a few hasty words I took my leave & repaired thither at the appointed hour, when a large party was assembled, & of course nothing more could then pass between us.

Give my kindest love to all [the?] little girls as well as to Miss Page for her letter; [tell ?] Louisa† that I have sent Lady Hobhouse‡ two excellent catalogues of the pictures & statues in the Louvre. With Sir Benjamin Hobhouse you are of course acquainted by character. He & his family have been making a short visit to Paris & the death of a beloved son who was in this regiment and fell at Waterloo,§ a particular friend of mine, was the melancholy means of making me known to him. They promised to take charge of any little packet & deliver them safely. I wish you would call on Sir B[enjamin] for his civility & attention towards me. He expressed also *a particular desire* to become acquainted with you & I wish it also very much. Lady H[obhouse] is a charming agreeable woman & so indeed are the four daughters, who accompanied them. God bless you my dearest father, believe me ever to be your most dutiful & affectionate son.

G. U. Barlow

We have every reason to believe that the British Army will winter in this

---

* Captain James Frederick Love received four wounds at Waterloo but survived.
† His sister Louisa who was to die in 1821 at the age of only 23.
‡ Lady Amelia wife of Sir Benjamin Hobhouse, 1st Bt.
§ Captain Benjamin Hobhouse, 69th Foot.

country. I shall therefore endeavour & pay you a visit in the course of the autumn & am not without hopes of being able to succeed.

No. 81   From the Same

Paris 5 November 1815

My dearest father,

I take this, the earliest opportunity since my arrival here of presenting you with some account of my proceedings. The beginning of the journey was not attended with very auspicious circumstances; that is to say the stage broke down about four miles on the London side of Cuckfield.* We were fortunately about to descend a hill & proceeding rather slowly when the axle tree of one of the fore wheels snapped; it was fortunately a moonlight night and the driver immediately perceived the accident and drew up; another step & we would have been upset. The horses were immediately taken from the carriage & the guard proceeded on and returned with two post chaises from Cuckfield; into which we put the luggage and passengers & thus we arrived at Brighton on Tuesday morning.

At two o'clock the same day the packet sailed and after a very tempestuous passage we all landed at Dieppe on Wednesday noon, about twelve o'clock. At *two* the diligence set out for Rouen; by this therefore you will see that I had not time to write a line with the information of my precious self having been safely conveyed across the water, that short space having been occupied in clearing our baggage from the custom house, breakfasting &c., besides there is a regular English post by way of Dieppe.

Thursday I spent at Rouen in rambling all over the town, which is a sad dirty place & contained nothing worthy of notice but a fine cathedral. I left it at night by the diligence & arrived here on Friday morning. Upon enquiry I found that the whole army had broken up from camp and was gone into cantonments, my regiment is at a small village about nine miles from hence on the road to Orleans called Visus [Wissous?] & whither I shall proceed this day.

Yesterday about twelve o'clock I waited on the Adjutant General, upon announcing my name and being ushered in, he immediately remembered my business and without any preamble he said that the Duke proposed to put me on the Staff, in the event of a favourable opportunity offering itself; nothing therefore remained for me to say, but that I had taken the earliest opportunity of waiting on him (the Adjutant General) to thank him for his kind advice and to show [that?] I had paid to it every possible attention, [and a?] trifling conversation followed and then I took my leave, such therefore is the present state of affairs.

---

* Cuckfield is one mile west of Haywards Heath.

I am writing at present in much haste and in a coffee room which is a perfect Babel among a sad confusion of tongues; present therefore my very best love to Miss Page and all the dear little girls and accept the same my dearest father, your most dutiful & affectionate son,

G. U. Barlow

No. 82 From the Same

Paris 19 November 1815

My dearest father,
We are now fast approaching to the conclusion of the present month, and from certain intelligence which has lately come to my knowledge, I am strongly led to believe that we shall return to England ere the ensuing Christmas. The long contemplated measure of reducing the inefficient second battalions is shortly about to take place and the present state of politics admitting of such a step, there is every reason to imagine that it will be no longer delayed. From a person who has the means of procuring good information, I learn that all the necessary arrangements had actually been made, and were about to be published in the General Orders, when an officer arrived from England and prevented the same being put in execution. The report at present in circulation is that the British Army will not move from the neighbourhood of Paris until that article of the treaty has been fulfilled which stipulates that certain fortresses shall be put into the hands of the allies. These are expected to be delivered up in the course of the ensuing week and then the British Army will be put in motion for the frontiers of Belgium, and that portion which it is intended to send home is to take the route of Dieppe, which is only 120 miles from this metropolis. Sir H. Torrens arrived three or four days ago and no doubt his journey is in some degree connected with the important arrangements which are shortly to be made.

In my last I omitted to mention a circumstance of which it will be therefore necessary here to notice Sir B. Hobhouse repeated his former kind offer of using his interest in my behalf and alluded to Lord Sidmouth* by name, who is a particular friend; I of course returned my best thanks. Possibly by this time you have been so fortunate as to meet him; he is generally to be found at the Carnatic Office in Manchester Buildings, Westminster, about twelve o'clock; it is the last house on the right hand side of the street & as it were suspended over the water. He expressed a strong wish to become acquainted with you; in the event of his coming to Streatham let the armour be put out of sight and everyone be cautioned against mentioning either my name as connected with

---

* Henry Addington, 1st Viscount Sidmouth, politician and previous Prime Minister.

Waterloo or anything relative to those transactions. That subject is yet a fertile source of affliction and is the source of correspondence between me & his relative Mr H.[enry] Hobhouse.* It was only this morning that I received a letter from Mr H. respecting a gun the property of my late friend; & his accounts I have yet to [obtain?] from Sir B[enjamin] [from whom] I have also lately heard. He of course relates on other subjects and gives me a very entertaining account of the journey homewards; he corresponds like any young friend of my own age, rather than as one who is old enough to be my father; so much notice does he take, & so grateful are his feelings for a circumstance which really merits nothing like the consideration that it has received.

The winter has now commenced in earnest; we have had two falls of snow, not very heavy and the mornings become extremely cold, so as to impede your usual walk before breakfast. There is no temptation here to practice that beneficial custom, the roads in general being so very bad and execrably muddy.

Offer to all the school room my very best love and accept the same, my dearest father, of your most dutiful & affectionate son,

G. U. Barlow

No. 83   From the Same

Paris, 7 December 1815

I have to acknowledge the receipt of your two kind letters dated the 22nd & 27th & which I have thus long deferred answering for the purpose of being able to communicate the result of those steps which you recommended me to take. I shall commence a detail of my proceedings with transcribing the following letter written & left by me early on Monday morning left at General Barnes' house. 'Sir, at moments like the present, when the time of his Excellency the Commander-in-Chief is doubtless sufficiently occupied, it is with some diffidence I bring myself to intrude either upon his or your attention, in soliciting you to call His Grace's notice to anything concerning an individual so humble as myself. His kind intentions, however, which you were so good as to signify in a letter dated the 30th of September last, induce me to address you on the subject of the present communication. My regiment being under orders to proceed to England during the course of the ensuing week, this circumstance, I trust will excuse the liberty I take in requesting to be informed, whether any opportunity is likely to offer for the fulfilment of those kind intentions'.

---

* His son, Henry William Hobhouse was in the Honourable East India Company Service.

I am writing the present in a very noisy coffee room, and from memory commit the above to paper, it is almost word for word the same as the original which you shall shortly see. Today (Thursday) is almost passed by, & I have not received any answer whatever; this application is not therefore likely to meet with success, the more so as instead of any augmentation being made to the Staff, a reduction of no less than twelve or fifteen officers has taken place in the Adjutant & Quarter Master General's departments & my old brigade, Sir P. Belson's* is likewise broken up. Upon calling to pay my respects to General Torrens, I found also that he had quitted Paris ten days previous. To Lord Hill I presented my letter and had the honour of dining with his lordship yesterday. He said, however, nothing calculated to inspire any hopes & after some trifling conversation regarding Lord Teignmouth[†] & one or two other personages known to himself & me we parted.

It now remains for me to add that the regiment marched off from hence this morning for Boulogne & I shall follow in the course of an hour or two. We shall reach the sea coast on the 20th instant, Dover is to be the place of our debarkation or Harwich I have yet to learn.

Remember me most kindly to Miss Page for her letter of the 7th December [and her?] little difficulty. I am glad that circumstances placed me some distance from home when this affair came before the court, even in reading Miss Page's letter I was agitated by a thousand conflicting emotions, that it would be in vain for me to attempt to describe but no more of this horrible subject.

I have taken advantage of your goodness also to draw upon [a] bill at ten days [only?] for fifty pounds payable at Messrs Glyn & Co. and will feel much obliged by your honouring the same, but more of this when we next meet. Give my kindest love to all, accept the same my dear father of your most dutiful & affectionate son.

G. U. Barlow

---

* Lieutenant Colonel Sir Charles P. Belson, 28th Foot, took command of the 8th Brigade after Waterloo.

† John Shore, 1st Baron Teignmouth (1751–1834) was a British politician who served as Governor General of India from 1793 to 1797.

Fourth Division of Lieutenant General
Sir Charles Colville
4th Brigade of Colonel Mitchell
1st Battalion 23rd Foot

No. 84   Unknown Officer*
From The Regimental Records of the Royal Welch Fusiliers, 23rd Foot,
by C. H. Dudley Ward, vol. 1, 1929

In a letter written by 'a British officer of the 23rd Regiment, dated
June 20th 1816, to his friends in Dumfries' with reference to his late
lamented colonel, occurs the following:

'Almost his last words to me were, 'I am happy, I am content, I have done
my duty'. I buried him, on the evening of the 23rd of June, with honours
of war, on the mound of the only windmill at Braine l'Alleud, about one
mile and a half to the rear of the right of the position. To show how
much he was beloved by his men and officers, I may give the following
anecdote: Among several of the soldiers of his regiment, who were at the
same farmhouse with him, mortally wounded, and inquiring anxiously
after their colonel, there was one who supported a very bad character,
and he had been frequently punished. To this man I said, to learn his
attachment, 'He is just dead; but why should you care? You cannot
forget how oft he caused your back to be bared?' 'Sir,' replied he, his eyes
assuming a momentary flash and his cheek a passing glow, 'I deserved the
punishment, else he would never have punished me.' With these words,
he turned his head a little from me, and burst into tears.'

No. 85   Lieutenant Colonel Thomas Dalmer,
Regarding the death of Captain Thomas Farmer, killed at Waterloo
From The Regimental Records of the Royal Welch Fusiliers, 23rd Foot,
by C. H. Dudley Ward, vol. 1, 1929

To Edward Farmer Esq. Bacheldore

Hamelincourt, February 1816

---

* It is impossible to be entirely certain of the identity of this officer. However, no
uninjured officer would have retired from the battle without being disgraced. This
leaves another wounded officer (although neither officer returned as wounded in the
regiment had obvious Scottish connections) or a surgeon. This leads me to suspect he
is no other than Surgeon John Munro, already famous for saving Colonel Ellis from
a blazing hut.

Sir,

In reply to your inquiries relative to the effects of the late Captain Farmer of the 23rd Regiment, Royal Welch Fusiliers, I have the honour to inform you that in consequence of my not being acquainted with the residences of my late friends' connexions, I was under the necessity of directing his personal property to be disposed of, according to military custom, by public sale. A statement thereof together with Captain Farmer's accounts, have been transmitted to Messrs Greenwood & Co. by the regimental paymaster, and the balance of £9 3s 3d paid into their hands.

I am sorry it will not be in my power to recover the canteen you have described, but from my recollection of the articles specified, I am well aware that among the plate there was not any article but what was quite modem and almost new, if any article of an old date had been found, it would have been kept, until an opportunity might have offered of returning it to his family.

I am not in the least aware of what property Captain Farmer may have left at Ostend or at the depot in England. An officer has been detached to the former place to ascertain what baggage belonging to officers may be there, and if any of the late Captain Farmer's can be found. I will direct his regimental and company accounts to be delivered to the paymaster, and will attend to any instructions you may wish to give relative to all his private property that may be found there.

I have the honour to be sir, your most obedient servant,
T. Dalmer Lieutenant Colonel*

No. 86   Lieutenant John Enoch, Regarding Captain Farmer
From The Regimental Records of the Royal Welch Fusiliers, 23rd Foot,
by C. H. Dudley Ward, vol. 1, 1929

Hamelincourt, France 27 May 1816

Sir,

I beg to inform you in reply to your letter of the 12th April on the subject of prize money due to the late Captain Farmer my much lamented friend, that it is not necessary you should be in possession of certificates from the commanding officer of the Royal Welch Fusiliers to enable you to apply for the shares due to him. I find on referring to the page lists (duplicates of which are in possession of Archibald Campbell Esq, Suffolk St., London, the general prize agent for captures made in the Peninsula and to whom you are to make application) that your brother was serving in the 23rd Regiment during the periods of the *Second* and *Third* payment and that

---

* Lieutenant Colonel Thomas Dalmer commanded the regiment at Waterloo after Sir Henry Ellis was fatally wounded.

he was also serving as a captain during the periods of the *Fourth* and *Fifth* payment of the prize money alluded to. With respect to the *Sixth* payment, I find he was not present with the regiment at that period. I have now Sir to apologise for not answering your letter at a much earlier date and to assure you that the hurry of business and numerous applications of the same nature occasioned my mislaying your letter, and which alone caused the neglect. I further beg to assure you of my readiness at any future time to afford you any information and assistance in my power. I have the honour to be, Sir, Your very obedient humble servant,

John Enoch Lieutenant & Adjutant Welch Fusiliers

No. 87   Private Thomas Jeremiah
By kind permission of Llyfrgell Genedlaethol Cymru/
The National Library of Wales, ref. NLW MS 22102A

… On the 23rd of March 1815 we embarked at Gosport for Ostend where previous to our disembarkation for the first time to the greatest part of us we got served out with 60 rounds of ball, we 2nd battalion lads begun by this time to smell powder. I forgot to mention a circumstance that occurred to me a little previous to this period above mentioned, in those days they were particularly strict about the soldier's necessaries and on one occasion at the inspection of our regimental necessaries I was found with one other soldier deficient of a shirt. Neither of us upon being asked what we had done with the above articles of regimental necessaries could give any satisfactory account to our sergeant who failed not to make and forward a report to the officer commanding the company. Some of those non commissioned officers are without exception the most artful rogues in existence, they are generally encouraged by their superiors to give every information and report every little tittle tattle that is done in and out of quarters by the multiplicity and the artfulness of their reports they generally turning themselves to [the] readers notice and promotion. I do not mean to give a swearing censure to all the non commissioned officers in the army for there are some among them who are men of integrity and honesty. But to proceed, this officer without further [ado] ordered us both to confinement. Next morning our adjutant came to our guard room and warned us for a court marshal [*sic*] when at 10 o'clock of the same day we were brought [before] a tribunal or court of officers and there tried, found guilty, sentenced and then after returning to our imprisonment. There was nothing left undone but our enduring [the] utmost rigour of the law, at 4 o'clock the same evening we were both brought out of the guard room when we saw the regiment drawn up in punishment order, that is in square, the flogging apparatus or the triangle was fixed ready in all its serious, to me indeed it had a most powerful influence. The adjutant* had commenced to read our court marshal, the other soldier was first to strip and tied up while my situation was very little more agreeable than my comrade who was already cringing under the terrific lash, he received 3 hundred lashes in the usual way, the commanding officer ordered the drummer to take him down, then I was to strip; soon after I had stripped and the drummers began the disagreeable office of tying up I was striving to summoning up all the little remaining courage that was left; after standing trembling with anxiety at my approaching fate. By this time [the] drummer had taken his place with the instrument of torture in his hand and the word 'one' quivering on the drum major's lips when all of a sudden an escort of the 88th Regiment† marched in to the regimental square. The commanding officer gave order to suspend the punishment for a moment and ordered the escort to march the prisoner into the square, who was a deserter from our regiment. He deserted 2 or 3 days previous to my confinement, when he came back the commanding officer questioned him as to where he'd been and what induced him to desert. He answered the colonel rather abruptly, having a bundle in his hand. I was all this [time] tied up waiting to receive my punishment, when the colonel ordered this deserter to open his bundle wherein was a pair of stockings and a shirt; the stockings a sergeant's name on them, when they were returned to the owner, and [what] was my surprise and joy when my colonel came to the drum major and desired him to take me down and produced the lost shirt for which I was so unjustly going to be punished, for it had my name in full on it. My joy on this occasion is better imagined than described, the shirt never the less was not returned to me until [I] had undergone the sentence of another court martial who after investigating into every circumstance relating to it they sentenced me to be honourably acquitted from all imputation of making away with the shirt, thus ended this almost fatal adventure.

I must now return to the bay of Ostend where as I said before, the young soldiers begun to smell powder and talk of the cannon fever which, however, by the cheerful and undaunted advice [of] our old and tried soldiers, the young ones soon learned to dispel those tremendous fears and soon showed that they were as great a [set of] fire eaters as their more fired veterans. We after disembarking we were taken [on] boats along the canal to Bruges, from whence we proceeded to Ghent where we had the honour to be doing duty over Louis the 18th as a guard of honour, the Welsh Fusiliers always at the post of honour and that without tarnishing [it]. In Ghent our regiments was quartered on the inhabitants

---

* 1st Lieutenant John Enoch.
† The Connaught Rangers.

of whose conduct during our stay I shall never forget, for their most kind and hospitable behaviour towards us, as we were quartered on the most respectable of the inhabitants of the town. Some of us poor soldiers found a strange contrast when sitting at table with and by the side of the most wealthy gentlemen or the greatest Van Tromps* in the Netherlands; and the same time surrounded by the most fashionable and the greatest blaze of female pride and beauty that the kingdom could produce and where the strictest etiquette of table discipline was maintained. Thus surrounded by such a brilliant blaze of beauty and fashion stood the untutored and rustic British soldier, among which were some of our sister isle's, who in the field of battle never found themselves so awkwardly situated as at the table of a rich burger where everything that was good and delicious was smiling them in the face and inviting him here for the first time, badly found his courage fail him; he said he would sooner be after taking a good meal of 'file oyes' and a flagon of decent butter milk at home in old Ireland with his own sisters & mother. We got the [taunt?] of none of these good people whose kindness I never can appreciate [enough].

We proceeded from here to Grammont where we were brigaded with the 51st and 14th Regiments, the command of which devolved on the colonel of the 51st, Colonel Mitchell;† these 3 battalions remained in brigade until we arrived at Paris. In Grammont we were quartered on the most respectable of the inhabitants who as well as the good people of Ghent were very kind and hospitable to us. Here we were destined to be under a variety of sensations from the many conflicting reports that daily and hourly arrived from the French frontiers. Some stated that the French army under Napoleon in person were moving down upon the English in terrible force, threatening like a deluge to overwhelm everything before it, others stated that the Prussians were the object of their attack which subsequently proved to be so.

From the beginning of April until the 16th June we remained among these good people who were never tired of administering comfort to the British soldier and generally speaking their kindness in some degree rewarded by the simple homely and good and cheerful good disposition of the British soldier who those good people found to be very agreeable guests. People at home will scarcely believe the good understanding that prevailed between those good natured Flemish people and the rustic English soldier; were I to state all the pleasing circumstances that occurred to my knowledge it would extend the limits of my little book. I even

---

* Dutch Admiral Maarten van Tromp had made this name famous in England.

† Lieutenant Colonel Hugh Henry Mitchell commanded the 4th Brigade of the 4th Division, comprising 3/14th, 1/23rd and 1/51st his memoirs are published as *The Life of a Regimental Officer* published in 1913.

to this day cannot forget those kind people who in some measure made amends to the young soldiers for the loss of their mothers. I cannot forget how comfortably I was situated in my billet when the restless ambition of Napoleon caused the war trumpets to sound and to rouse me from the circle of this good family where the first sound that saluted my ears in the morning before I was out of my bed would be by little Maria about my own age [&] little Thomas up getting coffee, dunking bread and butter, eaten, which would be prepared on a scale more fitting for my colonel than for me. If my reader has not been in Holland he will be a little surprised when I tell him that they use no shugar [*sic*] with their coffee which they make use of 4 or 5 times a day, but instead of shugar everyone is supplied with a piece of shugar candy which completely softens the bitterness of the coffee. Thus, happily situated the time rolled along in harmony, never did I put away such pleasant days as I did among those kind hearted Flemish, who were never easy unless they were contributing something towards the happiness of the British soldier, if my blessing can make them happy they have long got it.

But to proceed, the 3 regiments above mentioned were employed over a large plain, filling up holes and levelling the hills and preparing it for the passage of cavalry for the whole of the British artillery and cavalry were to be inspected by Lord Wellington and Prince Blücher and the greatest part of the most distinguished generals of the allied army were present. England never produced such a heap of cavalry as on this occasion for all their disposable troopers were on the ground even to a man. Well I remember the day for being then a young soldier and not being used to see large armies, I longing for this day to come. The display of such a fine body of cavalry could not fail to produce a degree of national pride and anxiety not only among the young soldiers but likewise among some of the most tried and experienced officers of the army. This grand display if report says truth did not fail to attract the notice of Napoleon himself who it was sayed [*sic*] that he was in disguise in the apparel of a fruit monger, it was inserted in the news of the day that he had the satisfaction to inspect the British cavalry, for whom he expressed the greatest admiration for their martial and soldier like appearance and at the same time expressing his deep regret that such a fine body of men should be brought from their happy homes to be marched against him. More experienced and tried soldiers who knew nothing but victory, he might ask, as the Russian General Miloradovitch did to Murat when at Moscow, if the French had no air to breath in their own country, no water to drink, no earth to cover their remains and if they had, why leave their fine country to fertilise the desolate waste of Russia with their remains, when you are dead.

I believe about the 23rd of May the roads leading towards the plains where the review was to take place were crowded with dense masses of horse and foot as far as the eye could reach; the sight was truly grand and tended to rise [*sic*] the spirits of the young soldiers to see so numerous a body of cavalry and composed of the flower of the youths of England, Ireland and Scotland, well clothed, fed, paid and drilled, and I think almost matchless in their native courage as well as physical strength to put their valour in force which the French found to their cost on the 18th of June 1815. But about from 10 to 11 o'clock the troops were streaming from every direction until by ½ past 11 the plains seemed literally choked up, by ¼ to 12 the whole of the artillery and cavalry were drawn up in three lines which extended nearly an English mile. Every eye was now on the stretch bent on the direction where the heroes of so many battles were expected to come from. At this time I was on the spot and the men were dismounted, every man standing by his horse ready to obey the signal, conversing and shaking hands with their countrymen belonging to the infantry who came by thousands to see this grand display of their native cavalry. The scene was truly affecting to see, brothers, cousins and not unfrequently [*sic*] you see the father and son belonging to different regiments embracing each other and while the father was holding his son by the hand and giving his fatherly advice to be a faithful and obedient soldier, he little thought that at the same time that was the last as it happened to many, yes they little thought that in 26 days more their worldly affairs would be all over. While looking [at] these affecting scenes, I all of a sudden could see a dense column of smoke and dust arising to the south of the plains. We were immediately informed that these were the two champions who subsequently conquered Napoleon [who had] defied the united efforts of all Europe for more than 15 years. Thus about 5 minutes before 12 o'clock noon, when the advanced squadrons of Prince Blücher's Cossacks entered the area followed closely by all the Allied generals and a large concourse of people among whom were the above mentioned heroes. At this time the British trumpet sounded to prepare to mount, in a moment all was silent as the grave, not a word; we could hear a pin fall when in an instant 18 thousand men were in their saddles and steady. By this time the allied generals had reach[ed] the front of the centre where they received the salute according to custom. The martial bands and trumpets had a most striking effect and the whole had a most imposing effect and it went off with the grandest éclat without any accident. So ended this grand review, the morale effect of this scene was very great on the inhabitants who had formed and entertained rather an unfavourable idea of the British prowess, but after witnessing the display of such a fine body of men as our cavalry are generally composed of, the opinion of the Netherlanders were unanimously in our favour, the spirit that prevailed among the military and civility were such as the time called for.

We remained in our respective quarters subject to the most strict military discipline particularly the maintaining of good order in our quarters, notwithstanding the unremitting vigilance of our active and good colonel and the unceasing attention of our officers to prevent crime, still there were a great deal of offences committed and but for the humanity of our colonel many of us would undoubtedly have felt the weight of the law. There were very few instances of corporal punishment in our regiment in comparison with other corps, not as I can pretend to say that there were less crimes committed amongst us than others but Colonel Ellis* was in possession of those rare qualifications without which no man can ever hope to aspire to honour and dignity among his superiors or be even popular among his men and officers, but Colonel Ellis was respected by his superiors, he was loved by his officers and loved and feared by his men, so that the whole regiment lived in harmony under his mild administration and although that he ruled with an iron rod, it was covered with velvet. I remember one morning after 2 men, countrymen of my own, were tried by court martial we marched out of town to see the sentence into execution, it being the custom of the service at this time to tie the culprit to a tree or any convenient place in [the] middle of the field about 2 miles out of town , those 2 men were tied up and flogged, the first of those men was one of those hardy Welsh mountaineers who generally have more courage than judgement, received 3 hundred lashes in the usual manner. As terrible as this punishment was it could not as much as extract one sigh from this hardy Briton, the next was a man of more delicate feeling for he shouted loud before the lash had touched him but the word was that he cried out in Welsh which caused us all to blush to think that the Irish and English should ridicule us because that one Welsh could not stand the lash, but to prove them wrong, the man who had already received his punishment volunteered to take this fellows punishment so he should not disgrace the hardy Welsh by cringing from the lash. Our good and kind colonel wisely observing the effect this fellow's conduct had on all the young Welsh lads, caused him to be taken down and took him by the ear and gave him such a kick as became a coward who could not stand his punishment without disgracing his country.

The punishment being over we returned to our quarters, I observed as soon as we left the field the owner came with his axe and cut the fatal tree down, this I have seen done in France and in Portugal several times, nor will they make use of the timber of such a tree to any other use than

---

* Lieutenant Colonel Sir Henry Walton Ellis.

to consign it to the flames, to show their aversion to such a cruel system of punishment.

The time was fast approaching to rouse from this life of inactivity to active service. Our time between the 23rd of May and the 16th of June was spent in comparative tranquillity. During this interval of time we were employed in exploring and ascending the mountains to see if we could see or hear any of the French army whom we expected to see moving down upon us every day.

At last the long looked for day came when the regiment was assembling on the 16th of June, the orderly dragoon galloped up to our colonel; every eye was turned on him for we expected something extra. Our colonel lost no time after he read his orders in issuing orders to march for Quatre Bras, we were allowed 10 minutes to retire to our quarters and bring all with us. During this time the town was crowded with horse and foot, regiment after regiment of cavalry and artillery came thundering through the streets, all blazing with anxiety to meet the French this day.

We marched about 7 leagues in our white jackets,* we bivouacked on the open field by the road until next morning, when at day break a cheerful sight appeared, the whole of the German cavalry were filing off by us for the plains of Waterloo. As soon as these had cleared our front our colonel gave the cheerful word to throw away the white jackets and put on our fighting coats. This done we proceeded on our march, in about an hour we passed the 52nd Regiment who were serving their men out with one ration of spirits. We marched by them in gloomy silence cursing our quartermaster for not having provided us with the same dose. But the object was [be]fore us and with us every eye was bent forward in the direction that we supposed the enemy layed [sic]. This day being the 17th we commenced our march pretty cheerfully considering that we had no rations since we started the previous morning. We begun to feel the wolf biting, formed hard marching and little sleeping is none so pleasant without nourishment. By the evening of the 17th we were greatly fatigued from the extreme inclemency of this day's weather and from marching nearly 8 French leagues† since 6 o'clock in the morning in the greatest rain that ever I saw, the heavens seemed to have opened their sluices and the celestial floodgates bursted open, so showered the 17th on us. I need not mention that all we had about us was completed soaked; by the same our blankets which was on the back of our knapsacks were completely drenched. Then where was our dried beds, but that was not the greatest of our thoughts, for hunger bites harder than a wet shirt. By 6 o'clock in

---

* When in barracks soldiers were dressed in 'fatigue jackets' of white.

† The French league has differed over time; but the most accepted usage was that one league measured three miles. Therefore they marched twenty-four miles that day.

the evening we arrived near a town of considerable size where we halted a short time when the word forward was given we passed through this town where we saw [a] great number of soldiers of different nations and among the rest we could see for the first time the wounded coming in upon cars and wagons. All of a sudden the town was put in great confusion by seeing a great body of cavalry approaching at full canter all expecting them to be the French; however, they proved to be the Belgian cavalry, to the eye as fine a body of men as ever I saw. The men appeared to be of the first order and their horses not inferior to any of our cavalry. However, I do not answer for their prowess in [the] field, time will show that. When they had passed by we moved forward at a considerable pace up to our knees in mud and it continued to rain with the utmost fury all the time until we arrived near another town outside of which we camped and began to pitched [*sic*] our blankets up to shelter us from the rain, for we had no tents up. We had marched with such rapidity as to outstrip all the baggage and stores. We had now orders to send parties of men for rations in the town that was quite convenient to us. I was one of the party, when we arrived in town all we could see was the points of bayonets and [famished?] soldiers and all busy employed in getting rations not by a regular distribution out but by marauding.* It was utterly impossible to get anything for love or money, for those [famished?] soldiers had stripped the town of every kind of provisions. By much to do we got about half a ration of spirits, not one ounce of bread could be obtained in all the place, so we returned to our camp with this half ration of spirits per man. This was poor comfort after 2 days hard marching and not as much as a mouthful of anything except water. When the men got this liquor, some of them it made quite drunk, for not having anything on the stomach, you would wonder to see a man apparently strong after taking about 3 table spoonful of spirits dropping down quite drunk. Just as we arrived in camp the bugle sounded to arms and we were ordered to move to the front to a position that the Duke of Wellington had chosen for the night while we were giving the spirits out to the men. They were all ready by this time to move off, it was high time for me to look after my things and accoutre myself, but when I came to the spot where I had left my arms and accoutrements they were not to be found. It was useless to enquire of my messmates if they knew anything of my things for they themselves were too busy with their own things to be concerned about

---

* It would seem that Wellington's legendary strict controls of the soldiery to avoid marauding did break down during this sequence of the campaign. It is hardly surprising with the commissariat having been left far behind and with little chance of detection, that regimental officers appear to have turned a blind eye to marauding and even partook of the food thus obtained.

mine, so that I became rather an object of merriment among my comrades, than of commiseration, one would ask how the blankets sold in town, others would ask if my gun was at the armourers and so forth, this is the kind of pity they have for a young soldier in trouble. There were some who were good enough to assist me to find my appointments but my search was all in vain. But when all the regiment was accoutred there was necessarily one suit of appointments left, so glad I was after shedding a profusion of tears to be clad in my full uniform, but not my own, but this was no time for choose [choice], for it was any fish that came to the net, while the enemy was quite close. So now I was in the ranks as well another, we moved to the ground appointed for us, where we laid upon our arms that night. The rain continued with the same unabated fury during the whole of the night, towards the morning the weather got a little lighter and as the day dawned it had nearly ceased. Raising then we were ordered to light fires and clean our arms & our appointments, by this time hunger began to be felt pretty generally. Myself and my comrade took 2 wooden [cudgels?] each and our haversacks and went to seek for something to eat; when we got about a couple of fields beneath of the camp we saw a pig and calf closely pursued by 4 or 5 German soldiers, some with knives and others with their bayonets. When we thought to become partakers of this banquet we thought that those Germans would share with their allies, but I do not know if we did not go away if they would not make us share the fate of the 2 beasts. We passed on to [a] little village when we saw a wagon of flour disposed in large casks and others of these Germans were busy filling their vessels and we pushed up among the rest and commenced storing our little haversacks. You must know that our coats must be drenched with the previous days and nights rain. In the struggle to get at the casks of flower in the scuffle I tumbled into the flour cask, the flower stuck to the wet coat [&] I was as wet if not as white as a miller. When I had filled the haversacks we were yet at a loss what to mix our dough in, on a dresser in a large farm house we saw the very thing we wanted, a fine large milk pan, we brought it with us. By this time we had succeeded very well, but our canteens were yet empty and wherever that to fill them we did not know where to get anything to put in them, water there was none in the camp, so we were nearly despairing of getting anything not only to drink but to wet the flour although there were a draw well in the yard, but it was said that the French had poisoned the water. In our way back to camp we saw a little to our left a very large gentleman's house, we immediately made for this house, we immediately commenced our search more for something to eat than for money, but to our great mortification the house had undergone a complete ransacking and plundered of every portable article and what they could not be carried away, they smashed in pieces, so that our hopes to get something to eat was blasted. It certainly was a great pity to see the damage done to this superb mansion which was of the most exquisite taste in its architecture together with its outhouses and extensive and well laid out gardens, which formed at once a little paradise on earth.* Even the fine statues that decorated the front of this house were with the turrets and obelisks as well as the beautiful fountains and cascades that had been the admiration of ages were demolished by the soldiery. By looking with wonder at this great work of art we had almost forgot our necessity we were now bent upon getting, something to put in our canteens. At last we thought that there must be a cellar of wine and spirit vault belonging to this house which upon examination we found the house was well furnished with all sorts of viands & spirits. When we came to the vault door we were agreeably surprised to see the cellar filled with the choicest beverage but like everything else, this place had undergone the severe discipline of the German soldiers, a most disagreeable proof of which was there to be seen to bear testimony of the unguarded and gluttonous propensity of 2 German soldiers who after drinking so excessively as to render themselves totally insensible and laying themselves down and there slept while the wine and liquors out of about 40 or 50 pipes was flowing on them where it appears that after they had drunk all they could drink & no more they neglected to turn the key of the vessel. When we entered we approached the men we found them dead, without any mark of violence. This had an effect on me, up to this time I had not been fond of tippling and up to this day I have not been drunk or if I have the faculties of my understanding never for a moment left me. Be this as it may I do not think that the sight of those drowned men was the effect of my temperance, neither do I think that it was out of any religious principles, for this great vice which [is] almost universal among English soldiers & sailors. I must not run away with my story for now my comrade and myself commenced filling our canteens with wine & brandy, this done we thought a little money would not be amiss, so we went and examined all the apartments without finding anything. We then shouldered our cargo and as we were passing through the courtyard we saw the first living thing we saw about the house, this was a large hound dog who seemed to have been the faithful guardian of this noble mansion, tied up by a chair and lying on a heap of straw. We to prevent starvation to the poor animal loosed him from his chain; while I was loosening the staple which was very fast I lifted the little cot up off the ground which was sunk about a foot in the earth when to my agreeable astonishment I saw

---

* This description would indicate that they were in the château of Mon Plaisir on the Nivelles road.

2 leather bags full of silver in dollars, each contained about 130 pieces. Thus happily supplied with money and good provision we lost no time to proceed to our camp where we saw our remaining 4 messmates half starved. They begun to open to their eyes at the sight of such a fine cargo of flour, brandy and here we commenced to mix our flour not with water but wine and brandy. When we had mixed our flour we made cakes of it and laid it on the cinders and before they were scarcely browned, when the old saying was verified that hunger breaks through stone walls, for there was no less than half the regiment looking as if they would rob me of what I had so much trouble in getting. The officers seemed as anxious to partake of our casks, some of them thought it rather strange that gentlemen like them should stoop to ask a common soldier for something to eat. Others thought that the men would consider it an honour to give an officer anything he might want, but they found out that there was no use of looking on in silence or think that their presence was sufficient to terrify the soldiers out of their dear earned progg.* At last they saw that if they intended to get any of the cake that they must lay aside that lofty distinction and submit to say 'comrades will you share with your officers in this time of need, and if a couple of dollars can be of service to you, here they are'. While the officers and soldiers were pressing very hard on us I was afraid that the crowd being so great and they were still increasing they would make a rush on me and deprive me of all. One of the officers offered 2 dollars for a small piece of the cakes, at this crisis I heard a rumour in among the crowd that in the case of hunger, everyone had a right to whatever was at hand. I immediately took this hint and took my cakes in my hands and at this time a circumstance occurred that saved me as well as my cakes, for it was not me having them in my hands that could save them for just as I cased them in my hands their fury was increased to such a point that they were on the point of rushing on me when the bugle sounded to arms and the colonel calling for the officers to fall the men in and march off immediately, so that was the very thing that saved my cakes. I gave one of the officers a small piece of the half toasted dough for which he gave me 2 large pieces of silver; he had not gone many yards before some of his comrade officers robbed him of the greatest part of it. Our orders was now to march to the front and occupy a position near the ever memorable Hougoumont. When we were told that we were going to action my mess mates threw away the 3 haversacks of flour saying that [it would] be useless for them to carry that which they should never live to eat, but I thought of the 2 proceeding days hunger and threw the flour on my pack and we marched off to the part of the field of battle allotted for us, which as usual [is] in the front line of the British infantry and moreover

---

* Army slang for food

than that, we had another mark of our general's confidence by placing a brigade of artillery in our charge, a confidence that is never placed in any except in most distinguished battalions who like the Roman Praetorian Band or the Grecian Myrmidons* on whose courage and bravery the fate of half the world depended. When we arrived on our destined ground a grand sight opened to our view, the whole British as well as Brunswick, Hanoverian, Dutch & Belgians were marching to occupy their respective position, this must be one of the most cheerful and glorious sights that ever a British soldier saw, to see nearly 100,000 men moving with the regularity of a mass line, every regiment moved as steady as if on a parade in St James's Park, I shall never forget this grand sight.

About 10 o'clock on Sunday the 18th day of June 1815 the whole of the allied forces under the command of the Duke of Wellington were drawn up in order of battle in 3 lines extending something short of 2 miles, the sight was at this time truly grand and imposing, it would be folly in me to attempt to describe the glorious sight, awe brung at this moment when all was silent as the grave, not a word or whisper to be heard, all waiting for the signal from our noble commander. About this time the light infantry of all the front line were ordered to the advance and cover the front of the line, this done immediately there appeared coming over the opposite heights a line of tirailleurs or French riflemen, both lines were now descending and approaching each other from their respective hills and in the valleys between the 2 armies they met and commenced skirmishing. The French videttes were then approaching quite fast when the Marquis of Anglesey ordered our light cavalry to counteract the French videttes. This you may depend is a very handsome sight, while we were anxiously looking at those skirmishers as far as the eye could see each side. We could see coming over the opposite hill the tops of lances quivering in the air and the men and horses appeared and showed us a long line of Polish lancers supported by immense bodies of cuirassiers, horse grenadiers, light cavalry of all description. By this time our officers of the army thought that it would be a cavalry affair and that we infantry would be as mere spectators, but all was not done yet. All our cavalry were held in readiness but we were soon undeceived by seeing immense columns of infantry coming over the hills supported by a great force of artillery and cavalry. By this time the skirmishing was very hot and [the] French began to throw round shot at our columns and reinforce their skirmishers, our light infantry began to give way on all sides and the French kept pouring fresh troops into the plains. Hitherto our army were lying down on the ground to avoid the shot & shell, the French seemed

---

* The Myrmidons were the soldiers of Achilles in the Trojan war, elite troops like the Praetorians.

to be quite awake to the British being in square threw shot & shell into our columns so that our colonel ordered us to form line so as to reduce the chance of hitting us. At this time the French cavalry approached and galloped up to our very bayonets. One circumstance I shall ever remember, that was a French regiment of cavalry headed by a bold and intrepid officer, he rode up in front of his regiment and when within a few yards of our front company. He exclaimed in English 'Come on you English cowards' this he said several times, this irritated our soldiers and our noble colonel was not one to put up with a language of this description and from a Frenchman who we were taught to despise as our natural enemy for many years. Our colonel seemed a little irritated by the bravado of this audacious soldier and immediately gave the word 'Fusiliers forward' this cheerful order was obeyed with alacrity, we moved in close column until we arrived at the summit of the hill from whence we could see the whole of the French army moving down in dark black masses. We were scarcely arrived in our position on the hill when the above mentioned officer came at the head of his brigade of cavalry of horse grenadiers. He made up to our very bayonets under a most tremendous fire of musketry; at the same charge they drove the 23rd Light Dragoons in some confusion on the 2nd line. The both 23rd's horse and foot were together all this day to bear witness of each others valour. At this we expected to be attacked by the infantry who were manoeuvring in front of us who we thought to pursue, now the same dragoons headed by the same intrepid general came again at full charge, the French advanced with the utmost speed and corresponding fury and charged with horrible yells. They passed us after failing to break in [to] our square and was very nearly annihilating one of our regiments who were all composed of inexperienced soldiers. However, this 2nd charge was beaten off as well as the 1st and now we were to prepare for the 3rd which was not long coming. It appeared that as long as this brigade and its daring commander occupied the plains in our front that there would be no peace for us, so we were to a man anxious to lay their commander low in the dust, at this time the enemy's infantry were manoeuvring in great force in our front and we expected a serious attack on the whole of our right. An extensive line of infantry were advancing in quick time towards us when we began to form line, they gave us a volley and immediately wheeled into open columns and under cover of the smoke which their fire occasioned, they [cavalry] came at full gallop with dreadful yells and but for the maturity of our colonel and officers we should to a man [have] been cut to pieces before we could form square as like the 42nd on the 16th who were severely cut to pieces for not forming square in time. This 3rd and last charge for this desperate French fire eater for just as he had arrived in front of our square he was shot dead. I had the satisfaction to see him lie wounded on the ground within 2 yards of me, he had received 3 balls, I was one myself who fired at this hero, for a hero indeed [he] proved himself and had the whole of the French generals and bands being so determined on conquest and victory as [he] was, I question I think with some justice whether the house of Hanover or a Corsican would hold the reign of government in old England. With this man's fall fell likewise the courage of his soldiers who though they charged they were less audacious from formerly, in short they only showed themselves twice more after the death of their brave commander. This brigade was relieved by a body of cuirassiers who annoyed us very much during the remainder of the day. The first effort of the French was on our right to force their passage to Brussels but after repeated charges and displaying the most desperate valour they were met with equal courage and bravery by the British who baffled all their exertions. When they found their attempts failed on their left they made a desperate attack on our left with immense forces and with such fury that it appeared that nothing short of victory would satisfy their desperate courage. Several of our regiments staggered by this dreadful onset of the French led on by the celebrated French General Lobau.* Victory seemed more than once to [have] appeared with the French standards. Where she had late so gay remained glorious in spite of the united efforts of Russia, Austria, Prussia, Italy, Holland, Belgium, Switzerland and Sweden for more than 15 years and for the first time the fickle goddess seemed to tremble in the scales and seemed willing to decide with the sons of the ocean in spite of the determined valour of the British to repulse the French who forced themselves headlong over a hedge that the English had made use of for a covering and drove the whole of our left wing [at] the point of the bayonets. The eagle [eye] of our commander saw the critical condition of our left wing & not only ordered the whole of the reserve to advance to support their comrades. The whole of the reserve marched in close columns of divisions within half a mile of us, these were headed by one of our best generals who when all was ready rode on his horse in front rank, his hat in his hand and gave the word forward in treble quick. This indeed was the grandest sight I ever saw from the hill where we stood gazing at the havoc the French was making among our left wing. We turned our heads towards the valleys where we beheld 16,000 men coming up in double quick and the charging steps. When they came to about 40 yards of the French they opened a most tremendous fire which staggered the French in their turn, it would require a better pen man than me to describe

---

* Georges Mouton, Comte de Lobau did not lead this attack, his troops being engaged with the Prussians, this refers to the advance of D'Erlon's attack.

this melee. The British saw that [it] was no use to waste their ammunition & time on them & they had recourse to the never failing weapon in the British soldier's hand, the bayonet. When we came to measure steel with them they faced about, the French not yet dismayed they brought up deep masses of fresh troops, but at this critical moment Sir Thomas Picton came up next his fighting 2nd* Division and threw the front line of the enemy upon the 2nd and at this moment, the British cavalry under Sir William Ponsonby seized the favourable moment of confusion among the enemy and thundered among the enemy and cut them to pieces and they became an inexorable confusion†. At this moment when victory was completely wrested from the French a large body of French cavalry came to check the retreat of their beaten comrades. Sir William Ponsonby leading his cavalry was speared by a Polish lancer through the body and England while victory smiled on her banners she met a great reverse by the loss of one of [the] bravest and best generals, Sir Thomas Picton a man whose worth is too well known to make any comment on his character, as general of a soldier he was our commander, right hand man and the talisman of the army among his men. The French finding their utmost efforts baffled on the left determined on another attack on our right, deep masses of combined horse and foot and artillery were seen manoeuvring down towards Hougoumont, this great force was headed by Count Reille, they amounted to upwards of 36,000 men who were determined to force their passage to Brussels, this attack was made with the most determined bravery and repulsed with equal courage but at a dreadful expenditure of human life. The attack on Hougoumont is too well described by Sir Walter Scott and others for me to attempt it, the flanks of this sweeping charge reached our regiment. This dreadful onset so beautifully described by one of our poets, 'from roaring guns the bellowing [unreadable] flamed whose throats of brass the work of death proclaimed, from bursting shells that excavate the ground and like hurling thunder spread destruction around and on the heights along our right at large the trembling earth announced their coming charge, before the sword played by the cuirassiers or hulans [sic] lance, whole thousands disappear, from mangled heaps the soaking blood distils and down the slope runs thick in crimson rills where the fields of verdant tincture were, now groans with death and floats a sea of gore, but on the heights along our right at large the trembling earth announced the coming charge, their steel-clad troops, resistless in their course destruction spread with more than mortal lance in vain, our guns their advancing columns tear and

---

* Picton commanded the 5th Division and was killed outright in this attack.

† Here Jeremiah's statement ceases to be completely his own first-hand account and therefore the sequence of events is jumbled somewhat.

vomit death on each approaching square in vain their ranks are by our sabres hewed, in vain the ground is with their blood imbued, as when a torrent with resistless sway down some high mount precipitates its way, nor tree nor rocks, its lawless force oppose, still moving foaming to the valley's floor, so rushed the French, o'er their companions dead'.* Our light troops routed and desolation spread, as I said that the flank of the columns of attack reached our regiment whose iron ranks stood so firm as although they might kill us they could never rout us, at this trying moment our brave colonel told us to be steady and wait well for his word of command and which was strictly obeyed until they were within 30 or 40 paces of us when we opened a most destructive fire which staggered their advancing columns and while our brave and beloved colonel was reminding us of our former exploits on the peninsula he received his mortal wound† just as he saw his commands obeyed. It required all the attention of our officers to restrain our men, for they were burning with revenge for the loss of their most beloved commander who had on so many actions led the regiment to victory and conquest in former campaigns, by reference to Lord Wellington's dispatches from the peninsula, you will see his personal worth as well as his most distinguished character as a soldier, he was after his death conveyed to his native country to be interred in his own native city of Worcester, when every man in the regiment gave a day's pay to raise a monument suitable to the magnanimity of the spirit that once inhabited the corpse of that brave Ellis. The 14th Regiment was nearly annihilated by the desperate charge on our right wing; however, this confusion was only momentary for they immediately rallied into a regular formation under a most murderous fire which made a considerable havoc among them but stimulated by the example of the Welch Fusiliers they resumed their position in the line from whence they were so nearly routed.‡ At this critical juncture the attention of our brave Wellington was directed to our right wing which was all but destroyed by those chosen cohorts of the French Imperial Guards and led on by their

---

* He probably refers to Sir Walter Scott's poem, *The Field of Waterloo*, but these lines are not from there. I have been unable to discover their origin.

† Lieutenant Colonel Ellis was severely wounded by a carbine shot in the chest and further was thrown from his horse whilst being led to the rear. Placed in a hovel it caught fire on the 19th from which he was rescued by Assistant Surgeon Munro. He died of his wounds on the 20 June and was buried at Braine l'Alleud. Jeremiah is mistaken as Ellis's grave was eventually moved to the Wellington Museum at Waterloo. That at Worcester is simply a memorial.

‡ I have found no mention of this attack on the 14th Foot elsewhere; it is true they were very inexperienced and could have been caught out of formation by the cavalry, but their casualties that day (only 36 casualties of which 7 rank and file killed) indicate that nothing too serious befell them.

most distinguished generals whose names had been a terror to all Europe for more than 15 years, and whose ability and bravery in the field was inferior to none, their master, Napoleon, alone excepted. However, notwithstanding their invincibility they found for the first time their victorious career put a stop to by the almost matchless and consummate ability of our commander and the able assistance of his brave officers together with the native courage of his soldiers which rendered that day so famous in history, that the determined bravery and courage that was displayed on that day will serve as a stimulus to encourage the youths of old England to follow the example of those who conquered the invincible legions of France on the [savage?] and far famed field of Waterloo. Thus the French found themselves baffled on all points in spite of their promised plunder of Brussels to reward their dear bought victory and toil to beat the English at Waterloo, but this was a miscalculation on the part of the French, who had displayed prodigies of valour but here they found in the plains of the Netherlands not as the Austrians was at Austerlitz when their two wings were separated and by one bold charge under Marshal Davout and supported by Murat's cavalry the Austrians thrown into utter confusion and the French becoming completely masters of the field, they found British soldiers firmly stationed and whose wings could not be forced, nor was our troops laying down their arms by whole divisions and surrender prisoners of war as at Ulm under the Austrian General Mack who surrendered with 25 thousand to Napoleon at the summons of the first shower of bombs from the French; but Wellington was no General Mack nor was the sons of Britain to be terrified at a 1000 showers of bombs, but firmly stood the brunt of battle, nor did they leave it while there was a soldier remaining to dispute with them the palm of victory, and although there were on the field troops of other nations who fought side by side with the British, still there were some among them who deserved not to be called soldiers, for I was witness to a superb body of cavalry who were ordered to charge alongside of our dragoons, but when they found themselves opposed to a smart body of French cavalry the Belgians faced about and fled to the rear and left the British to seek more faithful followers than they.* This was taken advantage of by the French who poured in the gap made by the desertion of the Belgians, the enemy were nearly benefiting by this but it was but momentary for the British closed on the French and were nearly capturing the commander. The French paid dearly for their temerity and rode off without affecting their purpose of breaking through the British lines; this was about 4 o'clock p.m.

---

* This would appear to refer to the Hanoverian Duke of Cumberland's Hussars, who left the field.

Fifth Division of Lieutenant General Sir Thomas Picton
8th Brigade of Major General Sir James Kempt

No. 88   Major General Sir James Kempt
By kind permission of Sir Michael Bunbury Bt, KCVO, DL, and
Suffolk Record Office, Bury St Edmunds, ref. E18/740/4

To Major General Sir James Willoughby Gordon, Quartermaster General
to the Forces.*

Bivouac near Genappe,19 June 1815

My dear Gordon,
I have just time to tell you that I am well and in the land of the living,
for at present I am quite unable to enter into the particulars of the great
battle fought yesterday in which a most glorious victory was gained over
Bonaparte, who attacked *us* with his *whole force* and with a degree of
fury that it is quite impossible to describe. When you learn the details
they will excite your *astonishment* and *admiration* of the invincible
spirit of the British lion. My late lamented friend Picton was killed in
the *first* attack. He commanded the left of the position and the charge of
the whole devolved on me *throughout the day*; a most impossible and
arduous situation but such was the undismayed and unconquerable spirit
of the British troops that though assailed by *20* times their numbers and
in every possible way, with a degree of fury and enthusiasm approaching
to madness, yet the enemy never gained for one moment a footing on
the little ridge where they were posted. It does indeed appear romantic,
but I do assure you on the faith and honour of a soldier, that 3 British
regiments in *line, very weak* (for they had lost upwards of 800 men and *42*
officers two days before in the action near Quatre Bras†) absolutely met,
charged and repulsed a mass of the enemy *not less* than 8 thousand just as
they had gained the crest of the position. After the 1st line of Dutch,‡ &c.

---

* This letter in the archives is headed 'To Colonel Gordon, Military Secretary to
the Commander-in-Chief'. However, this is clearly a mistake, this was Gordon's
previous rank and position way back in 1809 and he became a major general in 1813.
† The returns for Quatre Bras published in Siborne's *History of the Waterloo
Campaign* actually show that Kempt's 8th Brigade lost 588 rank and file killed,
wounded and missing, and 49 officers.
‡ Almost every map of the Battle of Waterloo mistakenly shows three lines of troops
on Wellington's right, but inexplicably only shows two lines on his left; the infantry
all in one line the cavalry behind, with no reserve. It is clear from such statements as
Kempt's that this was not the actual case. Bijlandt's Brigade formed the first line here
and Picton's troops were initially placed in their rear as the second line; the cavalry
forming a third line and therefore corresponding more with Wellington's dispositions

&c. had given way, and at a time when they were without any *support whatever*; it was an act of desperation but it succeeded, there was for one moment a struggle and as example is everything in our profession, I placed myself in the front at this particular crisis. The enemy were on one side of the hedge, we on the other; and how I escaped alive I cannot imagine. In every part of the position the attacks were equally furious and *all* had I believe, to exert themselves in an equal degree, on these occasions you must excuse a little egotism. I was wounded slightly in three places although I fear one in the knee, the ball having entered to the bone, will be unpleasant and tedious, but I have left the division for an instant and write with great pain and difficulty. My brigade major was killed[*] after losing three horses and both myself and ADC.[†] had the same number shot under us. I shall write to you in greater detail when I get into a house, for I am still in bivouac and have been so for some days. I have written to no person but yourself, but pray show these hasty lines to Torrens and Sir Harry C.[‡] and tell them that I trust I shall be continued in the command of the division till we get to Paris. Farewell, give as usual my kind regards to Lady Gordon and believe me ever &c. &c.

James Kempt.

No. 89   From the Same

Arnouville [les Gonesse], 3 July 1815

My dear Bunbury,[§]

I must in my turn snatch a moment to thank you, which I do most cordially, for your very kind letter and hearty congratulations on the late glorious events; you have in a few words expressed yourself strongly and said everything that we all feel, both as to the nature of the battle and its mighty consequences. Would to God that our illustrious leader had expressed himself something in the same manner. His dispatches are records for history and in his accounts of the battles of the 16th and 18th, he neither does justice to himself or the army that fought under his orders in the field of Waterloo. We are all, however, quite satisfied that these services will be fully appreciated in England and throughout Europe; but

---

on the right. For further evidence of this statement see Letter No. 175 by Captain Gore in the editor's *Letters from the Battle of Waterloo*, London 2004.

[*] Captain Charles Eeles, 95th Foot, was killed.

[†] Captain the Honourable Charles Gore, 85th Foot, Aide de Camp.

[‡] Lieutenant General Sir Harry Calvert, Adjutant General.

[§] Major General Sir Henry Bunbury, Under Secretary of State for War and the Colonies.

you must not treat us as we do our great coats, called for when the storm approaches, but laid aside with very little ceremony when it is dispersed. I cannot but consider myself particularly fortunate in escaping the dangers of such a day and my having had more than my usual share in the two battles. On the 16th my brigade happened to be particularly distinguished and on the 18th my lamented friend Picton was killed in the *first attack* when the command not only of the 5th Division, but the 6th and all the troops in position upon and from the left of the *great road* devolved on me. *Throughout* the *day*, upon this point, the principal efforts of the enemy were made under the direction of Ney, with a degree of fury and perseverance quite unexampled but without the least success; and the duke having been an eye witness himself of the spirit and determination displayed by the troops in repulsing the *first* great attack *never sent me one order through the day*. The right, he considered was the weak point and there he was the whole day in a dreadful fire superintending every movement. The loss of the 5th Division alone in the two days was quite tremendous, upwards of 200 officers and 2,250 men killed and wounded.*

In detailing such events a man cannot avoid being something of an egotist and you will with your usual charity excuse me I know, for having said so much about myself, although to tell you the honest truth I have on the present occasion rather an interested motive in doing so. I am very ambitious you must know to possess the ribbon which poor Picton wore† and from the circumstance of my having succeeded to his command in the great battle *almost at its commencement* and there being, I believe, but one officer senior to myself in the army eligible for it (old xxx‡) who had not equal good fortune having remained in the command of a brigade during the whole day, I trust that I may not be considered too presumptuous to look to his honour. At all events I feel quite satisfied that you will with your usual kindness give me all the aid in your power and act with all the zeal and *discretion* which you always display in the service of your friends.

We invested Paris on this side yesterday and the Prussians crossed the Seine near Saint Germain [en Laye] to attack it on the other. The negotiation still continues and we are still fighting; but all will be finished in the way we could wish, probably today and Louis again re-established on the throne of France, 18 days from the opening of the campaign!!

I was delighted to hear that our friend Adam's Brigade highly distinguished

---

* Siborne shows that the returns for killed wounded and missing in the 5th Division over the three days totalled 2,156 rank and file and 179 officers.

† Picton was a Knight Grand Cross of the Order of the Bath (GCB); Kempt did succeed Picton to the order as he hoped.

‡ I suspect he refers to Sir Denis Pack here.

itself, its leader behaving most conspicuously. Farewell, give my kind remembrance to Lady B[unbury] and believe me to be, ever faithfully yours,

James Kempt

I have had a pretty *jump* from the command of a brigade to that of a Corps d'Armée, having since the battle had in my column the 5th and 6th Divisions and [the] Brunswick Corps.

1st Battalion 95th Foot

No. 90   Unknown Officer[*]
Kindly supplied by John Lagden

Camp of Clichy

The following account, written by a rifleman after Waterloo, is from a book of account by eye-witnesses; it is contributed by Captain J. E. H. Neville late 43rd Light Infantry.

All the sharers of my tent having gone to Paris, and my servant having manufactured, a window shutter into a table, and a pack saddle into a seat, I will no longer delay answering your two affectionate, letters, and endeavour to comply with your demand of an account of the battle such as it offered to my own eyes.

On the 15th June, everything appeared so perfectly quiet, that the Duchess of Richmond gave a ball and supper, to which all the world was invited; and it was not till near ten o'clock at night that rumours of an action having taken place between the French and Prussians were circulated through the room in whispers: no credit was given to them, however, for some time; but when the general officers, whose corps were in advance, began to move, and when orders were given for persons to repair to their regiments, matters then began to be considered in a different light. At eleven o'clock the drums beat to arms, and the 5th Division, which garrisoned Brussels, after having bivouacked in the park till daylight, set forward towards the frontiers. On the road we

---

[*] In the statement, he describes himself being wounded in the thigh at Quatre Bras but not severely enough to go to the rear and remained with the battalion during the retreat and Battle of Waterloo. Two officers from the battalion are known to have been hit in the leg at Quatre Bras; 1st Lieutenants Gardiner and Fitzmaurice were so severely wounded that they went to Brussels and therefore can be eliminated. It is therefore most likely to be either 1st Lieutenants Orlando Felix, William Chapman or 2nd Lieutenant William Shenley who were all wounded but remained with the battalion.

met baggage and sick coming to the rear; but could only learn that the French and Prussians had been fighting the day before, and that another battle was expected when they left the advanced posts. At two o'clock we arrived at Genappe, from whence we heard firing very distinctly; half an hour afterwards we saw the French columns advancing and we had scarcely taken our position when they attacked us. Our front consisted of the 3rd and 5th Divisions, with some Nassau people, and a brigade of cavalry, in all about 13,000 men: while the French forces, according to Ney's account, must have been immense, as his reserve alone consisted of 30,000 which, however, he says, Bonaparte disposed of without having advertised him. The business was begun by the First Battalion of the 95th, which was sent to drive the enemy out of some corn-fields, and a thick wood, of which they had possession: after sustaining some loss, we succeeded completely; and three companies of the line: they, however, were driven out immediately; and the French also got possession of a village which turned our flanks. We were then obliged to return and it took us the whole day to retake what had been lost. While we were employed here, the remainder of the army were in a much more disagreeable situation: for in consequence of our inferiority in cavalry, each regiment was obliged to form a square, in which manner the most desperate attacks of infantry and charges of cavalry were resisted and repelled; and when night put an end to the slaughter, the French not only gave up every attempt on our position but retired from their own, on which we bivouacked. I will not attempt to describe the sort of night we passed, I will leave you to conceive it. The groans of the wounded and dying, to whom no relief could be afforded, must not be spoken of here, because on the 18th it was fifty thousand times worse. But a handful of men lying in the face of such superior numbers, and being obliged to sleep in squares for fear the enemy's dragoons, knowing that we were weak in that arm, might make a dash into the camp, was no very pleasant reverie to soothe one to rest. Exclusive of this, I was annoyed by a wound I had received in the thigh, and which was become excessively painful. I had no great coat, and small rain continued falling until late the next day, when it was succeeded by torrents. Boney, however, was determined not to give us much respite, for he attacked our picquets at two in the morning; some companies of the 95th were sent to their support; and we continued skirmishing until eleven o'clock, when the Duke commenced his retreat, which was covered by Lord Uxbridge. The Blues and Life Guards behaved extremely well.

The whole of the 17th, and indeed until late the next morning, the weather continued dreadful; and we were starving with hunger, no provision having been served out since the march from Brussels. While five officers who composed our mess were looking at each other with the most deplorable faces imaginable, one of the men brought us a fowl he had plundered, and a handful of biscuits, which though but little, added to some tea we boiled in a camp kettle, made us rather more comfortable; and we huddled up together, covered ourselves with straw, and were soon as soundly asleep as though reposing on beds of down. I awoke long before daylight, and found myself in a very bad state altogether, being completely wet through in addition to all other ills. Fortunately I soon after this found my way to a shed, of which Sir Andrew Barnard (our commandant) had taken possession, where there was a fire, and in which with three or four others I remained until the rain abated. About ten o'clock the sun made his appearance, to view the mighty struggle which was to determine the fate of Europe; and about an hour afterwards the French made their dispositions for the attack, which commenced on the right. The Duke's despatch will give you a more accurate idea of the ground, and of the grand scale of the operations, than I can do; and I shall therefore confine myself to details of less importance which he has passed over.

After having tried the right, and found it strong, Bonaparte manoeuvred until he got forty pieces of artillery to play on the left where the 5th Division, a brigade of heavy dragoons, and two companies of artillery, were posted. Our lines were formed behind a hedge, with two companies of the 95th extended in front, to annoy the enemy's approach. For some time we saw that Bonaparte intended to attack us; yet as nothing but cavalry was visible, no one could imagine what were his plans. It was generally supposed that he would endeavour to turn our flank. But all on a sudden his cavalry turned to the right and left, and showed large masses of infantry, who advanced up in the most gallant style, to the cries of '*Vive l' Empereur*', while a most tremendous cannonade was opened to cover their approach. They had arrived at the very hedge behind which we were-the muskets were almost muzzle to muzzle, and a French mounted officer attempted to seize the Colours of the 32nd Regiment,* when poor Picton ordered the charge of our brigade, commanded by Sir James Kempt. When the French saw us rushing through the hedge, and heard the tremendous huzza which we gave, they turned; but instead of running, they walked off in close columns with the greatest steadiness, and allowed themselves to be butchered without any material resistance At this moment, part of General Ponsonby's brigade of heavy cavalry took them in flank, and, besides killed and wounded, nearly two thousand were made prisoners. Now Bonaparte again changed his plan of attack. He sent a great force both on the right and left; but his chief aim was the centre, through which

---

* A French Officer attempted to seize the colour of the 32nd Foot, but was instantly run through by Sergeant Switzer's pike and by the sword of Ensign John Birtwhistle.

lay the road to Brussels, and to gain this he appeared determined. What we had hitherto seen was mere 'boy's play' in comparison with the 'tug-of-war' which took place from this time (3 o'clock) until the day was decided. All our army was formed in solid squares; the French cuirassiers advanced to the mouth of our cannon, rushed on our bayonets: sometimes walked their horses on all sides of a square to look for an opening, through which they might penetrate, or dashed madly on, thinking to carry everything by desperation. But not a British soldier moved; all personal feeling was forgotten in the enthusiasm of such a moment. Each person seemed to think the day depended on his individual exertions, and both sides vied with each other in acts of gallantry.

Bonaparte charged with his Imperial Guards. The Duke of Wellington led on a brigade consisting of the 52nd and 95th Regiments. Lord Uxbridge was with every squadron of cavalry ordered forward.

Poor Picton was killed at the head of our division, while advancing. But in short, look through the list engaged on that day, and it would be difficult to point out one who had not distinguished himself as much as another. Until eight o'clock, the contest raged without intermission, and a feather seemed only wanting in either scale to turn the balance. At this hour, our situation on the left was desperate. The 5th Division, having borne the brunt of the battle, was reduced from 6,000 to 1,800. The 6th Division, at least the British part of it, consisting of four regiments, formed in our rear as a reserve, was almost destroyed, without having fired a shot, by the terrible play of artillery, and the fire of the light troops. The 27th had four hundred men, and every officer but one subaltern, knocked down in square, without moving an inch, or discharging one musket; and at that time I mention, both divisions could not oppose a sufficient front to the enemy, who was rapidly advancing with crowds of fresh troops. We had not a single company for support, and the men were so completely worn out, that it required the greatest exertion on the part of the officers to keep up their spirits. Not a soldier thought of giving ground; but victory seemed hopeless, and they gave themselves up to death with perfect indifference. A last effort was our only chance. The remains of the regiments were formed as well as the circumstances allowed, and when the French came within forty paces, we set up a death-howl, and dashed at them. They fled immediately, not in a regular manner as before, but in the greatest confusion.

Their animal spirits were exhausted, the panic spread, and in five minutes the army was in complete disorder: at this critical moment firing was heard on our left, the Prussians were now coming down on the right flank of the French, which increased their flight to such a degree, that no mob was ever a greater scene of confusion; the road was blocked up by artillery; the dragoons rode over the infantry; arms, knapsacks, everything was thrown away, and *'sauve qui peut'* seemed indeed to be the universal feeling. At eleven o'clock when we halted, and gave the pursuit to Blücher's fresh troops, 150 pieces of cannon and numbers of prisoners had fallen into our hands. I will not attempt to describe the scene of slaughter which the fields presented, or what any person possessed of the least spark of humanity must have felt, while we viewed the dreadful situation of some thousands of wounded wretches who remained without assistance through a bitter cold night, succeeded by a day of most scorching heat; English and French were dying by the side of each other; and I have no doubt, hundreds who were not discovered when the dead were buried, and who were unable to crawl to any habitation, must have perished by famine. For my own part, when we halted for the night, I sunk down almost insensible from fatigue; my spirits and strength were completely exhausted. I was so weak, and the wound in my thigh so painful, from want of attention, and in consequence of severe exercise, that after I got to Nivelles, and secured quarters, I did not awake regularly for thirty-six hours.

No. 91   First Lieutenant George Simmons
Permission kindly granted by the Council of the National Army Museum, journal of First Lieutenant George Simmons, 1st Battalion 95th Rifles[*]

Officer's names who embarked at Dover on the 25th April 1815 for Ostend with 6 companies of the 1st Battalion 95th or Rifle Corps.

> Commanding Officer, Colonel Sir Andrew Barnard slightly wounded at Waterloo.
> Major Cameron brevet Lieutenant Colonel badly wounded at Waterloo.
> Captain Leach brevet Lieutenant Colonel[†]
> Captain Beckwith brevet Lieutenant Colonel, lost a leg at Waterloo.[‡]
> Captain Glasse, Deputy Judge Advocate joined after the battle.
> Captain Lee
> Captain Smyth, killed at Waterloo.

---

[*] This is a much more detailed account by Simmons of the Waterloo campaign than that published by Lieutenant Colonel Willoughby Verner as *A British Rifle Man* (London 1899).
[†] Dalton states that Leach was wounded, but he remained with the regiment.
[‡] Captain Charles Beckwith was acting as an Assistant Quartermaster General.

Captain Chawner, severely wounded in the leg at Waterloo.

Lieutenant Layton,[*] wounded in the wrist & side at Quatre Bras.

Lieutenant Molloy, slightly wounded at Waterloo.

Lieutenant Stewart.

Lieutenant Freer,[†] on baggage guard from Quatre Bras to Waterloo.

Lieutenant Lister, wounded through the abdomen at Quatre Bras and died next morning.

Lieutenant Simmons, wounded badly through the liver, two ribs broken at Waterloo.

Lieutenant Stilwell, wounded through the body at Waterloo, died on arriving at Brussels.

Lieutenant Haggup

Lieutenant Fitzmaurice, wounded in the leg at Quatre Bras

Lieutenant Johnstone, wounded severely & killed by a round shot on leaving the farm yard of Mont St Jean on horseback in company with Lieutenant Simmons.

2nd Lieutenant Church[‡]

2nd Lieutenant Allen Stewart. Stabbed through the arm, and wounded in the shoulder at Waterloo.

2nd Lieutenant Wright. Slightly wounded at Waterloo.

Lieutenant & Adjutant Kincaid. Joined at Brussels before the Battle of Waterloo.

Surgeon Joseph Burke

Assistant Surgeon Robson

Assistant Surgeon Heyt

Paymaster John Mackenzie

Quartermaster Bagshaw

Lieutenant Orlando Felix joined at Brussels[§]

Mr Charles Smith. Volunteer placed in the company with me by his brother now Sir Harry Smith.[¶]

---

[*] Dalton does not show Layton as wounded.

[†] Misspelt Frere in Dalton.

[‡] Dalton states that Church was wounded.

[§] Dalton states that Felix was wounded at Quatre Bras.

[¶] He omits Captain William Johnstone (w), 1st Lieutenant John Cox, 1st Lieutenant Archibald Stewart, 1st Lieutenant William Chapman, 1st Lieutenant John Gardiner, 1st Lieutenant John Gairdner, 1st Lieutenant George Drummond, and 2nd Lieutenant Wiliam Shenley (w); who all served with the 1st Battalion during the Waterloo campaign.

'Fifth' or General Picton's Division

8th Brigade
28th 1st Battalion
32nd 1st Battalion
79th 1st Battalion
95th or 1st Rifle Corps

9th Brigade
1st 3rd Battalion
42nd 1st Battalion
44th 2nd Battalion
92nd 1st Battalion

Mr & Mrs Overmann[*]
Sons Monsieurs Jacques, Albert, Edward, Gustavus.
Daughters, Mademoiselles Julia, Harriett, Eulalie.

Embarked at Dover on the 25th April 1815 on board of the *Wensleydale* packet, the company was commanded by Captain Beckwith, brevet Lieutenant Colonel, and the following officers viz. Lieutenant Layton,[†] Lieutenant Stewart,[‡] Lieutenant Simmons, 2nd Lieutenant Wright.[§]

My friend Beckwith gave me the payment of his company, he having done so during the Peninsular War, which made it incumbent on me to use my utmost zeal to keep it in good order. Two officers of the Staff Corps, Major Sturges[¶] and a lieutenant also embarked with us. Our vessel being very small, the sea rather rough & the wind contrary, made the most of us feel rather uncomfortable & soon began to mystify ourselves. I forced myself to joke & laugh & shake off if possible the unpleasant feeling which was creeping over me. I requested a sailor to hand up a bucket of salt water & place it on the deck before me, sailors like fun, it was instantly done, I then took a pint and said 'men, here is the antidote for seasickness, consequently you wish to stop it, follow my example'. Suiting the action to the word, I dipped it into the bucket, when brimful I swallowed the contents saying 'look men, there is no mistake', the

[*] The family he was billeted on in Brussels and who cared for him when severely wounded.
[†] First Lieutenant Jonathan Layton.
[‡] First Lieutenant Archibald Stewart.
[§] 2nd Lieutenant William Wright.
[¶] I cannot identify an officer of this name in the Army List. I believe it may be a mistake for Major William Staveley of the Royal African Corps who was with the Royal Staff Corps in Belgium in 1815.

effect was quite electrical, the whole company staggered forward, each man took a dose, making very wry faces. At this performance Colonel Beckwith laughing convulsively explained, 'If you knew that fellow as well as I do, you would not let him take such a rise out of you.' The Staff Corps major heard this remark, but he could not resist my plausible argument in favour of the remedy, particularly as the men called out it was doing them good. It is human nature, when men are in a scrape, they like to lug others into it, I handed the major a brimmer which he swallowed, I now thought it necessary to put a bold face on my antidote, ordered more salt water, took off another pint, but I had no more volunteers, the joke was out. I now saw the gallant major winding up his accounts and cascading handsomely, groaning & muttering between his teeth 'What a fool I was to be humbugged in this way, why that rifleman has a stomach like an ostrich.' On the 26th the wind became more favourable & on the 27th we landed at Ostend. Previous to leaving England, the colonel had issued a most stringent order to the 6 companies that no soldiers wife would be allowed to accompany her husband on service under any pretence whatever. You may guess his astonishment, standing on the wharf to see the companies land, he observed Corporal Pitt with his wife leaning on his arm, he said, 'Corporal, you have disobeyed my order, put your wife onboard the vessel instantly, or I will bring you to a court martial.'

'Sir, my wife was separated from me, when I went to the Peninsular War & I had rather die than be parted from her again.'

'Very well then, take the consequences', the woman was put in charge of a party & taken onboard. A drum head court martial was held on the spot, the corporal was reduced to a private soldier* & sentenced to receive *300 lashes*. The companies that had arrived were formed to witness the punishment, we were all very sorry for the corporal, as he was a good & brave soldier. I knew him well, he had been in a great many actions in the peninsula with me but there was no help for it, orders must be obeyed. Accidentally the two doctors had not yet landed or was their vessel in sight & the man was tied up to receive his punishment. The colonel in this dilemma observed me, 'George Simmons you see how disagreeably I am placed with you, act as surgeon,' (it flashed across me that by doing so I could abridge the number of lashes), so I agreed to do it & stepped forward to superintend it. After the man had received 100 lashes I said 'Stop', I addressed the colonel saying, 'It is my opinion the man has had enough.'

'Do you say so?'

---

* Private William Pitt of Captain Johnston's Company fought at Waterloo and survived.

'I do Sir!'

'Then take him down.'

I think at the moment, I gave pleasure to every man present, for they knew well that if the surgeon had been there he would not have dared to do so. Some short time after, the colonel said 'George Simmons you are a good fellow, you did exactly what I wished you to do. I was very sorry to be compelled to punish that man, but for the force of example & landing in a foreign country, I had no other alternative, although I dislike flogging as much as any man.'

By this time all the companies had arrived, we marched & embarked in Dutch schuyts on the canal & drawn by horses, we got to Bruges about dark. Our boats were moored for the night, we had no opportunity of seeing the place, so we rolled ourselves up in our boat cloaks & passed the night comfortably.

28th [April]

Moved forward at 4 o'clock in the morning but not at a slapping pace, the country was flat but seemed well cultivated, the people as we flitted by, looked squalid & dirty. Arrived at Ghent about 3 o'clock p.m. In the evening I got a billet upon Mr Barth, sugar merchant, Quai de la Grue no 29, I found my folks very kind & civil. Louis XVIII having cut *his stick* from Paris, held his court here, & had a motley group of followers with him. Sir A Barnard our colonel, was requested by the king to let him see the officers, so we paid him a visit, & were received most kindly. He paid us some very flattering compliments indeed. I was quite astonished at his enormous dimensions, they were marvellous, he was really a moving mountain of flesh, but under all this, his countenance displayed great animation & intelligence. We passed our time very agreeably here.

On the 7th May we were reviewed by our old commander, now the *Great Duke of Wellington*, he was pleased to express his satisfaction at our soldier like bearing. We looked at him with pride & pleasure when we remembered the battles & sieges we had gained under his command & were now looking forward to see him & his army pitted against the *Great Napoleon* & astonish him as he had already done to so many of his marshals.

10th May

Marched to Aalst, which being filled with Louis's people, we were compelled to move on to the village of Welle.

11th

Halted.

12th

Assembled & marched to Brussels, arrived there about 11 o'clock in the morning. The weather being very hot & the road covered with a light black dust, we marched along in a cloud of it, which gave us the appearance of chimney sweeps. After billeting off the company, I got a billet for myself upon a Guernsey man of the name of Jeune, he told me he had been detained for many years by Napoleon in France. He ushered me into a very handsome room, an elderly lady & two daughters, very nice girls, gaped & stared at me in amazement. I presented my billet, they timidly said 'Sir, we will give you a billet upon an inn, we are not in the habit of receiving officers into our house'.

'How is it then, that the authorities have had the impudence to give me a billet upon an English family, I will soon give them a little of my mind. For the last two hours I have been billeting soldiers & to be served in this way is not pleasant.'

'Oh!' said Mr Jeune 'I entreat you Sir, not to make a complaint of us at the *Mairie* or we shall have two German officers sent & we shall have to feed them.'

I now walked towards the window, at the moment I saw my face in a pane of glass, which made me exclaim 'Oh, Murder!' I certainly was an ugly rogue. At this moment I espied my young friend Wright* looking as clean & handsome as possible, I threw up the sash, telling him to come here directly. He entered the room, 'Have you got a billet?'

'Yes'.

'Give it to me, now Mr Wright, I install you here, take care of the ladies.' I waited for no apologies but bolted into the street with his billet in my hand. I met Richard Freer mooning about. 'Holloa! Have you got a billet?'

'Yes, here it is, but I do not like the look of the place, it has a sombre appearance, change with me.'

'Very well', I seized it & started off on my travels. I came to a large gloomy-looking door at the end of a narrow street. I struck it smartly with the handle of my sword. A very gentlemanly person opened a small wicket, receiving me most politely.

'Well I am glad they have not forgotten me at the *Mairie*, I began to despair of having one of your distinguished corps billeted upon me.' These words, he spoke to me in good English. 'Now Sir, what may you require?'

'A bed & sitting room, a kitchen & stable for 3 animals. Four officers grub with me, as I am caterer, I should like to feed at home, in consequence.'

'I can accommodate you & add my summer house as a dining room.'

---

* 2nd Lieutenant William Wright was his junior.

Nothing could be better. My landlord was a German, a merchant & banker named Overmann, Rue de l'Etoile, no. 819.* He had a very extensive connection abroad & generally from 15 to 20 people at dinner daily, from different parts of the world. 'There will always be a vacant chair kept for you at my table while you remain under my roof.'

'It will be quite impossible for me to accept your kind offer, as my mess mates would cut me if I did not generally dine with them. I will do so now & then provided you return the compliment to us.'

'Agreed'.

Sir Andrew Barnard put his young friend Lieutenant Orlando Felix into the company to be with me & Sir Harry Smith placed his brother Charles under my care, he was a Volunteer, an aspirant for a commission.† We passed our time most agreeably, I dined with Mr Overmann on Sundays, he had only his family circle on that day.

On the 15th June I had my baggage animals paraded in the yard, to see & adjust the pack saddles properly in case of a sudden start, as we had had rumours that the enemy was concentrating in vast numbers on the frontier & that we might expect to be attacked soon by the *Great Napoleon* himself. Mr Overmann saw my preparation to take the field which made him very gloomy. He asked me if I thought we should move soon. 'Most decidedly & in a very great hurry, too.'

'Oh Sir! If the French enter Brussels I am a ruined man, what will become of my poor wife & family? God in his mercy help them, for I shall be powerless.'

'Keep up your heart, you do not know what stuff Englishmen are made of, there will be many wigs on the green before the French enter Brussels & I tell you that for your comfort.'

His heart wavered towards me & he told me the following story.

'In the French Revolution, one horrid night I was dragged from my bed leaving my poor wife more dead than alive, by a body of fierce soldiers, who exclaimed to her "If you make any noise, we will bayonet you." I was marched with several other most respectable citizens to Valenciennes & put into a loathsome dungeon crowded with unfortunate beings, who had done no crime that they were aware of; daily the roll of names was

---

* This is quite clear in the text, it is incorrectly stated as 119 by Verner.

† Young gentlemen without a fortune to purchase a commission nor a family connection able to use their influence to gain one; could attempt to gain a commission by the 'Volunteer' system, being unpaid but receiving rations. The gentleman would carry a musket or rifle and fight in the ranks, but would mess with the officers (if allowed into a mess, if not they dined alone); hoping that by showing bravery before the enemy, they would be noticed and chosen to fill the vacancy that arose which was within the colonel's power to appoint to. Their chances of success were limited; many losing their lives whilst attempting it.

called & off they were marched to satisfy the hungry guillotine. In this way we went on from day to day, causing me a living death until only 3 of us remained. You may judge what my feelings were when the gaoler roared out our names, adding to it "Go about your business". I staggered along scarce knowing whether I was on my head or my heels to an inn, & there learnt that Marat had been assassinated by *Charlotte Corday* that blessed woman. Oh I soon returned to my wife & happy home. Now Sir, if such scenes as these are again to fall upon this land, may the Almighty in his infinite mercy, protect us.'

I went to bed as usual, about 10 o'clock I was startled from sleep about 11, our bugles sounding the Assembly, an old Peninsular trick, that had the effect of rousing the most sleepy fellow in an instant. Our men were very soon at their alarm post. The company formed close to my quarters when each man received two days rations of biscuit & meat. Mr Overmann was astonished to see the men in such high spirits joking about Napoleon to each other. 'Come we shall at last have a look at the fellow, we could not find him in Spain or Portugal.'

Previous to marching off, he said 'Mr Simmons I really feel a father's interest in you, should you be wounded, endeavour to get back to my house, I will receive you as I would my son. Do not forget what I now say, my house shall be a home to you & my wife & daughter will be proud to nurse you.'

'God bless you, Mr Overmann, accept my grateful thanks & best wishes towards you & yours. Men, attention, trail arms, threes left, shoulder forward, forward quick march.'

I marched close to the park, where the 6 companies soon formed in column at quarter distance, piled arms, took off their packs, made pillows of them & were soon asleep, waiting for further orders. Our Division, the 5th under General Picton were assembling here, I now observed to my friends Felix, Wright & Smith, 'Let us take time by the forelock & take the men's example & have a nap while we may.' I selected the lower step, as a pillow, of a gentleman's house. We laid down & slept very comfortably until about 2 o'clock when a respectable old man & two young ladies preceded by a man servant carrying a brilliant lanthorn, wanted to enter the house. The light awoke me, I rose up from my lair & apologised for obstructing their passage. The young ladies exclaimed 'Do not mention it Sir, there is room enough for us to pass, but how sad it is to see such nice young gentlemen lying down on the cold stones in the street at such an hour as this.'

'Ladies it does not rain, they ought to feel very comfortable.'

'We have just returned from the Ball' the old gentleman said, 'Will you have some blankets, or will you come into the hall, we will give you mattresses.'

'This is surely the commencement of the campaign & we ought to be satisfied that the weather is fine, so good night, pray for our success ladies & we shall feel obliged to you.'

At daylight, our division fell in & marched off through the Porte Namur, drumming & trumpeting in fine style for the amusement of crowds of natives who were gaping & staring at us. I heard no vivas, they appeared to treat the whole concern very coolly indeed. We marched direct to Waterloo & halted among some trees on the left side of the road. The men began to cook their breakfasts being sharp fellows at that sort of work. A 7 years apprenticeship had been of great service to them. They were a good deal like Sancho Panza, who found out in his severe trials, that the belly kept up the heart & not the heart the belly. I slipped into a little shop, bought some ham, eggs & milk. The baggage now came up, my cook a shrewd old peninsular man, had the tea kettle hissing on a fire, I paid him a compliment for his zeal, we soon had a glorious breakfast. Lieutenant Colonel Beckwith had gone on the Staff, Lieutenant Layton commanded the company, Lieutenant Stewart, Lieutenant Simmons, Lieutenant Felix, 2nd Lieutenant Wright, Mr Smith Volunteer, these officers constituted the mess, for whom I had to provide. In times gone by I have often found it a very difficult matter, but now everything was in abundance, so that we were all perfectly happy & contented. I now laid down under a tree, took a nap noise & bustle never discomposed me in the least. Some time after, the Duke of Wellington & Staff passed us to reconnoitre the enemy. We were now on the line of march to our front, the high road to Quatre Bras. I now found I had lost my neck tie, which was just as well, I undid my collar & made my neck free from ligatures, which is a great blessing on the march on a dusty road, under burning sun. The heat was so oppressive that one of the men was driven furiously mad with one excitement or other, he struck a comrade with his rifle, fell down & died instantly, so much for Prussian collars & stocks.* Many a brave soldier has died of apoplexy from having his neck ligatured in this frightful way. We moved on rapidly in spite of the heat & began to meet men, women & children travelling towards Brussels, poor people having left their homes in terror of the French. They appeared under sad excitement & very forlorn, they wanted to tell us a long story, but honest folk we could not understand them. The road now traversed fields of standing corn looking very luxuriant & ripe for the sickle, the companies as they came up, extended & passed through the corn waving above our heads. We were soon greeted by a few round shot *Johnny*† having found us out which caused many jokes among the men, such as 'Ah!

---

* The use of leather stocks was not discontinued in the British Army until 1855.

† Johnny Frenchman.

Ah! my boys, you are now opening the ball in good earnest.' We were now abruptly brought up by a thick quick set hedge. I peered through & found the ground much lower on the other side, being grass land intersected with ditches. Some French infantry commenced firing at the hedge, a man near me was wounded, several men were poking their rifles into it, but the thorns were so sharp that there was much hesitation as [to] how they were to pass through. I saw no time must be lost, or we should have several men injured. I espied at the moment, Sergeant Underwood,* a rough & ready peninsular man, I roared out 'Underwood, the devil do you not dash through!'

'Sir the pricks are very sharp.'

'Why man, you are like a fine lady.'

At the same time keeping my eye on him & taking a few steps to the rear, I rushed forward & struck him in the centre of his knapsack with my right shoulder. It had the effect of a battering ram, through it he went, I of course was in his wake, for a moment we were both sprawling in the field, Underwood gathering himself up, 'Who the hell sent me through the hedge in that manner?'

'I did Sir! We must have no fine ladies here, look at these rascals, the field is too small to hold us. Underwood deliberately fired at one of them, the company rushed through the gap like a flock of sheep following its leader. The French were now hounded along very unceremoniously through several fields intersected with ditches & low embankments affording us good ground for rifle practice. The enemy were now in force behind some straggling houses, so we called a halt in a good position, behind an embankment with a ditch in front. Lieutenant Layton who was close to me received a hit in the wrist & side by musket balls, the wounds were not severe, but they bled freely. I tore off part of the sleeve of his shirt & wound it round his wrist, telling him to go to the doctor. 'George Simmons you must hit the fellow first, I see him now pointing with his finger.'

I took a rifle, laid down & fired over the stump of a tree, several men were doing the same from the embankment. I knew some of them were punished because they began to hide themselves. After firing in this way 3 or 4 shots a sergeant said 'Fire my rifle Sir',

I sprang up & said 'Fire it yourself.' Layton entreated me to do so, not this time. The sergeant then placed his rifle over the stump, I pointing at (almost bent over him) a man at the corner of a wall. At this moment a round shot struck him in the face, dashing his head into long shreds or ribbons, throwing him backwards a distance of 10 yards. It was quite marvellous, his smashed head did not touch me, only a little sprinkling

---

* Sergeant Daniel Underwood of Captain Beckwith's company.

of blood. Layton & Felix were close by [&] observed 'George Simmons, you really have a charmed life.'

In my excitement I said 'Men look at that glorious fellow, our comrade & brother soldier, he now knows the grand secret. He has died nobly for his country & without a pang of suffering. My boys I trust he is on the high road to heaven. May *God* in his mercy bless *him.*'

A column of Germans now came near & halted. General Sir Charles Alten commanding the 3rd Division was on horseback in front with his Staff. This great & kind man commanding the Light Division in Spain, I no sooner espied him than I ran & seized his hand, saying 'God bless you my general.'

'Ah! My light division officer. I wish I had my old division here *now* gentlemen, this is one of my dear old friends.' There was no time for further greeting, the round shot were booming over the column handsomely. 'Simmons where is Barnard? I want him to cover my advance.'

'Look Sir, there he is & you know he will be pleased to do so. I hope we shall soon receive the order to clear your front.' Soon after we jumped the ditch & drove the enemy from the houses as riflemen are want to do, reader this was not done without having some wigs on the green, a necessary evil connected with glorious war. Several columns advanced covered by riflemen & light infantry. The columns were now & then compelled to form square to resist the French cavalry, our cavalry was not in the field. The 42nd were charged in line by a body of cuirassiers which passed through them. The highlanders closed in, faced to the right about & when they returned to the charge gave the French such a deadly volley that made those untouched scamper off at a furious rate. A fierce engagement took place in the vicinity of Quatre Bras. We entered a wood in skirmishing order supported by columns of infantry but were handsomely handed out of it by an overwhelming force & no mistake. The sight of our masses stopped them as it was now evening the enemy took up their position for the night throwing out along their front for miles videttes & double sentries alternately. Marshal Ney commanded here. We brought away poor Lieutenant Lister who was shot through the body. We now halted & laid on the ground & talked over our exploits. Sir Andrew Barnard pointed to a poor rifleman laid a little in front of the French advanced sentries, observing both his legs were sadly shattered. 'Gentlemen, if one of you would remain here with 2 or 3 men & when it is dark try to bring him off, it would be a glorious act indeed. Otherwise the poor fellow will be left to die in great misery.'

I said 'I will Sir'.

'George Simmons you are a good fellow, it is just what I expected from you.'

My folks soon moved away to occupy a position for the night. I *now* kept my eye on the poor fellow, stuck two forked sticks in the ground in a line with him, laid another across them, which in the dark was of great service to me. It luckily was soon very dark, I advanced a man some distance, marched upon him, we then crawled forward close to the ground & soon found him.

'My good fellow, Sir Andrew sent me to carry you off. You must make no noise or we shall be slaughtered.'

'God bless you Mr Simmons, I am in a sad forlorn state indeed.'

The French sentries were now making a great row, I suppose some officer of rank was visiting them, this was all in our favour. I now felt the poor fellows smashed legs which only hung together by lacerated muscles & tendons, he was hoisted on the back of a comrade not uttering a groan. I tried to comfort the maimed fellow, by saying 'I will never leave you until I have put you into a house & got you a doctor.'

The Germans had placed their advanced sentries in front of their position for the night, which we now had to pass through. There was a tremendous hubbub amongst them, being very young soldiers, luckily the darkness was beginning to clear off a little, which enabled them to ascertain our numbers. They called out 'Halt! Halt!'

I consequently stood still & sung out 'Englishmen, Englishmen what the devil do you want more?'

[An] Officer & 20 men approached us very cautiously with their bayonets at the charge. I pointed to the legs of my wounded man. The officer was satisfied that we were not enemies, the sentries allowed us to pass, we only understood each other by signs. I soon found myself on the high road & deposited my poor wounded friend in a house already nearly filled with wounded & dying soldiers. I handed him over to a doctor.

'Oh Sir! Give me your hand, a thousand, thousand thanks.'

Poor Lister was here in a dying state & unconscious of my presence. I turned away & quitted this house with an aching heart & was scrambling along through the country meeting with dead highlanders & cuirassiers. At last I found my battalion just in rear of the farm house of Quatre Bras in open column of companies right in front, arms piled, the men asleep, the officers laid down on the inner flank of their respective companies, in case of a sudden alarm. The men had only to jump up, stand to their arms, wheel into line & be ready for anything required of them. When I had satisfied myself why the men were thus formed I laid down by the officers of the company very hungry, having had nothing since breakfast. I soon fell into a sound sleep, I forgot everything connected with this world. Before daylight we stood to our arms, wheeled into line; when the day dawned some sharp firing began in front, our company occupied the farm yard. I took 20 men & relieved a company of the 69th under Captain Cuyler,* the light infantry company. He gave me a hearty shake of the hand, having been a rifleman. 'What are you blazing away so at each other?'

'Why the French fire at us & we like the fun, so we return the compliment. Good morning.' Off they went.

I placed my men in a ditch in front of an orchard & some behind a wall, directing them not to fire, which quieted the French also. I now recommended the men to cook; those in reserve cooked for the men opposed to the French. Our fellows knew their business well, I called two peninsular men & said 'the officer's baggage has not arrived, we must have something to eat, try if you can find something for us. The inhabitants have left their houses generally, do not be long about it, for I can see with half an eye that the French are bent upon mischief. Felix took charge of the men, while I examined our position. The farm house was filled with French wounded & the straw yard had numbers laid down about wounded in a sad state also, many horses some sadly wounded & others dead. I now satisfied myself who supported us in case we should be driven out of this advanced post, on returning, among some bushes I saw a pair of legs booted & spurred. Curiosity made me have them hauled out, when to my astonishment appeared a splendid cuirassier officer. Our men said 'he is dead, un-strap the cuirass', which was done, a ball had passed through it into his breast, the blood began to ooze from the wound, I felt his pulse, 'he is alive', gave him some water, bared his neck, he now breathed, which delighted me. I had him carried into the house, turned two men off a bed not so badly wounded, gave him a little wine, then returned to my men. The French had begun to fire occasionally, I saw some officers looking at us & more men assembled. A whim now crossed the spirit of my dream, I put on the cuirass & the huge gloves, it was not wide enough for my brawny shoulders, but much too long. I strutted about, which caused my men to laugh, Johnny took it as an insult, I had 3 or 4 shots, knocking up the dust pretty near me, [at] which I retired. The farmer came to see the fun, a handsome looking fellow & possessed a deal of pluck. Sergeant Fairfoot,† a brave peninsular man who was at the storming of Badajoz, on the breach near me, he was knocked down by a musket ball striking & fracturing his skull above the right temple; he now received a sharp wound which fractured a bone in his fore arm & bled freely. He sung out 'Oh Mr Simmons, the game is up with me for this campaign anyhow.'

'Never mind, your travelling is not spoilt, you can find your way to

---

* Captain Charles Cuyler had previously served with the 95th.
† Sergeant Robert Fairfoot of Captain Lee's Company.

the doctor in spite of them; take a pull at my calabash Fairfoot.' Which he did.

'Now Sir I have a favour to ask, let me take a shot at one of those rascals from your shoulder, it is not the first time I have done so.'

'Well then fire away'. He laid his rifle over my shoulder & with his left hand from his left shoulder took delicate aim & fired. I am convinced that the reader can well appreciate the worth of this splendid soldier. I was very sorry to lose him, the firing again subsided. I was glad of it, as I wanted breakfast. My foragers had got fowls, eggs, bacon, some tea & sugar. *All sorts* as they were pleased to say, 'but we want a frying-pan', off went the cuirass, the back part was perfect, the edges were embossed with silver; the skewered fowls & bacon were hissing & spluttering upon it in gravy, when Sir Andrew Barnard & a general, a friend of his, rode up.

'Well George Simmons, there you are, I told you general I would find you a breakfast. We are very hungry.'

'Well gentlemen go to work', which they did & when satisfied Sir Andrew said, 'Now let the French come on, as soon as they like, I am ready for them.'

The general began to apologise, 'Sir Andrew do not give yourself any trouble.'

'He is fully capable of taking care of himself', giving me a knowing nod, 'George you had better look sharp, for you will not remain quiet much longer.'

I took the hint & soon satisfied myself, [&] my comrades, I bought some excellent wine at a shilling a bottle from the farmer & put it into the canteens of men I could trust with it, told him to sell as much as he could, which advice he adopted.

The French in our front were becoming very lively, I went & took leave of my wounded friend. I was ordered to leave the farm & form my men upon the Charleroi road & remain until further orders. I soon began to perceive much activity amongst the French in my front, which caused me to look round for my support in case of an attack from cavalry, the country being quite open, to my surprise all had taken their departure, which satisfied me that I had no business here. I now saw in a dip in the road, masses of infantry collecting, which augured no good. An aide de camp galloped near me, I pointed out the columns of French in my front, 'Have you any orders?' 'No!' going off as quickly as he came.

'Now', I observed, 'We have no business here any longer', facing to the right about & retiring fully expecting every moment to be attacked by dragoons. I suppose we were too contemptible at this moment. I now saw a most splendid sight, my heart bounded with delight, as far as the eye could reach, a line advancing towards us. Columns of infantry came on, intersected with masses of cavalry; it really had the appearance of a splendid field day.

'Look at them my lads, tomorrow if it pleases God, we will have a regular turn up with them.' The men were struck with amazement & bandied jokes with each other. As we came near to Genappe, the Duke of Wellington with several general officers & the Staff were on a rising ground looking at the French.

My battalion was standing in column, Sir Andrew Barnard said, 'I began to be anxious about you, you stayed too long.'

'I received no orders to retire.'

'Is it possible George, this hot day has made me very thirsty?'

'I have some capital wine', calling to a sergeant to hand me his canteen.

The colonel took a good pull at it, exclaiming 'You have saved my life.'

This part of our army was soon in full retreat to Waterloo. The riflemen occupying the houses & stone walls nearest to the enemy. I was with a party behind a wall on both sides of the high road, leading into the town, with a good house close by. My cook had a pot on the fire with our ration beef & other comestibles, I made a man survey the garden & collect vegetables etc so that I anticipated a right good dinner. The French had halted about half a mile from us & most likely some of them were also cooking. I now washed & shaved myself jokingly, even asking that Johnny would respect me for it, if I fell into his hands & bury me decently. The rain now began to come down in torrents, the French moved forwards & away we went, I took a farewell look at the pot of soup, groaned in spirit; however, there was no help for it & luckily I had something else to take off my attention, for we were as wet as if we had gone through a river. I now picked up a blanket, leaving a third of it as a cape & fixing it round my neck with a strap, so that I was wet & warm. A blanket used in this way was an old peninsular trick. In the heavy ground, as we retired on our own left, a body of cuirassiers charged the 7th Hussars, but our Life Guards, not before some of the hussars had been made sad examples of, came up & charged the French. Many of their saddles were soon tenantless much to our satisfaction. We arrived at Waterloo about dark, where our army got into position for the night. The French fired a few cannon shot which ceased with the darkness. The ground we now occupied was in the morning a corn field in full bloom, now squashed into clay & mud.

The rain still coming down heavily, I told Smith to bring along a muddy blanket. I pitched upon a bit of rising ground to locate upon for the night. A soldier brought me a little straw, a valuable present, poor young Smith tired & jaded, crouched down upon it. I gave him some biscuit & wine, the good fellow who had my wine in charge was not forgotten. At this moment my colonel's orderly came & told me, that he wanted me directly. I followed the soldier & found the colonel had made a lodgement in a weaver's shop & had plenty of good things just arrived from Brussels. 'Now feed away my boy'.

I obeyed orders & laid hold of a plump bird of some sort & finished off with other solid eatables, good wine & porter in abundance. I saw a fine bundle of cigars, they took my fancy, I laid my hand upon them when Sir Andrew said 'Stop, Sir, you may have 4,' which he counted & pocketed the rest. 'Now you may take up a position for the night near the fire, make yourself as small as possible, I have many to accommodate'. He had some of the first men in the army with him.

'Why Sir, if I were to stay here the company would have a contempt for me, I must go & rough it with them.'

'George you are a strange fellow.'

Major General Sir John Elley* said, 'Barnard, we made a famous charge with our heavies, I do not know that in my life I made better practise', half drawing his sword which was red with blood. 'I made several of them bite the dust, they really went down before me like children.' He was very powerful & a splendid swordsman.

I wended my way to the bivouac under pelting rain, I now found my young friend crouched up exactly as I had left him. I called a soldier to bring a couple of knapsacks for pillows, requested Smith to lie down, I then took the wet blanket off me & put it nicely over him, I borrowed another & laid the blanket, I plastered over [it] with thick clay, fortunately we had plenty of it, I now laid close to Smith. The soldier dragged the loamy one carefully over all, we were now as comfortable as possible. We heard the rain pelting upon the clay in an agreeable manner which soon lulled us to sleep. When the rain ceased, I do not know, but I do know that we awoke after a good night's rest & quite dry. The people I conversed with said what a dreadful night they had passed. The men now made large fires, dried themselves & went to work & cooked their breakfasts, after which they put their rifles in order & carefully examined & dried their ammunition. Our friends the French being mounted on higher ground were doing the same, that we perceived very clearly. I now got another order to go to the weaver's shop & partake of a splendid breakfast, which made me as light hearted & fit for work as any man in the army.

The army went into their fighting position, the right in the chateau & wood of Hougoumont & the left ran beyond & in rear of La Haye Sainte which place was occupied by a battalion of Hanoverians commanded by Colonel Baring. In the Peninsula he was aide de camp to General Sir

---

* Actually Colonel Sir John Elley, Royal Horse Guards, at Waterloo, Deputy Adjutant General.

Charles Alten & well known to us. About 11 o'clock we formed column (not for prayers – being Sunday), a cannon shot from the French singled out a man in the rear rank of the rear company & smashed his head to pieces. Some men of a red regiment were cutting up a bullock for rations close by, this shot started them off to their corps. The meat looked so inviting that I called my servant & in a few minutes we deposited a large piece in a hole, I telling him to mark the spot as I meant to send him for it in the evening, this made the men laugh heartily, Sir Andrew shook his head at me.

I was now sent with a party to cut wood & form an abattis* on the Charleroi road, near a gravel pit which was occupied by Captain Leach & his company. I found a number of Germans at the same work; after depositing the wood, the battle now began in good earnest, I went back as fast as possible to my folks, a battery of ours was firing on the enemy. The young Germans were so alarmed that they blunderingly crossed in front of the guns, much to our amazement; men who do not know their business are often killed by their own people.

The columns were soon beaten back, we heard continued peals of musketry about Hougoumont & the French cavalry were moving about, which obliged our infantry to remain in square, fearful objects for cannon practise, of which the French cleverly took advantage. The farm of La Haye Sainte now became the object of attack as it overlooked our part of the position. Masses of men attacked & carried it, the Germans fought gallantly until all their ammunition was expended, some lively fellows bolted, but most of them were bayoneted. Guns were now brought up to this point, they made fearful havoc, in the square of the gallant 28th Regiment, who literally fell as they stood by hundreds, there was no mistake about it, as the regiment was on our left & near us.

My young servant, a handsome Englishman was struck by a grape shot, close to me, just after he had fired, his poor arm was sadly shattered. He sung out lustily.

'My good fellow, giving tongue in that way will do you no good, go off to the doctor.'

He turned to go, but was shot down. We now from time to time had terrible tussles with the enemy, I was generally sent forward with a party to meet the French skirmishers, who covered their advancing columns. A mass of men again approaching, Orlando Felix said, 'I have been shot through the cap, my jacket torn across the breast by a ball & a spent ball which hit my thigh & partially lamed me. George Simmons I shall be killed today.'

'Nonsense! I have a charmed life & feeling myself in the full vigour of

---

* An obstacle formed from felled trees, etc., usually laid across a road.

manhood, the devil a feather will they touch of me.'

'You have indeed, take my watch & pocket book. You will find letters, send them by the post. You will also find some instructions.'

We were soon after fiercely attacked, a musket ball grazed my arm, entered my side, broke two ribs, went through my liver & lodged in my breast.* Felix said I jumped as high as myself & fell near the hedge of La Haye Sainte on the left side of the road. On came the French & were soon travelling over me, however, they were unceremoniously handed back again, followed by our Life Guardsmen who galloped over the very place where I was deposited & gave a good account of a number of the unfortunate infantry who had the ill luck to taste their sabres. The shock I received brought my watch to a full stop at 4 o'clock, the works were broken.

Felix told Sir Andrew my deplorable situation, 'Where is he? Let me see him instantly, poor, poor George Simmons.' He ordered a corporal & 4 men to take me with the greatest care to the farm house of Mont St Jean, to return & report to him when he had done so. I was carried to the place & through the straw yard into a large cow house or stable, the premises were covered with great numbers of dying & wounded soldiers. Doctors were performing their evolutions with knife & saw in hand, most vigorously. Several of my brother officers were congregated together, laid upon straw in the right corner of the building. Poor Stilwell[†] exclaimed 'Dear George, how white you look, lie down by me', which I did. My body soon became so swollen that I had great difficulty in breathing, the warm blood was still oozing from my side into my trousers, the ends of the broken ribs gave me excruciating pain.

At this moment Fairfoot, that glorious fellow, had found me out, he was so shocked that the big tears ran down his manly countenance. 'Oh lift me up, I am suffocating,' he had poor fellow, only one arm at my service, I managed to get upon my knees & clutched a low crib with one hand & a sack with the other, I soon slided [sic] down. Our Assistant Surgeon Heyt[‡] came & tried to bleed me in the arm.

I now espied my dear old friend *Robson*,[§] a capital operator & a peninsular surgeon; he saw me & came instantly. 'Old fellow I am hard hit at last, cut the ball out of my breast directly as my game will soon

---

* In his journal Simmons states that the ribs were broken near the backbone indicating the wound was in the back rather than the side. However, in Appendix II of the same book the medical certificate states 'the ball entered the right side', confirming the statement he made in 1855.

† First Lieutenant John Stilwell

‡ Assistant Surgeon Robert Heyt.

§ Assistant Surgeon James Robson.

be up.' I could bear nothing on but my shirt, so I had no difficulty in placing my finger over the very spot where the ball was lodged, he made a wide & deep incision into my breast, & with a pair of forceps pulling out a musket ball which was nearly flattened against my broken ribs, he put it into my trouser pocket. A quantity of clotted blood followed the ball, which relieved my breathing. Fairfoot sat upon the straw supporting me during the operation, he appeared as happy at the result, as if one has been extracted from his own carcase.

The battle was still raging & some stray shots knocked the dust off the roof, some of the debris falling into the place. Some surgeons were operating when suddenly a cavalry officer, he appeared to be of rank, entered our location, accosted an officer of dragoons who was wounded, saying 'It is all up with us', in a very agitated manner, 'You must leave this, or you will fall into the hands of the French in a few minutes. The English are in full retreat, I have a horse waiting, here is some money', taking out his purse, away they both went. This cowardly rascal's words acted like magic, he has much to answer for, if he had been doing his duty like a man & a soldier, many lives might have been saved, that were lost by this false alarm. Doctors & wounded were moving off as speedily as possible, I saw poor fellows who had lost a leg a few moments before, now crawling like crabs out of the place. I glanced round me & I really think all that had life had departed with the exception of Stilwell & myself, he seized my hand convulsively, 'George Simmons, our race is nearly run, has it come to this? Napoleon then has conquered us, beaten! beaten! 'the tears running down his face 'Well then the French will soon give us a taste of the cold steel.'

'Stilwell my brave fellow, you & I have often been in terrible scenes together, I never loved you half so well as I do at this moment.'

'George you shall see me laugh at them & tell them to do the worst, you know I can speak a little French.'

We lay in a state of half stupor for some time when Fairfoot came & said 'Our fellows are fighting like devils. I have picked up two horses, now Sir you must try to ride.' I was raised on my legs but I fainted. Stilwell was put on the horse, I remained in this state quite unconscious. I was again roused & put upon a cuirassier's horse, the man had been killed by a cannon shot & the white woolly shabraque was covered with blood. I was in my shirt in the same state with a silk handkerchief tied tightly round my trousers to keep them up. I was a most fearful sight, I left the yard with Lieutenant Johnston* into the main road, the cannon shot from the French was hopping about at this moment very vivaciously, one struck poor Johnston just as I remarked the circumstance he fell a lifeless

---

* First Lieutenant Elliott Dunkin Johnston.

corpse, I could do him no good, so I pushed on in company of two men wounded in the arm as my protectors. We ran the gauntlet until a little turn in the road took us out of the range of our unpleasant companions, the road was crowded with Belgians running away & our wounded soldiers, I saw several men knocked over. I passed through Waterloo & wended my way to Brussels, I saw a whole regiment of Belgians marching away from the field of battle, I have no doubt that if the French had beaten us, the Belgians would have fought better against us than for us.

Captain Havelock* a friend of mine, aide de camp to Sir Charles Alten, told me the French were beaten & driven off the field, this news gave me fresh courage to proceed on my journey. I arrived at Brussels fearfully jaded, the broken ribs hurt me most cruelly, being raggedly fractured. The good people were running about with flambeau in their hands, begging both wounded officers & men to go to their houses. They stared at me with horror, mingled with pity, I remembered what Mr Overmann [had] said & proceeded at once to his house. On arriving at the good man's gate, the men rapped, it appeared ages before the gate was opened when a woman screamed out '*Mon Dieu* Monsieur Simmons' & started back & told him.

Mr Overmann came forward looking very sad 'Oh! Sir! I am very sorry indeed to see you in such a bad plight, you are welcome, heartily welcome to my house, but I shall soon be no longer master here, the French will be masters & I & my family driven out & homeless.'

'Who dared tell you this falsehood? The French are driven off the field & now are on the high road to the devil, or anywhere else you please. I am quite exhausted, take me off or I shall die in the saddle.' This was not an easy matter, my limbs were sadly swollen & my drawers & socks were glued to me with blood. A high table was put near the horse, I was raised bodily out of the saddle by two stout fellows, laid upon a mattress & carried back to the quarters I had left only 4 days before, then in the full vigour of health & manhood, now a broken down helpless creature. Such is too often the result of Glorious War! I fainted & remained in a state of stupor for some days with occasionally slight consciousness. My colonel had sent us a good soldier servant who did his duty by me. The day after the fight my noble, kind friend Sir Andrew Barnard rode over to see me & told Mr Overmann to spare no expense in my service, saying a great deal more in my praise, than I mean to publish here. I could not help observing to Mr Overmann, this is just as it ought to be, I saved that great & glorious man's life when badly wounded, I removed him from under a murderous fire from a body of French infantry, at the Battle of the Nivelles in the Pyrenees & in a month brought him back to the battalion

---

* Lieutenant William Havelock, 43rd Foot.

convalescent. The Duke of Wellington would have sent his surgeon to see him, but he would have no one but myself, to attend upon him.

I had 3 times 30 leeches put upon my body, which still increased. My good friend Robson was a constant attendant on me, I was entirely given up & laid in a comatose state for many days, when suddenly a large abscess in my liver burst its contents in vast quantities found vent at my breast, after this I became nearly exhausted, my pulse scarcely perceptible. Doctors Somerville* & John Bell† came with Robson to see me, they complimented me upon the narrow escape I had had, they had seen many of the wounded, whose livers had been injured, 'You are the only one likely to get better. This discharge is quite miraculous, now you must remain perfectly still, take a little tea & toast when you like.'

In a few hours my appetite became quite ravenous & I felt sinking into my grave, my mind was not very clear. I told my servant 'If I have not some solid food, I shall soon die, do go & buy me some good beef & make me a steak, also get a dozen bottles of porter. Be alive & let me have the meat fried quickly.' I ate heartily & swallowed the contents of a bottle of porter, I now felt much better.

In the morning I had another copious discharge. I took my beef & porter with the same good effect. Robson was astonished when he felt my pulse, to find it so strong, 'You took the tea & toast?'

'Of course I did.'

'Well you cannot have anything better, you do not know how happy I am to see you going on so wonderfully, good night!'

My servant had placed before me another savoury mess, when Robson accompanied by the doctors bolted into my room. 'Holloa! What is all this about?'

'Gentlemen, if I had only taken tea & toast I should not now be alive, remain here a few moments & I will convince you that I can feed as well as ever I did in my life.'

They laughed heartily & said I was an astonishing fellow indeed & fully capable of taking care of myself.

One day my servant said 'I found some articles in your trouser pockets, I placed them in a drawer, here they are.'

I was surprised to see two watches, when I opened the pocket book it brought Felix back to my recollection, he was disappointed in not being killed & I was too confident on that occasion. My constitution had been sadly tried by wounds & often very hard work in the peninsula, but

---

* Deputy Inspector William Somerville (Drew, *Medical Officers*, number 1499).

† This might be Assistant Surgeon John Bell 84th Foot, (Drew, *Medical Officers*, number 3111) although the regiment was in England, but could he have been one of the many doctors that arrived following the call for medical help?

thanks to a good & hardy frame, I gradually came round to health again.

In October I made an excursion with Mr Overmann & his family to the battle fields, I showed my friend where I fought in front of the orchard at Quatre Bras. The farmer now came & knew me at once, he had his arm in a sling, he had been badly wounded in protecting his property from the French after our departure. Mr Overmann wished to talk to the man, so I moved off & joined the ladies, when he joined us again, he told his family a long story in German, they complimented me highly for my attention to the cuirassier & my services to the farmer, it gave me great pleasure that I had risen in their estimation. I owed them much, one or other of the family never left me, night or day, until I was out of danger. In short, if I had been their own son I could not have had more kindness or attention shown me. Every night & morning this good man, with some members of his family came & prayed fervently to the Almighty to give me strength of mind to bear my affliction. I went to see my best friend Lieutenant Colonel Charles Beckwith, whose leg was shattered by a grape shot nearly as the Battle of Waterloo finished; 4 days after, it was obliged to be amputated below the knee to save his life, he was still suffering very much & sadly attenuated. I found him in bed propped up with pillows, he put on his rifle jacket to receive me in due form, as I entered his room, he took off his night cap & gave *three cheers*. I was so shocked at his broken down appearance that I could not respond to him. 'Oh George my career as a soldier is wound up, forever!!!' This highly talented & good man was a splendid soldier, he was Quarter Master General to the Light Division in Spain at the age of twenty three years. My suffering brother officer, Lieutenant Allen Stewart,[*] a very tall & powerful highlander & a most plucky fellow, was stabbed through the arm by a French officer whom he finished in an instant, he then received a musket ball in his shoulder which passed through & lodged close to the shoulder blade, he entreated me to come & see him. I found him in a very sad state, with continued fever, his shoulder fearfully swollen & burning hot, the wound looking very unhealthy. My good fellow the accursed ball is working all this mischief. 'You ought to have had it removed the very day you got it, & if I can find it, you shall soon be relieved.' I soon put my finger upon the very spot, the surgeon was sent for, the ball extracted, a poultice was put over both wounds & continued as long as was necessary. He took a decoction of Peruvian bark 3 times a day & soon added a little port wine. This treatment very soon put him on his legs again.[†]

We travelled to England together vowing eternal friendship. The day came at last & I most reluctantly took my departure from this good

---

[*] Second Lieutenant Allen Stewart.

[†] Simmons had been a medical practitioner before joining the army.

& amiable family, their marvellous kindness to me under such trying circumstances even without a murmur will bloom & blossom in my heart for ever, unless by some misfortune old age shall remove from my memory the last ray of feeling. May the Almighty in his infinite mercy bless & prosper this good & kind family. My son being a chip off the old block & fixedly determined to be a soldier, a flash crossed the spirit of my dream, to look for a small journal I had written 6 months after the Battle of Waterloo, from it & from memory I have made this statement for my boy's edification, trusting that in the day of battle, he may endeavour to tread in his father's steps to make as many friends of men of rank & at the same time not to be a toady's distinction & try to exceed him if possible in the duty he owes to his country.

I wrote a statement of the kindness I had received from Mr Robson, & headed the list with my subscription recommending him to two officers who had profited by his abilities as a surgeon. I had the satisfaction to see him in possession of a very handsome silver cup value 100 guineas with an appropriate inscription written upon it.

THE RESERVE FORCES

54th Foot

No. 92   Lieutenant Dixon Denham*
Journal of the Waterloo Campaign
By kind Permission of the Foyle Reading Room, Royal Geographical Society,
London. Reference DD/1 (Denham Collection)

[Following] The escape of Napoleon Bonaparte . . . officers belonging to the British regiments then on leave of absence who [*sic*] lost no time in reporting to their respective corps in the hope which was soon confirmed that Flanders would be the seat of the approaching campaign.

With these reports before me I took leave of my friends in the month of April and passing through Kent on my journey to Margate where I proposed to embark for Ostend. I put myself into a packet at that place and after 10 hours sail stepped on Flemish ground with which I was not much prepared on its first appearance, that day was one of the most unpleasant I ever experienced, it rained incessantly & blew a hurricane. To everybody who ever has been to Ostend on such a day my feelings will come home.

Travelled by trechschuyt, you pay 5 francs which includes an excellent dinner and coffee. If the weather is fine you pass an uncommon pleasant day. From here (Bruges) to Brussels diligences run daily and for about 7s/6d English you are transported there in a few hours.

The British and that part of the Allied army that had reached the frontier had been for some time cantoned along the Belgian frontier of the Netherlands, when on the 15th of June Bonaparte acting with all that

---

* Dixon Denham (1786–1828) was an English explorer in West Central Africa. He joined the army in 1811, first serving in the 23rd Royal Welsh Fusiliers, and afterwards in the 54th Foot, with whom he served in the campaigns in Portugal, Spain, France and Belgium, and received the Waterloo medal. This is an extract from his journal of the Waterloo campaign.

decision of character and energy of mind, which he is known to posses with five corps d'armee, together with his Guard and other cavalry, made an attack upon the Prussian posts at daylight, that led to the ever memorable Battle of Waterloo; the effect of which was the surrender of Paris to the Duke of Wellington and the allies on the 4 July following.

Bonaparte imagining himself in circumstances to assume the offensive, threw himself on the 15th in one condensed mass on the long and interrupted line of the allies and necessarily spread over a great circuit of country, for the double purpose of vigilance and easier subsistence and upon his first march had the advantage of a body acting upon a line, a body choosing its point of contact, whilst its enemy not knowing where such attack would be made, were compelled to be everywhere on the alert.

On the 16th Bonaparte recommenced the attack on the Prussians with three divisions and on the English with two. The English repelled every effort but the Prussians were obliged to retreat during the night; a corresponding movement becoming absolutely necessary on the part of the English. On the morning of the 17th the Duke of Wellington also fell back, although it appears with extreme reluctance, and on the evening of that day took up the position of Waterloo, having the Prussians at a long interval on the right [left] of the English.

It appears that the scheme of the enemy over the two first days was so little decided as not to have put them in a situation of either harassing Marshal Blücher on his night retreat or of the Duke of Wellington on the 17th on his march by bad roads.

On the following morning, the 18th of June and the fourth day of the battle [campaign?], the great conflict commenced and so fully and distinctly are the particulars related in the dispatch that to recapitulate them in any other words would be as unnecessary as it would be presumptuous, to attempt an explanation of that which must have come to the understanding of everyone. The grand effect by the Duke at the end of the day and which was crowned with success, was made with an energy of mind and example of person that rendered it certain but much would be effected, but from that example it is dreadful to reflect on the risks to which his venerable life was exposed. In fact, such was his dauntless activity that he was much more exposed than any private soldier who would only bear the hazard of a single spot, but the Duke was everywhere, at least wherever danger was and although probably the discomfiture of the French army might not have been so complete had not the Prussians made their appearance, at the time they did, yet that the enemy were repulsed at all points, by the firmness and undaunted bravery of the British infantry and the whole army in a situation to act on the offensive in their turn before the arrival of Marshal Bülow's Corps[*] is beyond a doubt. But nevertheless most critical was the period when the Prussians came to the attack, the peasant who guided Bülow's army resolved not to come out of the wood at Frichermont but to descend into the valley lower down and to penetrate by Planchenoit [Plançenoit]. The Duke of Wellington was hard pressed, his reserves already in action and Bonaparte was probably watching, should the opportunity occur, when with his Guards he could decide the day. Can we help shuddering when we reflect that at this important moment all depended on the local knowledge of a single peasant! Had he guided him wrong, had he led them into the hollow way through which the cannon could not pass, had Bülow's army come up an hour later, the *seal* possibly might have descended on the other side.

On the 19th the allied army advanced, the Duke of Wellington pursued its march on the left bank of the Sambre and on the 22nd the headquarters were at Le Cateau. Marshal Blücher having crossed that river in pursuit of the enemy, after the battle both armies entered the French territory on the 20th, the Prussians by Beaumont and the allied army by Bavay. On our march we daily encountered parties of deserters from the French army returning to their homes; those of the cavalry and artillery previously selling their horses to the natives or whoever would purchase them.

The French army had retired upon Laon, we were bivouacked just outside the town of Le Cateau and having since the 16th lived entirely on bread and eggs. The appearance of the town on our advancing raised strong hopes of finding a restauranteur and something like a dinner. This feeling I believe was pretty general as on arriving at the Singe d'Or, though scarcely 9 o'clock in the morning, every frying pan and gridiron had long been requisitioned. I was however sumptuously regaled with *cotelette de veau*[†] and a bottle of Burgundy. (I was much amused while following a party of soldiers into the town and what occurred to one of the 91st Regiment). He was giving an account of his having been some time a prisoner here and on passing two young women who were on the side of the street, one of them ran towards the soldier exclaiming '*Bien! Bien! Voilà Flack*'[‡] and taking him round the neck embraced him most cordially, the other followed her example. Their salutes were returned with interest by the honest soldier and on our coming up, declared with tears in his eyes, that for the two years that he had been a prisoner there, he had lived in the house of their mother and that the kindness with which he had been treated though during part of the time suffering from

---

[*] He is in error here, Bülow was actually a general.
[†] Veal chop.
[‡] There is no Flack listed in the 91st but there was a Private Flockhard.

a severe fever, could not be exceeded, they took him home with them to see their parents with as much glee as if one of their nearest relatives had returned after a long absence.

For the last three days we had been pushed down close to the batteries on the Canal de l'Ourcq and the Prussians had so completely pillaged every place in the neighbourhood previous to our arrival that not a single inhabitant was to be seen or article of provision procured. Indeed such an idea had our worthy allies given them of what they might expect that although during the whole of our march from the frontiers, the villagers had followed our line of march selling articles to the men with the greatest confidence, yet during our three days sojourn in front of St Denis not a soul came near the bivouac. It is rather a curious fact that although within 6 miles of Paris, the second city in Europe, I absolutely rode several miles for a bottle of wine and a paper of salt.

On the 6th the barriers were officially given up and on the 7th the Prussians took possession of the Tuilleries and bivouacked on the Place de Carousel to the no small annoyance of the Parisians.

The British army after bearing all the hard knocks were bivouacked in the Bois de Boulogne for their pains while the Prussians were put into quarters in the capital.

THE SUPPORT SERVICES

Royal Staff Corps

No. 93   Private Alexander Taylor, Royal Staff Corps
By kind permission of Glasgow Archives, ref. AGN 2219

To Mr James Taylor, Musical Instrument Maker,
114 John Street, Glasgow,
North Britain

Cambrai, 9 March 1817

My dear Jemie,[*]
I received your loving letter and was happy to hear of your & Mary's
welfare, as well as the rest of our family. I received a letter apiece from
mother & Nancy a few days before yours reached me, at the time I
received yours I had some little hopes that I was mending and indeed had
the presumption to take my duty (although in a very weak state) but I
had soon to relinquish the task, for I was taken so ill on guard that I was
obliged to be relieved and with the assistance of a comrade soldier got
home with great difficulty. I brought up a quantity of blood in the middle
of the night of the 4th instant, and has been in a very low state since,
surely my dear brother I am in a very bad state in my inside, but what can
I do, I am fearful some blood vessel is broke in me and that some night
or other I will bring up my heart's blood before any assistance can be
rendered. If ever I wanted the assistance of a tender mother, it is now, but
I am far, far from that, all the help I have to beg for, is from the hands of
my heavenly father. I can expect no one else to give me any help where I
am, it is dreadful to be in a bad state of health in a foreign country and to
depend upon the help a soldier gets. I have lately had cause to curse the
unhappy day that ever I left my father's warm fire side.
    If God of [*sic*] his infinite mercy spares me till the fine weather comes,

------
[*]   His brother.

and I can see no hopes of my recovery, I intend asking application to Colonel Nicolay,* to solicit the Duke of Wellington for my transfer to our headquarters in England, where perhaps the change of air may recruit me a little, but if this cannot be granted, God's will be done. I am perfectly resigned to the dispensations of the Almighty. You will please my dear Jemmie to let father & mother know how I am, which will save me the trouble of writing them a letter, as I have no news to send them, only above all my sincerest love and duty to them.

I received an apparent very affectionate letter from Nancy, wherein she assure me of her love, but my dear Jemmie, if she has any love for me, she has a very strange way of showing it, and I will give you an instance; I received a truly loving letter from her when I was in Brussels, wherein she seemed to say, that she had the greatest concern for my safety. I received it the 2nd June 1815, the very day fortnight before our first attack on the French on 16th June at Quatre Bras, near Brussels, now, I should have thought that if she had the regard for my safety, or the love that she hinted, she would have instantly wrote the moment she heard of the Battle of Waterloo and what thousands of men fell on these trying days, I say she might have wrote to ascertain if I was among the slain, but it clearly evinced that it gave her very little concern, whether I was or was not, as if I was, there was an end of me, and no more about it. Mother wrote me instantly and I received her letter the day after I arrived in Paris, she has indeed been a good mother to me and great indeed will be her reward hereafter for it, but instead of hearing from Nancy immediately after, I was obliged to wait till the month of August 1816. 14 months after the battle, this is no way of showing affection, if it is, I would rather be without it, I may write to her but I can never have the attachment that I used to have for her, she has entirely drawn my warm heart away from her. I sent her after a day or two before I got hers, she has the whole of my mind in it and it has not altered yet, she may be affronted or pleased, which ever suits her, and may make a vow never either to write when I am abroad or speak to me when I am at home, it will not give me the smallest concern. You may give her my love *if it is acceptable*, not otherwise, and tell her I love her as a brother ought to do, but no other. I have this long time left off cawker drinking† and I am sure if I was to live 100 years I would never take to it again, it (along with my late accident) has nearly proved fatal to me. You want to know if I could get leave for 2 or 3 months to come to Glasgow, that my dear Jemmie is impossible in this country, but if I get to England I will try, that is, if I am able to undertake

---

* Lieutenant Colonel William Nicolay commanded the Royal Staff Corps at Waterloo.

† A 'cawker' was slang for a drink, presumably meaning strong liquor.

the journey. You tell me to keep up my spirits, my dear Jemmie I wish I could, I can have nothing here to make me cheerful. Please to present my warmest love to Mary, and regrets much that I am not in England that I could get leave for a short time to see her, it is all my prayers to God that I may once more see you all before my dissolution approaches, whether that prayer will be answered I know not, but as I told you before, I am quite resigned. I have made my will and has bequeathed all my money and effects to Sergeant Cameron, who will forward them to you, this I thought best, as if the Lord would call me hence, all my effects would go to the government if I did without a will, but let us hope my dear James, that I may live to see you all and then I will die happy, at all events my dear Jemmie as long as I am able to sit at a table you shall always hear from me regularly and I an occasion to remind you of answering my letters as I always found you punctual ever since I received the first letter from you in Hythe, Nancy had something to tell me concerning John, but I am unfortunately denied knowing what it is, unless you can get it from her and send me word next letter. I wish you could get me the [news?] of all the family the same as you did in your last and now having almost filled my sheet I have nothing more to say only my kind love to Helen, so till I hear from you I must close with my blessings to you & Mary, I remain your heartfelt affectionate brother,

   Alex Taylor

Let me know if my letters come to you post free.

Medical Services

A Series of Letters to Sir Charles Bell
By kind permission of Wellcome Library and the Trustees of the Army Medical Services Museum, ref. RAMC630

No. 94   Staff Surgeon Charles Collier

Brussels, 5 August 1815

Dear Sir,
I feel much flattered by your communication & request which was received a few days since, and, although sadly in arrears in correspondence to my near friends, & yet much harassed by public duties, I take the first vacant moment to reply to your enquiries. I shall feel doubly gratified in the results of this short, & particularly speaking, splendid service, if, in addition to great professional opportunity, it shall have opened for me an acquaintance with yourself, ranking so highly as you do. Acquaintance, I might say, I

had already, in some degree, attained, but I mean that greater intimacy, which should permit me having recourse to your opinion, wherever I meet with any circumstance novel, or intricate to my own practice. In a few words I may reply to your questions, respecting these cases.

Frederick Meyer died a few hours after you saw him; and I regret that the pressure of duty, at that time, allowed the case to pass without examination.* There was no doubt, I believe, of the liver being the injured viscus, but I suspect there was also some *épanchement*† of blood into the abdomen.

Wanstell,‡ of the *10th,* lived some six days after you saw him, and appeared to be improving physically, but still with that impaired memory, and *confused judgment.* It is odd that he always described himself as belonging *to the 17th,* in which he had *formerly* served, and *then,* as if aware of the error, would *struggle,* to correct himself, but could never articulate, or recollect that it was the tenth. It is wonderful, to think that general life, & even some *combination of sense,* could be carried on, under the immense, & extensive injury done to this brain, which was examined by me in presence of Dr Thomson,§ & some brother Staff surgeons. As far as the operation had been concerned, the surgery was perfect, for there was no pressure from bone, or blood on the brain, but we found a fissure running from the upper part of the parietal bone, towards the base of the skull; the membranes were ruptured & bloody at that point where the fungus was protruded. There *might,* or there might *not be,* inflammation of the pia mater. You will understand that it was not very decisive; down to the roof of the ventricle, on the injured, (the left) side, the medullary substance was much softer than the corresponding hemisphere, & of a bloody colour, gradually [losing?] itself, as if blood had been thrown out in large quantities & there had been efforts at absorption; the thalami corporal striata & plexus appeared to be natural, nor did any mischief appear to have been done in the cerebellum or *posterior* parts of the organ. He died somewhat suddenly, I had bled him the overnight for some slight increase of pain in the heart, in the morning, there was a little oozing of blood from the fungus, enough to tinge the bandage, and, after sitting up to take some breakfast, he fell back, & expired.

I had anticipated this result for two days before, because the sensorial power appeared rather less and because he was more inclined to sleep. His life was correctly rescued at the time of the operation, and that it did not

---

* Examination was the term for an autopsy.
† French term meaning an accumulation of blood/fluid.
‡ Private William Wanstell, Captain Grey's Troop, 10th Hussars.
§ Doctor John Thompson taught military surgery at Edinburgh University, and became Regis Professor, the only chair for military surgery in the UK at the time.

ultimately succeed I attribute *to the shock given to the brain*, rather than to the immediate physical injury; to contusion, rather than to compression.

On Voultz of the German Legion I performed the operation we talked over & I add, with justification, successfully, ie, it now offers every prospect of a speedy case. I cannot immediately recall, whether, at the time you saw him, he had appearances of tetanic spasms, but, prior to my undertaking anything, *it was so confirmed*, that I deemed it necessary to call a consultation, & having then our opinions confirmed of its absolute necessity for any chance of life, I carried, what had been before conned over, into execution. I found no difficulty in dissecting the muscle from the bone, & *very little* in sawing it off *close* to the head; with two incisions; I removed all those splinters of bone which had been driven in among the muscles, and those portions of soft parts which appeared thickened & diseased. There was very little haemorrhage as the axillary artery was not touched; two ligatures were all, I think, which were required. But the head in the socket was some impediment to the meeting of the flap, and I rather regretted afterwards & now regret this also had not been taken away. The spasm appeared neither augmented, nor diminished by the operation, the counter arm became strongly tetanic, jaws were fixed; the least effort to swallow, produced the most frightful convulsion. His tongue, caught between the teeth, was badly lacerated; the emprosthotonos was succeeded by the opisthotonos* & of as marked a character as I ever witnessed. When sitting on the side of the bed, I have seen him thrown on his back, & the body arched by the power of the muscles; and though all this, & though some sloughing of the stump, which ensued, he has struggled, is now free, for some days, of spasm, which gradually subsided, after three weeks hold, the stump is fast closing up, & he walks about his ward & is considered as a convalescing patient. Although I know every attention was paid to this man by the young gentleman who does duty under me, & I obtained every opinion to see if I could gather any fresh view of the subject, and tried whatever offered a reasonable chance, I cannot say I attribute his cure to medicine, but to one of those happy constitutions we sometimes see, which survives the most frightful injuries, & survives in spite of the most natural & certain prognostics. What think you of this case? Would it have been ameliorated by the removal of the head of the bone?

James Alexander did not survive 48 hours after you saw him. I was quite prepared, in the event of haemorrhage, to cut down upon, & secure the bleeding vessels, but he died exhausted; he died, as I have seen many, from the powers of life yielding to an injury they are unable to restore.†

---

* The drawing forward of the body was followed by arching backwards in spasm.

† James Alexander died from an air embolism, which was first diagnosed by the

He had no fever, nor cough.

Albrecht Heifer is doing well, & doing so, from our looking constantly to that point you regard as the probable cause of destruction; once he has been bled, and the putrid symptoms have been those constantly watched, & kept under by mild, but steady antiphlogistic* treatment. The sinuses are close, the wound is well granulated, his health is steady and I think there is yet enough of it to complete his cure.

Ball is quite well, & will be discharged to his regiment. Believe me to be very faithfully yours,

Charles Collier

PS Voultz's case will be submitted at length to the *medical public*, by a physician, on account of the *cure*, or *subsidence* of such *strongly featured* tetanus. There are but two cases living of all who had this affection, this man, & a French officer. His death was constantly anticipated by all, and by none more than myself, on account of the general ill success of our means in these cases. I shall not enter further at length into the treatment than I have done, as it is *none medical* & does not so immediately concern what you wanted I should think, besides having promised the details to a physician, it would be anticipating, perhaps, his interests. CC

No. 95   From the Same

Brussels, 20 August 1815

Dear Sir

You were kind enough, to offer me a copy of the sketch you took of Ball's case, and, as I have sent a statement of it to Sir James McGrigor,[†] for the Medico and Chirurgical transactions. I should feel most truly obliged if you could now favour me with it. Perhaps you would have no objection to send it at once to Sir James, at the Medical Board, Berkeley Street, and I think, if the case be worthy of notice, the committee will have an engraving taken from it; without some such context, the best description is very feeble.

Voultz will soon be well; the health is good, & Sparrow has long since yielded, stump nearly healed.

---

famous French Surgeon Larrey.
*   Anti-inflammatory, induced by bleeding, purging and vomiting.
†   Director General Sir James McGrigor (Drew, *Medical Officers*, number 1182). It should be noted that McGrigor was only appointed 4 days before Waterloo and hence the medical services were clearly ill prepared. The survival rates for casualties at Waterloo were markedly worse than those at Toulouse, when the Army Medical Department was at its zenith.

Heifer* (who had the breast struck by a round shot) is convalescent.

I have had a most interesting case since I saw you, in the Life Guard's man, in Ward 14, who had the 4th and 5th ribs broken, by a musket shot. I pointed him out to you as a case doing well by general treatment, bleeding, bandaging &c. He had twice had a reoccurrence of inflammatory symptoms which had yielded to the usual means, but towards the close of July, he began to exhibit signs of more permanent mischief. He had [evening?] exacerbations of severely flushed cheeks, a short cough & a breathing, as he described it, of air *like rotten eggs* & onions. Instituting (on the evening of the 27th July) a more rigid examination, I felt what appeared to be either a ball, or a detached portion of bone & as my patient was obviously losing ground, I determined on ascertaining whether any piece of the rib, pressing, or driven in to the pleura, cured to the cause of the excitant. I made a free incision, accordingly, extending obliquely from the 4th towards the angle of the 5th rib. I removed several pieces of the broken bone, & feeling a *bulging of the pleura*, I made a cautious opening into the chest; some very fetid air first escaped, & then, to my gratification, out flowed fully a quart of pus, of an almost insupportable odour. He has been bled four times since & kept on [a] spare diet†. A tent‡ is introduced twice daily to the bottom of the wound, which we find difficult to keep open. There is still slight oozing of pus, but gradually diminishing. A few bubbles of air sometimes escape, the constitutional symptoms all on the decline, & the patient appears to be fairly convalescing. I feared emphysema,§ but I have not observed the least, even around the edges of the wound.

That case of very badly fractured femur in Ward 16 is an old man, a Pole, which I consulted you about, is doing so remarkably well, that I expect to have him on crutches in a week. The bone was miserably broken, the ball had entered just above the great trochanter, when you saw it, I think it must have been shortened fully three inches. It does not now appear to be more than one inch less than the sound one.

All the compound fractures of the tibia *have done,* or *are doing*, well.

When you can find leisure from your many pursuits, to favour me with your opinions on these, or on other subjects at all connected with our profession, I should be much obliged. We have all had enough of learning, and he is the happier who feels the greatest necessity for it.

Accept my best wishes for your health, & believe me very truly yours,
Charles Collier.

---

* Albrecht Heifer, KGL
† A spare or low diet consisted of sago, rice pudding etc.
‡ A fabric stopper which allows drainage of the wound.
§ A collection of air in the tissues.

I crave your excuse, my dear sir, for this *disorderly* letter, but hurried as I am, it is something to be able to do so much.

If you would address any letter for me to my brother's care (J. Collier Esq, 30 Carey Street, Lincoln's Inn) it will be forwarded through the commander-in-chief's office.

PS 29 August. I have been delayed in sending off this until the present time, & I am sorry to say my Life Guards man is not quite so well. I was, I fear, too sanguine, as the cure will be tedious. I have had occasion to dilate the wound down to the thorax & to give issue to a large collection of pus, & again *the action gave relief*. This case is quite extreme, I shall give you further particulars here after for your information, & opinion, now it will be published I believe, by a friend of mine who has been much interested in the man's fate. I tied the external iliac yesterday, on account of femoral aneurism within about three inches of Poupart's ligament. The tumour was large & I feared disease had reached where I was to operate, but it was fortunately quite sound. The aneurism* was received by musket shot on the 18th June, I shall furnish particulars hereafter. This day there is great want of blood in the limb, but I hope to prevent ill consequence.

No. 96   Staff Surgeon Jordan Roche[†]

Brussels, 17 August

I regret very much, I had it not in my power to pay earlier attention to your wishes. [As] I was ordered to Mons to form a grand hospital, I lost an opportunity of following up many interesting cases, as well as the pleasure of immediately complying with your request. I beg to assure you, that I will always hold myself flattered, in being afforded an opportunity to forward you any medical or surgical intelligence from this place.

Sam Pritchard[‡] is alive and doing well all things considered; complains of occasional pain, in the left side of the head. The left eye is protruding from the socket, I apprehend the ball is lodged behind its orbit. The sight of the right eye is impaired as well as the hearing of the left ear. This is really a very extraordinary case; you will perhaps soon have an opportunity of seeing him in England, as he will, I believe, be soon sent home.

If I mistake not you had a sketch taken of Karl Vrieborg's wound of the King's German Legion. Recollect however you took particular

---

*   An aneurism is an enlargement and weakening of the arterial wall.
†   Staff Surgeon Jordan Roche (Drew, *Medical Officers*, number 1526)
‡   Private Samuel Pritchard, of Captain Erskine's No 4 Company of the 4th Foot.

notice of the case, the left thigh was fractured with very great muscular protrusion. It was apparently a hopeless case and an operation at the hip joint was contemplated. He is now in a promising way, though I do not consider his recovery certain. The protruded muscles reduced to a plain surface and the loss is comparatively small, there is some irritation from the protrusion of the pelvic extremity of the femur. All things considered, he is doing surprisingly well.

In my division, two cases of tetanus have occurred of that disease, I believe you saw them both; one had his left leg amputated close to the knee and his right ankle fractured by a musket ball; he is now so entirely recovered of tetanus & in other respect doing well. The treatment was not particular, the wound of the ankle joint was dressed with lint dipped in spirits of *Fenouil*[*] & a strong embrocation of tincture of opium &c. was used externally and we contrived to introduce by the mouth 'for the jaws were not firmly locked' some cordial and antispasmodic medicines.

The other case originated from compound fracture of the thigh, which it was not possible to put in splints from the irritable state of the hock. This man died of exhaustion from the local disease. He had recovered of tetanus some time before his death; his treatment had been similar to that of the former, except that a few mercurial frictions to the arm, had been used. The following may be considered an extraordinary case and escape.

J. Turner 3rd Battalion 1st Foot Guards[†] was wounded by a splinter of a shell on the 18th which entered the dorsum of the illium [sic][‡] and directing its course towards the regis umbiliac, lodged between the superficial and duplicated muscle that form the anterior parietes of the abdomen. His health was excellent till about the 9th July when infection and hardness appeared about the umbular and lumbar region, and a hard body, changing its position with the posture of the patient, was evident. An incision was made upon it, by Staff Surgeon Brownriggs,[§] who extracted a piece of a shell weighing 9½ ounces, with ragged margin, it had formed a cavity between the internal oblique and transversal muscles, nice & clean. His patient is now doing well; his wound looking healthy and his general health and spirits good. This, with cases that daily occur, tends to show, what efforts nature, and an educated surgical aid may do, for recovery. I recollect, at the battle before New Orleans a man presented himself to me with an apparently enormous tumour over the left clavicle. I cut down from it, and extracted an iron ball weighing one pound that had entered at the superior part of the left scapula and pushing forward,

[*] Fennel.
[†] Private Jonathan Turner of Lieutenant Colonel Reeve's Company.
[‡] The ilium is part of the pelvic bone.
[§] Staff Surgeon David Brownrigg (Drew, *Medical Officers*, number 1980).

smashed the clavicle and thus exhausting itself, had not sufficient force to break the integuments. This man was doing well when I left him but being ordered on other duty, I do not know, the result. Requesting you will always consider me at your service, I remain, dear sir, your most faithfully,

J. Roche

No. 97   Staff Surgeon John Hennen[*]

Brussels, 6 September 1815

My dear Sir,

Your kind letter of the 17th of July reached me only this day having travelled as I learn from the postmark to Paris & after going God knows how many rounds has slumbered till now in some of the native post offices. It was transmitted to me from Ghent! At the close of the surgical campaign I find that I have been more successful than on any former occasion, & I have operated less. The compound fractures have done much better than at any other period. In my own practise I saved exactly one half, & also four wounds of the liver, four of the bladder, three of the head (without trepanning) & one of the head where the operation was performed.

Captain Campbell[†] was my only death, I would not be permitted to open the body but he died spitting pus, & with a liver enormously distended.

Captain Elphinstone[‡] after copious general & surgical bleedings in a tedious interval of seven weeks, is gone home perfectly recovered.

Of three shattered shoulders two were operated upon & one (the worst, and that where I merely padded the wound and sawed off the end of the bone) was left un-operated on; of the former two, one died tetanic, the vein on dissection found inflamed up to the very oracle,[§] the other proceeded *this day* for England.

Your visit here, will I assure you be long & thankfully remembered by the seniors of this Staff. For myself, I have never had but one opinion & I feel happy in stating it now, by offering you the assurance that I am very sincerely, your obliged servant,

J. Hennen

---

[*]   Henne (Drew, *Medical Officers*, number 1971) was a superb technical surgeon and artist who unfortunately succumbed to an outbreak of yellow fever at Gibraltar in 1828.

[†]   Captain Neil Campbell 79th Foot died of his wounds at Brussels.

[‡]   Captain James D. Elphinstone, 7th Hussars.

[§]   A vein to the heart.

No. 98   Staff Surgeon John Boggie*

Brussels, 12 September 1815

My dear Sir,

I had the honour to receive your letter a long time ago, which I ought to have answered much sooner. However I trust that you will excuse me for the delay which I have made, as I hope to be able to give you more information about some of the cases which I have seen treated, than if I had written sooner.

Major Vernor's† wound was exactly as you suspected; the bone was injured; some time after you left this it became extremely painful, the whole arm swelled & he had a considerable degree of fever. At least two small pieces of bone were thrown off & since that he has been considerably easier. The matter was working down the arm & forming a sac under the deltoid muscle a little below the wound. An incision was made down to the bone by which the matter has been discharged & I am now keeping the wound open. His health is very much improved but as a farther exfoliation must yet take place, the cure is likely to be very tedious.

The man whom you mention, who had his shoulder torn off, belonged I believe to Mr Bell; he died, I am told, soon after you left this.

The case which you saw in my division of the shoulder torn off is now nearly well, he left this a few days ago for England, with other invalids. The acromion process which has been left bare, dropped off about a month ago.

I have had some very interesting cases of wounds of the intestines which are now quite well. In two cases the faeces were discharging by the wound for upwards of three weeks. The colon appeared to be the portion wounded.

I had also a case of wound of the bladder, the urine was discharged by the wound 25 days & at last the patient (a French officer) got completely well. What was curious in this was that as long as when the urine was discharged by the back, he scarcely ever passed a drop by the natural way. Mr Guthrie's case of hip joint operation is, I am told likely to recover.

A case of aneurism occurred a few days ago, high up in the thigh. The external iliac was taken up, but the man died in three days after.

The case I am told is to be published. The operation was done by Mr Collier.

---

* Staff Surgeon John Boggie (Drew, *Medical Officers*, number 2064) had served in Egypt in 1801 and retired in 1816.
† Major Robert Vernor of the Scots Greys, he retired from the army in 1817.

I do not know if you have any belief in the wind of a ball. A French soldier whom I had in my division for a wound of the leg with a musket ball; consulted me one day about his eye, he said a cannon ball passed close to his head on the 18th June, he was instantly struck blind of one eye & has never since recovered the sight of it.[*]

I shall do myself the honour of waiting on you, when I get to London. I remain my dear Sir, yours very faithfully,

John Boggie

No. 99   Hospital Assistant Henry Blackadder[†]

Outline of a case: injury of the brain

Dominique Modere at 27 was wounded at the Battle of Waterloo on the 18th June. He lay three days on the field without food, was then taken to a village and from there to one of the churches in Brussels. He was admitted into the Gendarmerie Hospital on the 30th June and came under my care on the 4th July.

A musket ball had entered at the anterior part of the squamous suture of the temporal bone on the right side and passing backwards and downwards fractured the parietal bone and lodged in the brain.

On the morning of the 5th July the wound was laid open by Mr Charles Bell; three portions of bone were removed and the ball extracted from the posterior lobe of the right hemisphere of the brain immediately over the anterior cerebral superexm [*sic*]. The ball when extracted was covered with the substance of the brain.

Notwithstanding this extensive injury of the head, his constitution could scarcely be said to be at all affected. His pulse before laying open the wound was 72 and on the day after 80. He made no complaint but a slight headache and deafness of the right ear, appetite strong, tongue clean, belly regular, skin cool, slept well.

The wound was carefully cleaned of blood and small portions of the brain, the lips were then brought together and retained by means of two stitches and adhesive straps, over which a uniform compress and bandage.

His head was kept constantly cool and moist with cold water, his bowels were freely opened, diaphoretic medicines[‡] regularly administered

---

[*] Injuries caused by the pressure of a passing cannonball was a contentious issue. Memoirs of the period give copious examples but medical personnel were generally sceptical.

[†] Henry Home Blackadder (Drew, *Medical Officers*, number 3658) a hospital assistant who became an assistant surgeon on the Staff in September 1815.

[‡] These promoted sweating.

and he was rigidly kept on the lowest diet.

Under this management (his bowels kept constantly loose) he continued free from any uneasy feeling until the 16th when he complained of concentary [*sic*] pains in the back of the head and of uneasiness from the light of a candle and noise. The wound looked extremely well, the lips nearly united, very little discharge of matter, the pulse somewhat more full but not more frequent.

A fresh cathartic entirely removed these unfavourable symptoms and from that time till the 24th [July] he continued improving. On that day however the expression of his eyes and fullness of his countenance indicated some new visitation of the system. His pulse for the first time was found as high as 96 and hard, skin very hot, considerable disposition to sleep. Upon making enquiry it was found that the officer under whose care he had been placed for the last three days had omitted giving him his usual laxative and had given him wine, eggs and other extras. These were immediately stopped and a fresh cathartic of air administered by which means he was in the course of a few hours again restored to his former state of convalescence.

From this time he has again been under my immediate care, he makes no complaint but of slight deafness of the right ear and this he thinks is diminishing gradually. He says that from his present sensations he could not know that he had been wounded. He has all along been permitted to smoke tobacco freely, he uses it to remove the sensation of hunger, having a strong appetite and being at the same time kept on a very spare diet, of the propriety of which he is completely satisfied. The wounds are now (6th August) nearly all cauterised, to all appearance the remaining part will be skinned over in the course of four or six days at the farthest. The pulsation of the brain is distinctly visible at two different parts of the ceatrix, in every other respect he enjoys perfect health.

H. H. Blackadder, Hospital Assistant to the forces

NOT AT WATERLOO

Armed Forces

No. 100   Lieutenant Colonel John Burgoyne, Royal Engineers
From Life and Correspondence of Field Marshal Sir John Burgoyne, *vol. 1,*
pp. 327–9, by Lieutenant Colonel George Wrottesley, London 1873

Waterloo: Remarks made on a visit to the ground in 1816

The field of Waterloo in front of Mont St Jean is frequently accounted as no position, and does not show to very much advantage, even on Craan's plan, although that appears to be an accurate survey. On inspection, however, without which it is impossible to have a perfect idea of ground, it is certainly favourable for giving battle on, and if a little work could have been done on it, might have been made excellent.

It was not that commanding kind of position that is sometimes found, and which strikes the eye at once; on the contrary, the ridge occupied by our army is lower than the heights a mile or two in front, from whence the French army advanced. But it still had many of the essentials of a good fighting position. The flanks were on commanding points, that discovered the ground well all round them, at a fair distance from the main road by which the enemy approached and would have required him to make a considerable detour across the country to have turned them.

The real left of the position, at a turning of the cross road, was not more than three quarters of a mile from the Genappe chaussee in the centre, the right resting immediately above Goumont; the whole being about a mile and a half or two miles in extent; it, therefore, very compact. In front of the left the ground was well discovered, and with no very favourable points for the enemy's artillery. A road ran along the line in this part with thin hedges along it and a very slight bank, affording some little cover to the infantry if they laid down. This road continued along the centre and right of the position, out of sight of the enemy in those parts, but not affording any cover. The ground in front of the centre and right was more broken, but the hollows were well looked into by the chateau of Goumont in front of the right, and the farm of the La Haye Sainte on the high road. The whole line was on a ridge, which rounding back to the rear, covered the troops from the sight and from the direct fire of the enemy.

The chateau of Goumont and the Haye Sainte were strong buildings, not too far in front of the line, and situated in hollows, so as not to be much exposed to be cannonaded severely. They were both of very great consequence as posts. The first was occupied and defended so well as to be retained through the whole day, in spite of all the efforts of the enemy. The troops were put into the Haye Sainte only a short time before the action commenced. The approach to it from the position was very much exposed indeed. The men in it became a kind of forlorn hope; they fired all their ammunition away, and then, for want of communication and support, were overpowered. When the French were in possession of this point an extensive hollow was open to them, which could not be seen from any part of our line, and under favour of which, their great mass of cavalry remained for some hours within 400 yards of our line, from whence they advanced and made charges at their pleasure.

Such was the nature of our ground. Even a single company of sappers with their tools might in a few hours, have rendered most essential service in improving it, by preparing the two buildings for defence, and throwing up traverses for guns across the two chaussees. The Guards did to the chateau what was necessary for its defence. Had the Haye Sainte been loopholed, all its doors and approaches towards the front and flanks been strongly barricaded, and a communication made to the rear, it would probably have been held through the whole day. The traverse across the Genappe chausses would have given our artillery the command of that road by which the enemy brought down his troops to many of the most serious attacks, and still more so had the eighteen pounders been up, which had been prepared for the field.

Had there been an opportunity and means for more work, the points are clearly marked out where four or six detached works could have been placed to advantage, besides the cover that might be thrown up for the line. The Duke did not wish to have any ground entrenched beforehand which might give any clue to his intentions, but would have been glad to have had anything which could be thrown up at the time. Two companies of sappers and 3,000 men might, on the night of the 17th, in addition to the above mentioned posts, have thrown up such a line, as would have afforded great cover to our infantry and guns, have brought them more to the ridge of the hill and would have considerably checked and broken the advances of cavalry.

The French attacks do not appear to have been well judged, for want of union or combination. At one time, they made a great attack on Goumont on the right; at another, and for a considerable period, the great mass of cavalry were acting without support; at another, a powerful attack of infantry on our left; and last of all, when the cavalry was nearly annihilated and great part of the infantry of the line beaten, the infantry of the Imperial Guard, who had been in reserve, were brought up and shared the same fate. Each of these efforts appear to have been so powerful, that if united, in the style of the Duke of Wellington's attacks at Salamanca and Vitoria, certainly there would have been a better chance of success.

Had the Prussians and British, even on the morning of the 18th, been under one general, it is probable that many of the former, who marched by Ohain, might have been brought up regiment by regiment much earlier in the day; and they were much wanted in our line. As it was, it is probable that Blücher rather preferred bringing up his own army in mass together, as the Prussian army, than have portions of them falling in and beating the enemy off, under the Duke. As we were able to maintain our ground, the victory was more complete as it was, and Blücher gained great credit for acting so decisively respecting Grouchy's Corps. Had the enemy turned our left to separate us from the Prussians, the position would have been altered, with the left on the Forest of Soignes, the right probably where the left was in the battle, and the army would still have held a very good position.

J. F. B.

No. 101   General Francis Dundas[*]
By kind permission of the British Library, Mudford papers, Add. MS 19390 25–29

Query
1 I have reason to think the Prussians made their first attack about 7 o'clock in the afternoon of the 18th June though their troops were seen advancing at an earlier hour but without coming into action.

2 If the Prussians had remained at Wavre and not advanced to cooperate with the Duke of Wellington I fear the result of the battle would have been unfortunate as the Duke's army had made a great exertion, many corps were nearly annihilated so that he could not have maintained his

[*] General Francis Dundas was colonel of the 71st Foot, and a very experienced officer having served in the American War of Independence, the West Indies and the Cape. His last campaign had been to Germany in 1806.

position the following day even keeping his ground during the night if Bonaparte had persevered would have been a difficult task to perform with an army so reduced in numbers and fatigued.

3 Of the action at Quatre Bras on the evening of the 16th June I cannot give any particulars but they are well known. The few English regiments there engaged showed much courage and firmness which enabled the Duke of Wellington to keep the ground. I think his situation there on the morning of the 17th after the retreat of Blücher was extremely critical of which I believe he was himself aware and retired about noon accordingly. The French cavalry followed the Duke on his retreat and were charged from time to time by our cavalry under the command of Lord Uxbridge. I do not think the French columns made any movement until the whole of our infantry and guns had made good the passing through the village of Genappe which I conceive to have been the difficult part of the operation. It is necessary to explain here the French supineness I believe the Duke himself thought that Bonaparte had left the army.

4 The surface of the country is unusual and what may be called undulating without any hedges or enclosures but covered with crops. It is such as to enable cavalry to act in about every direction there being nothing to impede them in the open fields. Some gardens around the villages and houses seemed to form the only obstruction. There are many heights nearly equal in point of elevation consequently the advantage of ground is not very considerable.

5 The house at La Haye Sainte was defended by a battalion of the German legion. It was carried by the enemy in the afternoon.

6 I believe the engagement commenced soon after midday.

7 I have not heard that Bonaparte was ever on the point of being captured by the Marquis of Anglesey.

8 I was not employed on service last year in the continent therefore could have no opportunity of knowing exactly & officially the strength of the Duke of Wellington's army in the field. My conjecture is as follows:

British cavalry	6,500
German cavalry	4,000
British infantry	15,000

Hanoverians	20,000
Brunswickers	10,000
Sundry infantry	10,000
Total	65,500

9 It was said at the time Bonaparte marched and crossed the Sambre he had an army with him amounting to 130,000 men. He sustained some loss in his battles with the Prussians and as he had despatched two divisions to Wavre on the 18th I would suppose the troops under his immediate orders on that day might amount to 80,000.

10 The particulars of General Alava's report have escaped my recollection.

No. 102   Unknown Officer
By kind permission of E. & R. Shanahan of Australia

Plymouth Dock, dated 11 Aug. 1815

My dear Sir,
I have delayed writing so long under the expectation of being sent on the recruiting service and wished to give you an account of our destination. As the war however seems to have come to a close we shall remain for the present where we are.

I send you, as the greatest curiosity I have, the copy of a sketch of Bonaparte done about a week since on board the *Bellerophon* by his secretary Colonel Lanat.* Having had a very good sight of him myself I can pronounce it to be a strong likeness of the outline of his face and head. The day after he arrived here one of our colonels borrowed the general's boat and I was glad to seize the opportunity of taking Emily to see this wonder of the age. When we arrived near the ship we saw Bonaparte walking backwards and forwards in the cabin in conversation with General Bertrand.

Our boat (which was a very handsome one and filled with ladies and officers) having attracted his attention, he came forward and looked at us occasionally with an opera glass, for the space of five minutes. He was dressed in a green coat with red collar and cuffs and gold epaulettes and he wore a star. After staying good-naturedly long enough to satisfy the curiosity of the ladies, he sat down to a writing table and we saw no more of him.

You will have seen by the papers what an extraordinary sensation was

---

* Lieutenant Colonel Nicolas Louis Planat de la Faye who was part of Napoleon's entourage on *Bellerophon*, but did not sail to St Helena.

created here by Bonaparte's presence however the stories that related of him have no foundation; the fact is that he went away with a very good grace and having been invited to the *Northumberland* on Monday last, he immediately desired that all the officers should be introduced to him, and that same evening he was seated comfortably at cards with the admiral.

He is accompanied by Bertrand and three other superior officers and two ladies with their children and eight servants. Being desirous that the surgeon of the *Bellerophon* should also accompany him,* and the surgeon also being willing to go, he was allowed to have him and has promised him five hundred a year, in addition to his pay. He has taken with him about twenty thousand pounds sterling in French coin (Napoleons). He constantly regretted that he was not allowed to remain in England and domiciliate here, but on taking leave of Lord Keith, he expressed himself satisfied and obliged by his Lordship's civility and every person who has been near him is pleased with this manner and feels somewhat softened towards him. The *Northumberland* and the squadron bid a final adieu to our coast this morning and as regards Napoleon, Europe may be in peace. But the spirit still exists in France, and I do firmly believe the Bourbons will never reign in quiet.

I have been twice at St Helena and have dined often in the house which will be Napoleon's residence. It is a delightful spot and with half the comfort that he will have I could make my mind up to live some years there very easily,

As I do not wish to spoil my work below, I must conclude and Emily will scold me for not leaving room for her to say with how much pleasure she joins in love and every good wish to my aunt and yourself, your sincerely affectionate nephew [G W Tighe?†]

We continue in the same lodgings and pass our time very comfortably and peaceably receiving much attention from the gentlemen and ladies about us the markets which had risen a little, in consequence of so many ships being here will now fall again, necessaries of life in general are thirty percent cheaper here than to the eastward which may perhaps be accounted for by the immense quantities of fish which are constantly brought in. I wish we were near enough, I could supply your table with fish at very little expense.

---

* Barry O'Meara.

† This is my best guess at the signature and the only realistic option in the Army List of 1815. Captain George William Tighe of Bradshaw's Recruiting Corps was on half pay in 1815.

No. 103   Unknown Officer of the Royal Marines
Extracts from letters from an officer of the Royal Marines on board
HMS Northumberland, *dated 5 August 1815*

It is my guard, and I have to sit in the antechamber of Napoleon, to prevent communication between him and the ship's company, and also to be a check on his own domestics; it is now *one* and I must keep awake to *six* . . . Napoleon gets very sulky if he is not treated with that deference and respect to which he is accustomed: his own followers treat him with the same respect as if he was still emperor.

Beattie, my captain, was at Acre: Napoleon learnt this in conversation; seemed quite pleased, caught hold of his ear and gave it a good pinch (which is his custom when pleased), and seems to have taken a great liking to him. He is sometimes very communicative: today he mentioned the project he had formed for invading England in 1805, declared it had been his intention to lead the expedition himself; and said it might have succeeded.

The plan was this: he sent his fleet to the West Indies for the purpose of drawing our fleets there, which it did, Lord Nelson and Sir Robert Calder both following Villeneuve there; he was to return immediately to the Channel, and Napoleon said he calculated that Villeneuve would be in the Channel at least a fortnight before our fleets could get back.

His army was embarked (200,000 he says), but the plan was disconcerted by Villeneuve's going into Cadiz instead of coming to the Channel. His words were, ' He might as well have been in the East Indies as at Cadiz;' and he then declared that if Villeneuve had obeyed his orders, he should certainly have invaded England, be the result what it might.

Bertrand is the only one that seems to feel his situation; he speaks of Napoleon often with tears, and is extremely agitated when conversing on the state of France. He says Napoleon did not calculate upon fighting the English and Prussians at Waterloo. The Prussians were beaten on the 16th, and it was not supposed they could have been up to take part in the battle of the 18th. He thinks the French would have been victorious if the Prussians had not come up; but circumstances were not favourable. The French soldiers fought very well; the officers did not.

I asked him what became of the French army after the battle, why they did not retreat in some sort of order? He said, with a shrug, they were annihilated, there were none left; yet, notwithstanding these admissions, they break out gasconading about their victories.

Napoleon's spirits are better; he enters into conversation very freely on different parts of his life. The other day he was speaking of Waterloo: he said he had not the least idea of fighting on the 18th: he did not suppose Wellington would have given him battle; he so fully expected Wellington to retreat, that he had not even made preparations for battle, and was a little taken by surprise.

'But,' said he, ' I never was so pleased as when I saw he intended to fight. I had not a doubt of annihilating his army; it was the only thing I could have wished. I expected him to abandon Flanders, and fall back on the Russians; but when I found he gave me battle singly, I was confident of his destruction. My soldiers behaved well; my generals did not.'

He says it was dusk when his army was thrown into confusion; that if he could have shown himself, they would have rallied and been victorious; but that the rout was so great, he was carried away in the throng. He went to Paris to try to save the honour of France, but found he could not.

He positively asserts that previously to the Battle of Waterloo, and after his return to France, Austria proposed to him to abdicate in favour of Napoleon II, and promised to support him. His followers, too, have mentioned so many particulars respecting this, that I do not doubt the fact. This proposition had nothing to do with the forged letter of the Duke of Bassano, which they also speak of as a falsehood: none such was shown to him by Murat.

He has been talking this evening about his turning Mahometan: he said it was a long time before he could persuade them that he was a true Mussulman; 'but at last I persuaded them that Mahomet was wrong in some things, and I was right; and they acknowledged me to be the greater man.'* He says that in his retreat from Acre he lost nearly half his army.

Yesterday he remarked that Madame Bertrand was in much better spirits than when she attempted to drown herself, and added, ' A man of true courage will bear up against misfortunes, and finally surmount them, while common minds will sink under them. He converses sometimes on the subject of his making away with himself, and calmly reprobates the idea of his being supposed capable of it.

I believe the object of the guard is to prevent communication with the crew. Napoleon told the admiral that he did not doubt he could get many to join him if he tried; and, indeed, they are a set of as mutinous rascals as I ever heard of; though I don't think they would assist him to escape. What I am going to state must, for the credit of the country, be a secret: they mutinied, and refused to get anchor up at Portsmouth;† the artillery company, the 53rd [Foot], and ourselves, were under arms for three hours; that is to say, till we had sailed.

About twenty of the principal seamen were seized and confined, but sent away from the ship; and the conduct and language of the sailors now is beyond everything; they think nothing of striking the midshipmen.

---

* Quite a statement!

† I have been unable to find any corroborating evidence for this mutiny.

St Helena

We arrived at this barren horrid island yesterday, after a passage of ten weeks. In my former travels in these latitudes everything seemed animated; the sea swarming with fish, water brilliant and phosphoric, sky without a cloud. Now everything has been the reverse: since we left Madeira, the sun has been constantly obscured with clouds; the weather, even on the equator, as cold as you can have had it in England; scarcely a fish to be seen; and, what is still more extraordinary, the trade winds, which in the tropics are calculated upon as certain, have blown almost from the opposite quarter to what they were expected, and thereby opposed our progress.

We crossed the equator on the 23rd September, the same day as the sun; the greatest height of the thermometer was then only 75°, with a vertical sun; since it has been as low as 66°: today it is only 70°. Napoleon has been in pretty good health and spirits all the voyage, conversing on every subject without the least hesitation.

I have dined three times with Napoleon. I cannot say I think his manners have much of that elegance which might have been expected from a person of his ci-devant rank. He has a particularly disagreeable grunt when he does not understand what you say, and desires a repetition. He converses freely, but not at table, with the Frenchmen, and takes no more notice of the ladies than if they were a hundred miles off. I have not heard him speak once to Madame Bertrand at table, and seldom elsewhere.

Napoleon landed on the 17th of October: he appeared a good deal affected at leaving the ship, and spoke so.

Did I tell you that the band, who used to play every day, struck up of their own accord, a few days after we left England, '*Vive Henri Quatre*', upon Bonaparte coming [on deck] after dinner? Thinking it might hurt his feelings, we stopped them immediately; but he had heard enough to know what it was, and requested they would play that or any other French tune, as he liked it much; and afterwards they played the loyal and revolutionary airs indiscriminately.

Of the Duc d'Enghien's business he said, not a fortnight ago; (December 1815) and you may rely upon he did say, though I did not hear it; it was in dictating to his secretary, Las Cases, two days after the Duc was executed, he received proofs of his innocence, and that the Duc even solicited employment in his service, stating his poverty; but that the application was not received till after his death.

This Bonaparte certainly said; for I do not think his secretary would say so if it was not true: and he said he had it from Napoleon's mouth, as part of papers which he was dictating the day before I had it.

No. 104   Major General Sir Hudson Lowe
By kind permission of Sir Michael Bunbury Bt, KCVO, DL, and
Suffolk Record Office, Bury St Edmunds, ref. E18/740/4

London, 27 May 1815

To Major General Sir H. E. Bunbury KCB*

Dear Sir,
I beg leave to inclose an extract of the letter I received from General
Gneisenau previous to my departure from Brussels, with copy of
the remarks of the Duke of Wellington, which by his Grace's desire I
communicated to General Gneisenau. I apprehended the Prussian army
would be much gratified in having a rocket battery attached to it, in the
same manner as was done to the army of the Prince Royal of Sweden to
be used in the attacks of those towns where a defence might be attempted
without the inhabitants or the guards having the means of resisting a
regular siege. I have the honour to remain dear Sir, your most faithful &
most obedient servant.
   H. Lowe

Civilians

No. 105   Henry Lord Bathurst†

To General the Prince of Orange

War Department, 21 March 1815

Sir,
Since I had the honour of addressing your Royal Highness upon the 15th
and 16th instant, the circumstances of France have been such as to confirm
the expediency of making every exertion to place the Netherlands in a
good state of defence and every preparation to meet the attack which may
be expected in case Bonaparte should he acquire the dominion of France.
I am therefore to convey to your Royal Highness the commands of the
Prince Regent that you should take every measure of precaution and
preparation and that you should concert with the commander-in-chief
of the Prussian forces upon the Rhine a system of defensive measures,
placing your forces in such manner as may appear best calculated to
cover the Low Countries and to repel any irruption from the side of

---

* Major General Sir Henry Edward Bunbury was Under Secretary of State in the
Colonial and War Department.
† Henry 3rd Earl Bathurst, was Secretary for War and the Colonies.

France, but I am at the same time to desire that Your Royal Highness will not under any circumstances invade the French territory or engage in offensive measures without having received further instructions and authority from His Majesty's Government. I have &c.

Bathurst.

No. 106   Charles Greville*
By kind permission of the National Library of Wales, ref. Aston Hall (2) 2728

To Mrs Lloyd, Chigwell, Essex

Brussels, 5 July 1815

I feel quite ashamed my dear Mrs Lloyd & you must I fear think me a brute for having so long delayed obeying your kind commands & telling you of my thankfulness and happiness at the preservation of my boy in the midst of such a dreadful scene of carnage & desolation as I believe never was seen before. I did not receive the certain & welcome intelligence the next day after we parted when Mr James arrived at the Hague; had he not come I had determined on returning immediately to Brussels from which he dissuaded me and pressed me so much to stay on from day to day that I did not get home till Saturday last. Whilst I was at the Hague *par parenthèse*† is the dullest of all dull places, I did nothing but repose my harassed nerves & it did me a great deal of good & as I thought each day there would be the last I determined to put off writing to you till I arrived here that I might give you an account of our friends. Since my return however I have been passing all my days in going from one poor wounded friend to another & have literally done nothing else, they are going on well; the Prince‡ looks interesting & is very weak & I fear will never recover the use of his arm. Fred. Ponsonby§ is the worst of my acquaintance but rapidly improving. You can have no idea of the melancholy of this place so full of wounded mutilated beings that one cannot turn one's eyes without meeting some miserable object; it is quite painful to walk about. Lord Uxbridge¶ is gone, having recovered in an incredible short time. What is become of Mr Lloyd & his project of whinning [*sic*] immediately? The Conyngham's** are still here, he wants to

---

* Charles Greville (1762–1865) the father of the famous diarist who was in Brussels at the time with his family and attended the Duchess of Richmond's Ball.

† Literally, 'in brackets', i.e. 'by the way'

‡ Prince of Orange

§ Lieutenant Colonel the Honourable Frederick Cavendish Ponsonby 12th Light Dragoons; for his narrative see letter no. 19 in this volume.

¶ Lieutenant General The Earl of Uxbridge commanded the cavalry at Waterloo.

** General Sir Henry Conyngham, 1st Marques Conyngham was married to

go to spa & she is wavering. The George Seymours* are gone. If you are at Chigwell & see anything of Mr Dowdeswell pray remember me to him most cordially. I hope you found your children quite well & that Louisa continues to get about, my little girl is quite distressed at having kept 2 volumes of her Robinson, she will send them by the first opportunity. Adieu my dear Mrs Lloyd I hope you will soon come out again. Believe me very truly yours,

C. Greville.

No. 107 Charles Grenfell†
By kind permission of the Buckingham Archives, ref. D/GR/8/14

Brussels, Thursday 13 July 1815

My dear father,

I returned at 7 o'clock this evening from visiting the scenes of the late action; and though we had no other guides than the peasantry have been able to collect sufficient information to put me nearly au fait as to the positions of both armies, on the morning of the action of the 18th, and the general points upon which the contest & carnage was most severe [&] horrendous. The road to Waterloo is one of the finest things I ever saw. At about a mile and a half from the town the Forest of Soignes begins, and continues without any cessation for about 7 miles. The village of Waterloo is situated about half a mile from the termination of the forest & it was here that Lord Wellington & the other generals took up their quarters. The English army were posted on some rising ground about a mile in front of the forest, the line extending about 3 miles their right near Nivelles, their left centre at a country seat called Chateau Hougoumont, the right [left?] at a farm called La Haye Sainte, between which position the artillery were planted on a rising ground commanding several *chaussées* beyond which the French lines, at a distance of certainly not three hundred yards were drawing up. It was at the two last mentioned places that the action was most bloody. The attack began by the French endeavouring to dispossess the Guards of their position at the Chateau Hougoumont; and it is impossible to conceive anything more horrible that must have been the contest, from the effects that still remain of it.

Elizabeth (née Denison).

* Lord George Seymour and his wife Isabella (née Hamilton).

† Charles Pascoe Grenfell was born on 4 April 1790. He was the son of Pascoe Grenfell and Charlotte Grenfell. He married Lady Georgiana Frances Molyneux, daughter of William Philip Molyneux, 2nd Earl of Sefton and Hon. Maria Margaret Craven, on 22 June 1819. He died on 21 March 1867 at the age of 76, after serving as MP for Preston. He lived at Taplow Court, Taplow, Buckinghamshire, England.

The wood leading to the house may be about four or five acres, and there is scarcely a single tree standing in which the marks of bullets are not visible, and all the smaller trees are actually shot in two, in one trunk I counted eighty gun marks. The houses & buildings of every description are wholly destroyed, a few of the walls are standing, but so perforated with cannon balls that it is almost hazardous to approach too near. The gate at the entrance has not a square inch in it through which the shot has not passed and the whole presents a scene of desolation & ruin I never saw before. The remnants of many a poor fellow be scattered about in all directions; and I saw several skulls & bones which had escaped the notice of those employed to bury the dead. The garden walls were in many places covered with blood and even now the whole field of battle is showered with caps, scabbards, and a variety of things which the peasantry have not thought worth carrying away. I have seen many friends of mine among the wounded, and never was more shocked than at meeting on our road to Waterloo, the litters of two officers of the artillery, whose wounds had not permitted their removal from Waterloo till today. One was a Captain Napier,* brother I believe of the Napier's who have in almost every action been so unfortunate. When he passed us, I heard him pray to the men who were carrying him to let him stop, for that he could not bear it; he so bled also groaned with pain; I learned from the men who accompanied him that he had eight most severe wounds from shots & the pikes of the lancers. The farm of La Belle Alliance is on the high road and not above three hundred yards from La Haye Sainte, where also the battle was for a long time most severely contested. Here no further Bonaparte ventured to approach, his station having been during the greatest part of the day on an eminence behind his artillery, where the Prince of Orange some time before had constructed a sort of tower of great height for the purpose of viewing the movements of the enemy. There is no doubt but that the fate of the day was decided by the appearance of the Prussians towards the close of it; for our army was so diminished in strength, & that of the enemy so repeatedly recruited by fresh troops of which there still remained many corps in reserve that it would have been impossible to have continued the fight another day. The conduct of Lord Anglesey was heroic but a blunder or two exposed the light cavalry to severe losses, & they have been blamed for their leader's want of judgement. The French had 20,000 cavalry, we but six and a wounded colonel of the Greys[†]

---

* Second Captain Charles Napier RA of Captain Bolton's Battery; he commanded the battery following the death of Captain Bolton until wounded by shrapnel (8 wounds). He was not one of the famous Napier brothers.

† This could be either Lieutenant Colonel Clarke or Hankin, both were wounded at Waterloo.

whom I have been a good deal with, says it is impossible to conceive the fury with which the French, particularly the cuirassiers fought, though they were almost to a man annihilated by inferior numbers. He had four horses shot under him; the lancers did the most execution, their cruelty in striking every Englishman they found wounded on the ground, was well visited upon them by their total annihilation. But you will be tired, if I continue much longer, so I will leave the rest of my details to our next meeting. I will only add that I saw with pleasure the 133 pieces of canon, trophies of the day, which still remain upon the field of battle; though everything still both on the field and in the town & neighbourhood in which almost every house contains a mangled soldier, presents spectacles of horror and distress.

I have found many friends here. Dick Butler* among the rest. The Palace of Laeken belonging to the king is the only sight I have yet been able to see, tomorrow we devote to the lions of the town and if we find that the road to Paris is safe (which is very doubtful owing to the immense number of stragglers of French & Prussians, of which the latter are perhaps most to be dreaded) we intend starting on Saturday for France.

Strange rumours in this town about the opposition, which I hope to God are false, but the names of several leading members are publicly talked of and actually posted in print about the town. So I was thus today informed by an officer, though I myself have not seen them. They talk of ladies too busy concerned in treasonable communication with the enemy, but this I hope is nonsense. There certainly was a strong party in this town for Boney and it is well known that in more than 3 great houses, preparations were made on the night of the 18th for the entertainment of Boney & his officers and it is a curious fact, that at all the principal towns between this and Antwerp and indeed throughout the country reports were circulated at the same time on the evening of the 18th of our having lost the battle. Here it created such confusion that almost the whole town

. . .

[The remainder of the letter is missing.]

---

* I can only find a Lieutenant Richard Butler of the 91st Regiment in the Army List, which was at Hal during the battle. However, he is not mentioned as serving with the regiment during the campaign, so perhaps he visited Brussels after the battle.

BIBLIOGRAPHY

In any work of this kind, a great number of books have been used for reference, but a few have been particularly helpful and I list these here. The date of publication shown shows the version seen by me. The source and references for original unpublished material has been inserted at the relevant points for greater ease.

Anon. *The Army List,* War Office, various edns

Anon. *The Royal Military Calendar*, T. Egerton, London, 1820

Anon. *The Waterloo Medal Roll*, ed. C. J. Buckland, Naval and Military Press, Dallington, 1992

Adkin, Mark *The Waterloo Companion*, Aurum Press Ltd, London, 2001

Chandler, David *Dictionary of the Napoleonic Wars*, Arms and Armour Press, London, 1979

Crumplin, M. and P. Starling *A Surgical Artist at War: The Paintings and Sketches of Sir Charles Bell 1809–15 Royal College of Surgeons,* Edinburgh, 2005

Dalton, Charles *The Waterloo Roll Call*, Eyre & Spottiswoode, London, 1904

Drew, Robert *Commissioned Officers in the Medical Services of the British Army*, vol. 1, 1660–1897, The Wellcome Historical Medical Library, London, 1968

[Eaton Charlotte,] *Narrative of a Residence in Belgium during the campaign of 1815; and of a Visit to the Field of Waterloo*, John Murray, London, 1817

Eaton, Charlotte *The Battle of Waterloo by a Near Observer,* 10th edition (2 vols), John Murray, London 1817

Fraser, Alexander *The Frasers of Philorth*, privately printed, Edinburgh, 1879

Glover, Gareth *The Waterloo Archive, Volume I,* Frontline Books, Barnsley, 2010

Glover, Gareth *The Waterloo Archive, Volume III,* Frontline Books, Barnsley, 2011

Glover, Gareth *Eyewitness to the Peninsular War and the Battle of Waterloo: The Letters and Journals of Lieutenant Colonel James Hamilton Stanhope, 1803–25*, Frontline Books, Barnsley, 2010

Glover, Gareth *Waterloo Campaign Letters Written by Lieutenant Colonel Alexander, Lord Saltoun, 1st Foot Guards, 1815*, Ken Trotman Publishing, Godmanchester, 2010

Glover, Gareth *Recollections of My Life including Military Service at Waterloo by Colonel Blathwayt 23rd Light Dragoons 1814–17*, Ken Trotman Publishing, Godmanchester, 2004

Glover, Gareth *A Life Guardsman in Spain, France and at Waterloo: The Memoirs of Sergeant Thomas Playford, 2nd Life Guards 1810–30, Including Memories of Life Guardsman Shaw* Ken Trotman Publishing, Godmanchester, 2007

Glover, Gareth *Recollections of the Scenes of which I was a witness in the Low Countries & France in the campaigns of 1814 and 1815 and the subsequent occupation of French Flanders. The journal and letters of the Reverend George Griffin Stonestreet 1814–16*, Ken Trotman Publishing, Godmanchester, 2009.

Glover, Gareth *Letters From the Battle of Waterloo*, Greenhill Books, London, 2004

Glover, Gareth *A Short Account of the Life and Adventures of Private Thomas Jeremiah, 23rd or Royal Welch Fusiliers, 1812–37, Including his experiences at the Battle of Waterloo*, Ken Trotman Publishing, Godmanchester, 2008

Hall, John *History of the Peninsular War*, vol. VIII, Greenhill Books, London, 1998

Holme, N. and E. Kirby *Medal Rolls; 23rd Foot Royal Welch Fusiliers, Napoleonic Period*, Spink, London, 1978

Lachouque, Henry *Waterloo*, Arms and Armour Press, London, 1975

Mercer, Cavalie *Journal of the Waterloo Campaign*, Greenhill Books, London, 1985

Mockler-Ferryman, A. F. *The Life of a Regimental Officer During the Great War 1793–1815*, W. Blackwood & Sons, Edinburgh, 1913

Mullen, A. L. T. *The Military General Service Roll 1793–1814*, London Stamp Exchange, London, 1990

Siborne, H. T. *The Waterloo Letters*, Arms & Armour Press, London, 1983

Siborne, W. *History of the Waterloo Campaign*, Greenhill Books, London, 1990

Verner, Willoughby, *A British Rifleman*, London 1899, reprint Greenhill Books, 1986

Wrottesley Hon. George, *Life and Correspondence of Field Marshal Sir John Burgoyne*, R. Bentley, London, 1873

INDEX

of correspondents

Name, Rank at Waterloo and Regiment	Letters
Askew, Major Henry, 2nd Battalion 1st Foot Guards	58
Baillie, Mrs Sophia, civilian	62
Barlow, Captain George, 2nd Battalion 69th Foot	70–83
Barrington, Ensign the Honourable Samuel, 2nd Battalion, 1st Foot Guards	55–56
Bathurst, Henry Lord	105
Blackadder, Hospital Assistant Henry	99
Boggie, Staff Surgeon John	98
Bridgeman Captain Orlando, 1st Foot Guards, ADC to Lieutenant General Lord Hill	6–10
Burgoyne, Lieutenant Colonel John, Royal Engineers	100
Byng, Major General John	65
Campbell, Colonel Colin, Commandant at Headquarters	2
Clarke, Major Isaac, 2nd Dragoons, Scots Greys	16
Colgan, Sergeant Matthew, 18th Hussars	33
Collier, Staff Surgeon Charles	94–95
Critchley, Sergeant Thomas, 1st Dragoons	15
Dalmer, Lieutenant Colonel Thomas, 23rd Foot	85
Dawkins, Lieutenant Colonel Henry, 2nd Battalion 1st Foot Guards	59
Denham, Lieutenant Dixon, 54th Foot	92
Dickson, Lieutenant Colonel Alexander, Royal Artillery	52
Dundas, General Francis	101
Elton, Captain William, 1st Dragoon Guards	13
Enoch, Lieutenant John, 23rd Foot	86
Frazer, Lieutenant Colonel Sir Augustus, Royal Horse Artillery	50
Greenock, Lieutenant Colonel, AQMG	3
Grenfell, Charles, MP	107
Greville, Charles, civilian	106
Hennen, Staff Surgeon George	97

Hervey, Ensign James, 2nd Battalion, Coldstream Guards 68
Hume, Robert, Deputy Inspector of Hospitals 20
Jeremiah, Private Thomas, 23rd Foot 87
Kempt, Major General Sir James 88–89
Kennedy, Captain Arthur, 18th Hussars 25–32
Lowe, Major General Sir Hudson 104
Mackinnon, Lieutenant Colonel Daniel,
   2nd Battalion Coldstream Guards 66
Mackworth, Captain Digby, 7th Foot,
   ADC to Lieutenant General Lord Hill 5
Maitland, Major General Peregrine 54
May, Lieutenant Colonel Sir John, Royal Artillery, AAG 51
Murray, Lieutenant Colonel the Honourable Henry, 18th Hussars 24
Packe, Lieutenant George, 13th Light Dragoons 34–49
Payne, Captain Edward, 2nd Dragoons, Scots Greys 18
Phelps, First Lieutenant Samuel, Royal Artillery 53
Playford, Private Thomas, 2nd Life Guards 12
Ponsonby, Major General Sir William 14
Ponsonby, Lieutenant Colonel the Honourable Frederick,
   12th Light Dragoons 19
Price, Mr Ulysses, civilian 61
Roche, Staff Surgeon Jordan 96
Sadler, Mr John, civilian 17
Saltoun, Lieutenant Colonel Alexander Lord Saltoun,
   2nd Battalion 1st Foot Guards 57
Short, Ensign Charles, 2nd Battalion Coldstream Guards 67
Simmons, First Lieutenant George, 1st Battalion 95th Foot 91
Swan, Private Henry, 3rd Battalion 1st Foot Guards 64
Taylor, Private Alexander, Royal Staff Corps 93
Thain, Ensign William, 2nd Battalion 33rd Foot 69
Unknown Staff Officer 1
Unknown officer of 1st Foot Guards 60
Unknown officer of 1st Foot Guards 63
Unknown officer of 23rd Foot 84
Unknown officer of 1st Battalion 95th Foot 90
Unknown officer, Royal Marines 103
Unknown Officer 102
Vivian, Major General Sir Hussey 21–23
Whale, Captain John, 1st Life Guards 11
Woodford, Lieutenant Colonel John, 1st Foot Guards,
   extra ADC to Lord Wellington 4

INDEX

of officers and places mentioned in the letters

1st Cuirassier Regiment 39n
1st King's Dragoon Guards 38, 49–50
1st Foot Guards xiv, 3n, 4n, 6, 19n, 25,
  65n, 80n, 110n, 114n, 131–42, 236,
  143n, 144n, 146, 148
1st Foot 59, 60
1st Hussars KGL 63, 64, 68–9, 72, 91
1st Life Guards 4, 32–3, 38, 44
1st Royal Dragoons 31n, 44n, 53
2nd Division 12, 22, 23, 191
2nd Life Guards xv, 34–48
3rd Division 126, 129n, 198, 211
3rd Foot Guards 59n, 137n, 143n, 144n
3rd Hussars KGL 68
4th Foot 235n
4th Division 22, 23, 179n
5th Division 126, 191n, 196, 197, 198,
  199, 200
6th Division 197, 200
7th Hussars 22, 31n, 61, 67, 70, 72, 79,
  88n, 148, 149n, 215, 237n
10th Hussars 27n, 62–4, 68–72, 95, 98n,
  231
12th Light Dragoons 60, 251n
13th Light Dragoons xv, 96–120
14th Foot 179, 192
18th Hussars xv, 62–3, 66, 67–95
23rd Foot xvi, 175–93
23rd Light Dragoons 72, 189
28th Foot 174n, 203, 217
33rd Foot 150, 166
42nd Foot 158, 160, 189, 203, 211
44th Foot 203
51st Foot 179
52nd Foot 127, 153, 170, 183, 200
53rd Foot 248

54th Foot 13, 224
69th Foot 151–74
71st Foot 35, 243n
79th Foot 203, 237n
88th Foot 178
91st Foot 226, 254n
92nd Foot 203
95th Foot xvi, 195n, 197–223

Aalst 12, 205
Acre 20n, 247, 248
Acton, Lt Henry 13th Light
  Dragoons 101, 116
Adair, Lt Robert 1st Foot Guards 80
Adamson, Trooper 2nd Life Guards 40
Addington, Henry 1st Lord
  Sidmouth 172n
d'Alberg, Duc 87
Albuera, battle of 17
Aldegonde, Lt Quarter-maître Gen.
  Col. Comte van Sainte 17
Alten, Lt Gen. Sir Charles 159, 162,
  211, 217, 220
Ambrose, Assistant Surgeon James 122
Andreossy, Gen. Antoine 6
d'Angoulême, Duchess 88
Antwerp 3, 13, 14, 15, 16, 79, 102, 115,
  149, 150, 254
d'Arenburg, Duc 11
Arenschildt, Col. Sir Frederick 116
Arnold, Lt Robert 10th Hussars 64
Askew, Major Henry 1st Foot
  Guards 136
Ath 9, 154, 155
Aubervilliers 6, 83
Austerlitz, Battle of 75, 80, 193

Austrian troops 19, 34, 48, 52, 53, 72, 78, 110, 133, 140, 193

Bacon, Lt Anthony 10th Hussars 64
Bagshaw, Quartermaster 95th Foot 202
Baillie, Dr Andrew 138
Barclay, Col. Delancey 65
Baring, Major Georg 216
Barlow, Capt. George 69th Foot xvi, 151–74
Barlow, Sir George 151n
Barnard, Capt. Charles Scots Greys 56
Barnard, Sir Andrew 95th Foot 199, 201, 205, 207, 211, 214, 215, 216, 220
Barnes, Major Gen. Sir Edward 2, 9, 10n, 173
Barrington, Ensign the Hon. Samuel 1st Foot Guards xiv, 133–40
Bassano, Duke of 248
Bathurst, Henry 3rd Earl 250
Battersby, Capt. George 1st KDG 49, 51
Beamond, Quartermaster 2nd Life Guards 39
Bean, Major George RHA 122, 123
Beattie, Capt. RM 247
Beaumont 126, 226
Beckwith, Lt Col. Charles 95th Foot 201, 203, 204, 209, 222
Belgian troops 22, 54, 57, 60, 75, 78, 79, 83, 97, 106, 111, 113, 139, 146, 188, 193, 220
Bell, Assistant Surgeon John 84th Foot 221, 238
Bell, Sir Charles 230, 239
La Belle Alliance 24, 45n, 69, 114, 145, 159, 253
Bellerophon, HMS 86n, 245, 246
Belson, Lt Col. Sir Charles 28th Foot 174
Bergen op Zoom 13, 15, 16
Bernard, Cornet Hon. Henry 1st KDG 49
Berri, Duc de 9, 12
Berthier, Marshal 153
Bertrand, Gen. 245, 246, 247
Binche 61
Black, Troop Sgt Major William 18th Hussars 92n
Blackadder, Henry Hospital Assistant 239–40
Blackwood, Capt. Robert 69th Foot 167
Bloomfield, Major Gen. Benjamin RA 63
Blücher, Marshal Gebhard 2, 4, 20, 32, 33, 54, 71, 72, 76, 77, 78, 79, 82, 86, 87, 100, 110, 111, 114, 126, 127, 140, 145, 149, 159, 161, 180, 181, 201, 225, 226, 243, 244
Boggie, John Staff Surgeon 238–9
Bonaparte, Emperor Napoleon 1, 3, 4, 6, 9, 16, 19, 21, 26, 34, 35, 36, 47, 52, 57, 60, 61, 62, 72, 75, 77, 79, 80, 81, 82, 83, 84, 86, 87, 97, 102, 104, 105, 106, 107, 108, 109, 112, 113, 114, 125, 126, 127, 128, 133, 144, 146, 148, 140, 150, 152, 153, 157, 159, 161, 162, 164, 165, 194, 198, 199, 200, 224, 226, 244, 245, 225, 246, 249, 250, 253
Bonaparte, Jerome 3, 75
Bossu, Bois de 135, 146
Boulogne, Bois de 30–1, 128, 159, 167, 227
Bourget 5, 76, 84, 85
Bowater, Capt. Edward 3rd Foot Guards 137
Bowers, Lt Col. Patrick 13th Light Dragoons 119
Boyse, Capt. Jacques 32nd Foot 135
Braine l'Alleud 22, 23, 25, 121, 145, 161, 175, 192
Braine le Comte 7, 25, 61, 139, 145, 146
Breda 15, 16
Brereton, Lt RHA 124
Bridgeman, Capt. Hon. Orlando x, xiv, xv, 7n, 25–31
Bridgeman, Hon. Charles RN 28n
Bridgeman, Orlando 2nd Earl of Bradford 28n
Bridgeman, Rev. Hon. Henry 28n
Bringhurst, Capt. John 18th Hussars 80
Bringhurst, Major John 1st KDG 49, 51
Brooke, Lt Francis 18th Hussars 49, 80
Brownrigg, David Staff Surgeon 236
Bruce, Michael 142

Bruges 96, 98, 99, 152, 178, 224
Brunswick Oels troops 22, 23, 68, 69, 78, 79, 146, 160, 188, 196, 245
Brunswick, Duke of 4
Brussels x, xvi, 4, 7, 11, 12, 14, 20, 21, 22, 23, 26, 28, 29, 30, 31, 32, 33, 34, 35, 36, 42, 44, 67, 71, 73, 74, 76, 78, 79, 80, 84, 87, 91, 96, 100, 101, 102, 103, 106, 107, 109, 115, 126, 129n, 134, 136, 137, 138, 140, 142n, 146, 147, 149n, 151, 154, 160, 161, 166, 170, 190, 191, 193, 197, 198, 200, 202, 206, 207, 209, 216, 220, 224, 229, 239, 250, 251, 252, 254
Buckley, Lt Edward 1st Foot Guards 134, 136
Bull, Major Robert RHA 122, 123
Bülow, Gen. von 4, 80, 159, 161, 226
Bunbury, Major Gen. Sir Henry 195n
Burgoyne, Lt Col. John RE xvi, 241
Burke, Sugeon Joseph 95th Foot 202
Butler, Lt Richard 91st Foot 254
Byng, Gen. John 132, 142, 143, 147, 148

Cairnes, Major Robert RHA 122, 123
Calder, Adm. Sir Robert 247
Calvert, Lt Gen. Sir Henry 137n, 195n
Cambrai 81, 82, 89, 142, 228
Cambronne, Gen. Pierre xv, 24n, 151n
Cameron, Major Alexander 95th Foot 201
Campbell, Capt. Neil 79th Foot 237
Campbell, Col. Sir Colin xv, 1, 7
Canning Lt Col. Charles, 3rd Foot Guards 2, 125
Capel, Louisa 10n
Carnot, Lazare 112, 113
Carruthers, Lt James Scots Greys 55–6
Castlereagh, Lord 19, 84, 85, 87, 88, 89, 90, 91, 110
Cateau Cambresis 61n, 81, 82, 86, 96, 125, 135n, 226
Cathcart, Lt Hon. George 6 Dragoon Guards 5n
Chaplin, Lt Thomas 1st Foot Guards 103, 135
Chapman, 1st Lt William 95th Foot 197, 202

Chapman, Lt Col. Stephen RE 127
Charleroi 33, 73, 74, 78, 79, 126, 128, 148, 159, 214, 217
Charlotte, Queen 142n
Chawner, Capt. 95th Foot 202
Church, 2nd Lt 95th Foot 202
Clancarty, Richard 2nd Earl 31
Clarke, Lt Col. Isaac Scots Greys 55, 253n
Clichy 197
Clinton, Lt Gen. Henry 12
Coldstream Guards 6n, 103n, 136n, 140, 143, 144, 145
Cole, Sir Lowry 86
Colgan, Sgt Mathew 18th Hussars 91
Collier, Charles Staff Surgeon 230–4, 238
Colville, Lt Gen. Sir Charles 3n, 6n
Combermere, Lord 6, 110
Conran, Major Gen. Henry 116
Conyngham, Gen. Sir Henry 1st Marquess 28, 251
Cooke, Major Gen. George 3, 131, 143, 148
Coote, Lt Robert 18th Hussars 67
Cossacks 110, 181
Cotton, Lt Gen. Sir Stapleton see Combemere
Courtrai 13, 152, 154
Cox, 1st Lt John 95th Foot 202n
Craufurd, 1st Lt Donald RHA 123
Critchley, Sgt Thomas 1st Dragoons 53
Croft, Ensign Thomas 1st Foot Guards 138n, 139
Croix d'Orade 70
Croker, Capt. Richard 18th Hussars 88, 89
Cromie, 1st Lt Michael RHA 123
Currie, Lt Col. Edward 90th Foot 26
Cuyler, Capt. Charles 69th Foot 213

Dalmer, Lt Col. Thomas 23rd Foot 175–6
Dansey, Capt. Charles RHA 124
Dashwood, Ensign Augustus 137
Day, 1st Lt James RHA 124
Dawkins, Lt Col. Henry Coldstream Guards 136

Denderhoutem 51

d'Enghien, Duc 249

Denham, Lt Dixon 54th Foot 224

Dickson, Lt Col. Sir Alexander RA 127

Dieppe 171, 172

d'Ivry, Col. Baron 16

Doherty, Capt. Joseph 13th Light
   Dragoons 101, 117, 118, 119

Doherty, Lt Col. Patrick 13th Light
   Dragoons 99

d'Oyly, Capt. Sir Francis 138

Drouet, General 153

Drummond 1st Lt George 95th
   Foot 202

Duke of Cumberland's Hussars 49n,
   193n

Dumaresque, Capt. Henry 9th
   Foot 144

Dundas, Gen. Francis 243

Duperier, Lt Henry 18th Hussars 67

Dutch troops 15, 16, 23, 26, 39n, 66, 74,
   75, 79, 98, 101, 126n, 146, 150, 158,
   179, 188, 189, 194

Edwards, Capt. R 13th Light
   Dragoons 99, 101, 102, 108, 109, 111,
   112, 114, 115, 116

Eeklo 96, 99

Eeles, Capt. Charles 95th Foot 195n

Elba 7, 34, 75

Elley, Major Gen. Sir John Horse
   Guards 216

Ellis, Capt. Richard 18th Hussars 74

Ellis, Lt Col. Sir Henry 23rd Foot 175n,
   176n, 182, 192

Elphinstone, Capt. James 7th
   Hussars 237

Elphinstone, Col. 33rd Foot 166

Elton, Capt. William 1st KDG 49

Enghien 9, 11, 19, 25, 61, 73, 78, 103,
   134, 139, 140, 141, 145, 146

Enoch, Lt John 23rd Foot 176, 177

Evans, Major De Lacey 166

Fairfoot, Sgt Robert 95th Foot 213, 218,
   219

Farmer, Capt. Thomas 23rd Foot 175,
   176,

Faye, Lt Col. Nicolas Planat de la 245n

Felix, 1st Lt Orlando 95th Foot 197n,
   202, 207, 208, 209, 211, 213, 217, 218,
   221

Fitzmaurice, 1st Lt 95th Foot 197n, 202

Fitzroy, Lt Charles Royal Horse
   Guards 68

Fleurus 76, 78, 96, 126, 127, 141, 159

Forster, 1st Lt Henry RHA 123

Fouche, Duke of Otranto 87

France, King of xvi, 8, 12, 14, 31, 34,
   47, 52, 72, 82, 84, 86, 87, 91, 100, 109,
   113, 152, 165, 178, 196, 205

Frazer, Lt Col. Augustus RA 121, 125

Freer, Lt 95th Foot 202, 206

Fuller, Col. 1st KDG 50

Gairdner, 1st Lt John 95th Foot 202n

Gardiner, 1st Lt 95th Foot 197n, 202n,

Gardiner, Lt Col. Sir Robert RHA 65n,
   67, 124

Genappe 4, 23, 37, 75, 81, 128, 129, 147,
   149n, 161, 198, 215, 241, 241, 244

Ghent xvi, 8, 72, 84, 96, 98, 99, 102, 129,
   141, 178, 179, 205, 237

Glasse, Capt. 95th Foot 201

Gneisenau, Gen. August 250

Godley, Trooper Samuel 2nd Life
   Guards 45, 46

Gonesse 5, 29, 30, 77, 195

Gordon, Lt Col. Hon. Sir Alexander
   3rd Foot Guards 2, 59, 125

Gordon, Major Gen. Charles 53

Gordon, Major Gen. Sir James 194

Gore, Capt. Hon Charles 85th
   Foot 195n

Goulburn, Capt. Frederick 13th Light
   Dragoons 98

Graham, Capt. Henry 1st KDG 49, 51

Graham, Sir Thomas 3, 6

Grammont 12, 13, 16, 17, 25, 71, 73,
   103, 179,

Grant, Capt. James 18th Hussars 88,
   89

Greenock, Lt Col. Lord 3–6, 69

Grenfell, Charles MP 252

Greville, Col. Hon. Charles 38th
   Foot 10n

Greville, Ensign Algernon 1st Foot
  Guards 146
Greville, Lady Charlotte 10,
Grey, Capt. John 10th Hussars 64, 231
Grey, Charles 2nd Earl 53,
Gronow, Capt. Rees 58n
Grouchy, Marshal Emanuel 79, 243
Gunning, Lt George 10th Hussars 27,
  30, 64
Gunning, Lt George 1st Dragoons 31
Gurwood, Capt. John 10th Hussars 64

Haggup, Lt 95th Foot 202
Hake, Col. 1st KDG 49n, 193n
Hal 1, 6, 22, 25, 26, 254n
Halkett, Col. Hugh 151n
Halkett, Major Gen. Sir Colin 150, 166,
  170
Halle *see* Hal
Hamilton, Col. James Scots Greys 55
Hanbury, Capt. John 1st Foot
  Guards 110
Hankin, Lt Col. Scots Greys 253n
Hanoverian Landwehr 13, 74, 97, 113,
  117, 161, 188, 245
Hardinge, Col. Sir Henry 1st Foot
  Guards 19
Harris, Capt. Thomas 18th Hussars 67,
  94
Harvey, 2nd Lt William RA 130n
Haughton, Sir Simon 166n
Havelock, Lt William 43rd Foot 220
Hay, Capt. Lord James 1st Foot
  Guards 3, 145
Hay, Ensign James Lord 1st Foot
  Guards 80, 132
La Haye Sainte xvi, 23, 42n, 216, 217,
  218, 242, 244, 252
Heathcote, Cornet Lionel Horse
  Guards 110
Hennen, John Staff Surgeon 237
Hepburn, Col. Francis 3rd Foot
  Guards 143
Hervey, Col. Felton 14th Light
  Dragoons 59, 68, 139
Hervey Ensign James Coldstream
  Guards 149
Hesketh, Lt Robert 3rd Foot

Guards 137
Heyland, Major Arthur 40th Foot 81
Heyt, Assistant Surgeon 95th Foot 202,
  218
Hill, Clement 7n
Hill, Lt Gen. Lord Rowland x, xiv, xv,
  7, 8, 9, 10, 11, 12, 13, 14, 16, 17, 20,
  22, 24, 25, 26, 27, 28, 29, 30, 31, 116,
  117, 162, 174, 131
Hillier, Capt. George 74th Foot 7
Hilton, Trooper 2nd Life Guards 40
Hincks, 1st Lt John RHA 123
Hindley, Trooper Joseph 2nd Life
  Guards 42
Hobhouse, Capt. Benjamin 69th
  Foot 170n
Hodge, Major Edward 7th Hussars 149
Hodgkinson, Lt William 62nd Foot 5
Hougoumont 6n, 23, 39n, 126, 145, 147,
  162n, 187, 191, 216, 217, 252
Howard, Major 10th Hussars 63, 64
Hume, John Inspector of Hospitals 60
Hutchinson, Capt. John 1st Foot
  Guards 142

Imperial Guard xiv, 3, 18, 24, 26, 50, 62,
  66, 70, 75, 79, 81, 105, 121, 126, 127,
  132, 140, 144, 148, 151n, 157, 158,
  161, 163, 192, 200, 225, 226, 243

Jebb, Capt. John Horse Guards 106,
  117
Jeffs, Sgt Major Thomas 18th
  Hussars 70
Jeremiah, Private Thomas 23rd
  Foot xvi, 177
Johnson, Trooper John 2nd Life
  Guards 46
Johnstone, Capt. William 95th Foot 202

Keane, Capt. Edward 7th Hussars 67
Keith, Adm Lord 246
Kelly, Capt. Edward 1st Life Guards 4
Kempt, Major Gen. Sir James 3, 194,
  196n, 199
Kennedy, Capt. Arthur 18th
  Hussars xv, 71
Kincaid, Lt 95th Foot 202

Knollys, Major 45

Lancers, French 4, 39, 41, 44, 50, 51, 57, 59, 62, 63, 70, 79, 118, 141, 148, 188, 191
Las Cases 249
Laussat, Baron de 58n
Lautour-Maubourg, Gen. Marie 6
Layton, Lt Jonathan 95th Foot 202, 203, 209, 210, 211
Leach, Capt. 95th Foot 201, 217
Lee, Capt. 95th Foot 201, 213n
Lennox, Lady Sarah 20n
Liège 17, 71
Ligny 36
Lisle 152, 153
Lister, Lt, 95th Foot 202, 211, 212
Lobau, Georges Mouton Comte de 76, 190
Londonderry, 2nd Marquess of 19n, 71n, 73
Louis XVIII see France, King of
Louis, Prince of Austria 87
Love, Capt. James 52nd Foot 170
Lowe, Major Gen. Sir Hudson 250
Luard, Capt. George 18th Hussars 91n, 92, 94
Lumley, Sir Robert 27
Lyons 140

Macdonald, Capt. Alexander RHA 124
Macdonell, Lt Col. James Coldstream Guards 143
Mack, General 193
Mackinnon, Lt Col. Daniel Coldstream Gds 145
Mackenzie, Paymaster John 95th Foot 202
Mackworth, Capt. Digby 7th Fusiliers x, xiv, xv, 7, 258
Maclean, Lt Allen 13th Light Dragoons 116
Macleod, Lt Gen. John RA 128
Mainwaring, Private 18th Hussars 92
Maitland, Major Gen. Peregrine 20, 22, 69, 131, 144
Malcolm, Col. Sir John 168
Malmaison 110

Marmont, Marshal Auguste 8, 100
Maubeuge 52, 61, 73, 76, 78, 82, 126, 159
May, Lt Col. Sir John RA 125
McGrigor, Sir James Director General of Hospitals 233
Mercer, Capt. Alexander RHA 123
Merlen, Major Gen. 66n
Metternich, Clemens von 87
Miller, Capt. William 1st Foot Guards 141, 142n
Miloradovitch, Gen 180
Mitchell, Lt Col. Hugh 179
Molloy, Lt 95th Foot 202
Mons 73, 75, 76, 81, 155, 157, 235
Mont St Jean 23, 33, 37, 61, 63, 67, 68, 96, 202, 218, 241
Montmartre 6, 29, 30, 76, 77, 83, 112, 113, 163
Mortier, Marshal 134
Mountnorris, Lady 20
Munro, Ass Surgeon 23rd Foot 175n, 192n
Murat 8, 18, 19, 180, 193, 248
Murray, Lt Col. Hon Henry 18th Hussars 67, 89, 92

Namur 20, 73, 78, 126, 128, 209
Nanterre 47, 48, 53, 56
Napier, Capt. RA 69, 253
Nassau Troops 69, 162, 198
National Guard 29
Needham, Selina 28n
Nelson, Adm Lord 247
Nesle 29
Neuilly 87
Neville, Capt. J 43rd Foot 197
Ney, Marshal Michel 9, 22, 72, 78, 91, 126, 159, 196, 198, 211
Nicolay, Lt Col. William Royal Staff Corps 229
Ninove 72, 100
Nivelles 2, 7, 23, 24, 25, 35, 61, 75, 77, 78, 79, 91, 96, 126, 131, 139, 143, 145, 146, 148, 159, 161, 186, 201, 220, 252
Northumberland, HMS 114n, 246, 247

Ohain 65, 126, 243

Orange, Prince Frederick of 16, 26
Orange, Prince William of xv, 8, 9, 11, 16n, 25, 78, 87, 102, 126, 131, 139, 148, 159n, 250, 251n, 253
Ostend 7, 96, 97, 99, 101, 138, 141, 176, 177, 178, 201, 204, 224
Oudenarde 13, 196n

Pack, Sir Dennis 60
Packe, Capt. Henry 1st Foot Guards 110, 114
Packe, Charles 103n. 113, 115, 119
Packe, Lt George 13th Light Dragoons xv, 96
Packe, Major Robert Horse Guards 100, 102, 104, 105, 106,
Paget, Henry *see* Uxbridge
Paris ix, xv, xvi, 3, 5, 6, 12, 19, 28n, 29, 30, 34, 46, 47, 48, 49, 54, 61, 62, 72, 76, 77, 82, 83, 84, 85, 86, 87, 88, 91, 96, 100, 106, 107, 108, 109, 110, 111, 112, 113, 115, 117, 128, 130, 136, 142, 150, 152, 158, 163, 164, 165, 167, 168, 169, 170, 171, 172, 173, 174, 179, 195, 196, 197, 205, 225, 227, 229, 237, 248, 254
Payne, Capt. Edward Scots Greys 56
Perceval, Lt Philip 1st Foot Guards 134
Picton, Sir Thomas 2, 22, 66, 126, 191, 194, 196, 199, 200, 208
Pierrepoint, Lt Col. Michael Rutland Militia 107n
Pitt, Private William 95th Foot 204
Plançenoit 226
Playford, Private Thomas xv, 34
Poland 157
Ponsonby, Lt Col. Frederick 12th Lt Drag 2, 3, 5, 57, 60, 251
Ponsonby, Hon George 52n
Ponsonby, Hon Mary 51n
Ponsonby, John Viscount 52n
Ponsonby, Lady Charlotte 52n
Ponsonby, Lady Louisa 51
Ponsonby, Major Gen. William 3, 51, 166n, 191, 199
Ponsonby, Rev Hon Richard 52n
Pritchard, Private Samuel 4th Foot 235
Prussia, King of 47, 54, 85, 110, 113

Prussian troops xvi, 2, 4, 5, 6, 7, 19, 21, 25, 26, 29, 30, 31, 33, 34, 35, 36, 44, 48, 54, 58, 59, 61, 62, 63, 65, 68, 73, 74, 77, 78, 81, 82, 83, 85, 86, 93, 101, 104, 105, 106, 109, 110, 111, 112, 113, 116, 117, 119, 126, 127, 128, 129, 134, 139, 140, 145, 146, 147, 148, 149, 150, 159, 161, 179, 190, 196, 197, 198, 200, 209, 225, 226, 227, 243, 245, 247, 250, 253, 254

Quatre Bras xiv, xvi, 4, 22n, 23, 35, 36, 39n, 61, 78, 79, 126, 127, 129n, 131, 133n, 138n, 140, 145, 146, 183, 194, 197, 202, 209, 211, 212, 222, 229, 244
Quentin, Lt Col. George 10th Hussars 64, 98n, 110

Ramsay, Major William RHA 122n, 124
Reille, Comte 191
Rhelps, 1st Lt Samuel RA xvi, 128
Richmond, Duchess of 21, 25, 33, 61, 134n, 197, 251n
Richmond, Duke of 20
Robe, Lt Col. RA 121, 122n
Robe, Lt William RHA 122n, 124
Robson, Assistant Surgeon 95th Foot 202, 218, 221, 223
Roche, Jordan Staff Surgeon 235
Roosendaal 15
Rosario HMS 7
Ross, Lt Col. Sir Hew RHA 124
Rouen 168, 171
Royal Horse Guards 7n, 25n, 38, 68n, 100n, 110n, 116n, 148, 216n
Royal Staff Corps 203, 204, 228
Ruille 49
Russell, Lord George 6th Duke of Bedford 30n
Russia, Emperor Alexander of 47, 54, 85, 109, 111, 113
Russian troops xvi, 19, 34, 48, 52, 53, 72, 74, 86, 101, 106, 110, 112, 113, 167, 190, 196, 248

Saltoun, Lt Col. Alexander Lord 132, 135, 143, 144
Saxony 157

Schendelbeke 96, 100, 102
Schwarzenberg, Field Marshal Charles
   Prince of 110
Scots Greys 55, 56, 68, 82, 238n
Senlis 82, 83
Seymour, Capt. Horace 66
Seymour, Lord George 252
Shaw, Corporal of Horse 2nd Life
   Guards xv, 36, 37, 40, 41, 45, 46
Shawe, Lt Col. Merrick 3
Shenley, 2nd Lt William 95th
   Foot 197n, 202n
Shore, John 1st Baron Teignmouth 174n
Short, Ensign Charles Coldstream
   Guards 146
Siborne, William 65, 82n, 194n, 196n
Simmons, 1st Lt George 95th Foot xvi,
   201–22
Simpson, Henry Bridgeman 31
Smith, 1st Lt William RHA 123
Smith, Sir Harry 95th Foot 202, 207,
   208
Smith, Mr Charles Volunteer 202, 209,
   215, 216
Smith, Vice Adm Sir Sidney 20, 142
Smohain 65, 68
Smyth, Capt. 95th Foot 201
Soignes, Forest of 79, 145, 243, 252
Soignies 150, 154–5, 159
Somerset, Fitzroy 2, 125
Somerset, Lord Edward 32, 49, 50, 68,
   80
Somerville, William Deputy Inspector
   of Hospitals 221
St Cloud 84, 85, 86
St Denis 6, 82, 83, 227
St Helena 47, 114n, 245n, 246, 249
St Quentin 82
Stanhope, Lt Col. Hon James 1st Foot
   Guards 4, 144
Staveley, Major William Royal African
   Corps 203n
Stewart, 2nd Lt Allen 95th Foot 222
Stewart, Lt Archibald 95th Foot 202,
   203, 209
Stewart, Robert see Londonderry
Stilwell, Lt 95th Foot 202, 218, 219
Stothert, Capt. William 3rd Foot
   Guards 144
Strangways, 1st Lt Thomas RHA 124
Stuart, Sir Charles 71n
Swan, Private Henry 1st Foot
   Guards 141

Talleyrand 84
Taylor, Private Alexander Royal Staff
   Corps 228
Thain, Ensign William 33rd Foot 150
Thompson, Dr John 231
Tighe, Capt. George Bradshaw's
   Recruiting Corps 246
Tolentino, Battle of 18n
Torrens, Major Gen. Sir Henry 1, 3n,
   90, 172, 174, 195
Tournai 8, 13, 19, 154
Trollope, Cornet John 10th Hussars 98
Tromp, Admiral Maarten van 179
Tuilleries 85, 86, 88, 164
Turner, Private Jonathan 3rd Foot
   Guards 236

Underwood, Sgt Daniel 95th Foot 210
Uxbridge, Earl of xv, 2, 5, 6n, 17, 18n,
   31n, 36, 38, 40, 50, 66n, 70, 72, 78, 80,
   100, 102, 148, 198, 200, 244, 251

Valence, Comte de 6
Valenciennes 9n, 52, 82, 207
Vandamme Gen. Dominique 76
Vandeleur, Major Gen. Sir John 6, 44n,
   65, 66, 69
Vendée, La 18, 52
Verd Coucou 68
Verner, Capt. William 7th Hussars xvi,
   88, 201n, 207n
Vernor, Major Robert Scots Greys 238
Versailles 77, 82
Victor, Marshal 100
Villeneuve, Adm 247
Vivian, Major Gen. Sir Hussey xv, 2,
   44n, 61, 63, 65, 67, 68, 69, 70, 79, 81,
   82, 89, 92, 93
Vyvian, Paymaster Philip 69th
   Foot 151, 156

Waldegrave, Lt Col. John 6th Earl 13

Walton, Lt William Guards 144

Wanstell, Private 10th Hussars 231

Waterpark, Lord 10

Wavre 4, 68, 126, 128, 145, 161, 243, 245

Webber, Capt. William RHA 123

Webber-Smith, Lt Col. James RHA 123

Webster, Corp William 2nd Life
    Guards 45

Webster, Lady Frances 17

Wellesley, Lady Charlotte 18n

Whale, Capt. John 32, 33, 34

Whinyates, Capt. Edward RHA 37n,
    124

Whittaker, Private Kendall Coldstream
    Guards 146

Wildman, Capt. Thomas 7th Hussars 31

Wilson, Gen. Sir Robert 142

Wood, Capt. Charles 10th Hussars 64

Wood, Col. Sir George RA 127n

Woodford, Col. Alexander Coldstream
    Guards 6n, 143, 146

Woodford, Lt Col. John 1st Foot
    Guards 6

Woolley, Cpl John 18th Hussars 94

Wright, 2nd Lt William 95th Foot 202,
    203, 206, 208, 209

Wynne-Pendarves, Edward MP 61

York, Duke of 4n, 88, 89, 90, 131, 141,
    143

Youeson, Trooper John 2nd Life
    Guards 40

Ypres 151, 153

Ziethen, Gen. 65

Zottegem 16, 17